The Legal Protection of Databases

Mark Davison examines several legal models designed to protect databases, considering in particular the 1996 European Union Directive, the history of its adoption and its transposition into national laws. He compares the Directive with various American legislative proposals, as well as the principles of misappropriation that underpin them. In addition, the book also contains a commentary on the appropriateness of the various models in the context of moves for an international agreement on the topic.

This book will be of interest to academics and practitioners, including those involved with databases and other forms of new media.

MARK J. DAVISON is Associate Professor in the Faculty of Law at Monash University. He has published articles on intellectual property and restrictive trade practices in Australia, China, England, Germany, Indonesia and Thailand.

T0269319

Cambridge Studies in Intellectual Property Rights

As its economic potential has rapidly expanded, intellectual property has become a subject of front-rank legal importance. *Cambridge Studies in Intellectual Property Rights* is a series of monograph studies of major current issues in intellectual property. Each volume will contain a mix of international, European, comparative and national law, making this a highly significant series for practitioners, judges and academic researchers in many countries.

Series editor
Professor William R. Cornish, *University of Cambridge*

Advisory editors
Professor François Dessemontet, University of Lausanne
Professor Paul Goldstein, Stanford University
The Hon. Sir Justice Robin Jacob, The High Court, England and Wales

A list of books in the series can be found at the end of this volume.

The Legal Protection
of Databases

Mark J. Davison

Monash University

CAMBRIDGE
UNIVERSITY PRESS

CAMBRIDGE UNIVERSITY PRESS
Cambridge, New York, Melbourne, Madrid, Cape Town, Singapore, São Paulo

Cambridge University Press
The Edinburgh Building, Cambridge CB2 8RU, UK

Published in the United States of America by Cambridge University Press, New York

www.cambridge.org
Information on this title: www.cambridge.org/9780521802574

First published 2003
This digitally printed version 2008

A catalogue record for this publication is available from the British Library

ISBN 978-0-521-80257-4 hardback
ISBN 978-0-521-04945-0 paperback

For James, Sibyl and Sara

Contents

Foreword by William R. Cornish		*page* xv
Acknowledgments		xvi
Table of cases		xvii
Table of legislation		xxiii
Table of European Union legislation		xxxiv
Table of treaties, conventions, other international and regional instruments		xxxviii

1	**Introduction**	**1**
	Why have databases become an important issue	2
	The structure of this book	3
2	**Some basic principles**	**10**
	Basic copyright principles concerning databases	11
	Compilations and collections	11
	Originality	13
	The 'sweat of the brow' approach	14
	An intellectual creation	15
	European standards of originality	16
	The spectrum of originality	17
	Originality as it applies to compilations and databases	17
	Authorship	21
	Some technical aspects of database creation	22
	Infringement	24
	A substantial part of a work: qualitative rather than quantitative tests	25
	Rights that are infringed	28
	Right of reproduction	29
	Right of rental	31
	Right of distribution	31
	Right of communication to the public	31
	Protection against circumvention of technological protection devices	32
	Exceptions to copyright	32
	Compulsory licensing	34
	Summary of copyright	36

Principles of unfair competition 37
Contract law and databases 40
Competition law 43
The paradigm does not fit 43
The legal model for protection may generate the possibility of
    legitimate market power being created 46
The logistics of government regulation 47
Government policy towards competition law 48
Aspects of distributive justice 48

3   Protection of databases in the EU   **50**
History of the Directive 51
The Green Paper 52
The First Draft 53
Justification for a Directive 54
Definition of a database 54
Copyright in a database 54
Relationship to copyright in computer programs 55
Exceptions to copyright 55
Relationship between copyright and contract law 56
The *sui generis* right 57
Compulsory licensing 57
Exceptions to the *sui generis* right 58
Term of protection 59
Protection for databases outside the EU 59
Retrospectivity 59
Preservation of other legal provisions 59
Summary of the First Draft 60
Opinion of the Economic and Social Committee of the Council 60
Definition of a database 62
Protection for databases outside the EU 63
Duration of protection 63
Authorship of databases and circumvention of technological
    protection of databases 64
Summary of the Committee's Opinion 64
Amendments to the Directive by the European Parliament 65
Definition of a database 66
The *sui generis* right 66
Compulsory licensing 66
Exceptions to the *sui generis* right 67
The duration of protection 67
Summary of the 1993 Amendments 67
The common position of 10 July 1995 68
The final version of the Directive 68
The recitals 69
The need for uniform laws 69
Explanation of the substantive provisions of the Directive 70
Scope of the Directive and the definition of a database 70
Computer programs 74
Copyright in databases 75

Authors of databases   76
Restricted acts   76
Exceptions to copyright in databases   77
The *sui generis* right   81
The maker of a database   82
A qualitatively or quantitatively substantial investment in
    obtaining, verifying or presenting   83
Right to prevent extraction and/or re-utilisation   87
Infringement of the right of extraction and re-utilisation 89
Exceptions to the *sui generis* right   91
Duration of the *sui generis* right   92
Retrospectivity   93
Territorial qualification for protection   97
Compulsory licensing and competition law   97
Saving of existing legal regimes   98
Final provisions   98
Summary of the Directive   99
Circumvention of protection measures   100

4   Transposition of the Directive   103
Belgium   109
Copyright before and after transposition   109
Unfair competition laws   111
Sui generis protection   111
Right to extract or re-utilise an insubstantial part   112
Exceptions   113
Term of protection   113
France   113
Copyright before and after transposition   113
Unfair competition law   115
Sui generis protection   116
Right to extract or re-utilise an insubstantial part   117
Exceptions   117
Term of protection   118
Germany   118
Copyright before and after transposition   118
Unfair competition laws   123
Sui generis protection   124
Right to extract or re-utilise an insubstantial part   125
Exceptions   126
Term of protection   126
Ireland   126
Copyright protection before and after transposition   126
Unfair competition laws   127
Sui generis protection   128
The right to extract or re-utilise an insubstantial part 128
Exceptions   128
Term of protection   128
Licensing schemes   128
Technological protection measures   129

Italy	129
Copyright before and after transposition	129
Unfair competition laws	131
Sui generis protection	132
The right to extract or re-utilise an insubstantial part	133
Exceptions	133
The Netherlands	133
Copyright before and after transposition of databases prior to the Directive	133
Unfair competition laws	134
Sui generis protection	135
The right to extract or re-utilise an insubstantial part	136
Exceptions	137
Term of protection	137
Spain	138
Copyright before and after transposition	138
Unfair competition laws	139
Sui generis protection	140
The right to extract or re-utilise an insubstantial part	140
Exceptions	140
Term of protection	140
Sweden	141
Copyright before and after transposition	141
Unfair competition laws	142
Sui generis protection	142
United Kingdom	143
Copyright before and after transposition	143
Unfair competition laws	146
Sui generis protection	147
Right to extract or re-utilise an insubstantial part	151
Exceptions	151
Term of protection	151
Licensing schemes	152
Summary of the transposition of the Directive	152
Harmonisation of copyright	152
The investment necessary to qualify for *sui generis* protection	153
Nature of the right and the test of infringement	155
Definition of a lawful user	156
Lack of harmonisation of the exceptions	156
The period of protection	156
Relationship to unfair competition laws	157
Single source databases	157
Conclusion	158
5 Protection of databases in the United States of America	**160**
Copyright	162
Some decisions since *Feist*	162
Circumvention of technological measures	164
The fair use defence	167
Summary of the copyright position	170

Nature and history of the American tort of misappropriation   171
  International News Service v. *Associated Press*   172
    Subject matter of protection   173
    Protection against whom   174
    Nature of the protection   174
    The dissenting judgment in *International News Service* v.
      Associated Press   175
    Summary of the position in *International News Service* v.
      Associated Press   176
  The chequered history of the decision in *International News
    Service* v. *Associated Press*   178
  Limitations on the scope of the tort of misappropriation   179
    Pre-emption by the Federal Constitution and intellectual property
      legislation   180
    Direct competition between the parties   183
    Time-sensitivity   185
    Reducing the plaintiff's incentive   187
  Summary of American unfair competition law   189
Legislative proposals for *sui generis* protection   190
  The Database Investment and Intellectual Property Antipiracy
    Bill of 1996   190
    Definition of a database   191
    The *sui generis* right   191
    Comparisons with misappropriation   192
    Comparisons with the Directive   192
  The Collections of Information Antipiracy Bill 1997   193
    Definition of a Database   194
    Prerequisite for *sui generis* protection   194
    Nature of the *sui generis* right   195
    Potential market   195
    Circumvention of database protection systems and protection
      of database management information   197
    Permitted acts   197
    Exclusions   198
    Preservation of contract law and other legal regimes 199
    Pre-emption of state law   199
    Comparisons with the Directive   199
    Comparisons with misappropriation   200
  The Collections of Information Antipiracy Bill of 1999   200
    Definition of a collection of information   201
    Material harm   201
    The market protected   202
    A substantial part   203
    Fair use   204
    Reasonable uses for educational, scientific or research purposes 205
    Other reasonable uses   206
    Special provisions for securities and commodities market
      information and digital on-line communications 207
    Special provisions regarding genealogical information 207
    Investigative, protective or intelligence activities 207

Computer programs and digital on-line communications   208
Government collections of information   208
Duration of protection   209
Retrospectivity   211
Remedies   211
Study and report   211
Comparisons with the Directive   211
Comparisons with misappropriation   212
The Consumer and Investor Access to Information Bill of 1999   213
Summary of the American position   213

6   International aspects of protection of databases   217
International agreements concerning copyright protection of
databases   218
National treatment, most favoured nation status and the
Directive   221
Public international obligations and the American legislation   226
Steps towards a WIPO Treaty on the Protection of Databases   226
The Draft Treaty   227
Further moves towards a database treaty by WIPO   228
WIPO information meeting on intellectual property in databases,
Geneva, 17–19 September 1997   229
Observations by WMO and UNESCO   229
Outcome of the information meeting   230
Summary of moves to adopt a database treaty   231
EU and bilateral arrangements   234
Conclusion   235

7   The appropriate model for the legal protection
of databases   237
The argument in favour of *sui generis* protection   239
Economic theory   241
Price discrimination   242
The costs of intellectual property rights   244
Rent seeking   245
Loss of public good benefits   247
Transaction costs   254
Enforcement costs   257
Limiting the costs of property rights   257
Summary of economic theory   258
Anecdotal and empirical evidence   259
Evidence of the Directive's impact   263
Non-economic roles of information   264
Limits of the tragedy of the commons   266
Examples of scientific cooperation   269
The Health WIZ project   269
World Meteorological Organization (WMO)   271
Some suggestions for protection of databases   272
Defining the subject matter of protection narrowly so as to avoid
unnecessary and unintended consequences   273

Separation of the subject matter of *sui generis* protection for sweat of
    the brow from copyright protection   274
Differentiation of *sui generis* rights from copyright   275
Exceptions to copyright to permit use of underlying
    information   276
Exceptions to prohibitions on circumvention protection devices   277
An equivalent to the fair use defence   277
Relationship with contract law and compulsory licences   278
Modification of competition law principles   280
Duration of the period of protection   280
Remedies   281
Excise some areas of scientific cooperation from any treaty
    or legislation   282
Government information   282
Conclusion   283
Addendum   285
Canadian approach to originality   285
Reports to WIPO on the impact of database protection
    on developing countries   286

Glossary   288
Bibliography   290
Index   296

Foreword

Mark Davison's book on database protection covers a vital aspect of the digital revolution. Indeed, the whole issue cries out for a place in this series. Databases stand at the juncture between information as such and the expression of literary and artistic ideas. From the first perspective, information appears to be a necessary element in social existence and so arguably it should be freely accessible to all. From the second, the need to provide an incentive for the costly business of assembling large databases argues for an equivalent appropriation to that given to creators and their producers by copyright. Deciding how to structure this crossroads – be it with filter lanes or with stop signs – calls for refined legal engineering. What has been done so far to regulate this space has in considerable degree depended on attitudes towards traffic which were formed in a horsedrawn era. Now, motorised vehicles bearing enormous loads of information bear down and have somehow to be accommodated. Hard-pressed legislators and courts have done what struck them as best, but it is far too early to say whether anything like a reasonable balance has been reached between free flow and controlled access.

It will be some time before we can see whether by and large we are offering stimulants to investment in data accumulation which are what is needed, but not evidently more than that. Mark Davison draws on the experience to date in the United States, the British Commonwealth and the European Union. He shows the effects of pressure groups on emerging solutions and, with a candid objectivity, demonstrates how much has as yet to be treated as experimental. His writing is a refreshing antidote to those who abjure any idea of intellectual property in this sphere, as much as to those who battle for extensive intellectual property rights as the one and only cause in the new and ever expanding market for organised data. The book deserves to reach a wide audience.

Series Editor   WILLIAM R. CORNISH

Acknowledgments

In writing this book I received help from a number of people and organisations. In particular, I would like to thank Keith Akers for his generous assistance and the Australian Research Council for providing me and Sam Ricketson with research funds. Sam Ricketson read and commented on a number of chapters and provided generous support in many ways. I also received comments from Tony Duggan, Philip Williams and Russell Smyth. A large number of other people were very generous with their time and/or in providing documentation or commentary, including: Teresa Arnesen, Christian Auingier, Toby Bainton, Stuart Booth, Clive Bradley, Andrew Christie, Charles Clark, Chris Cresswell, Peter Drahos, Sir Roger Elliott, Janet Ford, Jens Gaster, Teresa Hackett, Beth Heyde, Bernt Hugenholtz, Anne Joseph, Stephen Maurer, Wilma Mossink, Sandy Norman, Oliver Oosterbaan, Dennis Pearce, Jerome Reichman, Andrew Treloar and John Zillman. Stephen Parker read a number of chapters and, as Dean of the Faculty of Law at Monash University, supported me in many ways.

Bill Cornish supported the proposal for the book and provided valuable advice and assistance at critical times. Finola O'Sullivan and Jennie Rubio from Cambridge University Press were both patient and very understanding and helpful. Lisa Gardaro did excellent work in the final editing of the manuscript.

URLs

The publisher has used its best endeavours to ensure that the URLs for external websites referred to in this book are correct and active at the time of going to press. However, the publisher has no responsibility for the websites and can make no guarantee that a site will remain live or that the content is or will remain appropriate.

Table of cases

APRA *v.* Ceridale Pty Ltd (1991) ATPR 41–074   *page* 47

Addressograph-Multigraph Corp. *v.* American Expansion
Bolt and Manufacturing Co., 7th Cir, 124 F 2d 706
(1942)   179

Advanced Computer Servs *v.* MAI Sys. Corp., 845 F
Supp. 356, 362 (ED Va, 1994)   30

Algemeen Dagblad and Others *v.* Eureka President, District
Court of Rotterdam, 22 August 2000   156

American Geophysical Union *v.* Texaco Inc., 802 F Supp. 1, 17
(SDNY, 1992)   169

Apple Computer Inc. *v.* Computer Edge Pty Ltd (1984)
53 ALR 225   273

Armond Budish *v.* Harley Gordon, 784 F Supp. 1320
(1992)   164

Associated Press *v.* United States, 326 US 1, 65 S. Ct 1416
(1945)   176

BN Marconi SRL *v.* Marchi & Marchi SRL, Court of Genoa,
19 June 1993, 1994 Foro It. Pt 1, 2559   132

Baumann *v.* Fussell [1978] RPC 485   27

Bellsouth Advertising & Publishing Corporation *v.* Donnelly
Information Publishing Inc., 999 F 2d 1436 (1993)   162

Board of Trade *v.* Dow Jones and Co., 456 NE 2d 84
(S. Ct Ill., 1983)   179

CD Law Inc. *v.* Lawworks Inc., 35 USPQ 2d (BNA) 1352
(1994)   182

Campbell *v.* Acuff-Rose Music Inc., 114 S. Ct 1164, 1170
(1994)   169

Capitol Records Inc. *v.* Spies, 130 Ill. App. 2d 429, 264 NE
874 (1970)   179

Cheney Bros. *v.* Doris Silk Corp., 35 F 2d 279
(2nd Cir. 1929)   160

Columbia Broadcasting System Inc. *v.* De Costa, 377 F 2d 315
(Ct App. 1st Cir. 1967)   178
Commercial Bank of Australia *v.* Amadio (1983) 151
CLR 447   42
Compco Corp. *v.* Day-Brite Lighting Inc., 376 US 234,
84 S. Ct 779 (1964)   181
Continental Casualty Co. *v.* Beardsley US Dist Ct SD NY
151 F Supp. 28 (1957)   179
Data Access Corporation *v.* Powerflex Services Pty Ltd [1999]
HCA 49   75
De Costa *v.* Viacom Int. Inc., 981 F 2d 602
(1st Cir. 1992)   178
Decoras SA and L'Esprit du Vin SARL *v.* Art Metal SARL and
Marioni Alfredi [1991] PIBD 510 III-655 (CA Paris)   116
Del Madera Properties *v.* Rhodes and Gardner Inc., 820 F 2d
973, 976 (9th Cir. 1987)   181
Denda International *v.* KPN., 5 August, 1997, [1997]
Informatierecht, AMI 218, Court of Appeal of
Amsterdam   45, 136
Diamond *v.* Am-Law Corp., 745 F 2d 142 (2nd Cir. 1984)   169
Electre *v.* TI Communication and Maxotex, Tribunal de
Commerce de Paris, 7 March 1999   117
Erie Railroad *v.* Tompkins, 304 US 64 (1938)   178
Feist Publications Inc. *v.* Rural Telephone Service Co.,
499 US 340 (1991)   14, 15, 28, 83, 95, 162,
                                             169, 171, 175, 182, 196,
                                             219, 244, 256, 274, 276
Financial Information Inc. *v.* Moody's Investors Service Inc.,
808 F 2d 204 (1986)   186
Fixtures Marketing Ltd *v.* AB Svenska, Spel, T 99-99, 11 April
2001   155
Football League Ltd *v.* Littlewoods Pools Ltd [1959] 1
Ch 637   144
France Telecom *v.* MA Editions, Tribunal de Commerce de
Paris, 18 June 1999   117
Fred Wehrenberge Circuit of Theatres Inc. *v.* Moviefone Inc., 73
F Supp. 2d 1044 (1999)   187
Gilmore *v.* Sammons, 269 SW 861 (1925)   186
Goldstein *v.* California, 412 US 546 (1973)   182
Groupe Moniteur and Others *v.* Observatoire des Marches,
Public Cour d'appel de Paris, 18 June 1999   114, 116,
                                                                117, 157

Harper & Row, Publishers, Inc. *v.* National Enterprises, 471 US
   539 (1985)   168
Hawkes and Son (London) *v.* Paramount Film Service Ltd
   [1934] 1 Ch 593   26
Hodgkinson & Corby Ltd and Roho Inc. *v.* Wards Mobility
   Services Ltd [1995] FSR 169   38, 146
Illinois Bell Telephone Company *v.* Haines and Co. Inc., 932 F
   2d 610 (7th Cir. 1991)   162
Infinity Broadcast Corp. *v.* Kirkwood, 150 F 3d 104, 109
   (2nd Cir. 1998)   169
Information Handling Service Inc. *v.* LRP Publications Inc., 54
   USPQ 2d (BNA) 1571 (2000)   182
International News Service *v.* Associated Press, 248 US 215
   (1918)   39, 160, 161, 172–178,
                               180, 183, 184, 189, 198
Iowa State University Research Foundation Inc. *v.* American
   Broadcasting Co., 621 F 2d 57 (2nd Cir. 1980)   168
KPN *v.* Denda International and Others, District Court Almelo,
   6 December 2000   45
KPN *v.* Denda International, Court of Appeal Arnhem, 15 April
   1997   136
KPN *v.* XSO President, District Court of the Hague, 14 January
   2000   136
KVOS *v.* Associated Press, 299 US 269 (1936); 80 F 2d 575
   (1935); 9 F Supp. 279 (1934)   183
Kewanee Oil Co. *v.* Bicron Corp., 416 US 470 (1974)   182
Key Publications Inc. *v.* Chinatown Today Publishing
   Enterprises Inc., 945 F 2d 509 (2nd Cir. 1991)   164
Koninklijke Vermande BV *v.* Bojkovski, 98/147 Court Decision
   of 20 March 1998 (District Court of The Hague)   134
Kregos *v.* Associated Press, 3 F 3d 656 (2nd Cir. 1993)   12, 182
Ladbroke (Football) Ltd *v.* William Hill (Football) Ltd [1964] 1
   All ER 465, [1964] 1 WLR 273   37
Lego *v.* Oku Hobby Speelgoed BV/Frits de Vrites Agenturen BV
   Lima Srl, President District Court of Utrecht, 10 September
   1998   135
Loeb *v.* Turner et al., 257 SW 2d 800 (Ct Civ. App.
   Tex. 1953)   185
Lynch, Jones & Ryan Inc. *v.* Standard & Poor's, 47 USPQ 2d
   BNA 1759 (S. Ct NY, 1998)   187
MAI Sys. Corp. *v.* Peak Computer Inc., 991 F 2d 511
   (9th Cir. 1993)   30

MacMillan & Co. *v.* Cooper (1924) 93 LJPC 113   14
Mars UK Ltd *v.* Teknowledge Ltd [2000] FSR 138, [1999] ALL
    ER 600 (QB)   71, 194
Matthew Bender & Co. *v.* West Publishing Co., 158 F 3d 674
    (2nd Cir. NY 1998)   163
Matthew Bender Co. Inc. *v.* West Publishing Co., 158 F 3d 693
    (1998)   163
Maxtone-Graham *v.* Burtchaell, 631 F Supp. 1432 (SDNY
    1986)   169
McCord Co. *v.* Plotnick, 108 Cal. App. 2d 392, 239 P 2d 32
    (1951)   184
Mercury Record Productions Inc. *v.* Economic Consultants Inc.,
    218 NW 2d 705 (Wis. 1974)   178
Metropolitan Opera Association *v.* Wagner-Nichols Recorder
    Corp., 199 Misc 786, 101 NYS 2d 483 (S. Ct, NY 1950) at
    492   179
Mirror Newspapers Ltd *v.* Queensland Newspapers Pty Ltd
    [1982] Qd R 305   20
Montgomery County Association of Realtors Inc. *v.* Realty Photo
    Master Corporation, 878 F Supp. 84 (1995)   164, 262
Moorgate Tobacco Co. Ltd *v.* Philip Morris Ltd (1984) 156
    CLR 414   38
NFL *v.* Governor of Delaware, 435 F Supp. 1372, (US Dist Ct,
    1977)   185
NV Holdingmaatschappij de Telegraf *v.* Nederlandes Omroep
    Stichting, Court of Appeal, The Hague 99/165, 30 January
    2001   154
NVM *v.* De Telegraaf, Court of Appeal, The Hague,
    21 December 2000   136, 137, 154
National Basketball Association *v.* Motorola Inc., 105 F
    3d 841 (2nd Cir. 1997).   39, 160, 162, 179, 180,
                                          182, 185–188, 198,
                                          200, 201, 206, 214
National Business Lists Inc. *v.* Dun & Bradstreet, 552 F Supp.
    89 (1982)   196
National Council on Compensation Insurance Inc. (NCCI) *v.*
    Insurance Data Resources Inc., 40 USPQ 2d (BNA) 1362
    (1996)   163
National Exhibition Co. *v.* Tele-Flash Inc., 24 F Supp. 810
    (Dist Ct, SD NY 1936)   183
Nationwide News Pty Ltd and Others *v.* Copyright Agency Ltd,
    No. NG94 of 1995, Federal Court of Australia   37

Neal *v.* Thomas Organ Co., 241 F Supp. 1020 (US Dist Ct, SD
    Cal. 1965)   178
Oasis Publishing Co. *v.* West Publishing Co., 924 F Supp. 918
    (Minn. 1996)   163
P.I.C. Design Corp. *v.* Sterling Precision Corp., 231 F Supp. 106
    (2nd Cir. US Dist Ct, SD NY, 1964)   178
Philips Electronics NV *v.* Ingman Ltd and the Video Duplicating
    Company Ltd [1995] FSR 530   46
Pittsburgh Athletic Co. *v.* KQV Broadcasting Co., 24 F Supp.
    490 (D Pa. 1934)   183
R R Donnelly & Sons Co. *v.* Haber, 43 F Supp. 456 (1942)   182
Radio Telefis Eireann (RTE) and Independent Television
    Publications Ltd (ITP) *v.* Commission of the European
    Communities (*Magill's* case) [1995] ECR I – 743 [1995] 4
    CMLR 718   45
Re.: CBS Records and Gross, No. G337 of 1989, Federal Court
    of Australia 69   38
SARL Parfum Ungaro *v.* SARL JJ Vivier Paris, 18 May 1989,
    D 1990   116
Salinger *v.* Random House Inc., 650 F Supp. 413 at 425
    (SD NY, 1986)   168
San Fernando Valley Board of Realtors Inc. *v.* Mayflower
    Transit Inc., No. CV 91–5872-WJR- (Kx) (CD Cal.
    1993)   260
Sears, Roebuck & Co. *v.* Stiffel Co., 376 US 225, 84 S. Ct 784
    (1964)   181
Skinder-Strauss Associates *v.* Massachusetts Continuing
    Legal Education Inc., 914 F Supp. 665 (D. Mass.
    1995)   28, 182, 260
Standard & Poor's Corporation Inc. *v.* Commodity Exchange
    Inc., 683 F 2d 704 (2nd Cir. 1982)   196
Stewarts *v.* Abend, 495 US 207 (1990)   168
Synercom Technology Inc. *v.* University Computing Company
    and Engineering Dynamics Inc., 474 F Supp. 37 (ND Tex.
    1979)   179
Tele-Direct (Publication) Inc. *v.* American Business Information
    Inc. (1996) 74 CPR (3d) 72   162, 236
Telstra *v.* Desktop Marketing Pty Ltd [2001] FCA 612   10
The British Horseracing Board Ltd *v.* William Hill Ltd,
    (HC 2000 1335), judgment 9 February 2001   137, 147–159
Tierce Ladbroke SA *v.* The Commission, case T-504/93 [1997]
    ECR II 923   46

Transwestern Publishing Company LP *v.* Multimedia Marketing
  Associates Inc., 133 F3d 773   162
Triangle Publications Inc. *v.* New England Newspaper, 46 F
  Supp. 198, (Dist Ct, 1942)   179
UNMS *v.* Belpharma Communication, Court of Brussels,
  16 March 1999   112
University of London Press Ltd *v.* University Tutorial Press Ltd
  [1916] 2 Ch 601   37
US Ex Rel Berge v. Board of Trustees of University of Alabama,
  104 F 3d 1453 (4th Cir. 1997)   182
Victor Lalli Enterprises Inc. *v.* Big Red Apple Inc., 936 F 2d 671
  (2nd Cir. 1991)   163
Waterlow Publishers Ltd. *v.* Rose (1990) 17 IPR 493   28
West Publishing Co. *v.* Matthew Bender & Co., Cert. denied S.
  Ct, 522 US 3732 (1999)   163
West Publishing Co. *v.* Mead Data Central Inc., 616 F Supp.
  1571 (D. Minn. 1985); 799 F 2d 1219 (8th Cir. 1986); 479
  US 1070 (US S. Ct 1987)   163
West Publishing *v.* Hyperlaw Inc., Cert. denied S. Ct, 526 US
  1154 (1999)   163

Table of legislation

Australia

Copyright Act 1968
Part VB   *page* 34
Part VI, Divison 3   34
    s. 10   12
       14(1)   26, 34
       116A   220

Foreign Proceedings (Excess of Jurisdiction) Act 1984   48

Trade Practices Act 1974
Part V, Division 2   43
    s. 46   46

Belgium

Civil Code
Arts. 1382–1384   111

Law on Copyright and Neighbouring Rights, 30 June 1994
(as amended)
Art. 1, s. 1   105, 109
       3(3)   109
       4(2)   109
       8   109
       20(2)   109
       20(4)   109
       20*ter*   105, 110
       22   106, 110
       22(1)   106, 110, 153
       22(2)   106, 110
       22(4)   106, 110
       22*bis*(1)   106, 110

22*bis*(4)   106, 110, 113
22*bis*(5)   106, 110
23   106, 110
23(3)   111
59   111
60   111
61*ter*   111

Legal Protection of Databases Act 1998
Art. 2(1)   107
2(2)(3)   107, 108
2(4)   107, 112
2(5)   107, 111
3   107
6   108, 113
7(1)   107, 113
7(2)   107
7(3)   108, 113
8   112

Denmark

Copyright Act 1995
s. 5   12
71   59, 260

Finland

Copyright Act 1961
Art. 49   59, 260

France

Copyright Act
Art. L341–1   82, 107

Law No. 98-536 of 1 July 1998   82, 104, 225

Law No. 92-597 of 1 July 1992, Code of Intellectual Property
(relative au code de la propriété intellectuelle (partie législative))
L111-1   21
L112-1   16, 114

L112-3	105, 107, 113, 114
L122-10	115
L122-5	80, 105, 106, 114, 115
L122-5(2)	33
L122-5(3)	33
L211-3	107
L341-1	82, 107
L342-1	107, 117
L342-3	107, 108, 117
L342-3(2)	117
L342-5	108

Germany

Unfair Competition Act (Gesetz gegen den unlauteren
Wettbewerb, 7 June 1909 (UWG))

s. 1	39, 123

Law on Copyright and Neighbouring Rights 1965 as amended
(or Copyright Law of 9 September 1965, Urhebesrechtsgesetz –
UrhG)   12

Art. 1	119
2(1)	119
2(2)	80, 118, 119
4	118
4(1)	120
45	106, 122
53	80, 121
53(1)–(3)	122
53(5)	79, 121
54a	122
55a	105, 122, 125
87a(1)	107, 120
87a(2)	107
87b	107, 125
87b(1)	104, 125
87c(1)	107, 126
87c(1), para. 2	107
87c(1), para. 3	107
87c(2)	108, 126
87d	104, 108, 126
87e	104, 125

Law on Copyright and Neighbouring Rights (1965 as amended by
Law of 9 June 1993)   120
  s. 2(1)   120
     4(2)   105
     29   119
     46   106, 121
     47(4)   122
     49(1)   122
     49(2)   122
     51(2)   122
     53   80, 106, 121
     53(1)   106, 121
     53(3)   122
     53(5)   106, 121
     69a   120, 121
     69a(3)   120, 121
     69b   118
     87a(1)   108

Ireland

Copyright Act 1963
  Art. 2   126

Copyright and Related Rights Act 2000
  Art. 2   105, 107, 126, 128, 129
     17(2)(d)   106, 126
     50   127
     51   106, 127
     52   106
     53(3)   127
     53(4)   127
     54   127
     57   106, 127
     59–70   127
     71   106, 127
     72–77   106
     83   105, 107
     173   127
     320   107, 108, 128
     321   107, 128
     322   107, 128
     324   107, 128
     325   108, 128

327	107, 128
329	107, 128
330	107, 128
331–336	108, 128
370	129
374	129
375	129

Italy

Civil Code 1942
Art. 2598 — 132

Law for the Protection of Copyright and Neighbouring Rights
(Law No. 633 of 22 April 1941)

Art. 1	107, 130
2	107, 130
2(9)	105, 132
3	12, 13, 129
6	16, 108, 130
7	108, 130
12ter	130
38	130
42	130
64	108
64(a)	108
64(6)(b)	131
64(6)(2)	131
64(6)(3)	131
68	106, 131
69	106, 131
70	106, 131
101	106, 131, 153
101(a)	131
101(b)	131
102bis	132

Legislative Decree No. 169 of 6 May 1999 — 82, 104, 225

Malaysia

Copyright Act 1987
s. 7(3)	14
8(1)(b)	14

Mexico

Copyright Law 1996
Art. 108   242

Netherlands

Copyright Act 1912
Art. 10   105, 133, 134
   10(1)   133, 134
   10(12), para 2   133
   11   133
   15   106
   15c   106, 134
   15c(2)   134
   15c(3)   134
   16   80, 106, 134
   16a   134
   16b(1)   106
   16b(5)   134
   16b(6)   134
   17(1)   134
   24a   105, 134

Database Law of 8 July 1998
Art. 1(a)   135
   1(b)   107, 135
   1(c)   135
   3(1)   107, 136
   5(a)   107, 137
   5(b)   107, 137
   5(c)   108, 137
   6   108, 137
   8(1)   137

Law of Obligations, Civil Code 1992
Book 6, Art. 6:162(2)   134

Spain

Copyright Act 1987 (Law No. 22, 1987) as amended
Art. 6(2)(a)–(c)   138

10	105, 138
12	105, 138
13	106, 138
31(1)	138
34	139
34(1)	105, 138
34(2)(a)–(c)	106, 138
35	106, 139
35(1)	139
37	106, 139
37(1)	139
37(2)	139
133(1)	107
133(3)(a)	107
133(3)(b)	107
133(3)(c)	107, 108
134(1)	107
135(a)	107
135(b)	107
136	108

Unfair Competition Act 1991
Art. 11	139
11(2)	139
11(3)	139

Sweden

Act on Copyright in Literary and Artistic Works (Law No. 729 of 1960 as amended)
Art. 1	141
13	141
16	141
18	141
21	141
26	141
26a	141
26(b)	141
49	59, 141, 142, 258

Market Practices Act 1996	142

United Kingdom

Copyright and Rights in Databases Regulations 1997   104, 144, 225
   Regulation 4   152
         6   144
        12   151
        12(1)   148
        13(1)   147
        14   107, 147
        14(1)   147
        14(2)–(4)   147
        14(5)   147
        15   107, 152
        16   148
        16(2)   150
        17   108
        19   107, 151
        20   107, 151
        21   151, 152
   Schedule 1   108, 151

Copyright, Designs and Patents Act 1988   24, 143, 145, 147, 152
  s. 3   143
   3A   105, 143
   3A(1)   107, 145, 147
   3A(2)   145
   9(3)   24
   11   105, 147
   16(3)   105
   29   146
   29 (1A)(5)   146
   296B   105, 145
   30   146
     ss. 32–36   146
     ss. 37–44   106, 146, 152
  s. 38   146
   44   152
     ss. 45–50   106, 146
     ss. 50D   105, 145
     s. 50D(1)   145
   121   152
   163   147
   165   147

USA

Collections of Information Antipiracy Bill of 1997,
(HR 2652)   193, 197, 199, 200, 206, 208
  s. 1201(5)   208
  1202   194, 195, 198, 206
  1203(b)   197, 198
  1203(c)   198
  1203(d)   205
  1203(e)   206
  1204(a)   198
  1204(a)(2)   198, 207
  1205   207
  1205(b)   196
  1206(e)   198
  1208(c)   195, 210

Collections of Information Antipiracy Bill of 1999, (HR 354)
  1401(a)   204
  1401(3)   202
  1401(1)   20
  1401(4)   202
  1401(6)   201, 210
  1402   193, 202, 203, 205, 206, 209, 212
  1403   207
  1403(a)   205, 207
  1403(a)(1)   205, 207
  1403(a)(2)   205, 207
  1403(b)   207
  1403(c)   204, 207
  1403(d)   207
  1403(e)   206
  1403(h)   207
  1403(i)   207
  1404(a)   208, 209
  1404(b)   208
  1404(c)   208
  1405(g)   207
  1406   211
  1406(e)   206
  1407   211
  1407(a)(2)   206
  1408   210, 211

1408(b) 208, 209
1408(c) 208, 209, 212
1409 210

Constitution of the United States
Art. I, cl. 8 171

Consumer and Investor Access to Information Bill of 1999
(HR 1858 of the 106th Congress)
s. 102 213
103(d) 213
104 213

Copyright Act of 1976
s. 102 182
103 183
106 182
107 168, 204
301 182
1201 197

Database Investment and Intellectual Property Antipiracy Bill of
1996 (HR 3531 of 1996)
s. 2 191
3(a) 191
3(d) 191
4(a)(1) 191
4(a)(2) 191
4(b) 191
6 192
6(a) 192
6(b) 192
9(c) 193
11 192

Digital Millennium Copyright Act of 1998 (12 Stat. 2860 (1998))
generally 165, 200
s. 1201 165
1201(a)(1)(A) 165
1201(a)(1)(B) 165
1201(a)(1)(C) 165
1201(d) 165
1201(d)(2) 165
1201(f) 165

Restatement of the Law, Third, Unfair Competition 1995,
s. 38   161

Sherman Act, Statute 209 of 1890 as amended by 15 USCA 2
(1973), s. 2   45

Table of European Union legislation

Common Position (EC) No. 48/2000 regarding the proposal for a
Council Directive on the legal protection of databases,
OJ No. C 288, 30 October 1995, Art. 6(2)   *page* 220

Copyright Directive (2001//29/EC; OJ No. L 167, 22 June 2001)
   Art. 6   91, 101
      6(1)   91, 100
      6(2)   100
      6(3)   100
      6(4)   101

Directive 96/9/EC of 11 March 1996 on the legal protection of
databases, (OJ No. L 77, 27 March 1996)
   Recital 2   69
        3   69
        4   69
        6   69
        7   69, 82, 89
        8   68
      10   69, 71, 82
      11   69, 82
      12   71, 82, 89
      13   69, 82
      16   76
      17   72, 73, 85
      18   55, 73
      19   73, 82, 85
      20   91
      22   71
      23   71
      24   77
      34   77
      36   78

39	82, 89
40	69, 82, 83, 89
41	82
42	89
43	71
44	71
52	142
54	82
55	82, 93
Art. 1	54, 55, 105, 109, 130
1(2)	57, 66, 70, 107
1(3)	74
1.1	70
1.2	107
2(b)	77
3	105, 109
3(1)	75, 84, 136
3(2)	76
4	76, 105
5	31, 56, 76, 77, 105
5(a)	30, 56, 76, 137
6	77, 91, 101, 122, 130
6(1)	77, 78, 100, 105, 122
6(2)(a)	78, 79, 92, 106, 138
6(2)(b)	78, 79, 92, 106, 138
6(2)(c)	78, 79, 92, 106, 138
6(2)(d)	106, 139
6(3)	79, 100
7	87, 100, 124, 130
7(1)	6, 55, 81, 84, 89, 149, 155
7(2)(a)	87
7(2)(b)	87, 108
7(4)	81
7(5)	92
8	42, 91
8(1)	35, 107, 91
8(2)	91, 151
9	91, 92, 98, 151
9(a)	78, 98, 107, 126
9(b)	98, 107
9(c)	98, 108

10	92, 93, 108, 134, 138
10(1)	134
10(2)	92
10(3)	92, 93
11	5, 97, 98
11(2)	97
11(3)	97
13	98, 138
14	94, 242
14(1)	94
15	91
16	98
16(3)	97

Explanatory Memorandum to the Proposal for a Council Directive
on the legal protection of databases COM(92) 24 Final – SYN 393,
Brussels, 13 May 1992   2, 53, 54, 55,
                                                        57, 58, 61

Green Paper on Copyright and the College of Technology 1988, Doc.
Ref. Com(88) 172 final   52, 53, 54, 96

Opinion on the Proposal for a Council Directive on the
legal protection of databases of the Economic
and Social Committee   16, 60, 61, 62, 63,
                                                    64, 65, 66, 67, 68,
                                                    70, 83, 94, 95, 97,
                                                    99, 100, 224, 241

Proposal for a Council Directive on the legal protection of databases
COM(92) 24 final – SYN 393 Brussels, 13 May 1992

Art. 1(1)	54, 55
1(2)	57
2	58
2(3)	54
2(4)	54
5	56
6	56
6(1)	56, 78
6(2)	56, 78
7(1)	55
7(2)	55
8(1)	58

8(2)	58, 98
8(4)	98
8(5)	66, 67
9(3)	59, 242
9(4)	59
11	59
11(2)	59
11(3)	59
12	59, 96
12(2)	59

Table of treaties, conventions, other international and regional instruments

Agreement on Trade Related Aspects of Intellectual Property (TRIPS) (entered into force 1 January 1995), UNTS 31874

Art 1(1)	*page* 222
1(2)	223
1(3)	222
1–7	223
3	222
3(1)	221
4	222
9	223
11	29, 31, 89
13	79, 224
Part III	223, 281

Basic Proposal for the Substantive Provisions of the Treaty on Intellectual Property in respect of Databases Considered by the Diplomatic Conference on Copyright and Neighbouring Rights Questions, Geneva, December, 1996

Art. 2	227
3	227
5	227
6	227

Berne Convention for the Protection of Literary and Artistic Works (Paris Act of 24 July 1971, as amended), 8L8 UNTS 221

Art. 1-21	30, 223
2(5)	52, 54, 218
7	225
9	28, 29
9(2)	36, 79, 224
10(2)	36, 55
11*bis*(2)	36

13(1)   36
18   95

Convention for the Protection of Producés of Phonograms 1971
(UNTS 12430)   231

EEC Treaty of Rome (25 March 1957; entered into force 1 January
1958) [UNTS/ILM Ref]
Art. 86   45

WIPO Copyright Treaty 1996, 36 ILM 65(1997)
Art. 1(4)   29, 30
4   219
6   29, 31, 88, 89
7   29, 31, 89
8   29, 31, 88, 89, 219, 220
11   29, 32, 220
12   220, 221
12(2)   221

1   Introduction

We live in the Age of Information. Information is money. So is time. The economies of the First World are dominated by the creation, manipulation and use of information and the time it takes to do so. These economies do not suffer from a shortage of information; they suffer from the difficulties associated with collecting, organising, accessing, maintaining and presenting it. Databases are designed to help deal with these difficulties. They are collections of information arranged in such a way that one or more items of information within them may be retrieved by any person with access to the collection containing those items.[1] Therefore, databases are big business because they contain important and copious amounts of information and they reduce the time taken to access that information.[2] And where there is big business, the law and lawyers inevitably follow.

But information is more than money and databases are more than big business. Information and databases are critical to science, the legal system itself, education and all those aspects of life that are improved by them. Consequently, there are important issues of social and political policy to be considered in the regulation of access to, and use of, databases. Again, where there are such critical issues at stake, the law has a role to play.

There is an inevitable tension between the commercial and the socio-political role of databases that leads to complexities in developing an appropriate model for their legal protection. In fact, given the diverse range of areas in which databases can be used, any one of a variety of legal models may be appropriate in any given context. One of the criticisms of general references to the importance of information is that they fail

---

[1] This is a very rough working definition of a database. The various issues concerning the definition of a database are discussed in later chapters, especially Chapters 3 and 4.

[2] 'In 1989, the world-wide turnover for online database and real time information services accounted for around 8.5 billion ECU.' In 1996, the estimated size of the European Market electronic information supply market was £5.138 billion. A Consultative Paper on United Kingdom Implementation: Directive 96/9/EC of 11 March 1996 on the legal protection of databases copyright directorate, The Patent Office, DTI, August, 1997 at para. 2.1.5 and Annex 2.

to differentiate between different categories of information.[3] The same criticism could be levelled at any legal system that applied a 'one size fits all' approach to the regulation of databases. It is no surprise then that a number of different legal models for protection of, and access to, data and databases have arisen.

Why have databases become an important issue

The transition of many First World economies from industrially based economies to information-based economies is a relatively recent phenomenon. It is a consequence of an explosion in information and the means by which it can be disseminated that results in turn from far-reaching technological and scientific developments.[4] In particular, advances in digital technology have facilitated the creation of databases. Large amounts of data can be created in, or converted into, digital form, and scanners and other devices permit the digital conversion of data. Alternatively, data can be originally produced and stored in digital forms that are perceived by humans as text, pictures, tables, spreadsheets and other easily recognisable formats. The digitisation of data in turn reduces storage costs. For example, if the DNA structure of the human genome were compiled in hardcopy it would occupy 200,000 pages.[5] The physical storage of such documentation in digital form can be achieved with a few CDs.

This expanded capacity to store data is complemented by an increased capacity to access and use it. It is facilitated by computer programs that enable quick and reliable searching and retrieval of data. Computer networks also allow on-line use of databases, thus increasing ease of access and marketability. These increased abilities to store and disseminate information, in turn, have increased the production of information. This is due to the relationship between the production of information and the availability of existing information. Existing information and access to it are critical to the creation of new data and information.[6] This creative process is like a spiral in which the users of existing data actually add

---

[3] See Chapter 6 for a discussion of this point.

[4] 'It has been estimated that the volume of the increase annually in information generated today equals the total information in circulation in the world fifty years ago.' Explanatory Memorandum to the Proposal for a Council Directive on the legal protection of databases COM(92) 24 final – SYN 393, Brussels, 13 May 1992.

[5] Human Genome Project Information at http://www.ornl.gov/hgmis/publicat/primer/fig14.html.

[6] At this point, the terms 'data' and 'information' are being used interchangeably. Possible distinctions between the two and the relevance of those distinctions are discussed in Chapter 6.

value to that data in the process of using it, thus generating more new data and information.

The pressure to provide specific legislative protection for databases has arisen from the increase in the mass of raw data available in almost every area of commerce and science, the increased technological ability to create databases containing those data and to provide easy access to them. These are coupled with the increased technological ability of others to reproduce those databases and a perceived lack of adequate protection from existing legal regimes, such as copyright. The same technology that has expanded the role and usefulness of databases permits quick and easy reproduction of those databases or large parts of the data contained within them. 'Robots' and other computer technology can be used to download data from databases with little effort or human intervention. This reproduction can take place anywhere on the planet, provided the person arranging for the reproduction has access to the necessary computer infrastructure. Consequently, database owners have claimed that they require additional legislative protection to protect their investment in the creation and marketing of databases from free-riders who can quickly and easily reproduce the databases created and maintained by them.

The structure of this book

This book examines various models of legal protection for databases. A brief explanation of those models is given at the beginning of Chapter 2, where the various basic legal principles relevant to nearly all jurisdictions are covered. In particular, Chapter 2 deals with some basic principles of copyright, unfair competition law, contract and competition or anti-trust law as they apply to databases. These principles are referred to throughout the book.

Chapter 3 examines the European Union (EU) Directive on the Legal Protection of Databases 1996 (the Directive),[7] including both the copyright protection and the *sui generis* protection that has been conferred by the Directive. This examination includes the history of the Directive, the justifications provided for it and its important features. In addition, Chapter 3 examines the impact on database protection of the provisions of the EU Copyright Directive on the harmonisation of certain aspects of copyright and related rights in the information Society 2001 (the Copyright Directive).[8] The provisions of the Copyright Directive

[7] Directive 96/9/EC of 11 March 1996 on the Legal Protection of Databases, OJ No. L77, 27 March 1996, pp. 20–8.
[8] Directive 2001/29/EC, OJ No. L167, 22 June 2001, pp. 10–19.

concerning the circumvention of effective technological measures that are designed to protect copyright material also apply to the *sui generis* right conferred by the Directive. Consequently, those provisions are an important aspect of the protection provided for databases.

The examination in Chapter 3 of the history of the Directive reveals that the initial EU moves for *sui generis* protection proposed a very limited protection clearly separated from the copyright protection of databases. However, Chapter 3 also shows that the final form of *sui generis* protection under the Directive is, in fact, a hybrid of the generous scope of protection under former UK copyright law and the restrictive exceptions provided in the copyright law of many continental countries. The latter are probably quite justified in a copyright scheme that requires high levels of originality before conferring any copyright protection at all. However, they are inadequate in a legislative scheme that confers protection on un-original databases. The effect of this hybrid approach has been to confer an extraordinary degree of *sui generis* protection. The argument is also made that the *sui generis* protection provided by the Directive is inappropriately and inextricably entwined with copyright law and that, in a number of technical respects, the Directive is worded in such a way that it provides protection, even beyond its intended scope. An example of this latter point is the broad definition of a database.

Chapter 4 examines the legislation transposing the Directive in a number of the Member States and some of the emerging case law relating to that legislation. This examination further illuminates some of the ambiguities in the wording of the Directive and different approaches that have been taken to its transposition.

Chapter 5 examines the protection provided by copyright and the tort of misappropriation in the United States. Copyright and misappropriation principles have underpinned the different proposals that have been made in the United States for *sui generis* protection. Yet the tort of misappropriation has itself had a chequered history. Considerable judicial attention has been given to the theoretical basis of the tort and its consequent scope with resulting differences in the operation of the tort. Consequently, it is not surprising that different pieces of proposed legislation that have all been (allegedly) based on misappropriation have proposed quite different degrees of protection. The lesson to be learned from this is that if the concept of misappropriation is to be incorporated into *sui generis* legislation, it needs to be defined with some precision. Chapter 5 also examines the different pieces of proposed legislation and compares them with the tort of misappropriation and the Directive. This examination reveals a move away from the approach taken in the Directive towards one with wider exceptions to protection and a less restrictive approach to the use of information for transformative or wealth-producing uses of information. There are also provisions that are designed to ensure public access to information produced by government or with government funds.

Chapter 6 examines moves to provide additional protection for data-bases outside of the EU. In 1996, a draft treaty based on the Directive and legislation that had been proposed in the United States[9] was briefly considered at a diplomatic conference hosted by the World Intellectual Property Organization (WIPO). The draft treaty was not adopted but the issue has continued to receive consideration by WIPO since that time. The failure to pass any of the proposed pieces of legislation in the United States has no doubt hampered that process but once such legislation is in place, moves for a treaty are likely to intensify. To date, the EU has suggested its Directive as a template for a treaty on the topic but this has encountered considerable resistance from developing countries. Resistance has also come from international science organisations that are concerned about the potential impact of any *sui generis* legislation on the exchange of scientific information. The relevance of their views to *sui generis* protection is considered in Chapter 7.

In response to this resistance at WIPO, the EU has shifted its focus to its bilateral arrangements with other countries such as those seeking membership of the EU. Consequently, over fifty countries, including the fifteen Member States, either have *sui generis* protection for databases or will acquire it within the next few years.

There are other significant international aspects to the protection of databases associated with these moves. For example, the Directive pro-vides that *sui generis* protection for overseas databases will only be con-ferred if the nations from which those databases originate also provide materially the same protection for EU databases.[10] This use of reciprocity provisions in intellectual property regimes is a relatively rare departure from the usual international practice of according national treatment to nationals from other nations. One of the reasons for this approach is to place pressure on countries such as the United States to provide recipro-cal protection and to create a de facto international model for protection. The implications of this are discussed. In particular, Chapter 6 argues that the EU may be obliged by international agreements to provide na-tional treatment to overseas databases and, consequently, the pressure to provide reciprocal protection is not as great as it may seem. Part of the

---

[9] The Database Investment and Intellectual Property Antipiracy Act of 1996, HR 3531 of 1996.

[10] Article 11 of the Directive.

basis of this argument relates back to the point made in Chapter 3 that *sui generis* protection is inextricably entwined with copyright. While the Directive describes it as being separate from copyright, a close inspection of the subject matter of protection, the rights conferred and exceptions to those rights suggests that *sui generis* protection is, in reality, a form of copyright.

Chapter 7 analyses the arguments for and against the different models for *sui generis* protection from a theoretical perspective. As with every intellectual property regime, the law in relation to the protection of databases needs to achieve an appropriate balance between the rights of users and the rights of producers or owners of intellectual property. The ultimate objective of this balancing act is to achieve an optimal production and dissemination of the material that is, or could be, contained within databases. Hence, database owners have argued that greater protection is required for databases in order to protect their investment in production. This emphasis on protection of the database maker's investment undoubtedly underpinned the Directive, as making a substantial investment is the litmus test for whether the Directive's *sui generis* protection extends to a particular database.[11] However, this emphasis represents a significant shift in the general approach to the recognition and protection of intellectual property. At least in common law countries, the emphasis in other intellectual property regimes has been on the creation and maintenance of a social contract between creators and users. While encouraging investment is a desirable goal of this social contract, the real question is whether the investment in question is an optimal investment for public purposes. This in itself is a controversial issue, as what constitutes 'optimal' investment is debatable.

In the context of databases, this relationship between producers and users is complicated by the fact that in a number of contexts, the users themselves make significant contributions to the production of the information that is contained within those databases; and this information production is often subsidised by public funds. A particular concern is the relationship between protection of databases and the impact of that protection on research and education, activities essential to the continued production of the very information that finds its way into many databases. Consequently, the book examines the impact of the models for *sui generis* protection on research and education.

As the justification for *sui generis* protection of databases is primarily an economic one, an analysis of that justification inevitably requires some examination of economic arguments for protection; hence, some

---

[11] Article 7(1) of the Directive.

of Chapter 7 is taken up with this. However, the validity of such theories is ultimately dependent on empirical evidence.[12] At the present time, there is no clear empirical evidence justifying a strong form of *sui generis* protection.[13] Consequently, while those theories are important, they should be treated with some caution, particularly when they suggest the creation of strong intellectual property rights which, if created, will be effectively impossible to rescind. In addition, there are important non-economic aspects of the debate concerning protection of, and access to, databases that receive attention in Chapter 7. One example concerns the availability of information for news reporting and political debate.

The book concludes with a list of basic principles that need to be considered and incorporated into any *sui generis* protection of databases. This list is explained by reference to the preceding analysis in Chapter 7 of the arguments for and against different forms of *sui generis* protection, and is compared with particular aspects of the Directive and the various American bills on the topic that are examined in Chapters 3, 4 and 5.

A couple of points need to be made about the issues with which the book does not deal. In particular, it does not cover in any detail the law of confidential information or trade secrets as it applies to databases. This is because the emphasis is upon databases that are available to the public, or at least those members of the public with sufficient resources and interest to acquire access to them. Consequently, the emphasis in the legal analysis is upon proposals for *sui generis* protection for databases that cannot rely upon the protection of the law of confidential information. Legal issues surrounding privacy and databases are also not considered here, although obviously privacy in the context of databases is an important issue in its own right. Nevertheless, the emphasis in this book is on database owners, rights and their appropriate nature and extent, rather than the privacy rights of those whose details may be included in a database.

While it would be superfluous to repeat the details of Chapter 7 here, a couple of general observations about the book's conclusions are worthwhile to assist the reader in the course of the following chapters. The ultimate conclusion of the book is that there is justification for some *sui generis* protection of the investment involved in the creation and presentation of databases. This view is taken by various independent organisations and even those who have expressed concerns about the possibly excessive nature of any *sui generis* protection.[14] In many jurisdictions, the protection provided by copyright is insufficient. However, the justification

---

[12] P. Drahos, *A Philosophy of Intellectual Property* (Dartmouth, Aldershot, 1996), p. 7.

[13] US Copyright Office Report on Legal Protection for Databases, August 1997, pp. 76–7.

[14] Ibid., p. 78. Statements of Andrew Pincus, General Counsel, US Department of Commerce, Joshua Lederberg (on behalf of the National Academy of Science and Ors),

only extends to quite limited protection over and above that presently conferred by copyright, contract and other means. Any international agreement or legislation on the topic needs to acknowledge and respond to the diverse types of information in databases and the diversity of their potential uses. A simplistic approach which confers strong exclusive property rights in all databases and which applies to all uses of those databases does not meet that need. Such an approach runs the risk of treating all information as a commodity for all purposes.

In particular, there is a need to ensure that public access to information created with government funds or subsidies is not completely lost. This is an important issue. For example, governments, universities and other non-profit organisations supply more than one-third of the funds devoted to research and development[15] and the process of government also generates large amounts of information that are valuable both in a commercial sense and to the democratic process.

The latest American proposals for *sui generis* protection based on misappropriation principles have addressed some of the difficulties, and demonstrate an appreciation of the complexities associated with legislation concerning such a diffuse area. Hence, there are a number of exceptions provided for in the latest proposed legislation and protection is based on misappropriation principles. Nevertheless, it is too simplistic to just accept the view that any *sui generis* protection should be based on misappropriation principles. As argued in Chapter 6, misappropriation is a nebulous concept and it must be given a concrete form that is relevant to the area of its application. The latest American proposals still provide generous protection that approximates exclusive property rights, even though they are ostensibly based on misappropriation principles. In addition, the relationship between any prohibition on misappropriation, copyright and contract law needs to be addressed in some detail. While those proposals have considered these issues, there is some room for improvement.

In contrast to the more sophisticated American response to the issue of *sui generis* protection, the Directive adopts an approach conferring broad exclusive property rights with few, if any, meaningful exceptions.

and Charles Phelps (on behalf of the Association of American Universities and Ors) to the Subcommittee on Courts and Intellectual Property of the Judiciary Committee on the 1999 Bill (Collections of Information Antipiracy Act of 1999) on 18 March 1999, pp. 62–506 (Pincus, pp. 51–100; Lederberg, pp. 189–205; Phelps, pp. 223–53).

[15] E.g. between 1992 and 1997 more than 33 per cent of all research and development in the USA was funded by government, universities or other non-profit organisations. 'Statistical Abstract of the United States' (Bureau of Statistics, Washington DC, 1998). The same was also true for the UK between 1992 and 1996: 'Annual Abstract of Statistics No. 135 of 1999, Table 19.1' (Office for National Statistics, London, 1999).

forms of legal protection may supplement these models of protection. For example, various forms of unfair competition law may prevent parasitic copying of databases for the purposes of competing with the owner of a database.

As a number of basic legal principles underpin the different models of protection, an appreciation of them is crucial. Those principles are dealt with below and will be referred to throughout the book. For example, the *sui generis* protection offered by the Directive cannot be adequately understood without an understanding of copyright, as it draws upon a number of copyright principles. Indeed, in Chapters 3, 4 and 6, the argument is made that the *sui generis* protection provided by the Directive is a form of copyright protection and that the EU has failed adequately to differentiate copyright protection from *sui generis* protection.

The tort of misappropriation, part of American unfair competition law, forms the basis of the various bills that have been presented to the American Congress. Unfair competition law can also be relied on in a number of European countries to provide some protection for databases. Hence, some aspects are discussed in this chapter, although the term itself encompasses so many different types of conduct that particular attention needs to be given to the specific form of any unfair competition law. It is discussed in more detail in Chapters 4 and 5 when the unfair competition law of specific European and American jurisdictions is considered.

A further critical issue is the relationship between the laws that protect databases and the general law of contract. Increasingly, the contract providing for access to a database dictates the relationship between the owner and user, rather than laws concerning databases. This is particularly the case in a digital environment, where technological devices can be used to prevent access to anyone who has not formed a contractual relationship with the owner. Consequently, laws preventing the circumvention of technological protection devices are a key factor in protecting the efficacy of contracts for access to databases, and those laws need to be examined. Finally, as competition law has been held out as a means of ameliorating any significant difficulties flowing from the granting of *sui generis* protection, some aspects of competition law are considered in that context.

Basic copyright principles concerning databases

Compilations and collections

Until the members of the European Union implemented the Directive, few, if any, pieces of copyright legislation specifically protected databases as such. Their protection under copyright flowed and, in many jurisdictions, continues to flow from the fact that they are regarded as falling within a more general category of copyright work. In particular, databases are a form of compilation, collection, collective work or composite work.[2] In addition, a given database may be considered to be a literary work because it is a table, and tables are treated as a form of literary work in a number of jurisdictions.[3] For present purposes, the term 'compilation' will be adopted to refer to all these various descriptions.

The copyright nature of the compilation is derived from the process of gathering together and presenting pre-existing works or data. Copyright may well exist in the pre-existing works that are included in the compilation. For example, copyright may subsist in a compilation of selected poems and in the individual poems themselves. The copyright in each poem is distinct and separate from the copyright in the compilation itself.

Alternatively, the material within a compilation may not itself be subject to copyright. For example, a table of statistics containing data relating to the performance of baseball players may be a literary work, but individual data within the table are unlikely to be a literary works in themselves.[4]

However, not every compilation attracts copyright protection. The individual laws of various countries impose a range of other criteria that must be met before a compilation may acquire copyright protection. For example, a number of jurisdictions limit protection of compilations to those that constitute literary works. UK and Australian copyright legislation are examples of this approach.[5] They include compilations within their non-exclusive definitions of literary works, ensuring that a

[2] The term or terms used varies from jurisdiction to jurisdiction but these are the most commonly used ones. For example, Italy, Law for the Protection of Copyright and Neighbouring Rights, Law No. 633 of 22 April 1941 (as amended), Article 3 uses the term 'collective work'. Germany, Federal Copyright Act of 9 September 1965 uses the term 'compilation'. France, Intellectual Property Code, Law No. 92–597 of 1 July 1992 uses the term 'collections'. Denmark, Act on Copyright No. 395 of 1995, s. 5 refers to 'composite works'. The term 'collective work' is also used in another sense in some jurisdictions to refer to a work of multiple authorship where the individual contributions of each author cannot be separated from each other. See S. Ricketson, *The Berne Convention for the Protection of Literary and Artistic Works: 1886–1986* (Centre for Commercial Law Studies, Queen Mary College, University of London, London, 1987), p. 6.71.
[3] Section 10 of the Australian Copyright Act 1968, defines a literary work as including 'a table or compilation expressed in words, figures or symbols (whether or not in visible form)'.
[4] *Kregos* v. *Associated Press*, 3 F 3d 656 (US App. 1993).
[5] Section 10 of the Australian Copyright Act 1968, defines a literary work as including 'compilation expressed in words, figures or symbols (whether or not in visible form)'. Section 3 of the UK Copyright, Designs and Patents Act 1988 defines a literary work as 'any work, other than a dramatic or musical work, which is written, spoken or sung, and

compilation must be a literary work in order to attract copyright protection. In turn, this means that the compilation must be either a compilation of existing literary works, parts of literary works or pieces of material that, although not in themselves literary works, are in a literary or textual form such that the compilation of them constitutes a literary work.[6] This may exclude, for example, compilations of sound recordings, films and other material of a non-literary nature. Given the advances in digital technology, such material can be stored in digital form and combined into a digital compilation.

Prior to the implementation of the Directive and the Agreement on Trade Related Aspects of Intellectual Property (TRIPS),[7] another limitation on the copyright protection of compilations was that a number of jurisdictions limited protection to compilations of works or parts of works.[8] This would seem to exclude compilations of data that are not part of a work, but which are drawn together specifically to create the compilation in question. For example, a table of statistics may not constitute a compilation as any individual datum is not a work or part of a work. A third limitation on the copyright protection for compilations is the need for them to be original. This difficult and important requirement is discussed below.

Originality

Originality or intellectual creativity in a work is a requirement that is imposed in every copyright regime. The difficulty is that the meaning of originality or intellectual creativity differs according to the relevant legal standard in a particular jurisdiction, and the way in which that particular standard is applied in individual cases.

Much has been written on the topic of originality and it is not the purpose of this discussion to repeat all of what has already been said.[9]

---

accordingly, includes (a) a table or compilation [other than a database] . . . A database is included later in the definition of a literary work, generating the difficulty that a database may have to be a literary work in order to receive copyright protection.'

[6] See A. Monotti, 'The Extent of Copyright Protection for Compilations of Artistic Works' (1993) 15 *European Intellectual Property Review* 156 for a discussion of this issue.

[7] TRIPS is Annex 1C of the Agreement Establishing the World Trade Organization. The terms of TRIPS are available on the web page of the World Trade Organization at http://www.wto.org/english/docs_e/legal_e/final_e.htm.

[8] For example, Italy, Law for the Protection of Copyright and Neighbouring Rights, Law No. 633 of 22 April 1941 (as amended), Article 3 referred to collective works 'formed by the assembling of works, or parts of works'.

[9] L. Dreier and G. Karnall, 'Originality of the Copyright Work: A European Perspective' (1992) 39 *Journal of the Copyright Society USA* 289; G. Dworkin, 'Originality in the Law of Copyright' (1962) 11 *ASCAP Copyright Law Symposium* 60; J. Ginsburg, 'No "Sweat":

Nevertheless, some understanding of the various approaches to originality is necessary before one can adequately address its application to copyright in databases.

The 'sweat of the brow' approach   Perhaps the easiest form of originality to comprehend is the 'sweat of the brow' approach, where the author of the copyright work need only demonstrate that he or she has expended a significant effort in creating the work. In this sense, originality means that the copyright work in question has flowed from the author, has entailed a significant amount of work and is not the work of another. The UK copyright regime is widely regarded as possessing a sweat of the brow approach to copyright protection.[10] This view may be questionable as there is no definitive UK case authority upholding that proposition in as many words. Instead, the tendency has been to use the formulaic expression that the author must demonstrate that sufficient labour, skill and judgement have been put into the creation of the work.[11] The role of labour has not been segregated from the other components of the tests, namely skill and judgement. An examination of the cases suggests that a sweat of the brow approach may be the only explanation for a number of decisions but, at the very least, the UK has a relatively low standard of originality.[12]

One Australian decision that has confronted this issue directly held that sweat of the brow is sufficient to confer copyright protection on a compilation.[13] This decision was based on the view that prior to the implementation of the Directive, sweat of the brow was sufficient to confer protection on databases in the UK, and Australia had adopted the same standard as the UK. Another country that probably has a sweat of the brow standard of originality is Malaysia which specifically provides in s. 7(3) of its Copyright Act of 1987 that 'A literary, musical or artistic work shall not be eligible for copyright unless – (a) sufficient effort has been expended to make the work original in character'.[14] As with the Australian position, Malaysian copyright law is heavily influenced by UK

Copyright and Other Protection of Works of Information after *Feist* v. *Rural Telephone'* [1992] *Columbia Law Review* 338.

[10] The standard of originality for databases has been increased but the standard for other copyright works remains the same. See s. 3A(2) of the UK Copyright, Designs and Patent Act 1988 (as amended).

[11] E.g. *MacMillan & Co.* v. *Cooper* (1924) 93 LJPC 113, *Ladbroke (Football) Ltd* v. *William Hill (Football) Ltd* [1964] 1 All ER 465.

[12] See the discussion of this topic in S. Ricketson, *The Law of Intellectual Property: Copyright, Designs and Confidential Information* (Sydney, 1999) at p. 7.140–7.170.

[13] *Telstra* v. *Desktop Marketing Pty Ltd* [2001] FCA 612.

[14] The position is then complicated by s. 8(1)(b) which provides that collections are protected as original works provided that they constitute intellectual creations by reason of

copyright case law and principles, thus suggesting that sweat of the brow is probably the relevant standard in Malaysia.

An intellectual creation   A higher level of originality is the requirement that a copyright work should display a modicum of creativity and consequently can be regarded as an intellectual creation. This was the view expressed by the US Supreme Court in *Feist Publications Inc.* v. *Rural Telephone Service Co.*[15] when it considered whether copyright subsisted in a white pages telephone directory.

In *Feist's* case, the Supreme Court made a number of critical observations concerning originality for the purposes of American copyright law. It held that a compilation must be original in the sense that it has been independently created by its author, and that it displays a modicum of creativity before it can receive copyright protection.[16] It is the latter requirement of creativity that removes mere sweat of the brow or industrious collection from the scope of copyright protection. However, the Court also pointed out that this standard of creativity is easily met:

To be sure, the requisite level of creativity is extremely low: even a slight amount will suffice. The vast majority of works make the grade quite easily, as they possess some creative spark, 'no matter how crude, humble or obvious' it might be.[17]

Obviously, copyright did not subsist in the individual telephone book entries as they were no more than facts lacking any original written expression, so the question was whether the plaintiff 'selected, coordinated or arranged these uncopyrightable facts in an original way'.[18] The Court noted that the standard of originality was low and the facts need not be presented in an innovative or surprising way but '[i]t is equally true, however, that the selection and arrangement of facts cannot be so mechanical or routine as to require no creativity whatsoever'.[19] The Court went on to hold that the actual publication prepared by *Feist* was 'a garden-variety white pages directory, devoid of even the slightest trace of creativity'.[20] This was because the alphabetical arrangement of the subscribers was commonplace and there was no creativity in selecting the entries, as all the subscribers were included in the telephone book.

It is this standard of originality which has been adopted in the Directive for copyright protection of databases. It is also the standard of originality

the selection and arrangement of their contents. This raises the question of what type of effort is required as well as whether the effort is sufficient.

[15] 499 US 340 (1991). The approach to originality adopted in the decision was explicitly rejected in the Australian decision of *Telstra* v. *Desktop Marketing Pty Ltd* [2001] FCA 612.

[16] 499 US 340 (1991) at 346.   [17] Ibid., at 345.

[18] Ibid., at 362.   [19] Ibid.   [20] Ibid.

for compilations expressed in the most recent international agreements on copyright.[21]

The reason for this requirement for originality was based upon the Court's view of the purpose of copyright protection:

The primary objective of copyright is not to reward the labor of authors, but 'to promote the Progress of Science and useful Arts' ... to this end, copyright assures authors the right to their original expression, but encourages others to build freely upon the ideas and information conveyed by a work...As applied to a factual compilation ... only the compiler's selection and arrangement may be protected; the raw facts may be copied at will. This result is neither unfair nor unfortunate. It is the means by which copyright advances the progress of science and art.[22]

European standards of originality   The standard of originality in many European countries also requires an element of intellectual creativity. The wording of that requirement varies from country to country, as does the required degree of creativity and the manner in which the various tests have been applied.[23] In a number of countries, intellectual creativity is described as the author imprinting their personality on the work which, in turn, means the exercise of creative choice by the author in making a work.[24] The higher standard of originality in these European countries is a reflection of their different conceptual approach to copyright, where copyright works are regarded as an extension of the author's personality, and the emphasis of copyright is upon its protection. In contrast, common law countries have a greater emphasis on the role of copyright in providing an economic incentive to create the material in question.[25] This latter approach to copyright is beginning to dominate

---

[21] See Chapter 6.   [22] 499 US 340 (1991) at 349–50.

[23] The German Federal Copyright Act of 9 September 1965, s. 2(2) defines a work as a personal intellectual creation, Italy, Law for the Protection of Copyright and Neighbouring Rights Article, Law No. 633 of 22 April 1941, Article 6 states: 'Copyright shall be acquired on the creation of a work that constitutes the particular expression of an intellectual effort.' France, Intellectual Property Code, Law No. 92–597 of 1 July 1992 protects the rights of authors in 'all works of the mind' in Art. L112–1. The Belgian Supreme Court has held that the creation must be 'the expression of the intellectual effort of the one that realized it, which is an indispensable condition to confer to the work the individual character without which there would be no creation', Cass. 27 April 1989, Pas, 1989, I, 908.

[24] A. Lucas and A. Plaisant, 'France' in M. B. Nimmer and P. E. Geller, *International Copyright Law and Practice* (Matthew Bender, New York, 1999) at p. 4. A. Strowel, 'Belgium' in Nimmer and Geller, *International Copyright Law and Practice* (1999) at p. 2.

[25] These different approaches to copyright protection are becoming less important in the EU as copyright and other intellectual property regimes are harmonised through EU law. Greater emphasis is being placed on the economic role of copyright. See, e.g. Opinion on the Proposal for a Council Directive on the legal protection of databases of the Economic and Social Committee, OJ No. C 19, 25 January 1993 at p. 3, para. 2.6.3.

EU proposals for copyright and is clearly the basis for the *sui generis* protection of databases.[26]

The spectrum of originality   In reality, applying the different formulations of the requirement of originality leads to some inconsistency of results, both between and within different legal jurisdictions. The requirements of originality can range across a wide spectrum, from sweat of the brow at the lower end, to intellectual creation and imprinting of the author's personality on the work at the high end. It is difficult, if not impossible, to define with precision what is and is not required to meet the relevant standard in any particular jurisdiction, although some works will clearly be within the standard while others will be questionable. What can be done is to identify the general standard within a particular jurisdiction and to determine where that standard is on the spectrum; this will provide some general guidance on the question. After that, guidance can be derived only by considering some case examples and the application of the general standard to particular types of works. In this instance, our obvious concern is with databases and compilations.

Originality as it applies to compilations and databases   The above discussion of originality suggests that there are two key elements. First, the work in question must be created by the author in the sense that the work flows from the author and is not simply copied from another source. It is original in the sense that the author and nobody else has created the work. The issue of authorship in the context of databases is discussed below.

Second, originality does not require that the ideas or information contained in the work need be new, inventive or original. This will usually be the case with databases, as their contents will be pre-existing. Copyright purports not to protect ideas or information as such, only the expression of ideas or information. Consequently, as it is only the expression of ideas or information that is protected, it is only the expression that need be original. The difficulty comes at the point where the compilation of the contents of the database in question emanates from the author, has not been copied from anyone else, but it is arguably no more than information or data in a relatively raw form.

If we return to the first requirement, that the work emanates from the author, there are some potential difficulties in the context of copyright protection of databases. If we ignore the copyright in the

---

[26] Ibid. One of the initial concerns of the French government about the Directive was that the *sui generis* right may undermine the nature of copyright and the status of authors.

pre-existing works or data, that which then emanates from the author of the database can only be the product of the author obtaining, verifying, selecting or arranging those pre-existing works or data. However, there is a question about the relevance of the nature and extent of the effort and skills involved in these activities to the requirement of originality. This is one example where there is a divergence in the approaches of different jurisdictions to the issue of originality. At the low or sweat of the brow end of the spectrum, credit is given to an author for the effort expended in creating the database, regardless of the fact that that effort may not have involved the application of any significant intellectual skill. The extent of the effort can be measured quite easily, and the amount of time and money invested in the creation of the database would, in many cases, be self-evident. Even if that were not the case, actual evidence of the investment could easily be presented. Under this approach, copyright protection will be conferred on a database because of the amount of effort involved in creating it. The nature of the intellectual effort is not relevant to the question of whether copyright protection is conferred.

Consequently, the investment in obtaining the information may be sufficient to meet the requirement of originality, provided that the end result emanates from the author and even though the selection or arrangement of the works or data in the database involves no spark of creativity. There are some benefits of this approach. In particular, it is relatively easy to determine whether the database is entitled to copyright protection. Yet, even at this low end of the spectrum, it is sometimes difficult to determine the point in the process of obtaining the information at which that effort becomes relevant to obtaining copyright protection. If we take the example of a telephone directory, is the work in providing a telephone subscription to an individual relevant to the copyright in the directory? For example, at the time that the would-be subscriber applies for a telephone service, their details such as name and address are taken and their new telephone number recorded. These details are subsequently entered into the directory. Yet, the work in question was not undertaken specifically for the purposes of the directory but as part of the process of providing a telephone service. Similar issues of distinguishing between the preparatory work of collecting information and subsequently displaying it have arisen in many cases, with a tendency for Australian and English courts to favour the view that copyright subsists in the ultimate compilation.[27] Ultimately, those jurisdictions that adopt a sweat of the brow approach to originality or a standard that is close to it, do give the copyright owner

---

[27] See Ricketson, *Law of Intellectual Property*, at p. 7.170.

significant credit for their investment in creating the database, regardless of the intellectual nature of that investment. As explained in the section below concerning infringement, this has ramifications for what constitutes infringement of a compilation or database.

Those approaches to originality that reject the sweat of the brow approach involve an analysis of the nature of effort involved in making the database. Under this approach, there must be some intellectual creativity in the selection or arrangement of the pre-existing works or data. The actual application of this approach to a given situation requires consideration of two key questions. The first question is whether there has been sufficient intellectual creativity to meet the requisite level of originality. The application of this imprecise concept to particular factual situations leads to difficulties in grey areas, where it is not immediately clear that the relevant standard has been met. With databases, the actual selection of material often does not involve any significant intellectual input or, indeed, any significant effort at all. This is because the database will often be designed to provide and contain all the information within a given area. Creating a database of all the decisions of the US Supreme Court involves little or no skill in selection of material. The criterion by which particular court decisions are included or excluded from the database is clear and obvious. In fact, the very purpose of the database is to create a collection of every decision of that Court. Consequently, the very purpose for which a database is created often leads to a situation in which the author of the database cannot rely on selection of its contents as the basis for claiming that it is original. This only leaves the manner of arrangement as a possible basis for claiming copyright.

The second question is whether the type of creative or intellectual activity identified is relevant to the issue of originality of the compilation or database. This has particular relevance to the intellectual activity involved in preparing or generating material for inclusion in a database. There may be a considerable deal of intellectual activity associated with generating the information in question, but it may not be of the kind relevant to copyright protection. An example of this might be the scientific work associated with determining the biochemical structure of a human gene. There is no doubt that identifying a previously unidentified gene takes not only a great deal of labour, but also a great deal of intellectual skill in devising and undertaking necessary experimentation. Nevertheless, the nature of that effort is not of a copyright nature as it relates to discovering a natural phenomenon rather than expressing that phenomenon. Consequently, that labour is irrelevant to the issue of originality. But other types of intellectual effort cannot be quite so easily separated from the written end result; a number of cases suggest that this intellectual skill cannot or should not be separated from the creativity associated with the final literary outcome of that effort.

For example, there have been cases concerning the creation of sporting fixtures.[28] It can take a great deal of intellectual effort to organise sporting fixtures so that they meet the requirements of the competition in question. The fixtures must ensure that the teams play each other the correct number of times, that they play at particular grounds that other teams in the competition use from time to time and that the games do not clash with other relevant events, such as knock-out competitions or representative games. All these difficulties increase the intellectual skill required to prepare the fixture list.[29] Similar issues arose in relation to the creation of a bingo game run by a daily newspaper in respect of bingo cards distributed with the newspaper. The daily list of bingo numbers was held to be a literary work on the grounds that the mathematical skill involved in devising a game extending over a fixed period of days gave the list of numbers sufficient originality to be a literary work.[30] In that case, the connection between the intellectual skill of making the necessary mathematical calculations and the final literary result that was expressed was not as direct or apparent as other types of intellectual skill, and the correctness of the decision can be questioned. Nevertheless, it demonstrates the possible difficulties in this area.

Ultimately, the real difficulty flows from the potential for uncertainty in the way in which any particular standard of originality is applied in particular instances. The concept of originality is, almost by its nature, somewhat nebulous. At best, some general observations can be made about the particular standard of originality in any jurisdiction at any particular time. At the low end of the spectrum, the 'sweat of the brow', the investment of effort in producing the compilation or database in question will count in determining whether the work is original. This effort may be sufficient to confer the quality of originality upon the work in the absence of any intellectual creativity in production. Moving up from this low end of the scale, we come to a standard where originality is conferred when the database manifests a combination of effort and the exercise of some intellectual skills. Those intellectual skills are not analysed and separated from the sweat of the brow effort so as to focus exclusively on those intellectual skills that are directly connected with the creation and expression of the final product. At the higher end of the scale, no credit is given for

[28] *Football League Ltd v. Littlewoods Pools Ltd* [1959] 1 Ch 637 at 651–2.
[29] In contrast, there are Belgian decisions denying copyright protection to calendars of football matches, Brussels, 26 June 1954, Ing.Cons, 1954, 121; Trib. Antwerp 27 June 1951, Ing-Cons, 1951, 244
[30] *Mirror Newspapers Ltd v. Queensland Newspapers Pty Ltd* [1982] Qd R 305.

the sweat of the brow effort in producing the final database and/or for the exercise of those intellectual skills that are not directly connected with the ultimate expression of the database. One advantage of the sweat of the brow approach is that it does provide a reasonable degree of certainty in the law of copyright but certainty is not necessarily a desirable end in itself, particularly if the certain result that is achieved is one that is inconsistent with the objectives of copyright law.

Authorship

In the section above concerning originality, it was noted that originality requires a work to have emanated from an author. Authorship and originality are intimately connected and have been observed to be correlative in that one connotes the other.[31] Perhaps a better way of putting this is that a work cannot be original unless it has an author, a person or group of people from whom the work emanates. There is some argument that some databases do not have authors in the copyright sense. This argument is based on the proposition that electronic databases are arranged automatically by the computer program responsible for organisation of data within the database.[32] This computer software forms a layer or layers of software between the physical database itself and its author, who accesses it to add, update or remove data.[33] Copyright subsists in the computer program as a literary work and that copyright is quite separate from any copyright in the database. The operator may simply key in the data in an undiscriminating manner or insert data that are already in digital form, and the data may be organised by the computer program.[34] There may be no originality associated with the selection of the data included in the database, particularly if the selection consists of all the available material relating to a particular topic. It could be further argued that, as the arrangement has occurred automatically as a consequence of the operation of the computer program that manipulates the data, the supposed author of the database has not in fact authored it. In some jurisdictions, this argument is enhanced by definitions of authors that provide that an author is a person who has produced a work of personal character or that the work must be a product of the mind of its author.[35]

---

[31] Ricketson, *Law of Intellectual Property*, at p. 7.45.   [32] Ibid., at p. 7.175 and p. 14.35.

[33] C. Date, *An Introduction to Database Systems* (6th edn, Addison-Wesley, Reading, 1994), p. 7.

[34] Ricketson, *Law of Intellectual Property*, at p. 7.175.

[35] E.g. Article L111–1 of the French Intellectual Property Code 1992 (as amended) provides rights to 'The author of a work of the mind'. Article 1 of the Italian Law of Copyright 1941 as amended protects 'Works of the mind having a creative character'.

Some technical aspects of database creation   There are a number of possible responses to this problem of authorship, and they require some understanding of the process of creating and updating an electronic database. First, the actual creation and updating of a database is rarely as simple as indiscriminately keying new data into some form of digital storage such as the hard disk of a computer. A decision has to be made about defining the records and fields (or the rows and columns) that are to be contained within the database.[36] For example, if we take a database of the white pages of a telephone directory, a decision has to be made that each individual entry in the directory should be stored in a particular order. In this case, it would be the family name, followed by a given name or initial, the residential address and, finally, the telephone number. The final directory would then consist of rows or records consisting of an individual's family name, given name or initial, their address and telephone numbers while there would be columns of family names, given names or initials, addresses and telephone numbers.[37] Even though the final result is produced by the 'work' of a computer in arranging the material in this way, human thought went into the scheme of the database and the conception of how the material would look to the external user.[38] In addition, most databases contain indexes that have been prepared in order to assist searching through them. Indexes are crucial for this purpose. For example, while individual records of a telephone subscriber's details may not be arranged in any meaningful order in the database's storage system, the indexes will contain, in a humanly defined order, a particular field of each record in the database and a link from that field to another field of the same record. For example, one index may have family names in alphabetical order. There will be links or pointers to another preselected field in the same record such as the telephone number or address. When the database user searches for, say, 'Anderson', the computer software searching the database will be able to stop at 'Anderson' in the family name index. It will then be directed to the numbers for all the Andersons in the directory.[39] The family name file is then one of several possible indexes to the file of telephone numbers.

The database author has to make decisions concerning indexing by reference to what information is likely to be required and whether the

---

[36] A record would be, for example, the entire entry of information concerning a telephone subscriber while a field would be a particular part of that information such as the telephone number. The record therefore consists of a number of different fields. If the database is thought of as a table, the records in a database are the rows in the table and the fields are the columns. See Date, *Introduction to Database Systems*, p. 3.

[37] Whether the arrangement is sufficiently creative to be original is a separate matter.

[38] Date, *Introduction to Database Systems*, pp. 36–7.   [39] Ibid., at p. 724.

costs of indexing to permit quick retrieval of it are warranted.[40] This is because every time the records in the database are updated, the indexes must also be updated. For example, the small number of times that users of a telephone directory search for the name of a subscriber by typing in their telephone number may not justify creating an index of telephone numbers in descending numerical order that indexes to the subscriber details of a person with that number.

The process of indexing will be even more complicated in all but the most simple of databases. This is because the user may wish to search the database by reference to more than one criterion at a time or, in other words, by reference to a combination of fields. For example, let us suppose that the user of the telephone directory wants to search for a person called 'Anderson' with an address in Chelsea. Simply searching for 'Anderson' may result in a very large list of Andersons, few or none of which may live in Chelsea. If there is an index to the file of telephone numbers that contains both family name and suburb, this will greatly speed up the search for Andersons in Chelsea and eliminate other Andersons from the search. This would be the equivalent of a Boolean 'And' search. Other forms of indexing may achieve the same result or assist in other search tasks. In addition to indexing, the database may contain an electronic thesaurus. Hence, a search for 'Anderson' may provide details of people named 'Andersen' or 'Anderssen'.

So with the vast majority of commercial databases, there has been some thought put into the database design by its author, regardless of the extent to which that design has been automatically implemented by computers. For example, a computer may have been programmed to identify the individual fields in a record and to separate each record into the relevant fields, but the field and record design has still been carried out by the author of the database, as has the design of the indexing system.

The second response is related to the first. It is based on the proposition that the authors of databases can claim authorship by virtue of having considered the possible outcomes of their input into the database. They have chosen the software used in the database and therefore chosen the operations that it can carry out on the data included. The fact that one or more of those operations is achieved extremely quickly is not relevant, particularly if the view is taken that sweat of the brow is not a key ingredient of originality. There is no reason why authorship should be required to take a particular period of time. Provided that the author has envisaged the final arrangement of the data output within the database or, more accurately, the myriad of arrangements of data output that can

---

[40] Ibid., at pp. 725–6.

be made, the fact that the burden of spending an enormous amount of time in creating those arrangements has been eliminated by the use of software should not be an obstacle to claiming authorship.[41] This is also a logical result of the arguments in favour of rejecting sweat of the brow as a basis for copyright protection. If mere sweat of the brow does not confer copyright protection, lack of sweat of the brow should not deprive a work of copyright protection if the appropriate intellectual effort has been put into the creation.

The final response is that the issue of computer-generated works and their authorship has been considered in a number of fora.[42] For example, the copyright law of the United Kingdom already provides that the author of a computer-generated work is the person who makes the necessary arrangements for the creation of the work.[43] It is likely that similar approaches will be taken in other jurisdictions in the not too distant future. The end result is that the requirement of authorship is unlikely to be a significant obstacle to copyright protection for databases. The majority of databases with any commercial value will, by necessity, be more than just a great deal of data that has been compiled by a computer. In order to be accessible in any meaningful way, there will be some organisation of the material that has been planned by a human or humans. This will probably be sufficient to meet the requirement of human authorship in those jurisdictions that require copyright works to be the product of a human author. Whether that organisation meets the originality requirements of the particular jurisdiction is a separate issue.

Consequently, the vast majority of databases that are intended to have commercial value will meet the requirements of authorship. What may be at issue are some compilations created without any real intention to derive any commercial value from their exploitation at the time that the contents were simply combined, rather than compiled. The capacity to extract individual items subsequently via the use of computer programs may not be sufficient to confer authorship, but this will be rare in any commercially significant context.

Infringement

Even when one has identified that a database is an original work with an identifiable human author in which copyright subsists, there are still some significant copyright issues concerning copyright protection. The

---

[41] See *University of London Press Ltd* v. *University Tutorial Press Ltd* [1916] 2 Ch 601 at 609 where Peterson J stated that time taken to create a literary work is not the relevant test.

[42] Ricketson, *Law of Intellectual Property*, at p. 14.30.

[43] Section 9(3) of the UK Copyright, Designs and Patents Act 1988.

rights granted to the owner of the copyright in the database have to be considered, as do the acts that might constitute infringement of those rights. These two matters are closely linked. There is also a close relationship between these rights and their infringement on the one hand and the subject matter of copyright on the other. Consequently, we cannot leave the discussion of originality out of consideration of the rights of copyright owners and infringement of those rights.

A substantial part of a work: qualitative rather than quantitative tests   Obviously, if the entirety of a work is used by an alleged infringer in precisely the same form in which it was expressed by the author, the only question is whether this use comes within the scope of one of the copyright owner's exclusive rights. If it does, then it is an infringement. One slight complication in this regard is the potential difficulty of defining the boundaries that constitute the work. This is particularly the case with electronic databases. It could be argued that there is a myriad of databases within a database and that each of those databases constitutes a work in which copyright subsists. We could take one of the databases within the Lexis network of databases as an example.[44] The combined American federal and state case law database can be divided into a number of other databases such as the 'federal cases within two years', 'federal and state cases after 1944', 'all courts – by circuit' and 'all courts – by state'. Even within those databases, further subdivision could occur. 'All courts – by state' could be considered to consist of fifty separate databases relating to each individual state. The smaller the database that is considered for the purposes of infringement, the easier it may be to establish infringement. For example, if an infringer reproduces from Lexis all the cases for the state of Idaho, there will be an infringement if the collection of cases from the state of Idaho constitutes a copyright work in itself because the whole of that work will have been reproduced. There will be no question of whether a substantial part has been reproduced because the entirety of the database has been reproduced. In addition, there is some argument that the smaller the database within the larger database, the more convincing the argument that the smaller database has copyright. This is because the smaller database within the database is being 'created' by selecting more and more criteria that exclude parts of the larger database. The database user's capacity to apply these selection criteria will be a product of the database author's indexing, which foresaw the possibility of such searching. The more selection criteria are involved, the

---

[44] Ignore for the purposes of this exercise whether the database has the necessary selection and arrangement to qualify for copyright protection.

greater is the prospect of being able to argue that the selection involves the necessary creativity to confer copyright protection. Consequently, defining the database may well be determinative of the issue of infringement, and database owners will naturally take the view that they own many databases within databases. To the author's knowledge, this issue has not been litigated in the context of databases but it seems to be a likely future scenario.[45]

But if the issue of what the relevant database is can be satisfactorily resolved, the relationship between rights and infringement on the one hand and originality on the other becomes particularly important. Copyright legislation or jurisprudence within a particular jurisdiction provides that the doing of an act in respect of a substantial part of a copyright work is deemed to constitute the same act in respect of the whole work.[46] Consequently, defining a substantial part is often the key to determining whether infringement of copyright has occurred. If, in our example, the copyright work in question is considered to be the database of all federal and state case law from the United States of America, a preliminary issue is whether the cases from the state of Idaho constitute a substantial part of that database. Determining the substantiality of a part of a work requires a measurement or consideration of the quantity and the quality of that part. Measuring the quantity that is taken is a relatively simple empirical task but in determining whether the part taken is substantial, the emphasis is more upon quality rather than quantity.[47] The task of measuring quality is a far more difficult one that is intimately connected with the concept of originality.

'Quality' has two possible meanings: the standard or degree of excellence of a work, and the attributes or characteristics of the work. Any particular work may be considered as an excellent or high quality work and as having particular qualities. The first of these definitions is the one that is most commonly used in ordinary language, however, it is probably not the relevant meaning for the purposes of measuring a substantial part of a copyright work. This is because the courts decline to comment on or judge the standard of excellence of a work in deciding whether a work is original and entitled to copyright protection. A corollary of this point is that it is not relevant to consider the excellence of what is taken when

---

[45] See B. Sherman, 'Digital Property and the Digital Commons' in C. Heath and A. K. Sanders (eds.), *Intellectual Property in the Digital Age: Challenges for Asia* (Kluwer, London, 2001), pp. 95–109 where the issue is discussed in relation to copyright works generally.

[46] E.g. s. 16(3) of the UK Copyright, Designs and Patents Act 1988 and s. 14(1) of the Copyright Act 1968 (Australia). See also J. Sterling *World Copyright Law* (London, 1998) at p. 13.06.

[47] *Hawkes and Son (London)* v. *Paramount Film Service Ltd* [1934] 1 Ch 593, *Ladbroke (Football) Ltd* v. *William Hill (Football) Ltd* [1964] 1 All ER 465.

deciding whether a substantial part of the quality of the work is taken. In other words, it is not the taking of what makes the work 'excellent' in itself that constitutes a taking of a substantial part. It is the taking of those attributes or characteristics of the work that make it original that is the critical consideration[48] whether or not those attributes contribute to the excellence of the work. Another way of putting this may be to say that consideration needs to be given to what are the characteristics of the work's originality, when addressing the issue of infringement.

This leads in turn to a consideration of what makes the work original and this varies according to the approach to originality within any particular jurisdiction. At the low end of the spectrum, we have seen that sweat of the brow may confer originality on a work. Consequently, a taking of that part of the work that took a great deal of effort to put together will be a taking of a substantial part. In contrast, if originality relates only to the intellectual creativity associated with the creation of the work, the part that is taken must comprise the results of that intellectual creativity.

In the context of databases, this means that if the standard of originality is low, a quantitatively significant amount of data will constitute a substantial part of the work. This is because it will have taken a significant amount of sweat of the brow to obtain the material, verify its accuracy and place it in the database.[49] It is this effort, regardless of its intellectual attributes, that will confer originality on the database.[50] The quantitative and qualitative aspects of the test of substantiality merge as a consequence of the sweat of the brow approach. A very different view of what constitutes a substantial part emerges if a different approach to originality is applied. If originality relates only to the intellectual creativity associated with selection and/or arrangement of the contents of the database, then infringement will only occur if a substantial part of these aspects of the database has been taken. Hence, even if copyright subsists in the database, it is possible to take a large amount of the contents of the database without infringing the copyright in the database, provided the selection or arrangement of the contents has not been taken.

While the above discussion refers to originality in terms of either a sweat of the brow approach or a creativity-based approach, we need to bear in mind that these criteria of originality are really the two ends of

---

[48] *Baumann* v. *Fussell* [1978] RPC 485 at 487.

[49] As we will see later, the Directive provides *sui generis* rights in respect of a substantial investment in obtaining, verifying and presenting data.

[50] The same database may also display creativity in the manner of its selection and arrangement, in which case that too would be protected in sweat of the brow copyright regimes that protect both effort and creativity.

the spectrum. Towards the lower end, originality may be the product of a combination of a small degree of creativity coupled with sweat of the brow. The effect of this approach is that while mere sweat of the brow may not be sufficient to attract copyright protection in itself, once a small degree of creativity is established, copyright protection is conferred on both the sweat of the brow and the creativity. The taking of either the sweat of the brow or the creativity may lead to infringement, thus permitting sweat of the brow protection via the back door. A more rigorous insistence towards the higher end of the spectrum of discriminating between sweat of the brow and creativity eliminates that possibility. An example of the former situation is the English Court of Appeal decision in *Waterlow Publishers Ltd* v. *Rose*[51] in which the defendant allegedly infringed the copyright in a directory of solicitors. The layout of the defendant's competing directory was very different from the plaintiff's,[52] yet infringement was found on the basis of the amount of information taken from the plaintiff's directory. In contrast, the *Feist* decision, in applying a higher standard of originality, clearly held that information and facts could be taken freely provided their selection and arrangement were not taken.

Rights that are infringed

Copyright confers on the copyright owner a number of exclusive rights in respect of the work. In the section above concerning 'a substantial part', generic terms such as 'taking' or 'using' were used to refer to acts of infringement, but in any consideration of infringement it is necessary to identify the precise right of the copyright owner that has been infringed. The precise nature of these rights varies from jurisdiction to jurisdiction in the same way that the issue of originality is treated differently in different jurisdictions. Despite these differences, the general nature of the rights conferred on a copyright owner in different jurisdictions is very similar. This is mainly a consequence of international copyright treaties specifying the rights that must be conferred on copyright owners.

There are several rights that are highly relevant in the context of databases. They are the rights of reproduction,[53] communication to the

---

[51] (1990) 17 IPR 493. The decision can be contrasted with the American decision in *Skinder-Strauss Associates* v. *Massachusetts Continuing Legal Education*, 914 F Supp. 665 (D. Mass. 1995) in which copyright was held not to subsist in a directory of attorneys for Massachusetts.

[52] '[T]he fact that there is no infringement of the plan of Waterlow's work or of the arrangement and layout of the information does not mean that there is no infringement of the compilation' (1990) 17 IPR 493 at 507.

[53] Article 9 of the Berne Convention for the Protection of Literary and Artistic Works 1971 (the Berne Convention, 828 UNTS 221).

public, including making available to the public,[54] distribution[55] and rental.[56] In addition, copyright owners can prevent the circumvention of technological protection devices used by them to control access to their copyright material.[57]

Right of reproduction

The right of reproduction is a longstanding right of copyright owners but there are a few difficulties associated with its application to databases. One of those difficulties is deciding whether a substantial part of the work has been reproduced. This has been discussed above. Another pertinent issue that has arisen is deciding the point in time at which a reproduction has occurred in the course of viewing or reading the contents of a database on a computer screen. This is because the process of viewing or reading on-screen involves making a temporary computer copy of the contents. Opinion is divided as to whether such copies are sufficiently fixed to constitute reproductions and, hence, infringing reproductions if the display on the computer screen has not been authorised by the copyright owner. If they are, then reproduction occurs in the database user's computer and arguably that user is responsible for any infringing reproduction; however, the international obligations with regard to this matter are not clear. There was an attempt to resolve it at the Diplomatic Conference on Certain Copyright and Neighbouring Rights Questions in Geneva in December 1996 that adopted the WIPO Copyright Treaty of 1996 (Copyright Treaty). The Agreed Statements Concerning the Copyright Treaty included this statement about the right of reproduction as it appears in the Berne Convention for the Protection of Literary and Artistic Works 1971 (Berne Convention):

The reproduction right, as set out in Article 9 of the Berne Convention, and the exceptions permitted thereunder, fully apply in the digital environment, in particular to the use of works in digital form. It is understood that the storage of a protected work in digital form in an electronic medium constitutes a reproduction within the meaning of Article 9 of the Berne Convention.[58]

---

[54] Article 8 of the WIPO Copyright Treaty 1996 adopted by the Diplomatic Conference on Certain Copyright and Neighbouring Rights Questions on 20 December 1996 36 ILM 65 (1997), (the Copyright Treaty) imposes an obligation to provide a right of communication to the public.

[55] Article 6 of the Copyright Treaty.

[56] Article 11 of TRIPS requires such a right in respect of computer programs and cinematographic works. Article 7 of the Copyright Treaty also requires that right for phonograms as well as computer programs and cinematographic works.

[57] Article 11 of the Copyright Treaty.

[58] Agreed Statement Concerning Article 1(4) of the Copyright Treaty. CRNR/DC/96.

Signatories to the Copyright Treaty are required to give the right of re-production to owners of copyright in literary and artistic works[59] but the attempt in the Agreed Statements to clarify the application of the right in the circumstances described above has not succeeded. This is because there is no definition of what constitutes storage, and a temporary copy made for the purposes of viewing the database on a computer screen may not be considered to be stored. The other circumstance in which this issue is likely to arise in the context of databases is where a database user wishes to take all or most of the data in a database and arrange it in their own way. They may not wish to take the database author's arrangement. If the data is not protected under a sweat of the brow copyright regime, the user is entitled to reproduce that data if there is no originality in its selection.[60] However, if the reproduction right includes temporary copies of the arrangement, the actual process of reproduction by the user may necessarily involve a reproduction of the arrangement. A manual repro-duction of the data would be possible but expensive.[61] The most efficient and logical means of reproduction would be digital. In order to digitally reproduce the data, there would have to be a temporary reproduction of the data in the manner in which it is arranged before that arrangement could be stripped out.

There is no uniform copyright practice concerning the application of the reproduction right to temporary digital copies of works such as databases. However, it appears that American law and the approach taken in the EU favour the view that temporary reproductions of this sort do constitute reproductions for copyright purposes.[62] This has signifi-cant implications for those who wish either simply to view a database or

---

[59] Article 1(4) of the Copyright Treaty requires contracting parties to comply with Articles 1–21 of the Berne Convention.

[60] Ignoring, for the moment, the possibility of contractual restrictions or the application of principles of confidential information.

[61] See A. Raubenheimer, 'Germany: Recent Decisions on Database Protection under Copyright Law and Unfair Competition Rules' (1996) 1 *Communications Law* 123 in which he describes two cases. 1994 CR 473: 1994 NJW –CoR 169 1995 CR 85; 1994 WRP 834; 1994 NJW –CoR 303. In the latter of those cases, manual reproduction of a telephone directory was undertaken in China.

[62] *MAI Sys. Corp. v. Peak Computer Inc.*, 991 F 2d 511, 517 (9th Cir. 1993); *Advanced Computer Servs. v. MAI Sys. Corp.*, 845 F Supp. 356, 362 (ED Va. 1994). See generally J. Ginsburg, 'Copyright Without Borders? Choice of Forum and Choice of Law for Copyright Infringement in Cyberspace' (1997) 15 *Cardozo Arts and Entertainment Law Journal* 153 at fn 28. Article 5(a) of the Directive states that the author of a database shall have the exclusive right to carry out or to authorize temporary reproduction. On 28 September 2000, the Council of the European Union adopted a Common Position concerning the draft of a copyright directive. OJ 2000 No. C344, 1 December 2000, pp. 1–22. Article 2 of the Common Position defines reproduction as including temporary copies.

to reproduce the data within a database, without the permission of the database owner.

Right of rental

The right of rental was introduced in TRIPS and was implemented into domestic legislation in 1996 by developed countries; it had to be implemented by developing countries by 2000. It relates to fixed copies of computer programs and cinematographic works[63] that can be put into distribution as tangible objects such as CDs or DVDs. The Copyright Treaty also applies this right to works embodied in phonograms.[64] The Directive has gone one step further by providing a broad right of distribution to owners of copyright in a database that is defined so as to include a rental right.[65]

Right of distribution

A right of distribution is incorporated into the Copyright Treaty,[66] which also applies to fixed copies of works.[67] It provides that 'authors of literary and artistic works shall enjoy the exclusive right of authorizing the making available to the public of the original and copies of their works through sale or other transfer of ownership'.[68] This right may be subject to exhaustion and, in most jurisdictions, is exhausted, upon the first sale of an authentic copy of the work, such that subsequent sales of that authentic copy cannot be prevented by the copyright owner. However, it would cover the distribution of infringing copies of a database. The right of distribution under the Copyright Treaty is defined more narrowly than it is in Article 5 of the Directive, as the latter incorporates a rental right.

Right of communication to the public

The right of communication to the public is also a right that was incorporated into the Copyright Treaty.[69] The right of communication is designed to deal with the electronic 'distribution' of copyright works by wire or wireless means, and includes making the works available to the public in such a way that members of the public can access these works

---

[63] Article 11 of TRIPS.   [64] Article 7 of the Copyright Treaty.

[65] Article 5 of the Directive gives the copyright owner the exclusive right to carry out 'any form of distribution to the public of the database or of copies thereof'.

[66] Article 6 of the Copyright Treaty.

[67] Agreed Statements Concerning Articles 6 and 7 of the Copyright Treaty, CRNR/DC/96.

[68] Article 6 of the Copyright Treaty.   [69] Article 8 of the Copyright Treaty.

from a place and at a time individually chosen by them. It therefore covers making databases available on-line. Not all signatories to the Copyright Treaty have incorporated its requirements into their domestic legislation as yet but the right of communication, in one form or another, will be part of the copyright law of those nations in the not too distant future.

These rights of copyright owners in databases may also be relevant to an understanding of *sui generis* rights of databases. In Chapter 3, we shall see that the *sui generis* rights granted under the Directive are very similar, if not identical, to the exclusive rights of copyright owners described above.

Protection against circumvention of technological protection devices

Copyright owners are also entitled to protection against devices designed to circumvent technological protection devices. The obligation to provide such protection is imposed by the Copyright Treaty.[70] This protection supplements the right of communication by preventing circumvention of self-help measures employed by copyright owners to prevent un-authorised access to their copyright works. It has particular significance in the context of databases because it prevents a person from gaining access to a copyright work to deal with it in a way that may not infringe copyright. For example, a person with lawful access to a database could take some, or even all, of the contents of the database without taking a substantial part of its arrangement or selection. Copyright would not be infringed but, with the restriction on circumventing technological protection devices, it may not be possible to gain access to the database to deal with it in a way that is lawful. In addition, it may have the effect of preventing access to databases in which copyright does not subsist. The limitations on the manufacture and sale of circumvention devices limit the capacity of individuals to gain access to any material that is protected by technological devices, regardless of whether copyright subsists in that material.

Exceptions to copyright

Most jurisdictions provide some exceptions to copyright, but the nature and scope of those exceptions vary widely. Part of the explanation for these differences is diverse views on the reason for protection of copyright. These have an impact on what is protected and excepted from that protection. The higher standards of originality imposed in continental countries lead to copyright subsisting in fewer works, but the exceptions

---

[70] Article 11 of the Copyright Treaty.

to copyright in those works are themselves more restricted than in countries where a lower standard of originality applies. In countries such as the UK where copyright subsists in more works, wider exceptions exist. For example, the UK has fair dealing provisions that permit the fair dealing with a substantial part of a work for the purposes of research or private study, or the purposes of criticism, review or reporting current events.[71] In contrast, French law only permits copying for private use of the copier.[72] This would exclude copying for commercial research but the nature of the rights in the work, which would not include protection of the information contained within it, ameliorates the impact of such a limited exception. A similar approach to the French one is taken in other European countries.[73]

Further contrast is provided by the copyright legislation of the United States which does not seek to define the precise circumstances in which what would otherwise be infringing conduct is permitted. Instead, it takes a flexible approach via the statutory defence of fair use, which identifies relevant factors for the courts to consider in determining whether the defendant's use of the copyright material has been fair.[74]

These differences in exceptions become a difficulty at the point of attempting to harmonise standards of originality and exceptions to copyright. They also become a difficulty when attempts are made to extrapolate those exceptions to *sui generis* rights. Once the subject matter of protection is altered, either by altering the standard of originality or by creating a new *sui generis* right applying to a different subject matter, the nature and scope of the exceptions need to be reconsidered. As discussed in Chapter 3, the Directive has attempted to harmonise the standard of originality for copyright protection for databases and the exceptions to that copyright, and it has created a new *sui generis* right. An important

---

[71] Sections 29 and 30 of the UK Copyright, Designs and Patents Act 1988. See Chapter 3 for a discussion of how the UK defence of fair dealing with databases for research purposes has been narrowed as a consequence of the Directive, so as to preclude research for commercial purposes.

[72] Article L122–5(2) of the Intellectual Property Code, Law No. 92–597 of 1 July 1992 (France). Article L122–5(3) also permits analyses and short quotations for critical, educational and other purposes, press reviews and news reporting.

[73] E.g. Article 68 of the Italian Copyright Law of 1941 (as amended) provides in part that 'The reproduction of single works . . . for the personal use of the reader when made by hand or by a means of reproduction unsuitable for marketing or dissemination to the public, shall be permitted.' Article 70 of that legislation also permits quotation or reproduction of parts of a work for the purposes of criticism or discussion, or for instructional purposes. Article 53 of the German Copyright Act 1965 as amended permits the making of 'single copies of a work for private use', and single copies of a work 'for personal scientific use, if and to the extent that such reproduction is necessary for the purpose'.

[74] Section 107 of the American Copyright Act of 1976. This defence is discussed in detail in Chapter 4.

issue to consider is whether the exceptions to the *sui generis* right are appropriate in the light of the nature of that right.

Compulsory licensing

In addition to exceptions to copyright protection, there are circumstances in which copyright owners are required to permit reproduction of their copyright material in return for equitable remuneration. This is compulsory licensing. As with exceptions to copyright, provisions for compulsory licences usually relate to some public interest in ensuring access to, and use of, copyright material, or they are imposed because the transaction costs associated with individual parties reaching a licensing agreement would be prohibitively expensive. Public interest in access and use includes access to copyright material for educational purposes, reporting of news and current affairs and government information or information concerning the functions of government. Compulsory licences may also be desirable if only relatively small but nevertheless substantial parts of copyright works are to be used, or many different copyright works are to be used by the one user, such as a radio station that will broadcast a variety of sound recordings.

In some cases, both justifications of ensuring access and minimising transaction costs exist for a particular exception to copyright or a compulsory licence. For example, in Australia there is a compulsory licence system in place concerning copyright materials that are reproduced for educational purposes by educational institutions.[75] It permits the reproduction of substantial parts of literary and artistic works and films and broadcasts for educational purposes, without the need to obtain the copyright owner's permission. The licence fee to be paid for these reproductions is fixed either by agreement between the collecting society responsible for collecting the fee and distributing it to copyright owners or, in the absence of agreement, by the Australian Copyright Tribunal which has specific legislative authority to deal with the issue.[76] The scheme is justified by both the public interest in making copyright materials available for educational purposes, and the high transaction costs that would be associated with requiring individual licences to be negotiated between a multitude of users and a multitude of copyright owners.

In a digital environment, that latter justification is somewhat diminished. The accessing of copyright material in digital form, particularly when it is on-line, can be monitored and recorded automatically and

---

[75] Australian Copyright Act 1968, Part VB.
[76] Australian Copyright Act 1968, Part VI, Division 3.

electronically with a minimum of human intervention or surveillance. If standard fees are charged for access, charges can be calculated quickly and easily and records kept of which works have been accessed. In addition, collecting societies play a role in reducing transaction costs by representing large numbers of copyright owners and contracting collectively on their behalf.[77] This has led to calls by some copyright owners to abolish exceptions to and compulsory licensing of copyright material.[78]

This leaves the justification that there is a public interest in ensuring access to the copyright material in question. Access, in this context, has two components: one is whether an intending user has the financial means to obtain access to material; the other is whether the intending user has physical access to the material. Exceptions such as defences of fair dealing or fair use presently provide financial access, in that the copyright work or a substantial part of it can be used without making any payment to the copyright owner. However, they do not provide any guarantee of physical access. The defences of fair dealing and fair use justify certain acts that would otherwise constitute copyright infringement. They are not rights to have physical or virtual access to the copyright material in order to perform those acts. Unless the user can gain that access, the defence of fair dealing or fair use is of no avail. Indeed, the contractual terms upon which the physical access is given may exclude the possibility of relying on those defences at all.[79] The cost of physical access may therefore involve foregoing financial access to the material. This issue has particular significance in the digital environment, where technological means can be used to prevent access to databases and copyright laws can be relied upon to prevent the circumvention of those technological protection devices. One response may be to override contractual provisions that seek to exclude exceptions and this has been done to some extent in the Directive.[80]

Compulsory licences have a different impact on access to copyright material. They affect both aspects of access. They have an impact on

---

[77] See a discussion of this in R. Merges, 'Of Property Rules, Coase, and Intellectual Property' (1994) 94 *Columbia Law Review* 2655.

[78] E.g. submission of the cross-industry working party established by database producers to the UK government in October 1997 referred to in 'The Government's Proposals to Implement the Directive of the European Parliament and the Council on the Legal Protection of Databases: Outcome of Consultations' at p. 3, a document provided to and held on file by the author from the UK Copyright Directorate.

[79] J. Reichman and J. Franklin, 'Privately Legislated Intellectual Property Rights: Reconciling Freedom of Contract with Public Good Uses of Information' (1999) 147 *University of Pennsylvania Law Review* 875.

[80] Article 8(1) of the Directive.

financial access to the extent that the licence fee imposed by an independent body such as a tribunal or court may be less than what it would be if the parties negotiated a licence fee. In short, access to the material may be more affordable. Equally important, the compulsory licence gives an effective right to physical access to the material. The compulsory licence imposes the major contractual terms upon which the copyright owner may contract for access to the material in question. If the copyright owner wishes to enter into a contract at all for the supply of the material, it is required to accept those terms or to negotiate with the knowledge that those terms may be imposed upon it.

In addition to these theoretical considerations relating to compulsory licensing, there are significant restraints on compulsory licensing of copyright material that are imposed by the Berne Convention. The structure of the Berne Convention is such that it provides exclusive rights to authors, and compulsory licensing is considered to be generally antithetical to those rights.[81] While the Berne Convention expressly permits compulsory licensing of sound recordings and for broadcasting purposes[82] and some authority to impose compulsory licences can be inferred from Articles 9(2) and 10(2), the scope for compulsory licensing is quite limited.

This has particular significance for databases. The information contained within a database may have particular public interest uses. Financial and physical access to that database may also serve a use that is in the public interest. Consequently, any discussion of legal protection of databases needs to consider the issue of access and the circumstances, if any, in which it is to be guaranteed. If the information contained within a database is given copyright protection or protection that is equivalent to copyright, it become difficult to impose compulsory licensing because of the Berne Convention. However, if the information itself is not protected by copyright, and the investment in the sweat of the brow in collecting it is protected by a *sui generis* right, that *sui generis* right can be subject to compulsory licensing provisions. This is because it is a new right that can be crafted as its creators see fit.

Summary of copyright

The above discussion of copyright principles leaves us with a few conclusions. First, the vast majority of databases will be works for copyright purposes because they contain sufficient originality in their selection or arrangement to qualify for protection. The issue of originality is most

---

[81] Ricketson, *The Berne Convention 1886–1986* at pp. 16.27–16.28.
[82] Articles 11*bis* (2) and 13(1) of the Berne Convention.

likely to come into play when considering infringement, as originality will define what can and cannot be taken. Second, whether copyright subsists in these databases will usually depend on whether they are original and have a human author. The answer to the first of these questions varies between jurisdictions according to jurisdictional differences in the requisite standard of originality, while it is unlikely in many situations that the issue of authorship will be a major obstacle to obtaining copyright protection for a database. Third, while the issue of originality is closely linked to the question of infringement, other aspects of infringement that need to be addressed include defining the particular database, defining a substantial part of a database and the particular rights that may have been infringed. Fourth, issues of infringement also raise the question of the extent to which acts that would otherwise constitute infringement should be permitted for public interest purposes, and whether and on what terms copyright owners should be compelled to provide access to their copyright material.

Principles of unfair competition

The principles and law of unfair competition also have an impact on the models for protection of databases. General laws on unfair competition could be relied upon to protect databases, or those laws could be modified and adapted specifically to apply to databases so that *sui generis* protection could be based on principles of unfair competition. American legislative proposals for *sui generis* protection have been based on these principles and the first versions of the Directive adopted such an approach.[83] In addition, some commentators have suggested that in some countries there is a significant link between unfair competition principles and the approach to infringement of copyright. For example, Ricketson suggests that the approach to originality and infringement in England and Australia is influenced by principles of unfair competition, even though or perhaps because there is no general statutory or common law prohibition of unfair competition in either country.[84] Hence, the comment from the decision of Mr Petersen Justice in *University of London Press Ltd* v. *University Tutorial Press Ltd*[85] that as a 'rough practical test... what is worth copying is prima facie worth protecting' is often quoted in UK and Australian copyright cases.[86]

---

[83] See Chapters 3 and 4.
[84] Ricketson, *The Berne Convention 1886–1986* at pp. 9.34, 9.35 and 9.450.
[85] [1916] 2 Ch 601.
[86] E.g. *Ladbroke (Football) Ltd* v. *William Hill (Football) Ltd* [1964] 1 All ER 465 at 471, 481. *Nationwide News Pty Ltd and Others* v. *Copyright Agency Ltd*, No. NG94 of 1995,

Nevertheless, there is a fundamental distinction between the two legal regimes of copyright and unfair competition. Copyright provides exclusive rights to the copyright owner to perform various acts in relation to the copyright material, such as reproducing it or communicating it to the public. Any person who performs those acts without the permission of the copyright owner will be infringing copyright unless they can rely on a defence such as fair dealing. The consequences of their action, either in terms of the detrimental impact that they have on the copyright owner or the beneficial impact that they have on the infringer, are not relevant to the question of whether liability exists for infringement. They may be relevant to the question of what remedies should be given to the copyright owner, but that is a separate issue.

The term 'unfair competition' is at least as vague as those terms used in copyright such as 'intellectual creation' and 'originality'. An important aspect of unfair competition laws that is relevant in this context is the requirement or the lack of any requirement of misrepresentation or confusion. A number of jurisdictions such as the UK have limited the concept of unfair competition to circumstances in which there is deception or confusion.[87] In those jurisdictions where such a requirement is part of any law of unfair competition, unfair competition has little, if any, role to play in protecting databases. The reason why some jurisdictions insist on a requirement of deception or confusion is relatively easy to understand; there are sound theoretical bases for it. In particular, there is the economic justification that those engaging in deception or confusion are taking a free ride on the efforts of the original information provider. Consumers may believe that the information being provided to them comes from a particular source when, in fact, it is not from that source at all. In those circumstances, the actual provider is taking a free ride on the reputation of the person from whom the information was taken. The effect of this will be that the original provider of the information will reduce its investment in gathering information and there will be a general disincentive to provide information.

If there is no requirement of deceit or confusion, the justification for providing a remedy is not so clear. Early American decisions on the point

---

Federal Court of Australia at para. 77; *Re: CBS Records and Gross*, No. G337 of 1989, Federal Court of Australia at para. 25.

[87] See e.g. *Hodgkinson & Corby Ltd and Roho Inc.* v. *Wards Mobility Services Ltd* [1995] FSR 169 *per* Jacob J: 'I turn to consider the law and begin by identifying what is not the law. There is no tort of copying. There is no tort of taking a man's market or customers . . . There is no tort of making use of another's goodwill as such. There is no tort of competition.' The High Court of Australia took a similar view of a tort of unfair competition in *Moorgate Tobacco Co. Ltd* v. *Philip Morris Ltd* (1984) 156 CLR 414. See generally A. Kamperman Sanders, *Unfair Competition Law: The Protection of Intellectual and Industrial Creativity* (Clarendon Press, Oxford, 1997).

suggested that the provision of a remedy was based on a natural rights theory, that a person should not be permitted to reap where they have not sown because it was simply unfair to permit misappropriation of information.[88] Partly for this reason, the tort of misappropriation did not find favour among courts for a number of years[89] as they were concerned that a finding of unfairness was too subjective.

In other jurisdictions, the emphasis is not upon deception or confusion but upon the appropriation of another's efforts in circumstances that are considered to be unfair. An example of this is the now broadly recognised tort of misappropriation that is part of the law of most American states.[90] At its broadest, unfair competition law can be said to prevent a person from appropriating information, ideas or reputations without permission or without paying for their use. However, no jurisdiction applies such a sweeping principle without limitations. To do otherwise would stifle almost all creativity, given the dependence of 'new' knowledge on old knowledge. The limitations imposed on the principle where deception and confusion are unnecessary vary from jurisdiction to jurisdiction, but as a general rule unfair competition law focuses on not only the actions of the defendant but also the effect of those actions on the plaintiff. It may also point to the effect on those who might contemplate undertaking similar activities to those of the plaintiff.[91] For example, more recent American decisions have embraced the tort but have applied an economic approach to it, by imposing tests aimed at determining whether the defendant's conduct is likely significantly to reduce or eliminate the incentive to provide information in the first place.[92] It therefore requires an analysis of the relationship between the plaintiff and the defendant and the effect on that relationship before any liability can be found.

The approach to unfair competition law in a number of European countries also focuses on the relationship between the parties.[93] For example, in Germany, s. 1 of the Act Against Unfair Competition (Gesetz gegen der unlauteren Wettbewerb) will apply only if the plaintiff and defendant

---

[88] See the discussion of the American tort of misappropriation in Chapter 4.

[89] See the discussion of the history of the tort in Chapter 4. See also D. Baird, 'Common Law Intellectual Property and the Legacy of *International News Service* v. *Associated Press*' (1983) 50 *University of Chicago Law Review* 411.

[90] The tort is part of common law and therefore accepted or rejected on a state by state basis. (See Chapter 4.)

[91] *National Basketball Association* v. *Motorola Inc.*, 105 F 3d (2nd Cir. 1997).   [92] Ibid.

[93] Section 1 of the German Unfair Competition Act 1909 (Gesetz gegen den unlauteren Wettbewerb, 7 June 1909 – (UWG) (Germany)) provides: 'Any person who, in the course of business activity for purposes of competition, commits acts contrary to honest practices, may be enjoined from these acts and held liable for damages.' See generally, Kamperman Sanders, *Unfair Competition Law* for a discussion of unfair competition law in Europe.

are in competition.[94] Hence, gaining access to a database and using it for personal purposes will not be unfair competition. There would need to be some commercial exploitation of the database that competed directly with the plaintiff.

There are other limitations that may be imposed which are discussed later in this book, particularly in Chapter 4 in the context of American approaches to unfair competition. However, the end result is that the scope of unfair competition law is almost invariably narrower than any scheme of exclusive property rights that is enforced, regardless of the relationship between the plaintiff and the defendant.

Contract law and databases

Contract law is another regime that can be used to regulate the access to, and use of, databases. There are a number of advantages in the use of contract for this purpose. A particular economic advantage is that it permits differential pricing. Different groups can be granted access to the information contained in the database according to their capacity to pay, their desire for the product and the use that they will make of the information supplied.[95] For example, commercial users can be charged different rates to educational users. In addition, those commercial users who are using the information to produce their own informational product, such as a newer, bigger, better or different database could be charged a different rate from the rate imposed for a non-competing use. The contract can be tailored to ensure that the database owner receives an appropriate return on their investment, as the terms of the individual contracts will be a reflection of the market demand for, and supply of, the information in question.

While there are significant advantages associated with contract law as a model for protection, there are also significant disadvantages from the perspective of both the database owner and user. First, a major difficulty that the database owner has is that the protection derived from the contract only extends to its contractual relationship between itself and the contracting party. If the contracting party releases the information to a third party it is difficult, if not impossible, to enforce contractual rights against that third party. It may be possible to sue the contracting party for use of the information in the database that was not authorised by the contract, but that course of action will not be available against the third party.

[94] J. Mehrings, 'Wettbewerbsrechtlicher Schutz von Online-Dataenbanken' [1990] *Computer und Recht* 305 at 308.
[95] See the discussion on price discrimination in Chapter 7.

Second, the database owner needs some form of protection that prevents access to the database by anyone who does not have a contractual right to that access. If anyone can gain access without obtaining a contractual right, there is no or little incentive for them to enter into a contract to obtain such a right. There are two types of protection that are applicable in such circumstances. One is the use of practical measures to prevent access to the database. In the context of hardcopy databases, this would involve physical separation of the database from those without a contractual arrangement with the database owner. In the context of electronic databases, this will mean virtual separation of the database from others by the use of technological measures such as passwords, encryption or other means. Even this form of protection will not be effective if the cost of circumventing that protection is less than the cost of obtaining access via a contract. For some, particularly those with technological ability, it will be easier to circumvent the technological protection devices than to pay the contractual price of access. The other type of protection would be legal, making it illegal to obtain access without the database owner's permission. In the context of hardcopy databases, this can be achieved by laws of trespass, and with electronic databases, it can be achieved by laws outlawing circumvention of technological protection devices. Consequently, the database owner has to rely on both forms of protection in order to make effective use of contracts.

There are also disadvantages associated with the use of contract law as a model of protection. One of these is that contracts for access to databases may not in fact have the customised features and associated advantages that are mentioned above. This is particularly the case where the contracts are of the 'click-on' type (where the database owner's standard terms are presented to the user who either accepts or rejects those terms). The user signifies acceptance by clicking on the relevant icon or box on their computer screen. In such circumstances, there is no negotiation over terms. This situation has been described in academic writings as one in which a contract may be formed but in fact there is no agreement in the sense that there is no meeting of the minds of the individual parties and the terms are completely non-negotiable. Such situations are highly likely to arise in relation to electronic databases because of the possibility of automating the contractual process.[96]

Related to this are other issues concerning the content of contract law as it applies in this area. In particular, there are issues about the extent

---

[96] J. Reichman and J. Franklin, 'Privately Legislated Intellectual Property Rights: Reconciling Freedom of Contract with Public Good Uses of Information' (1999) 147 *University of Pennsylvania Law Review* 875.

to which a contract should be scrutinised if its terms greatly favour one particular party, such as the database owner. Such an imbalance would itself be a reflection of the different bargaining strengths of the parties concerned. There are circumstances in contract law where the validity of a contract, or certain terms in it, will be questioned by the courts if the process by which the contract was formed was tainted in some way. However, as a general rule, that will only occur if the court is satisfied that one of the parties is suffering from some disability known to the other party and they have taken advantage of that disability.[97] Mere inequality of bargaining power does not of itself lead to the invalidity of a contract. This may result in extraordinarily high levels of protection being conferred on databases via contracts. For example, the contract could place extremely strict conditions upon the use of information extracted from a database.

These restrictions may even override the application of other legal regimes for the protection of, and access to, the database. For example, copyright protection that may apply to databases contains various exceptions such as fair use or fair dealing. The contract may exclude the operation of these exceptions. This has prompted calls for restrictions on the extent to which contracts can override the legislative balance between intellectual property right owners and users that has been crafted by the political process over many years. Alternatively, there should be a general restraint on contractual terms that are held to be contrary to the public interest.[98]

As noted above, contract law as a model of protection is only effective if there is some form of physical or virtual protection and some other form of legal protection preventing unauthorised access to the database. Therefore, there are critical issues to be considered in determining the relationship between contract law and the underlying legal regime that provides the necessary support for contract law. For example, the Directive permits legislation that overrides contracts in some situations, whereas proposed American *sui generis* legislation has expressly provided that contracts are unaffected by the *sui generis* legislation.[99] There are also other examples from intellectual property regimes of situations in which statutory rights override private contractual arrangements.[100] Overriding

---

[97] Ibid., at 927. See also the decision of the High Court of Australia in *Commercial Bank of Australia* v. *Amadio* (1983) 151 CLR 447.

[98] Reichman and Franklin, ibid., at 929.   [99] Article 8 of the Directive.

[100] Examples of such terms include provisions concerning back-up copies of computer programs and reproduction for the purposes of achieving interoperability of computer programs. See, e.g. Article 6 of the Council Directive 91/250/EEC of 14 May 1991 on the legal protection of computer programs and Part 11, Division 4A of the Australian Copyright Act 1968, not constituting infringements of copyright in computer programs.

contracts is also common in other fields of law, notably consumer protection, where there is a perceived inequality of bargaining power between the parties to the contracts.[101] In order to determine whether contracts concerning databases should be overridden, it is necessary to consider whether the underlying justifications for overriding contracts are applicable in the context.

The legal justification for overriding contractual provisions may also be derived from competition law. If a breach of that law has been demonstrated, a potential remedy may be the imposition of a compulsory licence, whereby the owner of intellectual property is required to licence that intellectual property to particular users. As competition law could potentially apply to any *sui generis* rights, there is a separate discussion of the issues concerning competition law and its application to database owners below.

Competition law

Advocates of various models of *sui generis* protection claim that many of the difficulties associated with those models of protection can be overcome by the application of competition law or anti-trust law. (The term 'competition law' will be used in this book, except when specific reference is being made to the anti-trust laws of the United States of America.) The purpose of such laws is to prevent the abuse of market power or the illegitimate acquisition of such power via, for example, price fixing between competitors.

The theory behind competition law is that it will ensure the proper market operation, thus preventing market distortions. While competition law does have a role to play, particularly in relation to the regulation of intellectual property, that role is severely restricted for a number of reasons.

The paradigm does not fit

There is a genuine argument that a number of database industries or industries that are dependent on databases simply do not fit within the model of a perfect market that dominates competition law. Competition law is predicated on the neoclassical economic assumption that the ideal market situation is one of perfect competition[102] although economists

---

[101] See, e.g. Part V, Division 2 of the Australian Trade Practices Act 1974 which imposes certain terms on the sale of goods and services to consumers.

[102] 'In a perfectly competitive market, individual sellers have no control over the price at which they sell, the price being determined by aggregate market demand and supply

take a dynamic rather than static view of the competitive process. This means that while perfect competition may not exist at any particular point in time, the economists will be content if the market conditions are such that there is continual pressure on the participants in a market to provide services as efficiently as possible. Hence, it may be the case that one particular company or a small group of companies may dominate a particular market at any particular point in time. This will not be a cause for concern, provided that their dominance has been achieved and maintained as a consequence of their competitive excellence. That is, they have achieved their position because they are better than their competitors. So long as market conditions provide the opportunity for others to compete in that market, there are no problems from a regulatory perspective. The role of competition law is simply to ensure that those who temporarily dominate a market do not continue to do so by preventing or deterring others from competing via illegitimate means that harm the competitive process itself.

The end result of this analysis is that no legal action pursuant to competition law will be taken against a company simply because it holds a dominant position in a particular market. There must be some identifiably anti-competitive conduct in which it has engaged before action will take place. In turn, this requirement presumes that the nature of the market in question is one that naturally lends itself to perfect competition.

This is simply not the case with a number of database markets. Their very nature is to lend themselves to natural monopolies,[103] or natural oligopolies rather than perfect competition. This market structure may exist because the databases cater for a very discrete, niche market, or the market demand is for a huge database that necessarily contains almost every piece of information relevant to the area of inquiry in question. Hence, there is only room for one or two providers in that market.

The cost of creating such a database is a formidable barrier to entry to the market-place as it is an enormous sunk cost. A sunk cost is one that cannot be recovered in the event of the person incurring that cost choosing or being forced to leave the market in which the investment has been made. The importance of sunk costs as opposed to other costs

conditions.' C. Pass and B. Lowes, *Collins Dictionary of Economics* (2nd edn, Harpercollins, Glasgow, 1988), p. 399.

[103] 'A situation where economies of scale are so significant that costs are only minimized when the entire output of an industry is supplied by a single producer so that supply costs are lower under monopoly than under conditions of perfect competition', ibid. See also the US Copyright Office Report on Legal Protection for Databases, August 1997 at 106–12.

is that anyone investing sunk costs runs a considerable risk of obtaining no, or very little, return on their investment, whereas if the costs are not sunk the investment can be converted to use in another commercial endeavour.

Once one or two investors have made that large commercial investment, there is a very real barrier to any other company making a similar investment. The acquisition, maintenance, presentation and delivery of the information are an extremely expensive operation. Consequently, the natural position in many database industries is one in which there is minimal competition, and the market is dominated by one or two major players. As this domination does not arise through any prohibited anti-competitive conduct, competition law has little, if any, role in regulating the industry.

The only circumstances in which competition law would be effective are where there has been some abuse of the dominant position[104] or use of substantial market power for an unlawful purpose, such as preventing another person from competing with them.[105] In some circumstances, a failure to licence data to a competitor or someone who requires the information in order to operate in another market may infringe competition law. An example of this is the decision of the European Court of Justice in *Radio Telefís Eireann (RTE) and Independent Television Publications Ltd (ITP)* v. *Commission of the European Communities (Magill's* case).[106] RTE and ITP were television companies in Ireland. Each company published its own individual television listings and claimed copyright in those listings. Each company refused to licence a third party, Magill TV Guide Ltd, to use the listings to create a comprehensive weekly television guide.

The Court held that the television stations held a dominant position in the market in weekly television magazines because they were the only source of the necessary programming information. It went on to hold that

---

[104] Article 86 of the EEC Treaty of Rome 1957 which applies to all Member States of the EU.

[105] Section 46 of the Trade Practices Act 1974. The relevant American legislation is section 2 of the Sherman Act, Statute 209 of 1890 as amended by 15 USCA 2 (1973) which imposes a general requirement that a person shall not monopolise or attempt to monopolise any part of the trade or commerce among the several states, or with foreign nations. This general requirement is then interpreted and applied by the American courts.

[106] [1995] ECR I-743, [1995] 4 CMCR 718, judgment of 6 April 1995. See also *Denda International* v. *KPN*, 5 August 1997, [1997] *Informatie recent* / AMI 218, Court of Appeal of Amsterdam where a refusal to licence white pages telephone directories for re-publication on CD-ROM was held to be an abuse of a dominant market position.

the dominant position was being abused to prevent Magill from competing with them in the market for weekly television guides. In particular, the appellants were preventing the appearance of a new product, a comprehensive weekly guide with the programme listings of both appellants.[107] Consequently, it ordered that RTE and ITP should licence Magill and other third parties to reproduce and publish the television listings in return for a reasonable licence fee.

Both the decision itself and subsequent decisions confirm that the mere possession of intellectual property rights does not of itself constitute a dominant position in the market.[108] Nor does a refusal to grant a licence, 'even if it is the act of an undertaking holding a dominant position', constitute abuse of a dominant position.[109] It appears that in order to demonstrate abuse, the intellectual property owner must be doing more than simply exercising their intellectual property rights. There must be exceptional circumstances such as the prevention of the creation of a new product that is in demand by consumers,[110] or evidence that the refusal to grant a licence leads to a complete foreclosure of the market to competition.[111]

The legal model for protection may generate the possibility of legitimate market power being created

While competition law can provide a remedy in some circumstances, the decision in *Magill* and subsequent cases demonstrates some of the limitations of competition law. First, the owner of the intellectual property right must have a dominant position[112] in the market. This is often extremely difficult to establish.[113] In addition, a third party may wish to

---

[107] Ibid., at para. 53.

[108] [1995] ECR I, 743, judgment of 6 April 1995 at para. 46. *Philips Electronics NV* v. *Ingman Ltd and the Video Duplicating Company Ltd* [1995] FSR 530; Case T-504/93 *Tierce Ladbroke SA* v. *The Commission Case*, [1997] ECR II 923.

[109] [1995] ECR I, 743, judgment of 6 April 1995 at para. 49. See also D. Fitzgerald, 'Magill Revisited' [1998] 20 *European Intellectual Property Review* 154.

[110] See the analysis of this issue in D. Fitzgerald, 'Magill Revisited', at 160–1. See also N. Jones, 'Euro-Defences: Magill Distinguished' (1998) 20 *European Intellectual Property Review* 352.

[111] See Case COMP 03/38.0 44 – NDC Health / IMS Health Interim Measures, IP/01/941 3 July 2001, in which the European Commission ordered that IMS Health should license pharmaceutical sales data to competitors wishing to enter the pharmaceutical sales data market.

[112] In Australia the test is whether the company has a substantial degree of power in a market. See s. 46 of the Trade Practices Act 1974 (Cth).

[113] Undated submission from the Australian Competition and Consumer Commission to the Attorney-General's Department re: the legal protection of databases. Copy held on file by the author.

have access to a database because it has information relating to a particular industry. Yet if that database is part of a wider market and contains other information, the owner of the database may not hold a substantial degree of market power in their own market.[114]

Even if the relevant test of market power can be established, the intellectual property owner in question will always be able to argue that they are not abusing their market position, but simply exercising the intellectual property rights that have been granted to them by legislation. The onus will always be on the other party to demonstrate an unlawful purpose of the database owner in refusing to licence the intellectual property right.[115] The existence of intellectual property rights therefore complicates the application of competition law.

The logistics of government regulation

A further difficulty associated with the use of competition law to prevent abuses of intellectual property rights in databases is that governments have limited means at their disposal to monitor and litigate these abuses. While very large and important cases concerning the relationship between intellectual property and competition law have been brought and won by government bodies, the costs of those actions are usually enormous as they involve a rule of reason analysis.[116] The defendants in such actions often have access to greater legal resources than the relevant government department.[117] There are two consequences of this fact. First, if an action is brought, the defendant has a reasonable chance of avoiding an adverse outcome due to the vast legal resources at its disposal. Second, government bodies are reluctant to institute proceedings unless they are sure that they have a very strong case, both in terms of economic theory and in terms of actual evidence of infringing conduct. Hence, even in

---

[114] Ibid.

[115] *APRA* v. *Ceridale Pty Ltd* (1991) ATPR 41–074. In that case, APRA declined to licence the right of public performance because Ceridale, a nightclub, had failed to pay its licence fees. This reason for refusing the licence was accepted as legitimate and not prohibited under Australian legislation.

[116] A rule of reason analysis is one in which the competition law infringement is only established if there is a particular effect of the conduct on the competitive process. Hence, the regulatory body must prove that the defendant has a significant degree of market power as well as proving the alleged conduct in question, the intent behind the conduct and the anti-competitive effect of the conduct.

[117] The US Department of Justice has spent $12.6 million in litigation with Microsoft since late 1989. Reuters, 7 October 1999. While this was a small proportion of the Department's budget, other national governments may not have similar resources. In addition, it is unlikely that private litigants would have the means to pursue costly anti-trust litigation of this nature.

those situations in which competition law is applicable, there is a very real limit on how often the law will, in fact, be applied.

Government policy towards competition law

There are also other restraints upon the application of competition law. The limited means of government bodies to enforce it means that policies are developed concerning what actions will and will not be taken. These policies are themselves subject to change according to both the budget of the relevant government enforcement agency, and the policy of the incumbent government. For example, in the United States during the Reagan administration, there was very little emphasis on the enforcement of anti-trust law,[118] and President George W. Bush Jr has indicated a considerable lack of enthusiasm for applying anti-trust law to industries such as information industries that rely on new technologies.[119]

In the case of databases, the international dimensions of the problem may also complicate the position. The database owner's market power may be held in an international market. The enforcement of competition law may then require the cooperation of several governments with different attitudes to competition law.[120] While cooperation between national competition law regulatory bodies is increasing, the political and practical logistics of such cooperation restrict its effectiveness.

Aspects of distributive justice

A further limitation of competition law is its lack of emphasis on distribution of wealth which, in this context, can be equated with information. As indicated above, the ultimate outcome of a particular market structure for databases is not the primary concern of competition law. The emphasis is more upon the means by which that structure has been achieved or is being maintained. Hence, competition law has little, if anything, to say about the distribution of economic power. It certainly has nothing to

---

[118] See W. Shughart, II, 'The Fleeting Reagan Antitrust Revolution' (2000) 45 *The Antitrust Bulletin* 271, G. Bittlingmayer, 'The Antitrust Vision Thing: How Did Bush Measure Up?' (2000) 45 *The Antitrust Bulletin* 291. These two articles also suggest that individual antitrust actions in the US were the product of prevailing political views rather than transparent and coherent economic considerations.

[119] *The Australian Financial Review*, 5 April 2000, p. 13. The views expressed by the then presidential candidate suggest that his administration will return to the approach of the Reagan administration of an emphasis on horizontal restraints such as price-fixing.

[120] For example, in 1984 Australia passed legislation preventing the enforcement of American anti-trust judgments in Australia. Foreign Proceedings (Excess of Jurisdiction) Act 1984 (Cth).

say about non-economic objectives. For example, if compulsory licensing of databases were desirable in order to achieve objectives relating to research or education, competition law would have no role to play in achieving those objectives.

With these general principles in mind, we can turn to an examination of the specific provisions of the Directive, their implementation by Member States and the position in the United States. This is done in Chapters 3, 4 and 5.

3   Protection of databases in the EU

This chapter examines the history of the Directive and its final form. It provides an overview of the official process leading up to the adoption of the Directive, and emphasises its changes in direction from the first EU documentation suggesting separate protection for databases through to the final version. In so doing, it demonstrates the myriad of potential models for *sui generis* protection. The initial proposals were firmly based on unfair competition principles, while the final version of the Directive draws very heavily upon copyright principles. The chapter also undertakes an analysis of individual provisions of the Directive and examines some of the difficulties associated with their interpretation. Particular emphasis is placed upon the relationship between copyright in the structure of databases and the individual contents of databases on the one hand, and the new *sui generis* right provided by the Directive on the other. In the course of this analysis, reference is also made to the justifications provided by various organs of the EU for the Directive's approach to particular issues and the various provisions implementing that approach. Finally, the last section of this chapter discusses the provisions of the recently adopted EU Directive 2001/29/EC of 22 May 2001 on the harmonisation of certain aspects of copyright and related rights in the information society ("the Copyright Directive"). The Copyright Directive contains provisions concerning the prohibition of circumvention of technological protection devices designed to protect copyright material. These provisions also apply to the circumvention of technological protection devices designed to protect material in which the *sui generis* right subsists. Consequently, a consideration of them is critical to a full understanding of the *sui generis* right created by the Directive.

The chapter identifies a number of conceptual difficulties with the Directive. The first of these is that the Directive creates a situation in which there may be three different sets of rights applicable to a database. The first set of rights is the copyright that may subsist in the structure of the database, that is the selection and arrangement of the database. Another set of rights is the copyright that may subsist in the individual items constituting the contents of the database. In between these rights may be the *sui generis* right in the contents of the database. The conceptual difficulty with the *sui generis* right as defined in the Directive is in distinguishing between it and the other two sets of rights. While the terminology adopted as the test for protection via the *sui generis* right differs from those other rights, the application of that test involves and implicates the same tests that are applicable to determining whether copyright in the structure of the database exists, or copyright in the individual contents exists.

The other major difficulty with the Directive probably arises from the history of its making. In its first iterations, it was intended to provide limited protection based on the unfair competition principles of a number of European countries.[1] It was coupled with generous exceptions and provision for compulsory licensing. It ended up being based on English sweat of the brow copyright principles which led to part of the difficulty referred to in the previous paragraph. In addition, the exceptions were pared back so that they basically reflected the copyright exceptions of continental countries. The end result is that the *sui generis* right is a hybrid between English copyright with its low standard of originality, and continental exceptions to copyright that are designed for a copyright regime with high standards of originality.

Combined with these conceptual difficulties are a number of problems of interpretation that will be only finally played out in the legislation of Member States which implements the Directive and the case law applying that legislation. Those problems are referred to in the discussion below and dealt with in more detail in Chapter 4.

History of the Directive

The development and final iteration of the Directive involved a long and slow process. During that process, fundamental changes in direction were taken concerning the extent and nature of the protection to be provided to databases. The *sui generis* right that has been finally granted to database owners is considerably broader and stronger than the right that was originally envisaged. The original *sui generis* right for databases was intended to be limited to electronic databases. The right was not intended to apply if the contents of the database were protected by copyright. In addition, the right was to be one based on unfair competition principles. It was aimed solely at copying for commercial purposes, and was to be subject

---

[1] Initial German objections to the Directive were based on the view that Germany's unfair competition laws were sufficient to meet the problem being addressed.

to express provision for a compulsory licence for databases containing particular types of information. The initial proposed duration of the right was ten years.

The end result was a *sui generis* right that bears no resemblance to the right that was originally proposed. It is a broad exclusive property right unrelated to unfair competition principles or consideration of the impact of the defendant's actions on the database owner. The right applies to databases in any format, whether electronic or not, and whether or not copyright subsists in the contents of the database. The duration of the right is fifteen years, but with relative ease, this period can be restarted to effectively confer perpetual protection. It has been described as akin to a publisher's right and its introduction was heavily supported by major publishing companies.[2]

The Green Paper

The first official suggestion for specific protection for databases in the EU came from Chapter 6 of the EC Green Paper on Copyright and the Challenge of Technology 1988 (Green Paper)[3] which proposed harmonisation measures for the legal protection of databases. The Green Paper noted the different levels of protection provided to databases under the copyright laws of the various members of the EU[4] and stated that the Commission was considering 'whether to propose the introduction of measures to give some limited protection to the database itself, as a compilation'.[5] Obviously, a lack of uniformity of legal protection within the EU and its impact on the free flow of information between Member States was an issue,[6] as was the manner in which uniformity was to be achieved.

The Green Paper provided few specific details about the type of protection that was envisaged in order to achieve a level of protection that was both uniform and optimal, but it made a number of general observations concerning the issue. It made the somewhat obvious points that 'the scope of protection and the restricted acts would have to be carefully considered lest access to computerized information be unjustifiably restricted'.[7] In this context, one of the concerns expressed was the limited protection mandated by Article 2(5) of the Berne Convention, which only requires copyright protection for compilations of material that is itself protected by

---

[2] See C. Clark, 'Net Law: A Cyberspace Agenda for Publishers', paper prepared for the UK Publishers Association and the Federation of European Publishers, p. 20 available at http://www.alpsp.org/netlaws.pdf, 11 October 1999.

[3] Chapter 6 of the EC Green Paper on Copyright and the Challenge of Technology 1988, COM(88) 172 Final.

[4] Ibid., at 212–13.   [5] Ibid., at 213.   [6] Ibid., at 207.   [7] Ibid., at 213.

copyright.[8] Protection for the mode of compilation of databases was suggested, regardless of the copyright status of the material in the database.[9] This was discussed in the context of copyright protection and the reference to protection of the mode of compilation reinforced this aspect of the Green Paper. While there were references to *sui generis* protection, they were also made primarily in the context of providing protection to the mode of compilation of databases. However, there were suggestions that the more important aspect of some databases was not their mode of compilation but the raw data contained within them.[10] Further, there was a suggestion, perhaps for the first time, that the underlying basis for providing protection should be that the compilation of data represents an investment that should be protected.[11]

It appears that what was envisaged was a slight restructuring of existing copyright, or possibly the introduction of a *sui generis* right to protect the mode of compilation of databases.[12] In any event, the new measures would give only limited protection[13] and would be carefully considered to avoid unjustifiable restrictions on the access to computerised information.[14] It was also envisaged that the measures in question would be restricted to computerised databases.

The First Draft

Following the Green Paper and the taking of public submissions, the Commission drafted a proposed directive that encapsulated the points mentioned above. The Commission's draft (the First Draft), like all the subsequent drafts, contained a number of recitals indicating the purpose of the Directive and what it was intended to achieve. A comparison of the various draft recitals and the final recitals, together with some observations on their relevance, is undertaken in the analysis of the final version of the Directive that appears below. However, a reasonably close examination of the substantive provisions of the First Draft is warranted, as a comparison between the preliminary drafts of the Directive and the final document reveals a very considerable shift in the approach to achieving the Directive's policy objectives. The First Draft was also accompanied by an explanatory memorandum[15] (the Explanatory Memorandum) that sheds light on the justification for the proposed new directive.

---

[8] Ibid., at 214. See Chapter 6 for a discussion of the international obligations to protect compilations via copyright. At the time of the Green Paper, TRIPS and the Copyright Treaty were not in place.

[9] Ibid.   [10] Ibid., at 207.   [11] Ibid.

[12] Ibid., at 216.   [13] Ibid., at 213.   [14] Ibid.

[15] Explanatory Memorandum for a Proposal for a Council Directive on the legal protection of databases, COM(92) 24 final – SYN 393 Brussels, 13 May 1992.

Justification for a Directive   The Explanatory Memorandum clearly based the argument for the Directive on the economic necessity of protecting the EU database industry. This new sector was seen as being of considerable importance to the economic development of the Community, as information was increasingly treated as a tradeable commodity.[16] In 1990, about 'one quarter of the world's accessible on-line databases [were] of European origin compared with the US share of the world market of 56%'.[17] While the gap between the US and European markets was closing,[18] a directive was needed to provide a 'harmonized and stable legal regime protecting databases created within the Community'.[19]

Definition of a database   For the purposes of the First Draft, the definition of a database was restricted to electronic databases as the Directive was originally intended to deal with the specific problems associated with the use of electronic data.[20] Consequently, a database was defined as

a collection of works or materials arranged, stored and accessed by electronic means, and the electronic materials necessary for the operation of the database such as its thesaurus, index or system of obtaining or presenting information.[21]

Copyright in a database   As contemplated in the Green Paper, copyright protection for these databases was extended beyond the minimum required by Article 2(5) of the Berne Convention for compilations to include copyright protection for collections of both 'works or collections of materials which, by reason of their selection or their arrangement, constituted the author's own intellectual creation'.[22] The protection provided under the Berne Convention only applies to compilations of works and hence to databases with contents in which copyright subsisted. Therefore, the First Draft included within the protection of copyright, databases with contents in which copyright did not subsist, provided those contents were arranged or selected in such a way as to constitute the author's own creation. In other words, copyright protection would be provided if there was some intellectual creativity involved in the design of the database. This copyright in the database that subsisted due to the creativity associated with the selection and arrangement of its contents was separate from the copyright that might subsist in the contents.[23] However, some wording of the First Draft demonstrated confusion between the

---

[16] Paragraphs 1.2 and 2.1.1 of the Explanatory Memorandum, General.
[17] Paragraph 1.1.   [18] Ibid.   [19] Paragraphs 1.1, 1.4, 2.2.11.
[20] Paragraph 3.1.1.   [21] Article 1(1) of the First Draft.
[22] Article 2(3) of the First Draft.   [23] Article 2(4) of the First Draft.

individual works or materials contained in a database and what was referred to as 'the contents of the database'.[24] As will be discussed later in the context of the *sui generis* right created by the Directive, the distinction between copyright in the individual items in a database and the *sui generis* rights in the contents of the database is still a problem.

The standard of originality adopted for copyright in a database was to be the same as that adopted for computer programs via Directive 91/250/EEC of 14 May 1991 on the legal protection of computer programs,[25] although the originality in the database related to its selection and arrangement rather than the work as a whole.[26] This is but one aspect of the relationship between protection for databases and protection for computer programs which has continued to be a difficulty in the interpretation and application of the Directive.

Relationship to copyright in computer programs   The First Draft was not intended to apply to any computer program used in the construction or operation of a database[27] and these computer programs were expressly excluded from the definition of a database.[28] While the intent of the Directive in relation to this issue has always been clear, legislation implementing the Directive has already been implicated in the protection of computer programs.[29] In a number of jurisdictions there have been problems in distinguishing between protection for the data that is manipulated by a computer program and the computer program itself.[30] The Directive may not have helped in resolving those problems.

Exceptions to copyright   A number of provisions in the First Draft dealt with exceptions to the copyright in the database and their relationship to exceptions to the copyright that may subsist in the database contents. Article 7(1) imposed a requirement on Member States to make the same exception in relation to the contents of a database as those Member States made in respect of the works or materials themselves. This exception related to 'brief quotations, and illustrations for the purposes of teaching, provided that such utilisation is compatible with fair practice.'[31] The effect of this provision would have been to permit fair dealing with

---

[24] See Articles 7(1) and (2) of the First Draft that seem to adopt different wording concerning copyright in a database, copyright in the contents of a database and copyright in the works or materials contained in the database.

[25] OJ No. L122, 17 May 1991, pp. 42–6.

[26] Paragraph 2.3 of the Explanatory Memorandum, Particular Provisions.

[27] Recital 18 of the First Draft.   [28] Article 1(1) of the First Draft.

[29] *Mars* v. *Teknowledge* [2000] FSR 138, [1999] ALL ER 600 (QB).

[30] E.g. ibid., and *Data Access Corporation* v. *Powerflex Services Pty Ltd* [1999] HCA 49.

[31] This provision is based on a similar provision in Article 10(2) of the Berne Convention.

the materials contained within a database for these purposes, regardless of whether the fair dealing was in relation to the materials as they stood alone or as part of the database.

Primacy was accorded to any copyright in the contents of the database over the copyright in the database itself. Hence, Article 7(2) provided that where Member States already permitted acts that derogated from the copyright in the contents of a database, the performance of those acts would not infringe the copyright in the database itself. Again, this would permit fair dealing with any of the contents of a database without the possibility of any claim of breach of copyright by the copyright owner.

Relationship between copyright and contract law   Article 7(2) also provided that where contractual arrangements permitted the user of a database to perform acts that derogated from any of the exclusive copyright rights in the contents of a database, the performance of those acts would not infringe the copyright in the database. Again, this demonstrated the primacy of any copyright in the contents of databases and the subordination of any rights in the copyright in the database itself to the copyright in the contents. In this case, the primacy of the copyright in the contents was reinforced by making the copyright in a database subordinate to existing contractual arrangements concerning the copyright in the contents of a database.

Article 6 of the First Draft was a precursor to a perplexing provision in the final version of the Directive concerning the rights of lawful users of databases. Article 6(1) provided that 'the lawful user of a database may perform any of the acts listed in Article 5 [the exclusive rights of copyright] which is necessary in order to use that database in the manner determined by contractual arrangements with the rightholder'. This was supplemented by Article 6(2) that provided:

In the absence of any contractual arrangements between the rightholder and the user of a database in respect of its use, the performance by the lawful acquiror of a database of any of the acts listed in Article 5 which is necessary in order to gain access to the contents of the database and use thereof shall not require the authorization of the rightholder.

The effect of these provisions is dealt with below in the discussion of the final version of the Directive. However, it appears that Article 6 was intended to apply only to database users who had a contractual arrangement with the database owner or to those who acquired the database from such a user. This latter situation would only have applied to hardcopy databases or databases in CDs or other similar electronic format.

The sui generis *right*   A *sui generis* right was proposed by Article 2(5) that required Member States to provide a right 'for the maker of a database to prevent the unauthorized extraction or re-utilization, from that database, of its contents, in whole or in substantial part, for commercial purposes'. The right was to apply regardless of whether the database was entitled to copyright protection pursuant to Article 2(3). However, there were a number of limitations on, and exceptions to, the right. The primary limitation was that the right itself was restricted to 'unfair extraction', which in turn was defined as meaning extraction and re-utilisation for commercial purposes.[32] This was a very significant limitation on the *sui generis* right that was to be granted. It was clearly designed to provide limited protection[33] based on principles of unfair competition.

This protection against parasitic behaviour by competitors, which would already be available under unfair competition law in some Member States but not in others, is intended to create a climate in which investment in data processing can be stimulated and protection provided against misappropriation. It does not prevent the flow of information, nor does it create any rights in the information as such.[34]

For example, it was intended that users could continue to use databases for their own private purposes.[35]

Apart from the limitation inherent in the nature of the right provided, further limitations were also built into the First Draft. For example, the definition of a database included only electronic databases, excluding non-electronic databases from the new right. Another very significant limitation was that the right did not apply to databases if the contents of those databases were works already protected by copyright or neighbouring rights.[36] In such circumstances, the database maker had to rely either on their copyright in the selection or arrangement of their database, or on the enforcement of copyright in the contents of the database. This limitation on the *sui generis* right of unfair extraction was another example of the primacy given to the copyright in the contents of databases over any rights in the database itself.

Compulsory licensing   There was also provision for compulsory licensing of the contents of a database on fair and non-discriminatory terms, if 'the works or materials contained in a database which is made publicly available cannot be independently created, collected or obtained

---

[32] Article 1(2) of the First Draft.
[33] Paragraph 3.2.7 of the Explanatory Memorandum, General.
[34] Paragraph 3.2.8. See also para. 3.2.7.   [35] Paragraph 3.2.8.
[36] Article 2(5) of the First Draft.

from any other source'.[37] A similar requirement for compulsory licences was provided for in respect of databases made publicly available by a public body 'which is either established to assemble or disclose information pursuant to legislation, or is under a general duty to do so.'[38] As the *sui generis* right did not apply to databases with contents that qualified for copyright protection, there was no clash between these compulsory licences of use of the data and the restrictions on compulsory licensing of copyright material.[39]

Exceptions to the sui generis *right*   There were also two exceptions to the right of unfair extraction. These exceptions conferred substantive rights upon users of databases, rather than merely giving them a defence. Under Article 8(4), the lawful user of a database could extract and re-utilise insubstantial parts of works or materials from a database for commercial purposes, provided that acknowledgment was made of the source. The original right provided under the First Draft only applied to extracting or re-utilising the whole or a substantial part of the material in a database in any event.[40] Consequently, an exception to permit those acts in respect of an insubstantial part was not strictly necessary. Similarly, Article 8(5) provided that a lawful user of a database may extract and re-utilise insubstantial parts of works or materials from that database for personal use only, without having to acknowledge the source of the materials. Again, as the right of re-utilisation and extraction only applied in respect of such actions towards a substantial part of the database, and then only if the action was for a commercial purpose, that provision was arguably superfluous.

However, the advantage of the provisions was that they mandated the implementation of those exceptions in Member States' domestic legislation. Without this, Member States would otherwise have been free to provide a *sui generis* right that was broader or stronger than the right of extraction and re-utilisation referred to in Article 2. This broader or stronger right could have prevented use for private purposes, or use of even insubstantial parts of a database but for the presence of Articles 8(4) and (5). Alternatively, a database owner could have relied on contractual provisions to prevent the extraction or re-utilisation of insubstantial parts or particular acts constituting such extraction or re-utilisation. The exceptions would have overridden contractual provisions to some extent in that a contract for use of a database could not have prevented a user

---

[37] Article 8(1) of the First Draft.   [38] Article 8(2) of the First Draft.
[39] Paragraph 2.5 of the Explanatory Memorandum, Particular Provisions.
[40] Article 2(5) of the First Draft.

extracting and re-utilising insubstantial parts. Once it was lawful to use the database, whether pursuant to contract or otherwise, the user would have been entitled to the use of insubstantial parts.

Term of protection The period of copyright protection for databases was to be the same as for other literary works. The period of protection from unfair extraction and re-utilization was ten years according to Article 9(3). This was the same period of time provided under the catalogue laws of Sweden, Denmark and Finland prior to the implementation of the Directive.[41]

The First Draft was unclear as to whether the term of protection could be restarted if significant changes were made to a database. It seems that this was intended, as Article 9(4) stated that 'insubstantial changes to the contents of a database shall not extend the original period of protection of that database by the right to prevent unfair extraction', thus suggesting that substantial changes would have led to an extension of the protection period.

Protection for databases outside the EU Article 11 of the First Draft dealt with the jurisdictional scope of protection provided by the proposed new *sui generis* right. It restricted protection to databases made by nationals or residents of Member States, and databases made by companies and firms having a connection with the EU.[42] In the latter case, the company or firm had to be formed in accordance with the laws of a Member State and have their registered office, central administration or principal place of business within the EU.[43] Protection to other databases from third countries would only be provided pursuant to agreements concluded by the Council.[44]

Retrospectivity The protection provided pursuant to the provisions of the Directive was to be made available in respect of databases created prior to the date of the Directive's publication.[45] In another word, retrospectively.

Preservation of other legal provisions Article 12 provided that the Directive was without prejudice to copyright or other rights in the

---

[41] For example, s. 49 of the Swedish Copyright Act 1960 protected catalogues, tables or other similar productions in which a large number of information items had been reproduced for a period of ten years. See also s. 71 of the Danish Copyright Act 1995 and Article 49 of the Finnish Copyright Act 1961.
[42] Article 11 of the First Draft.   [43] Article 11(2) of the First Draft.
[44] Article 11(3) of the First Draft.   [45] Article 12(2) of the First Draft.

contents of a database as well as to other legal provisions such as unfair competition, trade secrets and the law of contract. In this context,
the law of unfair competition has two important and discrete components that may have an impact on the protection of databases. The first
of these is the competition law regulating monopolistic and other anti-
competitive practices. This law has been harmonised throughout the EU
and, as will be seen in the discussion of the final version of the Directive,
was relied upon as a primary reason for discarding the proposed compulsory licensing arrangements. The second component is the diverse unfair
competition laws of Member States that prohibit conduct constituting a
misappropriation of the labour and efforts of another party. This form of
unfair competition does not require any proof of conduct that deceives or
confuses consumers. In some Member States, unfair competition is not
recognised as a form of action at all while there are considerable differences in the approaches taken in those Member States that do recognise
it as a cause of action.[46] This lack of harmonisation is cited in the recitals
to the Directive as a reason for the Directive. The First Draft, with its *sui
generis* right of unfair extraction, can be seen as an attempt to provide a
uniform action of unfair competition in respect of databases.

Summary of the First Draft   The First Draft was, therefore, an
attempt to provide a minimalist solution to a lack of uniformity in protection for databases. It had a restricted definition of a database that did not
include non-electronic databases. The *sui generis* right given in respect of
databases was a limited right that only affected extraction or re-utilisation
for commercial purposes. The right did not apply if copyright subsisted
in the contents of the database, and was subject to a number of exceptions that were not only permissible but mandatory for all Member States
and subject to a requirement of compulsory licensing in certain circumstances. In short, it was designed to fill the gap that arose in protection
against commercial copying if the contents of a database were not subject to copyright. As can be seen below, that minimalist protection was
expanded to create a far stronger level of protection prior to the adoption
of the Directive.

Opinion of the Economic and Social Committee of the Council

The First Draft that was submitted to the Council was referred by it
to the Economic and Social Committee (the Committee). The Opinion
of the Economic and Social Committee (the Committee's Opinion) was

---

[46] A. Kamperman Sanders, *Unfair Competition Law* (Clarendon Press, Oxford, 1997).

adopted at a meeting of the Committee on 24 November 1992.[47] The Committee took the view that the Council should have the paramount objective of having a strong database industry[48] and ensuring that the legal protection envisaged lead to that objective.[49] It specifically recommended that the Council eschew a debate on legal philosophies that underlie the Directive, particularly on the subject of originality,[50] and questioned whether it was important to distinguish between databases that were the product of intellectual creativity or sweat of the brow.[51]

The Committee then went on to suggest a correlation between the success of the database industry in the UK and the high level of intellectual property protection via copyright in that country.[52] It claimed that the UK had 60 per cent of the Community market share.[53] The Committee's Opinion did note that Spain also had laws protecting databases but made no comment on the impact of those laws on its database industry.[54] This is curious, as the Explanatory Memorandum had identified Spain as having a small database industry.[55] In other words, both the UK and Spain had strong copyright protection for databases but they were at opposite ends of the industry.

Despite this, the Committee's Opinion concluded that a strong Community database industry required strong intellectual property protection and that the right of unfair extraction did not meet this requirement. In particular, the term of the right was too short[56] although no justification was given for that statement. In addition, the compulsory licensing provisions in the First Draft were criticised because they reduced unduly the extent of protection provided, and there was a lack of detail as to how a scheme of compulsory licensing would be implemented.[57] In addition, it stated that 'the sophistication of the Community's laws ensuring fair competition' ensured that those laws would deal with any misuse by the owners of any new exclusionary right.[58] It suggested that any new right should become one of the exclusive rights comprised within the copyright in databases as the Commission had previously rejected the concept of new *sui generis* rights on other occasions, particularly in relation to

---

[47] Opinion on the Proposal for a Council Directive on the Legal Protection of Databases of the Economic and Social Committee, OJ No. C19.
[48] Paragraph 2.1 of the Committee's Opinion.   [49] Ibid.   [50] Ibid.
[51] Paragraph 2.3(b).   [52] Paragraph 2.2.   [53] Paragraph 1.2.
[54] Ibid. 'In Spain, databases are protected as such and there is an elaborate definition of precisely what qualifies as a database.'
[55] Paras. 2.2.2 and 2.2.3 of the Explanatory Memorandum, General. The predicted UK turnover for on-line services for 1992 was 1,770 million ECU, whereas the predicted Spanish turnover was 26 million ECU.
[56] Paragraph 2.3.b of the Committee's Opinion.   [57] Paragraphs 1.6, 2.7 and 3.12.
[58] Paragraph 2.7.

protection of computer programs.[59] This suggestion that any new right should be incorporated within the existing copyright regime was coupled with the suggestion that copyright protection should be provided for sweat of the brow.[60] Part of the justification for this approach was that any intellectual property protection should be of a high standard:

It would be wrong to compromise on the question of whether or not something should be protected by allowing a measure of short-term intellectual property protection with a compulsory licence. It is preferable to take a decision on whether something qualifies for protection and, if so, then to grant intellectual property protection of a high standard.[61]

A second and less favoured option was the creation of a *sui generis* right. However, it stated that a *sui generis* right should be 'as effective a right as it would be if it were a restricted act under the copyright in the database'.[62]

Therefore, the Committee saw new rights in respect of databases as being far more important and stronger than the new right originally envisaged by the Commission. In effect, the Committee sought to incorporate a sweat of the brow doctrine into the copyright or neighbouring rights law of the EU. In contrast, the Commission's original proposal was intended to provide a far weaker right aimed at correcting market failure associated with commercial copying of database contents, where the copier was taking a free ride on the efforts of a database maker. The Committee's Opinion made a number of other specific points about the First Draft of the Directive that are worthy of mention.

Definition of a database   It recommended that the Directive not be restricted in its operation to electronic databases, because of the legal complications associated with having different legal regimes applying to the same database if it were stored in both electronic and some other form.[63] It also gave an example of white pages directories and suggested that the owners may end up without either copyright or *sui generis* protection. The analysis of that example bears repeating here because it may have led to a significant change in the scope of the Directive. It is also wrong.

For example, white pages telephone directories are protected under the law of copyright in some Member States. If, as frequently happens, these white pages directories are made available on CD-ROM as databases, the databases themselves would not be protected as 'original' databases (because there would be no intellectual creation in transposing them from paper to the electronic medium)

---

[59] Paragraph 2.6.   [60] Paragraph 2.3(b).   [61] Paragraph 2.6.2.
[62] Paragraph 2.7.   [63] Paragraph 3.2.

and would not be the subject of the unfair extraction right because, at least in some Member States, there would be copyright in the underlying materials.[64]

The error in this analysis is that if copyright did subsist in the hardcopy of the white pages directory, it would also subsist in the CD-ROM version. The necessary originality would not be lost if the copyright owner reproduced its directory in a different medium. The originality derived from the creativity in selection or arrangement, or from the sweat of the brow, would still be manifested in both versions. Copyright would subsist in both versions. If the reasoning in the Committee's Opinion were correct, it would apply equally to the second and subsequent hardcopies of the directory. The first hardcopy would have originality but the subsequent copies would not because there is no intellectual creation in printing subsequent copies. One can only hope that the impact of this analysis was less than what it appears to have been.

Protection for databases outside the EU The Committee also made an observation concerning the international implications of any new rights. It noted that if the unfair extraction right were incorporated into the copyright in a database, the EU Member States would be obliged to protect databases from other countries, particularly the United States of America, because of international copyright obligations.[65] The Committee took the view that this was not a serious obstacle as the dichotomy between the rights granted in the United States and those granted in some Member States already existed, and it did not provide any significant detriment to the database industry in the Member States concerned.[66] Despite this observation that no significant harm would flow from providing national treatment for legal protection of databases, the final version of the Directive did not provide protection for databases from other countries in the absence of reciprocal protection being provided by those countries. This issue is discussed in more detail in Chapter 5, where it is argued that the Members of the EU may be in breach of their international treaty obligations by not providing national treatment to foreign databases.

Duration of protection The Committee's Opinion expressed the view that the term of ten years of protection was too short.[67] No reason for this view was given, except to assert that 'the existence of the equivalent of an unfair extraction right as part of the copyright in some Member States' does not appear to have impeded the growth of the industry.[68]

---

[64] Paragraph 1.5.   [65] Paragraph 3.4.   [66] Ibid.
[67] Paragraph 2.3(b).   [68] Paragraph 3.13.

Presumably, this was a reference to the sweat of the brow copyright protection provided under UK copyright legislation, and the implication was that the copyright period of protection would be appropriate.[69]

The Committee's Opinion also discussed the question of when the term of protection should start to run and, perhaps more importantly, when a new period of protection would start to run after changes to the database.[70] It suggested that the 'most practical means of determining the start of a new term of protection would be for each item of data in the database to be electronically or otherwise "date-stamped" on its incorporation into the database. Each piece of data would be protected for the appropriate term from the date of its date-stamp'.[71] There are two issues arising from this recommendation. First, it created the possibility of protection expiring in respect of part of a database and being renewed in respect of the updated portion of the database, a proposal that has been subsequently put forward in the United States. This would seem to be preferable to a situation in which substantial updating of the database would lead to a new period of protection for the entire database. A further implication from the suggestion was that it seemed to indicate that individual pieces of data could be protected for the specified period of time. The First Draft clearly stated that infringement of the right of unfair extraction would only occur if the whole or a substantial part of the database were unfairly extracted,[72] but if protection were to be afforded to one piece of data, this would suggest that one piece of data could constitute a substantial part of a database.

Authorship of databases and circumvention of technological protection of databases   The Committee also indicated that the issue of authorship of computer-generated databases would have to be considered at some stage,[73] as should the requirement to protect databases from devices designed to circumvent technical protection.[74] However, it offered no solution to the issue of authorship of computer-generated databases.[75]

Summary of the Committee's Opinion   The cumulative effect of the First Draft of the Directive and the Committee's Opinion was to demonstrate the confusion about how to achieve the objective of a strong

---

[69] Database owners initially sought copyright protection along the lines of UK copyright protection.
[70] Paragraph 3.14 of the Committee's Opinion.   [71] Paragraph 3.14.
[72] Paragraph 2(5) of the First Draft.   [73] Paragraph 3.6 of the Committee's Opinion.
[74] Paragraph 3.15.
[75] See the general discussion of this issue in Chapter 2. See also the discussion at the end of this chapter on circumvention of technological protection devices.

database industry. The Commission originally adopted a minimalist approach designed to give limited protection against unfair extraction for commercial purposes to electronic databases that could not obtain protection indirectly via copyright, on the basis that copyright subsisted in the contents of those databases. This minimalist right would also have been subject to compulsory licensing in certain circumstances, and a guaranteed right to extract insubstantial parts of a database, both for commercial and private purposes.

The Committee took a totally different, protectionist view. Its preferred option was to harmonise the law concerning copyright protection for databases by introducing a uniform standard of originality based on a sweat of the brow approach. Then a new right was to be added to the existing rights of copyright owners. Alternatively, a new *sui generis* right could be created that would achieve the same result. Its preference was the establishment of a new exclusive right within the existing copyright regime. In addition, it objected to the presence of any compulsory licensing provisions and wanted a longer period of protection than that originally suggested by the Commission.

From a more general perspective, the Committee's Opinion made it very clear that the basis of, and justification for, the Directive was, and should be, solely economic.[76] It urged the Council to 'resist being sidetracked into a debate on legal philosophies which underlie the Directive...', as the paramount objective was to foster a strong database industry.[77] Hundreds of years of jurisprudence relating to copyright were to be disregarded as an unnecessary distraction in achieving this objective. Yet, at the same time a particular philosophical position was adopted which meant that once it was decided to protect something, intellectual property protection of a high standard should be conferred.[78] Rather than tailoring any protection as required in order to provide the appropriate mix of protection and availability to data necessary to achieve the required outcome, a fixed position was adopted that a high level of protection should be given.

Amendments to the Directive by the European Parliament

On 23 June 1993, the European Parliament issued a number of proposed amendments to the Commission's text (the 1993 Amendments).[79] A number of the amendments were designed simply to clarify the First Draft, and as the final version of the Directive was also significantly

---

[76] Paragraph 2.6.3 of the Committee's Opinion.   [77] Paragraph 2.1.
[78] Paragraph 2.6.2.   [79] A3–0183/93, OJ 1993 No. C194, 23 June 1993, p. 144.

different from the First Draft, little is gained by discussing all of those amendments here. However, some of the more important amendments are worthy of consideration because they were the precursors to important changes in the final version of the Directive and, as such, they signalled a shift in the approach to copyright or *sui generis* protection.

Definition of a database   The definition of a database was amended to define it as a collection of 'a large number of data, works or other materials arranged, stored and accessed by electronic means'. The addition of the words 'a large number of' was intended to ensure that the new rights did not apply to every collection of accessible data, and this expression was the precursor to the test of substantial investment in obtaining, verifying and presenting a database that appears in the Directive.[80] Definitions of the author of a database and the owner of a database for the purposes of copyright were introduced[81] although ultimately no definition of the owner of a database was included in the Directive.

The sui generis *right*   The *sui generis* right became a right of unauthorised extraction rather than unfair extraction.[82] This was the start of a major shift in the nature of the *sui generis* protection for database owners. Unauthorised extraction was still defined as extraction and re-utilisation for commercial purposes, but 'commercial purposes' was given a definition in the new Article 1(2). It was defined as 'any use – whether domestic or collective – aiming at economic activity or a remunerated transaction'. While the actual meaning of those words may never be known, they appeared to include any private use of a database that involved avoiding payment for that use.[83]

Compulsory licensing   Despite the recommendation in the Committee's Opinion that compulsory licensing provisions be dispensed with completely, they were retained in the 1993 Amendments in a slightly modified form. In particular, the compulsory licensing provisions concerning information supplied by public authorities were expanded to cover private firms or entities in some circumstances.[84] Hence, compulsory licensing provisions were extended to bodies, whether public or

[80] Amendment No. 3 of the 1993 Amendments.
[81] Amendments Nos. 4 and 5 of the 1993 Amendments.
[82] Amendment No. 6 of the 1993 Amendments.
[83] Curiously, there was a definition of non-commercial for the purposes of Article 8(5) of the First Draft that defined such use as 'domestic and non-collective'.
[84] Amendment 33 of the 1993 Amendments.

not, which were established or authorised to assemble or to disclose information pursuant to legislation, or which had a general duty to do so. In addition, 'firms or entities enjoying a monopoly status by virtue of an exclusive concession by a public body' were also made the subject of the compulsory licensing provisions.[85]

On the other hand, obtaining compulsory licences on the basis that the database owner was the sole source of the contents of that database was made slightly more difficult. Compulsory licences for works or materials that could not be independently created, collected or obtained from any other source would only be permitted if the compulsory licence was not being sought simply for reasons of economy of time, effort or financial investment.[86]

Exceptions to the sui generis *right*   The exception under Article 8(5) of the First Draft was amended to require an acknowledgment of the source of insubstantial parts used for personal non-commercial use.[87] More importantly, a definition of 'insubstantial parts' was also included which, for the first time, referred to quantitative and qualitative measures of an insubstantial part of a database.[88] One of the points made below concerning the Directive is that this introduction of a reference to qualitative evaluation also imported, necessarily, copyright principles into the *sui generis* right. The consequences of this are significant in themselves.

Duration of protection   The only significant aspect of the Committee's Opinion that was adopted in the 1993 Amendments was the extension of the period of protection to fifteen years, and that a fresh period of protection would begin if there were a substantial change to the contents of a database.[89]

Summary of the 1993 Amendments   The 1993 Amendments were not particularly significant in the context of the final form of the Directive, and a number of the key recommendations expressed in the Committee's Opinion were not adopted. In particular, the *sui generis* right was not incorporated into copyright and remained a quite limited right in the respects previously mentioned. Namely, it applied to electronic databases and only if the contents of such a database were not themselves subject to copyright. In addition, the compulsory licensing provisions were not only retained but also extended to apply to private organisations performing

---

[85] Clause 3 of the 1993 Amendments.   [86] Amendment 18 of the 1993 Amendments.
[87] Amendment 19 of the 1993 Amendments.
[88] Amendment 20 of the 1993 Amendments.
[89] Amendment 24 of the 1993 Amendments.

what have traditionally been viewed as public functions. The only key recommendation of the Committee's Opinion that was adopted was the proposal to increase the period of protection to fifteen years. The major significance of the 1993 Amendments is that they signalled an intention to continue on in the manner outlined in the First Draft. Yet the next substantive draft of the Directive was almost unrecognisable when compared to the First Draft and the 1993 Amendments.

The common position of 10 July 1995

On 10 July 1995[90] a common position[91] was adopted by the Council of the EU (Common Position).[92] This document was the primary basis of the Directive in its final form. A number of amendments were made to this document before the Directive was adopted in March 1996, but they were relatively minor in nature. As the differences between the Common Position and the Directive are minor, no analysis of the former document is undertaken here and the next section deals with the Directive. However, the Council did provide a statement of the Council's Reasons (Council's Reasons) that provides a commentary on the various recitals and articles in the Directive and they are referred to in the discussion below concerning the final draft of the Directive.

The final version of the Directive

The final version of the Directive was adopted by the EU on 11 March 1996. There are four key elements of the Directive. First, the recitals set out the justification for the Directive and provided some insight into its interpretation. Second, Chapter 1 dealt with the scope of the Directive, particularly the definition of a database. Third, Chapter II dealt with the copyright in databases, particularly the harmonisation of copyright protection throughout the EU. Fourth, Chapters III and IV created the *sui generis* rights and the exceptions to those rights, and dealt with a number of common provisions relating to implementation matters such as transition issues, remedies and reporting on the impact of the Directive to the Commission.

---

[90] [1995] EU Bull 7/8 para. 1.3.25, OJ No. C288.

[91] A common position is the position of the Council of the EU, usually known as the Council of Ministers. Each Member State is represented in the Council and at least sixty-two votes cast in favour of the Common Position. See 'Institutions of the European Union', at http://europa.eu.int/inst.en.htm.

[92] Common Position Regarding the Proposal for a Council Directive on the legal protection of databases, OJ 1995 No. C288, 30 October 1995, at p. 14.

The recitals   There are sixty recitals to the Directive. Their length exceeds the length of the substantive provisions of the Directive and they can be separated into a number of different categories. One category asserts the need for additional protection and the reasons why. The first recital states that 'databases are at present not sufficiently protected in all Member States by existing legislation; [and] such protection, where it exists, has different attributes'. Recital 7 provides that 'the making of databases requires the investment of considerable human, technical and financial resources while such databases can be copied or accessed at a fraction of the cost needed to design them independently'. The unauthorised extraction and/or re-utilisation of the contents of a database constitute acts that can have serious economic and technical consequences.[93]

The recitals also state that the exponential growth in the amount of information generated and processed annually in all sectors of commerce and industry calls for investment in advanced information processing systems.[94] They go on to say that there is a very great imbalance in the level of investment in the database sector between the Member States and between the EU and the world's largest database-producing third countries.[95] In addition, the investment necessary to rectify this imbalance will not occur within the EU unless a stable and uniform legal protection regime is introduced for the protection of the rights of database makers.[96]

These recitals clearly indicate that the Directive is justified by the need to maintain and increase the level of investment in databases in the EU. The Directive is then intended to do this by the creation of a *sui generis* right 'to ensure protection of any investment made in obtaining, verifying or presenting the contents of a database'.[97]

The need for uniform laws   A second category of the recitals deals with the need for uniformity of protection within the EU. These are a reflection of the fundamental tenets of the 1957 Treaty establishing the European Community which are designed to create a single common market for goods and services within it. Inconsistency in the laws of each nation impede this fundamental objective.[98] The recitals note that the existing levels of protection are not standardised or harmonised within the EU. In particular, there are differences in the nature of copyright protection for databases[99] and the protection provided by unfair competition legislation or case law.[100]

---

[93] Recital 8 of the Directive.   [94] Recital 10.   [95] Recital 11.   [96] Recital 13.
[97] Recital 40.   [98] Recitals 2 and 3.   [99] Recital 4.   [100] Recital 6.

Explanation of the substantive provisions of the Directive   The third category of recitals relates to the details of the *sui generis* protection to be granted and aspects of copyright protection. These details are then reflected in the substantive provisions of the Directive and will be discussed in the relevant sections below that deal with those substantive provisions. For present purposes, it is sufficient to note that the recitals appear to justify the creation of a *sui generis* right on the grounds that investment in databases must be protected and the existing protection in the EU, via copyright and unfair competition, is inappropriate, primarily because of the lack of consistency between the Member States in these areas of law.

Scope of the Directive and the definition of a database   Chapter 1 of the Directive provides the definition of a database. For the purposes of the Directive, 'Database' means 'a collection of independent works, data or other materials arranged in a systematic or methodical way and individually accessible by electronic or other means'.[101] In addition, Article 1(1) provides that protection is extended to databases in any form. This definition of a database is extremely broad. As noted above, preliminary drafts of the Directive restricted the definition of a database to electronic databases, but that approach was discarded in favour of the approach taken in the Committee's Opinion. The need for individual works, data or other material within the database to be individually accessible does suggest that the database must be fixed in some material form, so that retrieval of individual parts of it may occur. For example, a speech containing various pieces of information would not constitute a database for this reason unless it has been fixed in some form.[102]

Apart from the implicit requirement that the database be in a fixed form of some sort, there are few other restrictions on what collections of information may constitute a database. In particular, there is no requirement that the database be created exclusively or primarily for the purpose of retrieval and use of individual datum or information. The information may have been put together for a number of different purposes other than the accessing of individual pieces of information. For example, by not focusing on the purpose for which information is collected and organised, the definition may include material brought together in order to communicate a message, tell a story or accomplish a

---

[101] Article 1(2) of the Directive.
[102] Whether it would then be a database depends on other issues concerning the definition of a database.

result.[103] An example of this is the decision in *Mars UK Ltd* v. *Teknowledge Ltd*.[104] Mars UK Ltd (Mars) designed and manufactured vending machines that contained built-in discriminators that discriminated between different denominations of coins and between authentic and inauthentic coins. The discriminators contained electronically erasable programmable read-only memory (EEPROMs). These EEPROMs contained data that were then compared with information about coins inserted in the machine. Teknowledge reprogrammed the EEPROMs to update them to contain information concerning new coins. In the process, they reproduced the data in the EEPROMs. This was found to be an infringement of the database rights of Mars, although the point was conceded by Teknowledge without argument. Presumably, Mars's original purpose in collecting and organising the data was to achieve the desired result that the vending machines operate properly. There was no intention to make individual pieces of information accessible to someone interested in using that information for some extrinsic purpose. There is a myriad of other possible applications of this decision in the context of computer programs, as computer programs typically contain significant amounts of data or information primarily for the purpose of ensuring the proper working of the program.[105] The data are not there for any extrinsic purpose of informing someone who accesses the information. This point is taken up again in the next section concerning computer programs.

This broad definition of a database does not seem to be consistent with the purpose of the Directive, as espoused in the recitals. The recitals suggest that the purpose is to improve investment in the generation and processing of information[106] and modern information storage and processing systems.[107] These databases are intended to be a vital tool in the development of an information market within the EU. There is also a clear intention to provide protection for the on-line delivery of information or delivery via physical media such as CDs.[108] In contrast, the recitals suggest that there is no intention to increase or alter the existing protection provided by copyright to computer programs or parts of them.[109]

---

[103] See the Statement of Marybeth Peters, Register of Copyrights before the House Subcommittee on Courts and Intellectual Property on HR 354, 106th Congress, 1st Session, 18 March 1997 at http://www.loc.gov/copyright/reports.
[104] [2000] FSR 138, [1999] ALL ER 600 (QB).
[105] E.g. *Data Access Corporation* v. *Powerflex Services Pty Ltd* [1999] HCA 49.
[106] Recital 10 of the Directive.   [107] Recital 12.   [108] Recitals 22, 43 and 44.
[109] Recital 23.

There are other difficulties associated with other types of 'databases' such as anthologies or collections of works, particularly in hardcopy form. For example, legal casebooks would constitute databases as materials within them are usually arranged according to a systematic way via chapters, subchapters and headings within chapters dealing with particular aspects of the area of law being considered. Periodicals and journals could be considered to be a database, as they are collections of independent works arranged in a systematic way by volume and issue number and categories such as refereed articles, letters, notes and comments coupled with an index or table of contents. In addition, it is arguable that works of non-fiction such as biographies are databases within the meaning of the definition given in the Directive.

The one word in the definition that may provide some limitation on the broad construction of definition of the term 'database' is the word 'independent', depending on how that word is interpreted in the context of the Directive. Let us take the example of a film. It could be argued that the film constitutes a database although that conclusion would be counter-intuitive.[110] The argument would proceed on the basis that the film consists of a collection of individual frames that together constitute the film. Each would be individually accessible as demonstrated by frame-by-frame slow motion replay. Each would be a work or other material that have been arranged in a systematic or methodical way, namely to tell the story portrayed in the film. The only potential obstacle to a finding that the film is a database is the word 'independent'. If 'independent' requires that the individual frames of the film have a stand-alone function to play in terms of informing or entertaining people, then it may be that the film is not a database. This is because the frames are integral parts of the film and interdependent rather than independent. This conclusion in relation to films and other material such as musical works and audiovisual works is supported by Recital 17 of the Directive. However, Chalton has pointed out that the issue of independence and dependence may be more debatable in other circumstances such as in a collection of materials of related stock exchange transactions.[111] He suggests that 'the qualities of dependence...should be judged from consideration of the items in a collection from the standpoint of their mutual dependence within the collection, rather than consideration of each item without reference to the entity of the collection'.[112] To do otherwise could lead to some strange findings as to what constitutes a database.

---

[110] S. Chalton, 'The Copyright and Rights in Databases Regulations 1997: Some Outstanding Issues on Implementation of the Database Directive' (1998) 20 *European Intellectual Property Review* 178.
[111] Ibid.   [112] Ibid., at 179.

The broad scope of the definition of database is reinforced by Recital 19, although, on its face, that recital appears to limit the definition. It provides that:

[A]s a rule, the compilation of several recordings of musical performances on a CD does not come within the scope of this Directive, both because, as a compilation, it does not meet the conditions for copyright protection and because it does not represent a substantial enough investment to be eligible under the *sui generis* right.

Recital 19 states that a compilation of musical recordings is unlikely to receive either copyright protection or *sui generis* protection. However, it acknowledges that an ordinary CD with musical recordings does constitute a database. The lack of protection is a consequence of the minimal investment made in the obtaining, verification or presentation of the contents of the CDs. The requirement of a substantial investment in the database is discussed later in the chapter but, if this requirement were met, the CD would be protected by the *sui generis* right provided under the Directive. The definition of database is therefore so broad that one can legitimately wonder what is not a database for the purposes of the Directive. For example, are art galleries and libraries databases? They are collections of independent works, the independent works are arranged in a systematic way and they are individually accessible by electronic or other means.

There are no definitions of 'works' or 'data' in the Directive. Given the Directive's concern with copyright matters, 'works' presumably refers to individual copyright works such as literary or artistic works that are incorporated into the database. 'Data' are 'facts, especially numerical facts, collected together for reference or information'.[113] Arguably, the two terms both involve a concept of information or material that conveys information and therefore 'other material' refers to information generally. Recital 17 gives some insight into the issue by stating that 'the term "database" should be understood to include literary, artistic, musical or other collections of works or collections of other material such as texts, sound, images, numbers, facts and data'. Nevertheless, even with that limitation on the definition, art galleries and libraries would constitute databases.[114]

This definition of a database in the Directive can be compared with the definition in proposed American legislation (discussed in Chapter 5) that does have a purposive definition of a collection of information. It

---

[113] *The New Shorter Oxford Dictionary* (4th edn, Clarendon Press, Oxford, 1993).
[114] This in turn would lead to some interesting results when considering what might constitute infringement.

also contains a definition of 'information' so as to reduce difficulties concerning the subject matter of the legislation of the type described above.

Computer programs   All the drafts of the Directive provided that the protection granted to databases, either by copyright or the *sui generis* right, did not apply to computer programs used in the making or operation of databases accessible by electronic means.[115] Despite this attempt to separate the protection of the selection and arrangement of the database and its contents on the one hand from the computer program that assists in making or operating the database, difficulties have arisen concerning the application of the Directive's protection to computer programs. This issue has already been raised above in relation to the definition of a database where the decision in *Mars* v. *Teknowledge* was discussed. One of the main difficulties is that the very broad definition of a database in the Directive leads to a situation in which most computer programs are themselves databases or contain databases. This is because the nature of many computer programs is such that they contain a large amount of data. In order for the computer program to operate, the data in the program must be arranged in a systematic or methodical way. In turn, those data are individually accessible by electronic means, although they are usually accessed by another part of the computer program rather than a human being. Usually, there will have been a qualitative or quantitative investment in obtaining, verifying or presenting those data, the contents of the database. Consequently, the computer program containing large amounts of data is itself a database. This is so even though the data are there for the purpose of facilitating the operation of the computer program, whereas in most other databases the function of the data is to provide information to the user.

The facts of the decision in *Mars* v. *Teknowledge* demonstrate this point. Data concerning the dimensions and other qualities of coins of legal tender that could be used in the vending machine were a key component of the computer program that operated the vending machine. Without those data, the computer program could not determine whether the actual coins used were legal tender. But the data were primarily there in order that the computer program could perform its function. They were not there primarily for the information of human beings who would then use the information for some extrinsic purpose unrelated to the operation of the vending machine. Nor were the data arranged in a user-friendly fashion such that they could easily be accessed by a human being. As already indicated, one of the difficulties with the decision in the *Mars* case

---

[115] E.g. Article 1(3) of the Directive.

is that the defendant conceded that it had infringed the database rights of the plaintiff, and relied upon an alleged common law defence to justify its actions. The court refused to acknowledge the existence of that defence and hence found for the plaintiff.

Other cases from different jurisdictions concerning copyright protection of computer programs, or data within computer programs, also reinforce the point. In *Data Access Corporation* v. *Powerflex Services Pty Ltd*,[116] the High Court of Australia decided that a Huffman compression table constituted a literary work. A Huffman compression table, named after the first person to devise such a table, is a table that minimises use of a computer's memory by storing 'characters in a data file as bit strings which have a length which relates to the character's frequency of occurrence in the data file'.[117] The more frequently the character occurs, the shorter the bit string for that character and vice versa. Therefore, the creation of the table required its author to identify the most frequently and infrequently occurring characters and devise short and long bit strings for them respectively. The High Court found that the production of the compression table required the employment of substantial skill and judgement and a very great deal of hard work. Arguably, it would also constitute a database within the computer program as would look-up tables and the menu command hierarchy of a user interface.[118] One possible response to this argument would be that the substantial investment in such cases has not gone into the obtaining, verification and presentation of the data but into the creation of the data. This would certainly be the case with a Huffman compression table and a look-up table. The argument in this respect would be the same as that analysed above concerning the meaning of 'obtaining' in the Directive.

The end result is that the Directive actually fails to achieve its objective of divorcing the protection of computer programs from the protection of the selection or arrangement of a database and its contents.

Copyright in databases   Chapter II of the Directive relates to the copyright protection of databases. The approach taken on this issue is similar to that taken in the earlier drafts. Article 3(1) provides that 'databases which, by reason of the selection or arrangement of their contents, constitute the author's own intellectual creation shall be protected as such by copyright. No other criteria shall be applied to determine their eligibility for that protection'.

---

[116] [1999] HCA 49.   [117] Ibid., at para. 113.
[118] See S. Lai, 'Database Protection in the United Kingdom: The New Deal and its Effects on Software Protection' (1998) 20 *European Intellectual Property Review* 32 for further discussion of this issue.

Article 3(2) goes on to provide that: 'The copyright protection of databases provided for by this Directive shall not extend to their contents and shall be without prejudice to any rights subsisting in those contents themselves.' This Article attempts to harmonise the standard for copyright protection of databases throughout the EU. The differences in the standard prior to the Directive were a product of different standards of originality (as discussed in Chapter 2).

One curious aspect of this approach to copyright protection is the commentary on it provided in Recital 16, which states:

No criterion other than originality in the sense of the author's intellectual creation should be applied to determine the eligibility of the database for copyright protection, and in particular no aesthetic or *qualitative* criteria should be applied. [emphasis added]

In this context, 'qualitative' is being used in the sense of the standard of excellence or otherwise of the database. As previously discussed, 'quality', in a copyright sense, refers to the original attributes of a work rather than its standard of excellence. Consequently, it is surprising to see it being used as a reference to a standard of excellence in the recitals. The difficulty with this use of 'qualitative' is that the word reappears in the provisions concerning *sui generis* protection, but without a definition. This invites the conclusion that it is being used in the same sense as it was in Recital 16, although, as we will see when the *sui generis* rights are discussed below, this would create even greater problems than the use of the word necessarily generates.

Authors of databases   Article 4 of the Directive provides that:

The author of a database shall be the natural person or group of natural persons who created the base or, where the legislation of the Member States so permits, the legal person designated as the rightholder by that legislation.

Consequently, the legislative rules of the individual Member States concerning authorship dictate the issue of authorship and ownership of copyright in a database that qualifies for copyright protection.

Restricted acts   Article 5 of the Directive sets out the particular exclusive rights that must be accorded to the author of a database meeting the standard of originality as set out in Article 4. The rights are, in effect, those provided for in the Berne Convention and the Copyright Treaty,[119] although the right of communication to the public under the

---

[119] There is no specific obligation to prevent circumvention of technological protection devices or to protect rights management information.

Copyright Treaty was not actually created until after the adoption of the Directive. Hence, the owner of copyright in the database has the exclusive right to reproduce, translate, adapt or arrange the database, or to distribute, communicate, display or perform the database to the public. The owner also has the same rights in respect of any translation, adaptation or arrangement of the database. The duration of these rights is the term of copyright as already governed by Council Directive 93/98/EEC of 29 October 1993 harmonising the term of protection of copyright and certain related rights.[120]

Article 5 does not expressly confer the rental right that is part of TRIPS but Article 2(b) does provide that the Directive applies without prejudice to EU provisions relating to the rental right. In addition, Recital 24 notes that 'the rental and lending of databases is governed exclusively by Council Directive 92/100/EEC of 19 November 1992 on rental right and lending right'. Consequently, the rental right is conferred via other means than the Directive.

The relationship between these rights and the *sui generis* right is discussed below under the various headings concerning the *sui generis* right.

Exceptions to copyright in databases Article 6 provides for a number of exceptions to the copyright in a database. Article 6(1) is the most difficult to interpret and its meaning is obscure. It provides that:

The performance by the lawful user of a database or of a copy thereof of any of the acts listed in Article 5 [the copyright rights] which is necessary for the purposes of access to the contents of the databases and normal use of the contents by the lawful user shall not require the authorization of the author of the database. Where the lawful user is authorized to use only part of the database, this provision shall apply only to that part.

A lawful user is not defined in the Directive, although Recital 34 states in part that 'once the rightholder has chosen to make available a copy of the database to a user, whether by an on-line service or by other means of distribution, that lawful user must be able to access and use the database for the purposes and in the way set out in the agreement with the rightholder'. This suggests that a lawful user is a person with a licence from the copyright owner to use the database in some manner. If the definition is restricted to that situation then Article 6 is tautological in that it does no more than provide that a licensee is entitled to use a database in the manner permitted by the licence. It would be merely confirming, for example, that viewing the database on a computer screen, although

[120] OJ No. L290, 24 November 1993, pp. 9–13.

technically a reproduction, would not constitute an infringement of copyright if the viewer had a licence to view that part of the database.[121]

Article 6(1) probably also applies to third parties who acquire a copy of the database on resale so that they are not in a direct contractual relationship with the owner of the copyright in the database. For example, a database sold in CD-ROM format could be resold and the third party acquiring it would be a lawful user who would not be infringing copyright by viewing it on a computer screen.[122]

The broadest possible interpretation of Article 6(1) is that a lawful user is someone who does not have a licence from the rightholder, or has not acquired the database via resale, but is someone who is using the database for fair dealing purposes. Their use would be lawful provided it is within the limits of the permitted dealing. Arguably, they would be permitted to view the database, thus reproducing it, for the purpose of selecting and dealing with the relevant part. This may override any contractual provision to the contrary. However, it seems unlikely that such a broad exception was intended, and the limitation in Article 6(1) stipulating that the provision only applies to the part of the database that the lawful user is authorised to use mitigates against this view.[123]

The other exceptions in Article 6(2) are, thankfully, a little clearer, although even here significant difficulties arise. While the Directive provided protection to non-electronic databases, it did permit Member States to discriminate between electronic and non-electronic databases to some extent. Consequently, Article 6(2)(a) permits reproduction for private purposes of a non-electronic database.[124]

Articles 6(2)(b) and (c) permit the use of the database for the purpose of illustration for teaching or scientific research,[125] public security or administrative or judicial procedures. This exception for illustration

---

[121] This interpretation would also be consistent with Article 6(1) of the First Draft which provided: 'The lawful user of a database may perform any of the acts listed in Art. 5 which is necessary in order to use that database in the manner determined by contractual arrangements with the rightholder.'

[122] This is also consistent with Article 6(2) of the First Draft which provided: 'In the absence of any contractual arrangements between the rightholder and the user of a database in respect of its use, the performance by the lawful *acquirer* of a database of any of the acts listed in Art. 5 which is necessary in order to gain access to the contents of the database and use thereof shall not require the authorization of the rightholder.'

[123] Some of the implementing legislation clearly restricts the operation of Article 6(1) to licensees or owners and their successors while the UK legislation is unclear. See L122–5 of the Code of Intellectual Property which refers to the limits of use provided for in the contract. Section 50D(1) of the UK Copyright, Designs and Patents Act 1988 refers to 'whether under a licence to do any of the acts restricted by the copyright in the database *or otherwise*'.

[124] This is mirrored for the *sui generis* right by Article 9(a).

[125] Recital 36 states that scientific research includes natural and human sciences.

for teaching and research only applies to the extent that the use is justified by the non-commercial purpose to be achieved. Other exceptions to
copyright authorised under national law may also be made to the copyright in a database. All these exceptions are subject to the limit expressed
in Article 6(3), which reiterates Article 9(2) of the Berne Convention and
Article 13 of TRIPS, that do not permit exceptions to copyright which
unreasonably prejudice the rightholder's legitimate interests or conflict
with normal exploitation of the database.

As the exceptions in Article 6(2)(b) and (c) are mirrored in Article 9 in
respect of the *sui generis* right, some further consideration of them is justified here. In addition, scientific bodies and libraries have been among the
most vociferous opponents of *sui generis* legislation, suggesting that the
exceptions in respect of research, education and study are critical issues in
the debate for *sui generis* protection. There are a number of problems with
these provisions. The first problem is understanding what is meant by the
words 'use for the sole purpose of illustration for teaching or scientific
research'. In particular, no assistance is given in defining 'illustration' for
teaching or research purposes and no indication is given of why that particular aspect of teaching and research has been singled out for attention.
It may be that 'illustration' in the context of teaching restricts the use of a
database to providing an example of what is being taught. Alternatively,
it could be argued that all teaching is designed to illustrate in a broad
sense but, surely, a reference to the purpose of teaching would have suf-
ficed unless the intention is significantly to restrict the use of databases
in the course of teaching.[126] Nor is there any obvious reason for focusing on teaching, rather than the objective of teaching, namely learning.
No exception exists for study purposes, suggesting that only a teacher
may use the database, not students. This latter problem could have been
overcome by the exception for scientific research if a broad view of research, as opposed to research and study, had been taken. However, as
the use for research purposes is also apparently restricted to illustration,
that possibility is excluded by the wording of the provision.[127]

Both exceptions to use of a database for teaching or research only apply
to the extent justified by the non-commercial purpose to be achieved. This

---

[126] Prior to the implementation of the Directive, Belgian copyright law made an exception
for 'didactic purposes' without making any reference to illustration. The implementing
legislation amended s. 22(1), fourth paragraph, to delete this reference and insert a
reference to 'illustration for teaching'. See Legal Protection of Databases Act 1998
(Belgium).

[127] The requirement that the use be restricted to illustrative purposes was intended to apply
to both teaching and research. However, the provision has not been implemented in
this way. See, e.g. Article 53(5) of the German Copyright Act 1965 which applies to
any scientific use for non-commercial purposes.

also creates difficulties. Many teaching and research institutions have a commercial aspect to their operations, partly in response to reductions in public funding.[128] The potential for a mix of commercial and non-commercial purposes for which teaching or research may be undertaken has dramatically increased as a result. The elimination of use for commercial research is also a significant reduction of rights that existed in the UK. The UK fair dealing provisions referred only to 'research' and they still do so for copyright works other than databases.[129] The fair dealing provisions for databases are now restricted to non-commercial research in the UK.[130] Other European states have also reduced exceptions to the copyright in databases as a consequence of the Directive.[131]

The new provisions of the Directive are more in keeping with the copyright exceptions of other European countries such as France[132] and Germany,[133] which had relatively high standards of originality for copyright protection.[134] As the scope of copyright protection in those countries was limited by the higher originality requirements, the need for broad exceptions was correspondingly reduced. As we will see when discussing

[128] For example, Australian public universities on average receive only 65 per cent of their income from government sources, with fees from local and overseas students providing a significant percentage of the remainder. 'Unis Rely Ever More on Fees', *The Age*, 22 December 2000, p. 8.

[129] Section 29 of the Copyright, Designs and Patents Act 1988. The application of both copyright and database rights to essentially the same information has generated considerable difficulties for UK libraries. See 'Interpretation of Terms in the Database Regulations: Supplement to a Position Paper Submitted to the Database Market Strategy Group in 1999', Library Association Copyright Alliance, October 2000 (copy on file with the author).

[130] Section 29 of the Copyright, Designs and Patents Act 1988.

[131] For example, Belgian legislation previously had an exception for didactic purposes. Article 16 of the Dutch Copyright Act 1912 provided an exception for works clearly intended for use in education or for other scientific purposes. This exception for copyright appears to have been retained in the implementing legislation, but the narrower exception appears for the *sui generis* right. See Article 5(b) of Law of 8 July 1999 (Databases Act), conforming to an adaptation of the Dutch legislation on Directive 96/9/EC of 11 March 1996 concerning protection of databases.

[132] See Article L122–5 of the Code of Intellectual Property which refers to copies reserved strictly for private use and not intended for collective use.

[133] See s. 53 of the German Law on Copyright and Neighbouring Rights of 9 September 1965 (amended 1998) which refers to 'single copies for personal scientific use' and 'use in teaching, in non-commercial institutions of education'.

[134] C. Hertz-Eichenrode, 'Germany' in D. Campbell (ed.), *World Intellectual Property Rights and Remedies* (Oceana Publications, New York, 1999), at Ger-18: 'The essential prerequisite for copyright protection is set forth in Art. 2(2) of the Copyright Act, requiring that the work be a personal intellectual creation . . . The work must show an individuality of a certain creative level far beyond the average of a well-skilled and trained person in the area', citing Supreme Court, GRUR 1982 at 305, Buromobelprogramm and GRUR 1983, at 377, Brombeermuster. A. Lucas and A. Plaisant, 'France' in M. B. Nimmer and P. E. Geller (eds.), *International Copyright Law and Practice* (Matthew Bender, New York, 1999), p. 4.

the *sui generis* right created by the Directive, these limited exceptions, designed for copyright regimes with high standards of originality, have been transposed to the *sui generis* regime which is, in part, a sweat of the brow copyright regime.

The sui generis *right*   Article 7(1) imposes an obligation on Member States to:

Provide for a right for the maker of a database which shows that there has been qualitatively and/or quantitatively a substantial investment in either the obtaining, verification or presentation of the contents to prevent extraction and/or re-utilization of the whole or of a substantial part evaluated qualitatively and/or quantitatively, of the contents of that database.

This obligation exists independently of any copyright that may or may not subsist in the database or the contents of the database.[135] In this respect it is a significant departure from the First Draft, which provided that the *sui generis* right did not apply to a database if copyright subsisted in the contents of the database.[136] The Council's Reasons expressed the view that this limitation would create difficulties if a database consisted of both copyright works and materials that were not covered by copyright or other rights.[137]

Some academic writers have described the copyright protection provided by the Directive as protection for the structure of the database and the *sui generis* right as protection for its contents.[138] That analysis is superficially accurate but also misleadingly simplistic. There is now a supposed distinction between copyright in the individual items constituting the contents of the database, the copyright in the structure of the database and the *sui generis* right to prevent extraction or re-utilisation of a substantial part of the contents of the database. In fact, the tests for ownership of copyright and the *sui generis* right, the test for determining the subject matter of the *sui generis* right, the nature of the right itself and the exceptions to it have been defined in such a way that there is necessarily a considerable overlap between the copyright in the structure of the database and the *sui generis* right. The extent of an overlap between the *sui generis* right and any copyright in the individual items in a database depends on the actual interpretation of the Directive.

---

[135] Article 7(4) of the Directive.   [136] Article 2(5) of the First Draft.
[137] Paragraph 14 of the Council's Reasons.
[138] E.g. J. Sterling, *World Copyright Law* (Sweet & Maxwell, London, 1998) at 26E.06; P. Raue and V. Bensinger, 'Implementation of the Sui Generis Right in Databases Pursuant to Section 87 et seq. of the German Copyright Act' (1998) 3 *Communications Law* 220.

The overlap between the copyright that may subsist in a database and
the *sui generis* right over the contents of the database is a critical issue in
determining the appropriateness of the *sui generis* right as it is expressed
in the Directive. The various aspects of the Directive's *sui generis* right are
discussed below with particular reference to their relationship to copyright. In so doing, particular reference is made to a number of the points
discussed in Chapter 2 concerning the principles of copyright law.

The maker of a database   The Directive adopts the term 'maker'
of a database to differentiate the person who first acquires the *sui generis*
right in a database from the author who first acquires the copyright in a
database. Unlike the position with authorship, no definition of a maker
appears in the text of the Directive. Some assistance can be derived from
Recital 41, which provides in part that 'the maker of a database is the person who takes the initiative and the risk of investing; whereas this excludes
subcontractors in particular from the definition of maker'. This focuses
on the protection of the investment in the creation of the database, a focus
that is revealed by other recitals and the very nature of the right itself.[139]
It also suggests, along with the recitals and various other provisions, that
the *sui generis* right is designed to protect the investment in the making
of the database.

The recitals also reveal that the Directive identifies and seeks to protect different types of investment. For example, Recital 7 refers to the
investment of human, technical and financial resources, while Recital 12
refers to the investment in modern information storage and processing
systems. Recital 39 refers to the financial and professional investment
made in obtaining and collecting the contents of a database, and Recital
40 states in part that 'investment may consist in the deployment of financial resources and/or expending of time, effort and energy'. Clearly,
all of these investments are referring to the investments directed towards
obtaining, verifying or presenting the contents of the database. Equally
clearly, investment is contemplated as including financial investment, but
it also seems to go beyond that to include the investment of skill and effort
in making the database.[140]

---

[139] The Recitals are full of references to the investment of the database maker and the need
to protect it. See Recitals 7, 10, 11, 12, 19, 39, 40, 54 and 55.

[140] This is confirmed by various pieces of implementing legislation. For example, Art.
L341–1 of the Law No. 98–536 defines the maker of a database as a person who takes
the initiative and risk of financial or human investment in the setting up, verification
and presentation of the contents of a database. Article 102(2)(a) of the Italian legislative
Decree No. 169 of 6 May 1999 defines a maker of a database as 'someone who makes
a substantial investment for the creation of a database or in verifying or presenting it,
deploying, towards that end, financial resources and/or expending time and effort'.

There will be circumstances in which the making of a database will not constitute authorship of the database. For example, where the making involved mere sweat of the brow, there will be a maker, but no author. The concept of 'making' should also overcome any remaining difficulties with computer-generated databases, as the emphasis is on who made the investment rather than any demonstration of personal involvement in the actual creation of the database.

However, a comparison of this test for 'making' a database with the definition of authorship of a database for copyright purposes reveals the very real possibility that the same action can result in the copyright and the *sui generis* right vesting in the same person simultaneously. This is because the selection and arrangement of the database may well be the same thing as the investment in obtaining, verifying and presenting the contents of the database, particularly if the investment includes the investment of human intellectual resources in the creative arrangement and selection of the database.

A qualitatively or quantitatively substantial investment in obtaining, verifying or presenting   In the same way that not every database is entitled to copyright protection pursuant to the Directive, not every database qualifies for protection under the *sui generis* right. The database owner must demonstrate that a substantial investment was made in the obtaining, verification or presentation of the contents of the database. The prerequisite of a substantial investment in the making of the database replaced the previous requirement that a database be a collection of a large number of data, works or other materials.[141] The substantiality of the investment can be either a qualitative and/or a quantitative one. Little other guidance is given as to what constitutes a substantial investment, although it must be directed towards the obtaining, verification or presentation of the contents of the database.

The acts of obtaining, verification or presentation of the contents of the database include all of the activities involved in the sweat of the brow expended in creating a database. For example, the major investment in the *Feist* case related to the relatively mundane and labour-intensive tasks of obtaining the details of every subscriber to the plaintiff's telephone service, verifying them and presenting them in alphabetical order. It is clear that sweat of the brow activities can constitute the necessary substantial investment, as they constitute a quantitatively substantial investment in making the database. Indeed, this was clearly one of the objectives of the Directive.[142]

---

[141] Amendment 3 of the 1993 Amendments.
[142] Recital 40 of the Directive, and the Committee's Opinion, para. 2.3.

Despite the intention to focus on the protection of sweat of the brow via a *sui generis* right, the test for protection also includes what is, in effect, the same test as for copyright protection for the structure of a database. This is a complication caused by the introduction of the reference to qualitative as well as quantitative investment in Article 7(1). The necessary qualitative investment in obtaining, verification or presentation of the contents required to obtain protection under the *sui generis* right would include the 'selection and arrangement that constitute the author's own intellectual creation'[143] necessary to obtain copyright protection for a database. Presentation obviously includes the arrangement of a database and an arrangement that involves intellectual creation would constitute a qualitative investment in the presentation and thus meet the prerequisite for protection under the *sui generis* right. Obtaining the contents would also involve selecting them and, again, if there is significant intellectual creativity in that selection process this will constitute the necessary qualitative investment in obtaining the contents of the database. The net effect of this is that a database that qualifies for copyright protection will almost invariably qualify for protection under the *sui generis* right, and the author of a database for copyright purposes will also be the maker of the database for the purposes of the *sui generis* right. This is the case, even though the major investment may have been the intellectual investment in the selection or creation of the contents rather than in the labour-intensive aspects of making the database.

A database therefore qualifies for the *sui generis* right if it can be placed at any point in the spectrum of originality (referred to in Chapter 2) as Article 7(1) refers to a qualitative and/or quantitative investment. Hence, sweat of the brow confers *sui generis* protection, but intellectual creativity also confers protection as does a combination of sweat of the brow and intellectual creativity. In short, the test for protection is the same as the English copyright position prior to the Directive.[144] Hence, we have an unavoidable overlap between the copyright in the structure of the database and the *sui generis* right in the contents. This point will be made again later in the discussion concerning the nature of the right and the exceptions to it.

The introduction of qualitative concepts into the nature of the investment also introduces the possibility of an overlap between copyright in individual items in the contents of the database and the *sui generis* right. The issue is complicated by the strange reference to 'qualitative' criteria

---

[143] Article 3(1) of the Directive.
[144] This was in fact the intention of the UK database industry when it made its submissions concerning the Directive.

in Recital 17, already mentioned in the previous discussion of the Directive's copyright protection of databases. In that recital, 'qualitative' was used in conjunction with 'aesthetic', suggesting an emphasis on the standard of the work rather than its creative attributes. If a similar interpretation of 'qualitative' were taken in the context of the *sui generis* right, this would require a 'good' or high standard of investment in the obtaining, presenting or verifying of the database. However, given the difficulty of applying such an interpretation and the tenuous connection between Recital 17 which was referring to copyright issues and the *sui generis* right, it is unlikely that interpretation would or could be applied. If such an interpretation were adopted it would cover situations such as investing in the acquisition of important or valuable works, data or other materials, even if the effort in doing so would be minimal. For example, the purchase of a famous, highly regarded painting for an art gallery may constitute a substantial qualitative investment in the database constituted by the acquisition of this one piece. This has implications for what constitutes infringement of the database, which are discussed below. For now, it is sufficient to note that the *sui generis* right arguably applies to the extraction or re-utilisation of one item in a database, leaving an overlap between the *sui generis* right in that item and any copyright that may exist in it.[145]

Even if the 'qualitative' or 'quantitative' issue is resolved, it is still necessary to demonstrate that the investment is substantial. Some guidance about what constitutes a substantial investment comes from Recital 19 of the Directive, which states 'the investment in the compilation of several recordings of musical performances on a CD would not generally come within the scope of the Directive as it would not represent a substantial enough investment'. While this gives some guidance about what does not constitute a sufficiently substantial investment, it also raises more questions than it answers. As already discussed above, the recital confirms, rather than refutes, the possibility that such a CD constitutes a database. Hence, the only relevant issue is whether there has been a substantial investment in the obtaining, verification or presentation of its contents. Recital 19 also refers specifically to the act of *compilation* of several recordings of musical performances. But it does not state whether the investment in the individual recordings or the individual musical performances may constitute the necessary investment. Obviously, there can be a very considerable investment in making those recordings or in the performances

---

[145] The argument that use of one item may constitute infringement has been made by database owners in the UK and US. Notes of a discussion between the writer and Professor Jerome Reichman, December 1999, held on file by the writer concerning negotiations in the United States between database owners and users.

that are recorded, either by the person who pays for them to be made or by the actual recording artists. Arguably, this would be a substantial investment in obtaining the contents of the database. So there is an issue as to whether the concept of 'obtaining' the contents of a database includes the actual creation of the contents, or whether it is restricted to collecting or gathering pre-existing works, data or other materials. The literal meaning of 'obtaining' suggests that either of these meanings could be adopted.[146] The more restrictive view would generate considerable difficulties for some database makers seeking to establish a *sui generis* right in their database. They would have to differentiate between their investment in creating the contents of their database, and the investment in obtaining or collecting those contents. It would have particular implications for database makers who are the sole source of the contents of that database. For example, a telephone company could not count any investment involved in creating the original telephone subscription or the original recording of the subscriber's details.

An even greater difficulty would arise in relation to databases with a relatively small amount of information such as, for example, sporting fixture lists. The intellectual effort in the creation of the fixture list would not be a relevant investment, and the verification and presentation of the fixture list would not entail any significant investment. The same approach may be taken to television programme schedules, train timetables and similar documents where the majority of investment, whether monetary or intellectual, quantitative or qualitative, would relate to the creation of the information going into the database rather than the obtaining, verification or presentation. The difficulties here are identical to the difficulties discussed in Chapter 2 concerning the identification of the point at which the intellectual activities that lead to the ultimate creation of a work become relevant to the conferment of copyright protection.

The terms 'verifying' and 'presenting' may also present difficulties. Verification may be done on the occasion of the initial creation of the database but for on-line databases it may be necessary to check the continuing veracity of information. The information may not need to be altered, but a substantial investment may have to be made in ascertaining that this is the case. Arguably, verification after the creation of the initial database may satisfy the criteria for protection.

A similar argument applies in relation to the presentation of on-line databases. Unlike hardcopies of databases, the continued presentation of a database in an on-line format may require considerable ongoing investment in the maintenance of the database. There is then an issue

---

[146] 'Obtain: Come into the possession or enjoyment of, secure or gain as the result of request or effort', *The New Shorter Oxford Dictionary*.

as to whether the relevant investment in the presentation of the database is restricted to the investment in the initial presentation of the database, or whether it includes the ongoing costs of presenting or maintaining the database. In short, there is a question as to whether presentation of a database includes the concept of maintaining that database. This in turn has implications for the calculation of the period of protection as it runs from the making of a substantial investment. If the maker can argue that it makes a substantial investment in the ongoing presentation of the database, time may commence to run again and again.

Right to prevent extraction and/or re-utilisation   Article 7 provides for a right of extraction and re-utilisation. These are terms not usually used in copyright legislation and they give the appearance that a new type of right has been created by the Directive. This appearance is misleading. An examination of the definitions of extraction and re-utilisation reveals that the new terminology refers to rights that already exist and are well known in copyright law.

Article 7(2)(a) defines extraction as 'the permanent or temporary transfer of all or a substantial part of the contents of a database to another medium by any means or in any form'. In other words, it is the right of reproduction that is well known to copyright. Presumably, a 'transfer' in this context is not referring to a situation in which the contents of the database are removed from one medium and put in another medium, but instead refers to their reproduction in another medium while the original contents remain where they were located. The reference to 'temporary' transfer makes it clear that temporary digital copies also constitute extraction or reproduction of the contents of the database. Hence, reading a substantial part of a database on a computer would constitute an extraction.[147] Interpreted in this way, the right effectively becomes a right of access to an electronic database, as the mere act of accessing the database without the maker's authority would involve an infringement of the right of extraction.

The right of re-utilisation is defined in Article 7(2)(b) as:

Any form of making available to the public all or a substantial part of the contents of a database by the distribution of copies, by renting, by on-line or other forms of transmission. The first sale of a copy of a database within the Community by the rightholder or with his consent shall exhaust the right to control resale of that copy within the Community. Public lending is not an act of extraction or re-utilization.

---

[147] So would the repeated and systematic reading of insubstantial parts of the contents of the database.

It is a number of different rights expressed in the one word. In a copyright context, a right of 'making available to the public' applies to provision of material in an electronic form in such a way that users can access it at a time and place of their choosing.[148] The exclusive right within copyright of 'making available to the public' is a creature of the Copyright Treaty and part of a new right of communication to the public. This new right was created to respond to the convergence of communication technology which rendered obsolete the previous distinction between the communication of copyright material via the air or wires. It is intended to cover both the transmission of copyright material, whereby the copyright material is transmitted to users at a time determined by the transmitter, and making copyright material available to the public. In the latter situation, the material is simply made available electronically so that it can be accessed at a time chosen by the user. It covers the situation in which material is made available on the Internet.

It must be remembered that the Directive was adopted prior to the creation of the Copyright Treaty in December 1996. Although the proposals in respect of the ultimate treaty no doubt influenced the wording of the Directive, some care needs to be taken not to assume that the same words in the Copyright Treaty have the same meaning as in the Directive. At the time of the adoption of the Directive, there was still considerable international debate as to the appropriate wording of a new right to deal with the issues of convergence of technology and the emergence of the Internet.

In the context of the Directive, the concept of making available to the public within the re-utilisation right is a far broader concept than that envisaged by the Copyright Treaty. In the Directive, it includes the distribution of copies, renting, on-line and other forms of transmission. The distribution of copies in the Copyright Treaty refers to the distribution of the database in hardcopy form or a self-contained good such as a CD-ROM.[149] Similarly, the rental right referred to in TRIPS relates to rental of fixed goods such as CD-ROMs. The reference to making available by on-line or other forms of transmission in the Directive refers to the electronic provision of access to the database. The description of 'making available on-line' as a form of transmission is also a reflection of the fact that the distinction, on the one hand, between making copyright material available to end users at a time of their choosing and, on the other hand, transmission, had not been adopted as distinct aspects of the right of communication to the public at the time of the adoption of the Directive.

---

[148] Article 8 of the Copyright Treaty.   [149] Article 6 of the Copyright Treaty.

The right of re-utilisation is therefore an amalgam of the rights of distribution and communication to the public in the Copyright Treaty[150] and the right of rental contained within TRIPS.[151] It is a number of exclusive copyright rights rolled into one word. The net result is that the *sui generis* right is, in fact, the exclusive rights of copyright that are relevant to databases.

Infringement of the right of extraction and re-utilisation   The discussion in Chapter 2 concerning the relationship between the subject matter of copyright and its infringement argued that one defines the other. Defining what makes a work original simultaneously defines what cannot be reproduced or dealt with in a manner referred to in the exclusive rights of the copyright owner. That same synchronicity does not appear on the face of the wording of the subject matter of the *sui generis* right and what constitutes infringement of that right. The subject matter of the *sui generis* right is the *investment*, whether qualitative or quantitative, in the *obtaining, verification or presentation* of the contents.[152] The infringement is expressed to be in the extraction or re-utilisation of the whole or a substantive part, evaluated qualitatively or quantitatively, of the *contents* of that database.[153]

The assumption is that the extraction or re-utilisation of a substantial part of the database contents will harm the investment in the obtaining, verification or presentation of the contents. This depends in part on how one defines a substantial part of the contents. Protection for a quantitatively substantial part of the contents of a database provides protection for sweat of the brow. Taking a quantitatively substantial part of the database would presumably harm the sweat of the brow investment in the database.

But the word 'qualitative' creates problems. What is a qualitatively substantial part of the contents? Any of the potential means of determining what this is raises the possibility of an overlap between the copyright in the structure of the database or the copyright in any individual item in the database. For example, qualitative could mean one work, piece of

---

[150] See Articles 6 and 8 of the Copyright Treaty. It should be noted that the right of making available to the public pursuant to the Copyright Treaty is more restricted than the reference to 'making available to the public' in the definition of 're-utilisation' under the Directive. The former is restricted to situations where material is made available electronically at a time determined by the user. See Article 8 of the Copyright Treaty.

[151] Article 11 of TRIPS. Article 7 of the Copyright Treaty also confers a rental right. The Directive goes further by providing a right of rental in respect of databases, whereas TRIPS was restricted to computer programs and cinematographic works and the Copyright Treaty added works contained within phonograms to the rental right.

[152] Article 7(1) of the Directive. See also Recitals 7, 12, 39, 40 and 42.

[153] Article 7(1) of the Directive.

data or other material that is regarded as extremely useful or valuable. Its importance could flow from its time-sensitivity, its particular value for a limited period of time. For example, it might be the fluctuation in price of a particular share in the last five minutes or a report by company directors that has just been released that may affect the company's share price. The information revealed by the share price or the report may be extremely valuable to share traders. Arguably then, it is qualitatively a substantial part of the database, at least for a short period of time.[154] At this point, an overlap may exist in the copyright in the single item contained in the database and the *sui generis* right in the contents of the database. For example, copyright would probably subsist in the report, leading to *sui generis* rights in the report and copyright. Alternatively, the share price, which is unlikely to be copyright, would have the protection of the *sui generis* right even though copyright law would suggest that the information it reveals should be free.

Another difficulty with this is that it is unlikely that the investment in obtaining, verifying and presenting that one piece of information would be significant, at least from a quantitative viewpoint.[155] Yet it would still be protected. In other words, protection would be gained by making a relatively minor investment and the value of that protection would significantly exceed the cost of obtaining it. This difference between the cost of the investment and the value of the rights given over the product of the investment is one of the difficulties with the Directive that is discussed in Chapter 6.[156]

Of course, it is possible that courts would reject the proposition that one piece of information could be a qualitatively substantial part of a database. If so, then the qualitative aspect of the substantial part would flow from the collection of individual parts extracted or re-utilised. At this point, there is the potential for overlap with the copyright in the structure of the database. The qualitative substantiality of that taken would flow from its importance as a collection of items. At that point, the test of a qualitatively substantial part of the contents necessarily involves a consideration of the selection of the contents. Consequently, copyright in the structure of the database and *sui generis* protection merge and cover

---

[154] Whether the information could cease to be a qualitatively substantial part of the database once it ceases to be 'hot news' is itself an issue.

[155] The investment here would be the human cost of actually incorporating the information into the database, as opposed to any price that might be paid for gaining access to it initially.

[156] Another issue is why existing legal rights should not be sufficient to determine the protection for the item in question. For example, copyright should determine the nature and limits of protection for the painting and trade secret law or contract should be sufficient to protect the share price without an overlay of *sui generis* database rights.

precisely the same subject matter for precisely the same reason. This fact combined with the points above concerning authorship, the making of a database, the equivalence of the *sui generis* right and the exclusive rights of copyright, leads to one conclusion. In some circumstances, the creation of the same database by the same person will lead to the simultaneous creation of two separate but identical sets of rights in respect of the same database. One set of rights is called copyright. The other set of rights is described as a *sui generis* right.

A similar argument may be made in respect of the arrangement of the database. As stated in Chapter 2, the indices of a database are critical to its operation and effectiveness. They are a qualitatively substantial part of the contents, as well as a substantial part of the arrangement. An index may confer both copyright and *sui generis* protection on a database on the grounds that the index simultaneously involves intellectual creativity in the arrangement of the database, and a qualitatively significant investment in its presentation. The same act, such as reproduction of an index, may therefore constitute an infringement of both copyright and the *sui generis* right.[157]

Exceptions to the sui generis *right*   Articles 8 and 9 provide exceptions to the *sui generis* right, although Article 8 is described as the rights and obligations of lawful users. Article 8(1) provides a positive right for a lawful user to extract or re-utilise insubstantial parts of a database, if the maker of the database has made it available to the public. This right only applies to that part of a database that a lawful user is authorised to extract and/or re-utilise. Similar difficulties arise in defining a lawful user for the purpose of this Article as those that arise in Article 6.

What it clearly does do is override contractual provisions in database licences that seek to prevent any particular use of an insubstantial part of a database.[158] Whether it gives a right to the public at large, as opposed to licensees or those who buy a copy of the database, depends on the definition of a lawful user that has already been discussed above in the section concerning exceptions to copyright.

While Article 8(1) provides a positive right to use an insubstantial part of a database, there is an overriding obligation expressed in Article 8(2)

---

[157] The definition of a database in the First Draft included a reference to indexes, thesauruses and other systems for obtaining or presenting information. The definition in the Directive does not refer to this, but Recital 20 does provide: 'Whereas protection under this Directive may also apply to the materials necessary for the operation or consultation of certain databases such as thesaurus and indexation systems.'

[158] Article 15 of the Directive provides that: 'Any contractual provision contrary to Articles 6(1) and 8 shall be null and void.'

on lawful users not to perform acts which 'conflict with normal exploitation of the database or unreasonably prejudice the legitimate interest of the maker of the database'. A similar obligation is imposed by Article 7(5), which provides that: 'The repeated and systematic extraction and/or re-utilisation of insubstantial parts of the contents of the database implying acts which conflict with a normal exploitation of that database or which unreasonably prejudice the legitimate interests of the maker of the database shall not be permitted.'

Both these provisions adopt the terminology of the Berne Convention relating to exceptions to copyright. Following on from the previous discussion concerning the relationship between copyright and the *sui generis* right in a database, this re-emphasises the overlap between the copyright in a database and the *sui generis* right in the database.

The exceptions in Article 9 mirror for the *sui generis* right the exceptions for copyright as set out in Article 6(2)(a), (b) and (c). As we have seen in previous discussion, the *sui generis* right clearly includes protection for sweat of the brow, although it also extends beyond that to include intellectual creativity. The real difficulty in terms of the *sui generis* right is that the copyright exceptions designed for copyright based on a relatively high standard of originality have been imported into a sweat of the brow copyright regime that has been called a *sui generis* right. At the very least, UK exceptions prior to the Directive should have been made to the *sui generis* right.

Duration of the sui generis *right*   The period of protection under the *sui generis* right is fifteen years in accordance with the 1993 Amendments.[159] Time begins to run from 1 January in the year following the date when the database was first made available to the public, provided this occurs within fifteen years from the 1 January following the completion of the database.[160] If the database is not first made available to the public within that time, the period of protection runs only for the fifteen-year period starting on 1 January after the completion of making the database.[161]

The period of protection can start to run again if there is a substantial change to the contents of a database[162] which would result in the database being considered to be a substantial new investment. The requirement for changes to the database in order to qualify for a renewed period of

---

[159] Article 10 of the Directive.   [160] Article 10(2).

[161] Article 10(3). As with the original making of the database, the change may be evaluated either qualitatively or quantitatively.

[162] Article 10(3). As with the original making of the database, the change may be evaluated either qualitatively or quantitatively.

protection may have some implications for interpretation of the Directive generally. It would suggest for example that the investment in maintaining a database is not relevant either to a renewed period of protection or to the initial acquisition of the *sui generis* right. Therefore, maintaining a database does not qualify as presenting a database, one of the bases upon which the *sui generis* right is obtained. However, despite the wording of Article 10(3) which refers to a *change* to the contents of the database, ongoing verification – checking the continuing accuracy of the information in the database – may constitute a relevant substantial investment in the database.[163] Recital 55 specifically provides that 'a substantial new investment involving a new term of protection may include a substantial verification of the contents of the database'. This issue of what is relevant verification or presentation of the contents of a database has already been discussed above.

There is one other difficulty associated with the requirement that there be a substantial change in the contents of a database before a new period of protection may start to run again. This difficulty flows from the reference to the possibility that the substantial change can be evaluated quantitatively or qualitatively. A quantitative change is reasonably easily understood and partly explained by the reference in Article 10(3) to changes 'resulting from the accumulation of successive additions, deletions or alterations'. What is a qualitative change in the contents of a database? It may be a change in the selection or arrangement of the contents of the database. The necessary change is a change 'to' the contents of a database, which would seem to include a rearrangement of the same contents. Consequently, yet again, the very acts defined in the Directive as the acts that confer copyright protection on a database or, in this context, renewed copyright protection, also confer renewal of the *sui generis* protection for the database.

In any event, the effect of Article 10 is to ensure that a database that is continually updated (or even updated every fifteen years) will have perpetual protection pursuant to the *sui generis* right, even though the copyright in the database will expire seventy years after the death of its author. None of the contents of the database would ever fall into the public domain, even though works, data or other material in the original database may have been available for far longer than fifteen years.

Retrospectivity   An issue that is related to the duration of protection is the question of retrospective protection for databases made prior to

---

[163] W. Cornish, '1996 European Community Directive on Databases' (1996) 21 *Columbia-VLA Journal of Law and the Arts* 1.

the adoption of the Directive. As with the issue of the commencement of the protection, consideration needs to be given to both copyright protection and *sui generis* protection. The copyright protection for databases in existence prior to the adoption of the Directive varied between Member States. The standardisation of the level of originality potentially meant that some databases in the Member States with lower levels of originality would be deprived of copyright protection, while some databases in those Member States with the higher standards would now gain copyright protection that they did not previously have. This issue had to be addressed, as did the issue of the retrospective effect of the new *sui generis* right.

Article 14 provides the maximum protection in both areas. Existing copyright protection is retained and not curtailed by the new, harmonised standard of originality. Databases that would not have been protected by copyright before the Directive but which meet the originality requirements of the Directive become protected even if they were created prior to 1 January 1998.[164] The *sui generis* right is conferred on any database that meets the necessary investment criterion, provided it was completed within fifteen years of 1 January 1998. The protection so provided extends for a full fifteen-year period from 1 January 1998. For example, a database completed in early 1983 would be protected until the 1 January 2013 if a substantial investment had been made in obtaining, presenting or verifying its contents.

This analysis of the maximisation of retrospective protection raises the obvious question of why such a high level of protection would be conferred, particularly in light of the paramount objective of developing a strong database industry by ensuring sufficient protection for databases and the opportunity for new entrants to the market.[165] The provision of protection to databases that have already been completed seems a little incongruous in that context. It is difficult, if not impossible, to argue that the protection provided by the Directive acted as an incentive to create databases that were made prior to the Directive being adopted. This lack of incentive was exacerbated by the decision to provide fifteen years of protection from 1 January 1998 for databases created within the fifteen-year period prior to that date. In particular, this created an actual disincentive to update a database and thus to obtain the benefit of a new period of protection. In terms of producing a strong database industry, it was counterproductive.

In addition, the provision of protection to what may have been previously unprotected would have a detrimental effect on potential new

---

[164] Article 14(1) of the Directive.   [165] The Committee's Opinion at para. 2.1.

entrants to the market who, without the retrospective effect of the Directive, could have used existing databases for the purpose of making their own. The usual objection to this, that it would constitute free-riding on the efforts of the database maker, is not relevant in the context of the paramount objective of developing a strong database industry. It may be relevant on the grounds that the database users would be behaving in some morally reprehensible fashion contrary to the rights of database makers, but that is an approach that was supposedly rejected early on in the development of the Directive.[166] The makers of those databases knew that they did not have the protection of any *sui generis* right at the time of making those databases. They would also have had a very good idea of the nature and extent of the copyright protection provided to their database within various Member States as the state of copyright, at least in regard to the question of originality, was reasonably well settled. This is in contrast to the position in the United States of America in which, it is argued by some writers, the decision in *Feist* to reject sweat of the brow copyright came as a surprise to database owners.[167] Consequently, it is very difficult to find a justification for the retrospective protection provided by the Directive, at least in reference to the stated paramount objective of developing a strong database industry.

The actual justification provided in the Council's Reasons was to avoid any uncertainty.[168] The need for certainty is apparent. What is not apparent is how that need for certainty should be met. There was a myriad of options available concerning the starting point for protection. The Directive could have conferred *sui generis* protection only on databases completed after 1 January 1998 or databases first made available to the public after that date. Alternatively, in the case of databases made prior to the transposition of the Directive, protection could have expired fifteen years after the date on which they were made or, possibly, made available to the public for the first time.[169] Any of these provisions would have provided either no retrospective protection or less retrospective protection than what was actually conferred, while at the same time meeting the need for certainty. The expressed reason for the particular means of delivering certainty that was finally adopted was that 'the *sui generis* right was

---

[166] The Committee's Opinion at para. 2.6.3.

[167] See, e.g. the Statement of Michael Kirk, Executive Director, American Intellectual Property Law Association to The Subcommittee on Intellectual Property and the Courts of the Committee on the Judiciary, 18 March 1999, in which he claimed that the decision in *Feist* overturned nearly two hundred years of jurisprudence. Available at http://www.house.gov/judiciary/106-kirk.htm.

[168] Paragraph 22 of the Council's Reasons.

[169] This last possibility would have been consistent with the approach to retrospectivity pursuant to Article 18 of the Berne Convention.

a new right and therefore no database would have had the benefit of any identical right before transposition of the Directive'.[170] Such an explanation has almost no relationship to the professed objective of ensuring a strong database industry. Instead, it suggests a concern with the rights of makers and a desire to give protection for its own sake. For some reason, databases that had never enjoyed the right should now benefit from it, even though retrospective protection would have no impact on the decision to make those databases. It seems hard to avoid the conclusion that the final provisions on retrospectivity reflect a policy stance unrelated to economic considerations.

There are two possible arguments that the retrospective effect of the Directive was justified by the desire to provide an incentive for a strong database industry. One justification is that the promise of retrospective protection would have been an incentive for companies to continue to make databases during the lengthy period of time leading up to the adoption of the Directive. Without the assurance of retrospective protection, there would have been an incentive to refrain from further development of databases until protection was in place. The promise of retrospective protection from the very beginning of the process[171] ensured that the continued development of the database industry would occur through the critical period of the 1990s in which the commercial potential of the Internet began to be realised. The problem with this view is that it does not justify retrospective protection as far back as 1983. At best, it justifies retrospective provision from the time at which it was first seriously and officially proposed that protection be conferred. At the earliest, this would have been at the time of the release of the Green Paper on copyright and the challenge of technology in June 1988, but more realistically upon release of the First Draft in 1992.

A related but slightly different argument is that the retrospective provisions provided a particular type of certainty to the database industry and to the intellectual property industry in general. The retrospective provisions may send out a general message about not just retrospectivity but the approach to protection generally. They may be part of a general message that the EU had a protectionist disposition in relation to emerging areas of technology, and that those entering these areas could do so with confidence that legal protection would follow them. Inevitably, the political machinations of legal change move more slowly than emerging technologies but a general policy stance that protection would be forthcoming in due course may provide an incentive for those involved in such industries to invest in the EU rather than elsewhere. This in turn is a

---

[170] Paragraph 22 of the Council's Reasons.   [171] Article 12 of the First Draft.

statement that the particular provisions of the Directive are, in some respects, not as important as the generation of a culture of protection and assistance to those making a substantial investment in the industry. Nevertheless, despite these arguments, one is left with the impression that the decision was driven by other considerations than positive economic ones.

Territorial qualification for protection   One of the most controversial aspects of the Directive is Article 11 which places territorial restrictions on who may obtain the *sui generis* right in a database. Essentially, the right is extended only to makers or rightholders who are nationals or residents of a Member State. This is extended slightly by Article 11(2) to include companies and firms which have their central administration or principal place of business within the EU. In addition, companies or firms with a registered office in the EU that have a genuine ongoing link with the economy of a Member State also qualify for the right.

Article 11(3) contemplates the possibility that the Council may reach agreements to provide the *sui generis* right to other databases. As yet that has not occurred. Article 11 is clearly aimed at eliciting reciprocal protection from other countries, and the pressure to gain reciprocal protection has been one argument made in the United States for *sui generis* rights to be adopted there. This issue is discussed in more detail in Chapter 5 as the failure of the EU to provide national treatment may be a breach of the international copyright and neighbouring rights obligations of the Member States, depending on how one classifies the *sui generis* right.[172]

Compulsory licensing and competition law   The compulsory licensing provisions contained in the First Draft and the 1993 Amendments have disappeared. The Committee's Opinion that reliance should be placed on the competition law and principles of the EU rather than a system of compulsory licences has been accepted. Consequently, the compulsory licensing provisions have been replaced with a mechanism for the Commission to report on whether the provision of this right has led to 'abuse of a dominant position or other interference with free competition'.[173] The report shall consider whether measures such as a compulsory licensing scheme should be introduced.

The Council's Reasons provide other justifications for the removal of the compulsory licensing provisions.[174] None survives even cursory

---

[172] Database owners were divided on this issue. Some wanted to provide national treatment in order to avoid users preferring foreign databases.
[173] Article 16(3) of the Directive.   [174] Paragraph 16 of the Council's Reasons.

scrutiny. They state that compulsory licences became unnecessary because the *sui generis* right originally applied to insubstantial as well as substantial parts of a database, and because of the exceptions to the *sui generis* right in Article 9. The First Draft only applied to the whole or substantial parts of a database, it never provided that the *sui generis* right covered insubstantial parts of a database.[175] The exceptions set out in Article 9 of the Directive only marginally advanced the position of users as compared to their position under the First Draft. Article 9(a) makes an exception for non-electronic databases. Non-electronic databases did not receive any protection under the First Draft. Article 9(b) provides an exception for illustration for teaching or scientific research for non-commercial purposes. The original right under the First Draft only applied to extraction or re-utilisation for commercial purposes and, therefore, did not cover such uses in any event. The only arguable advancement of the position of users is Article 9(c) concerning extraction and/or re-utilisation for purposes of public security or administrative or judicial procedures. Even this advancement is limited, given that the First Draft only applied to extraction or re-utilisation for commercial purposes and there was provision for a compulsory licence of similar material.[176]

Saving of existing legal regimes   Article 13 of the Directive provides that other legal regimes relating to databases remain operative despite the new right. In particular 'copyright, rights related to copyright... subsisting in the data, works or other materials incorporated into a database... laws on restrictive practices and unfair competition, trade secrets, security, confidentiality, data protection and privacy, access to public documents, and the law of contract'. This may be significant, as the different unfair competition laws of Member States may also achieve the desired objective of preventing free riding on the efforts of a database.

Final provisions   Article 16 required Member States to implement the Directive before 1 January 1998. Not all Member States complied with this deadline, especially Ireland and Luxembourg, who did not do so until 2001.

Each Member State was also required to supply information to the Commission by the end of 2000 so that it could prepare a report concerning the operation of the Directive and, in particular, whether the *sui generis* right has led to abuse of a dominant position or other interference with free competition. Due to the delay of some Member States to

---

[175] Article 2(5) of the First Draft, Articles 8(4) and (5) of the First Draft.
[176] Article 8(2) of the First Draft.

implement the Directive and the work associated with other directives, the timeframe for submission of that report has been pushed back.

Summary of the Directive

An examination of the history of the Directive reveals a number of important points about the Directive. The first of these is that there was clear agreement throughout the process about the objective of the Directive. The stated and paramount objective was to provide legal protection for databases to encourage the development of a strong database industry within the EU that did not unduly hinder new entrants to that industry. In keeping with the fundamental tenet of the EU, this was to be done by both harmonising the protection for databases and increasing protection by the provision of a *sui generis* right. The early versions of the Directive aimed to do this via a minimalist approach, in order to prevent unauthorised use of the whole or a substantial part of the contents of a database for commercial purposes. The need to ensure new entrants were not unduly hindered was guaranteed by the limited nature of the new *sui generis* right and the availability of compulsory licensing.

What finally emerged in the Directive was a very different *sui generis* right. It can be categorised as a new form of copyright that applies to databases, covering both the sweat of the brow and creative aspects of making a database. This categorisation can be made on the basis of the relevant criterion for acquiring the *sui generis* right, the nature of the right, the nature of infringement of the right and the wording of the exceptions to the right. A very significant part of the subject matter of protection is defined by reference to actions by the database maker that are the same as those necessary for an author to acquire copyright protection. The rights conferred are referred to as one right, but a closer examination reveals that this right incorporates, and is identical to, the exclusive rights enjoyed by copyright owners. As it is in effect a copyright, it constitutes a strong, exclusive property right as recommended in the Committee's Opinion, and that right is untrammelled by any system of compulsory licensing. It is coupled with a high degree of retrospective protection which, together with the nature of the *sui generis* right itself, suggest a policy decision that high levels of protection are the most appropriate means of achieving the desired objective. The exceptions to this *sui generis* right are quite limited and are more appropriate to – and it seems were borrowed from – copyright systems with relatively high standards of originality. In particular, the exceptions for educational and research purposes are extremely limited, more so than the previous UK provisions for sweat of the brow copyright.

There are also particular difficulties with the actual wording of the Directive in a number of respects. Not least of these is the definition of a database that is extremely (and probably unnecessarily) broad to achieve even the stated objectives. This has particular implications for the protection of computer programs, an issue that is supposedly very separate from the scope of the Directive. In addition, while there has been an attempt to segregate completely the issue of copyright protection for the selection and arrangement of a database from the *sui generis* protection for the contents of the database, this has not been achieved. In part, this is due to the manner in which the *sui generis* right has been defined. In particular, the introduction of 'qualitative' aspects to the definition of a substantial investment and a substantial part of the contents of a database has seriously blurred the distinction between the *sui generis* right and copyright.

There are also a number of difficulties associated with interpretation of the Directive, such as Article 7 which prescribes the necessary criteria to obtain the *sui generis* right. For example, the meaning of the words 'obtaining, verification and presentation' is not entirely clear. Similarly, the relation between contract law and the copyright and *sui generis* protection for databases is somewhat unclear. While there was an obvious intention to limit the extent to which contract could derogate from the rights of database users, the wording of that prohibition on contractual derogation is unclear. This lack of clarity is exacerbated by provisions concerning the circumvention of technological protection measures, as introduced in the Copyright Directive in 2001. Those provisions are discussed below.

Circumvention of protection measures

The issue of preventing the circumvention of technological protection measures was raised in the Opinion but not dealt with in the Directive itself. Instead, that issue was directly addressed in the Copyright Directive that came into effect in May 2001. Article 6(1) of the Copyright Directive requires Member States to provide adequate legal protection against the circumvention of any effective technological protection measures. Article 6(2) also requires Member States to provide 'adequate legal protection against the manufacture, import, distribution, sale, rental, advertisement for sale or rental, or possession for commercial purposes of devices, products or components' or the provision of services for the purpose of circumvention. Article 6(3) specifically provides that the protection in question is to be provided to both copyright owners and owners of the *sui generis* right under the Directive.

These provisions are in keeping with the requirements of the Copyright Treaty concerning protection against circumvention of technological protection measures (as discussed in Chapter 2). Yet, they go beyond the requirements of the Copyright Treaty in a number of respects. First, the Copyright Treaty does not specifically require the prohibition of the manufacture of circumvention devices or other commercial dealings with them such as importation, offering for sale or rental.

Second, and perhaps more importantly, the Copyright Directive deals with the relationship between circumvention of technological measures of protection and the exceptions to the rights of copyright and *sui generis* right owners. Article 6(4) provides in part that:

In the absence of voluntary measures taken by rightholders, including agreements between rightholders and other parties concerned, Member States shall take appropriate measures to ensure that rightholders make available to the beneficiary of an exception or limitation provided for in national law . . . the means of benefiting from that exception or limitation, to the extent necessary to benefit from that exception or limitation and where that beneficiary has legal access to the protected work or subject-matter concerned.

The provisions of the first and second subparagraphs shall not apply to works or other subject-matter made available to the public on agreed contractual terms in such a way that members of the public may access them from a place and a time individually chosen by them.

The first paragraphs of Article 6 appear to require Member States effectively to override contractual provisions that eliminate a user's entitlement to statutory exceptions to protection unless publishers demonstrate that they have taken voluntary measures to preserve statutory exceptions. Yet that appearance is deceptive and the last paragraph quoted above may well render that requirement otiose. This paragraph was inserted in the Copyright Directive late in the negotiations at the suggestion of Finland. It was the subject of considerable controversy and library groups unsuccessfully sought inclusion of the word 'negotiated' rather than 'agreed'. Their concern was that database owners may impose contracts of adhesion that users either agree to or reject, but they will not negotiate on possible terms. If the database in question is an on-line database, the contract of adhesion need make no concession to the statutory exceptions or limitations.

In the context of the *sui generis* right, there is also a difficulty in determining the relevant 'exceptions and limitations' within the meaning of the Copyright Directive. For example, the Directive places the entitlement of a legitimate user to extract insubstantial parts of a database under the heading of 'Rights and Obligations of Legitimate Users'. This would suggest that Article 6(4) has no relationship with the right to extract insubstantial parts of a database provided for in the Directive. Consequently, the Directive's requirement that lawful users of a database be permitted to extract insubstantial parts of it would remain in effect.

On the other hand, the provisions concerning extraction for teaching or research are described as 'Exceptions'. The final paragraph quoted above most certainly applies to those exceptions. Consequently, the owner of an on-line database that users access at a time and place of their own choosing may contractually exclude any extraction for teaching or research purposes or require payment for such extraction, even if it would otherwise come within the scope of the Directive's exception.

4 Transposition of the Directive

This chapter examines the transposition of the Directive into the domestic laws of the EU Member States. It does so by focusing on the protection of databases in nine of the Member States: Belgium, France, Germany, Ireland, Italy, the Netherlands, Spain, Sweden and the UK. The section below describes the legislation and case law of those countries relating to copyright and unfair competition as they relate to databases and the *sui generis* right. In order to avoid repetition, only particular features of the transposing legislation that are of note are discussed.

These nine countries were chosen for a number of reasons. First, they represent a broad range of pre- and post-Directive approaches to protection of databases. For example, Ireland and the UK had sweat of the brow copyright protection for databases prior to transposing the Directive. Most other countries did not have such copyright laws but had other schemes in place that conferred at least some protection on the non-original aspects of databases. For example, Sweden had its catalogue laws that influenced the Directive. Germany and other countries had, and still have, unfair competition laws that prevent parasitic copying by a competitor. Second, these nine countries represent the vast majority of the population of the EU and, finally, the vast majority of EU investment in databases and publishing occurs in those countries.

After examining the nine individual countries, the main issues raised by the transposing legislation and related case law are summarised. The chapter begins with three tables. The first lists the transposing legislation of all fifteen members of the EU. The second and third tables compare the Directive's provisions concerning copyright and *sui generis* protection respectively with the legislation of eight of the nine countries dealt with below.

Table 4.1. *Transpositions of directive 96/9/EC in Member States of the EU*

Member State	Commencement date	Title of implementing legislation
Austria	1 January 1998	Law transposing Directive 96/9/EC and amending the Intellectual Property Code, Law No. 25 of 1998
Belgium	14 November 1998	Legal Protection of Databases Act 1998, s. 35 Moniteur Belge du 14 novembre 98, pp. 36913–14
Denmark	1 July 1998	Act No. 407 of 1998
Finland	15 April 1998	Law of 3 April 1998 (FFS 1998, p. 963)
France	1 July 1998	Law No. 98–536 transposing Directive 96/9/EC and amending the Intellectual Property Code
Germany	1 January 1998	German Information and Communication Services Act 1997 which amended Articles 4, 55, 87(a)–(e), 127a, 137g in the Law on Copyright and Neighbouring Rights Act 1965, as amended (Urheberrechtsgesetz, UrhG)
Greece	15 March 2000	Law No. 2819/2000, *Official Journal* 8/A 15 March 2000
Ireland	1 January 2001	Copyright and Related Rights Act 2000
Italy	15 June 1999	Implementation of Directive 96/9/EC on the Legal Protection of Databases, Article 8 Legislative Decree No. 169 of 6 May 1999 (which amended the Copyright Law of 1941)
Luxembourg		Law No. 4431 adopted by the Chamber of Deputies, 15 February 2001
Netherlands	21 July 1999	Database Law of 8 July 1998 amending the Copyright Act of 1912: Article IV
Portugal	4 July 2000	Decree No. 122/2000 of 4 July 2000
Spain	1 April 1998	Law No. 5 of 1998 transposing Directive 96/9/EC amending Spanish Copyright Act 1987
Sweden	1 January 1998	Law No. 790 of 1997 amending Law No. 729 of 1960 (Law on Copyright)
UK	1 January 1998	Copyright and Rights in Databases Regulations 1997 (SI 1997 No. 3032)

Table 4.2. *The Directive, transposing legislation and copyright in databases*

Copyright aspect	EU Directive	Belgium	France	Germany	Ireland	Italy	Netherlands	Spain	UK
Definition of a database	Arts. 1, 2	Art. 20*bis*, Part 4*bis*, Chapter 1	L112–3	s. 4(2)	Art. 2(1)	Art. 2(9)	Art. 10 of 1912 CL. Art. 1.1(a) (of Law 8 July 1999)	Art. 12(2)	s. 3A
Criteria for copyright protection	Art. 3	Art. 20*bis*, Part 4*bis*, Chapter 1	L112–3	ss. 1, 2	Arts. 2, 18	Arts. 12(2), 171(2)	Not expressly stated	Art. 10, Art. 12	ss. 3(1)(d)
Authorship and ownership provisions	Art. 4	Art. 1, Section 1, Chapter 1 and Art. 20*ter*, Part 4*bis*, Chapter 1	L113–1–L113–9	ss. 7–10	Arts. 21–23	Art. 12(2) (of Law of 8 July 1999)	Art. 7	Art. 5	ss. 9–11
Restricted Acts	Art. 5	Art. 1, Section 1, Chapter 1	L122–1–L122–12	ss. 15–24	Arts. 37–48	Arts. 12(2), 19, Art. 64(5)	Art. I. Art. 4, Art. 3(2) (Law of 8 July 1999)	Arts. 17–23	ss. 2, 16–27
Performance by a lawful user of acts for the purposes of access to the contents of the databases	Art. 6(1)	Art. 20*quater* (1994)	L122–5	s. 55a	Art. 83	Art. 64(b)	Art. 24a	Art. 34(1)	s. 50D, s. 296B

(*cont.*)

Table 4.2. (*cont.*)

Copyright aspect	EU Directive	Belgium	France	Germany	Ireland	Italy	Netherlands	Spain	UK
Exception for reproduction for private purposes of a non-electronic database	Art. 6(2)(a)	Art. 22*bis* (1), Part 4*bis*, Chapter 1 (1994)	L122–5	s. 53(1) (5)	N/A, but see Art. 50 (fair dealing)	Art. 68	Art. 16b	Art. 34(2)(a)	N/A
Use for the sole purpose of illustration for teaching or scientific research	Art. 6(2)(b)	Art. 22*bis* (2)(3)(4), Part 4*bis*, Chapter 1	L122–5 (but more restricted) private use family use	s. 46, s. 53(2) (1)(3)(1), s. 63	Arts. 50 research private studies, 53 inst. exams, 54 education, 57 education	Art. 64(b) (1)(a)	Arts. 16, 16b	Art. 34(2)(b)	s. 29(1A) ss. 33, 60
Use for purposes of public security for purposes of an administrative or judicial procedure	Art. 6(2)(c)	Art. 22*bis* (5), Part 4*bis*, Chapter 1	N/A	s. 45	Arts 71–77	Art. 64(6) (1)(b)	Art. 16b	Art. 34(2)(c)	ss. 45–50
Exceptions to copyright traditionally authorised under national law	Art. 6(2)(d)	Arts. 21, 22 and 23, Part 5, Chapter 1	L122–5	ss. 45–53	Arts. 51 – fair dealing, 52 – critical review, 91 – scientific or technical article	Arts. 68, 70, 101	Arts. 15, 15a–b, 16, 16a–b, 17, 17a–c	Art. 13, Art. 35	ss. 33–44
Public lending	Art. 6(2)(d)	Art. 23		s. 27	Arts. 58 and 40(1)(g)	Art. 69	Art. 15c	Art. 37	s. 40A(2)

Table 4.3. *The Directive, transposing legislation and the sui generis right*

Sui generis right	Directive	Belgium	France	Germany	Ireland	Italy	Netherlands	Spain	UK
Defn of maker or Creator (Neth) of D/b	Not defined	Art. 2(5) of the Legal Protection of Databases Act 1998	Art. L341–1 procedure	s. 87a(2)	Arts. 322, 323	Art. 102(2) 1(a)	Art. I(1)(b), (Law of 8 July 1999)	Art. 133(3)(a)	Reg. 14
Definition of a database	Art. 1.2	Art. 2(1)	Arts. L112–3 and L341–1	s. 87a(1)	Arts. 2, 321	Art. 2	Art. I(1)(a) (Law of 8 July 1999)	Art. 12(2)	s. 3A(1)
Rights of database maker or manufacturers (Spain)	Art. 7.1	Art. 4, Art. 2(2)(3)	Art. 342–1	s. 87b	Arts. 320, 324	Art. 102(2)(3)	Art. I, Art. 2 (Law of 8 July 1999)	Art. 133(1)(2)(3)(b), (c)	Reg. 15
Use of an insubstantial part by a lawful user	Art. 8(1)	Art. 2(4), Art. 8	L342–3	s. 87e	Art. 327	Art. I, Art. 3.1 (Law of 8 July 1999)	Art. I, Art. 3.1 (Law of 8 July 1999)	Art. 134(1)	Reg. 19
Extraction from a non-electronic database for private purposes	Art. 9(a)	Art. 7(1)	L342–3	s. 87c(1) (para 1)	N/A but see Art. 329	Art. 68?	Art. I, Art. 5(a) (Law of 8 July 1999), Art. I	Art. 135(1)(a), 34(2)(a)	N/A
Illustration for teaching or scientific research	Art. 9(b)	Art. 7(2)	Other exceptions in Art. L211–3	s. 87c(1) (paras. 2, 3)	Art. 330 for teaching but not research	64(b)(1)(a)	Art. I, Art. 5(b), 64(b)(1)(a) (Law of 8 July 99), Art. I	Art. 135(1)(b)	Reg. 20

(cont.)

Table 4.3. (cont.)

Sui generis right	Directive	Belgium	France	Germany	Ireland	Italy	Netherlands	Spain	UK
Use for purposes of public security or for the purposes of an administrative or judicial procedure	Art. 9(c)	Art. 7(3)	N/A	s. 87c(2)	Arts. 331–336	Nil but possibly Art. 64 *sexies*, 64(b) (1)(a)	Art. 5(c)	Art. (1) 135(c)	Reg. 20(2), Sch. 1
Duration of protection (including renewal)	Art. 10	Art. 6	Art. L342–5	s. 87d	Art. 325	Art. 102(2), 6, 7	Art. I, Art. 6	Art. 136	Reg. 17
Beneficiaries of protection	Art. 11	Art. 12	L341–2	s. 127a	Art. 326	Art. 102(2) 4, 5	Art. I, Art. 7	Art. 164	Reg. 18
Public lending right	Art. 7(2)	Art. 2(2), (3)	Art. L342–3	s. 27, s. 87b(2)	Art. 320	Art. 102, 69(1)(b)	Art. I(2), Art. I		Reg. 12(2)
Distribution of lawful copies	Art. 7(2)(b)	Art. 4	Art. L342–4	s. 17, 87b(2)	Art. 320(5)	Art. 102(2)(2)	Art. 2(3)	Art. 133(3)(c)	Reg. 12(5)
Retrospectivity	Art. 14(3)	Art. 6	Art. L342–5	s. 137g(2)	Sch. 1, Part VI, para. 46	Art. 7 of the Implementation of Directive 96/9/EC on the legal protection of databases	Art. I (Law No. 169 of 1999), Art. III	Para. 16 of the Transitional Provisions	Reg. 30

NB The Swedish legislation is not represented in the two tables above as its minimalist approach does not lend itself to easy identification of the relevant provisions that reflect particular aspects of the Directive. See the description of the Swedish legislation in the section below.

Belgium

Copyright before and after transposition

As with other national legislation, there was no specific provision for databases prior to the implementation of the Directive. Protection for compilations and databases flowed from the general protection of literary or artistic works.[1] Literary works are defined as 'writings of any kind'[2] but the Belgian courts have imposed a requirement of originality.[3] The Belgian Supreme Court has expressed this requirement by requiring that a work must be 'the expression of the intellectual effort of the one that realized it, which is an indispensable condition to confer to the work the individual character without which there would be no creation'.[4]

Chapter III of the Legal Protection of Databases Act 1998 amended the existing Law on Copyright and Neighbouring Rights 1994 in order to implement the Directive's requirements in relation to copyright. Consequently, the discussion here concerning changes to copyright refers to the Law on Copyright and Neighbouring Rights 1994 as amended.

The implementation of the Directive has led to the insertion of a new section 4(2) in chapter 1 of the Law on Copyright and Neighbouring Rights 1994. Article 20(2) reflects the requirements of Article 3 of the Directive to confer copyright protection on databases that constitute the author's own intellectual creation, by reason of the selection or arrangement of the subject matter. The same article reproduces the definition of a database in Article 1 of the Directive.

Employers are deemed to be the assignees of economic rights relating to databases created 'in the non-cultural industry'.[5] This contrasts with the usual position concerning ownership of copyright that requires specific provisions within the contract of employment assigning copyright to the employer.[6]

Article 20(4) of Chapter 1, part 5 of the Law on Copyright and Neighbouring Rights 1994 implements the specific exception required in the

---

[1] Article 1, Section 1, Chapter 1 of the Law on Copyright and Neighbouring Rights 1994 (Belgium).

[2] Article 8, Section 2, Chapter 1, of the Law on Copyright and Neighbouring Rights 1994 (Belgium).

[3] A. Strowel, N. Dutilh and J. Corbet, 'Belgium' in D. Nimmer and P. E. Getter (eds.), *Geller on International Copyright Law and Practice* (1998–9 edn) (Matthew Bender, New York, 1999) at p. 2.

[4] Cass 27 April 1989, Pas 1989 I 908 Cass 25 October 1989 Pas I 238.

[5] Chapter 1 Article 20*ter*, section 4*bis*, of the Law on Copyright and Neighbouring Rights 1994 (Belgium).

[6] Article 3(3), Section 1, Chapter 1 of the Law on Copyright and Neighbouring Rights Act 1994 (Belgium).

Directive to permit a lawful user to perform acts necessary for the purposes of access to the contents of a database and normal use of those contents. Interestingly, the same article defines 'a lawful user' as 'a person who effects acts authorised by the author or permitted by law'. This definition seems to include those who do not necessarily have a contractual relationship with the database owner, and who are accessing the database to engage in one of the permitted exceptions, such as reproducing for scientific purposes.

Articles 21, 22 and 23 of Chapter 1, part 5 of the Law on Copyright and Neighbouring Rights 1994 contain the general exceptions to copyright. Articles 22(2) and 23(2) have amended some aspects of Articles 22 and 23. In particular, the legislation makes a distinction between electronic and non-electronic databases as permitted by Article 6(2)(a) of the Directive.[7] Hence, reproduction of non-electronic databases for purely private purposes is permitted, provided that it does not prejudice normal exploitation of the work.[8] Reproduction of any database for the purposes of illustration for teaching or scientific research is permitted to the extent justified by the non-commercial purpose to be achieved, and provided that it does not prejudice normal exploitation of the work.[9] Communication of a database for the same purposes is permitted if it is done 'by establishments officially acknowledged or organised for that purpose by the authorities'.[10] Reproduction and communication to the public for the purpose of effecting acts related to public security or an administrative or judicial procedure are also permitted.[11]

Article 23 of the Law on Copyright and Neighbouring Rights 1994 deals with public lending of works and it has been amended to include databases within its provisions. Consequently, approved institutions may lend databases to the public and may import up to five copies of the

---

[7] This distinction is made by referring to databases 'enshrined in a graphic or analogue medium', and 'databases enshrined in a medium other than a graphic or analogue medium'.

[8] Article 22*bis*(1), section 4*bis*, Chapter 1 of the Law on Copyright and Neighbouring Rights Act 1994 (Belgium). A consequence of these new provisions is that the previous exception of copying for didactic purposes has now been removed altogether, replaced by general provisions relating to copyright material that permit copying for the purposes of illustration for teaching or research to the extent justified by the non-commercial purpose. See the new Articles 22 (4), (4*bis*) and (4*ter*).

[9] Article 22*bis*(2)(3), Section 4*bis*, Chapter 1 of the Law on Copyright and Neighbouring Rights 1994 (Belgium). The two sub-articles distinguish between non-electronic and electronic databases, partly to facilitate the equitable remuneration provisions that are discussed below.

[10] Article 22*bis*(4), Section 4*bis*, Chapter 1 of the Law on Copyright and Neighbouring Rights Act 1994 (Belgium).

[11] Article 22*bis*(5), Section 4*bis*, Chapter 1 of the Law on Copyright and Neighbouring Rights Act 1994 (Belgium).

database from outside the EU, even if it has not yet been published in the EU.[12]

The exceptions of copying of non-electronic databases for private purposes, illustration for teaching or research and public lending are associated with other provisions designed to provide equitable remuneration to copyright owners. Hence, Chapter V has been amended to provide equitable remuneration for reproduction of non-electronic works, including databases, for private purposes or for illustration for teaching or research. This remuneration is provided primarily via a surcharge on copying appliances and those who make them available for copying purposes.[13] In addition a new Chapter V*bis* has been introduced, which is designed to provide equitable remuneration for reproduction and communication of electronic works, including electronic databases. The equitable remuneration is payable either by those persons effecting the acts of exploitation, or 'the educational or scientific research establishments making the works and performances available to another, either free of charge or for valuable consideration'.[14]

The existing provisions for payments in respect of public lending were extended to include payments in respect of public lending of databases.

Unfair competition laws

Articles 1382–1384 of the Belgian Civil Code form the basis of general unfair competition law.[15] These provisions are similar to the provisions in the French Civil Code and Belgian principles of unfair competition have developed along the same lines as the French law of unfair competition.[16] In addition, the Law of 14 July 1991 on the practices of the trade and on information and consumer protection has specific provisions aimed at parasitic competition.

Sui generis *protection*

Chapter II of the Legal Protection of Databases Act 1998 implements the provisions of the Directive relating to *sui generis* protection. A maker of a database is defined as 'the natural or legal person who takes the initiative and the risk of investment from which a database originates'.[17] The relevant initiative and risk are presumably the initiative and risk

---

[12] Article 23(3).   [13] Chapter V, Articles 59 and 60.   [14] Chapter V*bis*, Article 61*ter*.
[15] A. Kamperman Sanders, *Unfair Competition Law* (Clarendon Press, Oxford, 1997), p. 55.
[16] Ibid., at p. 55.
[17] Article 2(5), Section 1, Chapter II of the Legal Protection of Databases Act 1998.

involved in obtaining, verifying or presenting the contents of the database, as database rights are created upon the making of a substantial investment in those activities.[18] This raises the possibility of at least two different legal persons being involved in the making of a database as taking the initiative of obtaining, verifying or presenting is presumably a different concept from that of taking the risk of doing so. The former suggests the actual activities of obtaining, verifying or presenting, whereas the latter suggests a financial risk associated with some financial investment in those activities.

The definition of a database is taken from and repeats the definition in the Directive.[19] A pamphlet listing 'self-help' groups has been held to be a database.[20] This decision suggests that the act of selecting material, in this case the 'self-help' groups to be included in the pamphlet, would constitute the relevant qualitative investment necessary to qualify for *sui generis* protection.

Similarly, the right of extraction and re-utilisation is defined in the same way that it is defined in the Directive.[21] Specific exceptions are made for public lending so that it does not contravene the right of extraction and re-utilisation.[22] Consequently, the limited importation of a database from outside the EU permitted by the copyright public lending provisions is unaffected by the *sui generis* provisions.

Right to extract or re-utilise an insubstantial part   Article 8 of the Legal Protection of Databases Act 1998 (Belgium) confers a right on lawful users to extract and/or re-utilise insubstantial parts of the contents of a database. The legislation has a broad definition of a lawful user. Article 2(4) defines a lawful user as 'a person who effects acts of extraction or re-utilisation authorised by the database maker or permitted by law'. Consequently, the definition is not restricted to those in a contractual relationship with the maker and includes those who are accessing a database in order to avail themselves of one of the exceptions to the right of extraction and re-utilisation, including the right to use insubstantial parts. The definition of a lawful user then confers considerable importance on the provisions for circumventing database protection devices that will be introduced pursuant to the Copyright Directive. While extracting or re-utilising insubstantial parts is lawful, it may not be lawful to circumvent database protection devices that prevent such extraction or re-utilisation in the first place.

[18] Article 3, Section 1, Chapter II of the Legal Protection of Databases Act 1998.
[19] Article 2(1).
[20] *UNMS* v. *Belpharma Communication*, Court of Brussels, 16 March 1999.
[21] Article 2(2)(3).   [22] Ibid.

Exceptions   Belgian legislation adopts the exception that is available under the Directive for private reproduction of non-electronic databases for private purposes.[23] Similarly, extraction for the purposes of illustration for teaching or scientific research is permitted, provided that such extraction is justified by the non-commercial purpose to be achieved.[24] As indicated in the Directive itself, this exception only relates to extraction, not re-utilisation, whereas under the Belgian copyright provisions, an exception exists for both reproduction and communication to the public.[25] The effect is that the copyright exception for communication of a database to the public for illustration for teaching or research purposes is pointless. Any communication to the public would infringe the right of re-utilisation and would not be protected by any exception. As envisaged by the Directive, extraction and re-utilisation for the purposes of public security or administrative or judicial procedures is permitted.[26]

Term of protection   Article 6 confers a fifteen-year period of protection. It also provides that any substantial change to the contents qualifies the resulting database for its own term of protection. It is not clear whether the resulting database is that database constituted by the new contents or whether it applies to the entire database, including contents that were previously part of the database, although the Directive itself probably provides the answer to this question. Article 6 specifically places the burden of proof regarding the date of completion of the production of the database and any substantial change to the database on the database maker.

France

Copyright before and after transposition

Prior to the implementation of the Directive, copyright protection for databases flowed from Article L112–3 of the Code of Intellectual Property 1992 which states:

The authors of translations, adaptations, transformations or arrangements of works of the mind shall enjoy the protection afforded by this Code, without prejudice to the rights of the maker of the original work. The same shall apply to the authors of anthologies or collections of miscellaneous works or data which, by reason of the selection or arrangement of their contents, constitute creations of the mind.

[23] Article 7(1).   [24] Article 7(2).
[25] Article 22*bis* (4) of the Law of Copyright and Neighbouring Rights 1994.
[26] Article 7(3).

French copyright law imposes a relatively high standard of originality. The Code of Intellectual Property 1992[27] protects the rights of authors in 'all works of the mind'.[28] This has traditionally been interpreted to mean that the work must involve an imprint of personality by the author which, in turn, means the author's exercise of creative choice in making a work.[29] Lucas and Plaisant have noted that this traditional view of originality has been eroded, partly as a consequence of the difficulties associated with determining originality in computer programs.[30] Hence, in the context of computer programs, the Cour de Cassation spoke of originality as an 'intellectual input'.[31]

Despite the confusion about the meaning of originality, French copyright law clearly does not confer protection on the sweat of the brow involved in creating compilations.[32] For example, protection has been refused for alphabetical listings of professionals,[33] the layout of annual tide tables[34] and a map of France indicating wine regions.[35] On the other hand, court decisions have conferred copyright protection on compilations such as address books, schedules of prices, a directory of medical laboratories and on-line databases where sufficient creativity existed in the selection or arrangement of materials.[36]

Article L112–3, which already provided protection for collections, now specifically refers to collections 'such as new databases which, through choice or layout of materials, constitute intellectual works'. Article L112–3 contains a definition of a database being 'a collection of independent works, data or other materials arranged in a systematic or methodical way and individually accessible by electronic or other means'. Since the implementation of the Directive, copyright has been denied in a compilation of advertised invitations to tender for public procurement.[37]

The exceptions to copyright appear in Article L122–5. A new paragraph 5 of that states that 'Acts necessary for the purpose of access to the

---

[27] Loi No. 92–597 du 1er juillet 1992 relative au code de la propriété intellectuelle (partie législative).

[28] Article L112–1.

[29] A. Lucas and A. Plaisant, 'France' in M. B. Nimmer and P. E. Geller (eds.), *International Copyright Law and Practice* (Matthew Bender, New York, 1999), p. 4.

[30] Ibid., p. 5. Germany faced similar difficulties although the initial response there was to maintain a requirement of a high level of originality.

[31] Cass, Ass. plen., 7 March 1986, RIDA 1986, no. 129, 136.

[32] Lucas and Plaisant, 'France', p. 11.

[33] Paris, 4e ch., 16 January 1995, Expertises 1996, 40, obs. Bertrand.

[34] Rennes, le ch., 16 May 1995, Juris-Data no. 047866.

[35] Douai, le ch., 7 October 1996, RIDA 1997, no. 172, 286.

[36] Lucas and Plaisant, 'France', see fn. 111.

[37] *Groupe Moniteur and Others* v. *Observatoire des Marches*, Public Cour d'appel de Paris, 18 June 1999, RTD COM 4, 1 December 1999, pp. 866–9.

contents of an electronic database for the requirements and within the limits of use provided for in the contract' are permitted. The reference to contract in this provision appears to confirm the view that a lawful user is restricted to someone in a contractual relationship with the database owner, or someone deriving usage rights from a contractual relationship.

Article L122–5, second paragraph permits reproductions for private use of non-electronic databases. It has been written so as to exclude private copying of electronic databases. Article L122–5 contains a number of other general exceptions to copyright that apply to copyright in databases. For example, authors may not prohibit 'analyses and short quotations justified by the critical, polemic, educational, scientific or informatory nature of the work in which they are incorporated'. Exceptions also exist for press reviews and the dissemination as current news of speeches intended for the public in various public settings such as political, administrative or judicial gatherings. However, there does not appear to be any exception for reproduction for the purposes of judicial or administrative proceedings or for the purposes of public security.

Compulsory licensing exists in respect of the right of reprographic reproduction as the publication of a work implies assignment of the right to a collecting society.[38] The right of reprographic reproduction seems to be limited to an analogue means, as it is defined as 'reproduction in the form of a copy on paper or an assimilated medium by means of a photographic process or one having equivalent effect permitting direct reading'.[39]

Unfair competition law

Unfair competition law can be relied upon to prevent slavish imitation of another's product.[40] This principle is based upon Article 1382 of the French Civil Code which provides that 'any action by one person which causes damage to another obliges the person whose fault it is to compensate the other'.[41] This general provision has been adapted by French courts to many different situations, including what is referred to as disloyal competition.[42] It covers conduct that a reasonable person would regard as contrary to the usages of the trade and professional honesty,[43] such as disparaging another trader's goods and creating confusion in the

---

[38] Article L122–10.   [39] Ibid.
[40] Kamperman Sanders, *Unfair Competition Law*, pp. 28–9.
[41] R. Clauss, 'The French Law of Disloyal Competition' (1995) 11 *European Intellectual Property Review* 550, at 550.
[42] Ibid.   [43] Ibid.

minds of consumers. The slavish imitation of another's product will often lead the courts easily to conclude the possibility of confusion.

More recent decisions have included decisions concerning parasitic behaviour or misappropriation of another trader's reputation, even where there was no confusion of the public.[44] This has led to suggestions that a new cause of action of parasitic competition has been established by the courts.[45] In any event, slavish imitation of another's product and consequent appropriation of the fruits of another person's labour is likely to lead to a finding of either disloyal competition or parasitic competition, particularly where the two parties are in direct competition.[46] For example, in a recent decision the copying and republication of advertisements published in a journal dedicated to announcing invitations to tender for public procurement was considered to constitute unfair competition. This was so, even though the court found that there had not been sufficient investment in the arrangement of the invitations to tender to confer *sui generis* protection under French database legislation.[47] A similar decision was made in relation to the copying of a collection of 400 collective bargaining agreements although the *sui generis* legislation may well also have been applicable in that instance.[48]

Sui generis *protection*

The *sui generis* provisions are incorporated into Book II of the Intellectual Property Code 1992 and form a new kind of neighbouring right. Some of the general provisions concerning neighbouring rights in Book II, Chapter 1 are applicable to the *sui generis* provisions.

The maker of a database is a person who takes the initiative and risk of financial or human investment in the setting up, verification and presentation of the contents of a database.[49] The definition of a database comes from Article L112–3 which deals with the copyright protection of databases. However, the *sui generis* provisions require that the investment in the obtaining, verifying and presenting of the database must

---

[44] *SARL Parfum Ungaro* v. *SARL JJ Vivier*, Paris, 18 May 1989 D 1990 340. *Decoras SA and L'Esprit du Vin SARL* v. *Art Metal SARL and Marioni Alfredi* [1991] PIBD 510 III-655 (CA Paris).

[45] Clauss, 'The French Law', p. 553. Kamperman Sanders, *Unfair Competition Law*, p. 28.

[46] *SARL Parfum Ungaro* v. *SARL JJ Vivier*, and *Decoras SA and L'Esprit du Vin SARL* v. *Art Metal SARL and Marioni Alfredi*.

[47] *Groupe Moniteur and Others* v. *Observatoire des Marches*.

[48] *Dictionnaire Permanent des Conventions Collectives Tribunal de grande instance de Lyon 18 December 1998* [1999] 181 RIDA 325. See also *Cadremploi* v. *Keljob and Colt Telecommunications* TGI Paris, 5 September 2001 for another decision combining references to unfair competition and *sui generis* protection.

[49] Article L341–1.

be substantial.[50] The investment in obtaining and verifying an electronic version of telephone white pages has been held to be a substantial investment.[51] On the other hand, it has been held that a journal specifically dedicated to publishing advertisements inviting tenders for building projects did not make a sufficient investment to be able to obtain database rights as it merely had to arrange typographically advertisements provided to it. However, the wholesale reproduction and republication of the advertisements was prevented under unfair competition law.[52]

The right of extraction and re-utilisation is conferred by Article 342–1 which effectively adopts the wording of the Directive. Public lending is not an act of extraction or re-utilisation. The reproduction of newspaper advertisements originally displayed on a newspaper's website has been held to infringe the database right.[53] On the other hand, an Internet service provider whose service hosted a website that was illegally displaying a database of bibliographic information has been found not to be in breach of the database right[54] although the service provider closed the infringing site upon receipt of notice.

Right to extract or re-utilise an insubstantial part The right of a lawful user to extract or re-utilise insubstantial parts of the database is also provided and contractual provisions to the contrary are prohibited.[55] As already noted, a lawful user is someone in a contractual relationship with the maker or deriving their right to use from that contract and in at least one decision, contract law has been used to prevent extraction from a database rather than resorting to *sui generis* protection.[56]

In one decision concerning an employment website displaying job offers, 12 per cent of those offers were considered to constitute a substantive part of the database.[57] An important factor in the court's decision was the fact that the plaintiff had lost a number of its clients to the defendant due to its parasitic behaviour.[58]

Exceptions An exception is made for the extraction or re-utilisation of substantial parts of a non-electronic database.[59] Other

[50] Ibid.
[51] *France Télécom* v. *MA Editions*, Tribunal de Commerce de Paris, 18 June 1999.
[52] *Groupe Moniteur* (CA Paris).   [53] *Süddeutsche Zeitung* (DC Cologne).
[54] *Electre* v. *TI Communication and Maxotex*, Tribunal de Commerce de Paris, 7 March 1999.
[55] Article L342–3.   [56] *Electre* v. *TI Communication and Maxotex*.
[57] *Cadremploi* v. *Keljob and Colt Telecommunications*.
[58] O. Oosterbaan, 'Database Protection in the EU and the US Compared: A High-Tech Game of Chicken?', April 2002, available at: http://lex.oosterbaan.net/docs.html.
[59] Article L342–3(2).

exceptions are contained in the general provisions for neighbouring rights in Article L211–3 which repeats the exceptions for copyright in Article L112–5.

Term of protection   The fifteen-year period of protection is conferred by Article L342–5. If a substantial new investment is made in a database, protection is conferred for the fifteen years following that new investment.

Germany

Copyright before and after transposition

Up until 1 January 1998, s. 4 of the German Law on Copyright and Neighbouring Rights 1965 (as amended) provided that:

Compilations of works or other contributions, which can be considered as personal intellectual creations due to the efforts of formation and selection they include, are protected as independent works irrespective of those works being compiled.

Prior to the transposition of the Directive, German copyright law[60] was regarded as having one of the highest standards of originality for copyright in the EU.[61] As will be seen in the following discussion concerning the impact of the Directive on copyright, there is a question as to whether it still does, at least as far as databases are concerned. The nature of copyright in Germany differs significantly from common law jurisdictions. Germany has a monistic view of copyright[62] in which the economic rights of an author and their moral rights are inextricably intertwined. For example, ownership of copyright inevitably follows authorship and there is no principle of work for hire in which copyright would automatically vest in an employer of an author.[63] Nor can an author assign their

[60] The French term 'droit d'auteur', or author's right may be a better translation of the title of the German law usually referred to in English as copyright. See A. Dietz, *International Copyright Law and Practice* (Matthew Bender, New York, 1999).

[61] C. Hertz-Eichenrode, 'Germany', in D. Campbell (ed.), *World Intellectual Property Rights and Remedies* (Oceana Publications, New York, 1999), at Ger-18: 'The essential prerequisite for copyright protection is set forth in article 2(2) of the Copyright Act, requiring that the work be a personal intellectual creation . . . The work must show an individuality of a certain creative level far beyond the average of a well-skilled and trained person in the area' citing Supreme Court, GRUR 1982 at p. 305, Buromobelprogramm and GRUR 1983, at p. 377, Brombeermuster.

[62] B. Hugenholtz, 'Electronic Rights and Wrongs in Germany and the Netherlands' (1998) 22 *Columbia Journal of Law and the Arts* 151 at 152.

[63] Ibid., at 152 and Dietz, *International Copyright Law*. There is an exception to this rule in respect of computer programs. See s. 69b of the Urheberrechtsgesetz UrhG.

copyright to another person although licences, including exclusive licences, may be granted by the author.[64]

The key copyright legislation is contained in the Law on Copyright and Neighbouring Rights of 9 September 1965 (as amended). It encapsulates the monistic view of copyright by its emphasis upon the protection of works of authors that are personal creations with some intellectual content. The basic principle underpinning the legislation is that 'authors of literary, scientific and artistic works shall enjoy protection for their works'.[65] Section 2(1) gives a non-exhaustive list of examples of works. The key provision in terms of the requirement of originality is s. 2(2), which provides that 'Personal intellectual creations alone shall constitute works within the meaning of this Law'.

The emphasis upon personal intellectual creations has led to a number of decisions that require a considerable degree of originality before a literary work will be considered to have copyright protection. In addition, these decisions emphasise the need for freedom of use of scientific information.[66]

In the context of compilations, the German courts have decided a number of cases concerning telephone directories, with inconsistent outcomes.[67] For example, in 1993, the Frankfurt District Court enjoined the distribution of a telephone book contained in a CD.[68] The defendants had directly copied the plaintiff's electronic telephone directory although they had added data from their own sources such as the postal codes of subscribers.[69] The Court held that the plaintiff had copyright in its telephone book and that the copyright had been infringed by the defendant. The effect of the decision is a little ambiguous, as the defendant also copied the plaintiff's user interface and search strategy.[70] This suggests that there was a claim for breach of copyright in the computer program used to search the telephone directory and that this was the basis of the plaintiff's success. This view taken by the District Court's decision is confirmed to a certain extent by a later decision of the Frankfurt Court

---

[64] B. Hugenholtz, 'The New Database Right: Early Case Law from Europe', paper presented to the Ninth Annual Conference on International IP Law and Policy, New York, 19–20 April 2001, p. 152, s. 29 (UrhG).

[65] Section 1 of the Law on Copyright and Neighbouring Rights 1965 (Germany) as amended.

[66] Federal Supreme Court, decision of March 12, 1987 GRUR 704, 705, P. Katzenberger, 'Copyright Law and Data Banks' (1990) 21 IIC 310 at 322–3.

[67] See M. Leistner, 'The Legal Protection of Telephone Directories Relating to the New Database Maker's Right' (2000) 31 IIC 950 for a detailed discussion of the issue.

[68] A. Raubenheimer, 'Germany: Recent Decisions on Database Protection Under Copyright Law and Unfair Competition Rules' (1996) 1 *Communications Law* 3, 123. 1994 CR 473: 1994 NJW–CoR 169.

[69] Raubenheimer, 'Germany', p. 123.   [70] Ibid.

of Appeal.[71] In that case the defendants had manually modified the official telephone books and had scanned only the data on the telephone connections in Germany.[72] The Court held that the 'mere data such as names, addresses, telephone numbers was...not susceptible for copyright protection'.[73]

The Directive was transposed into German law by the Act on Information and Communication Services of 22 July 1997 which effected amendments to the Law on Copyright and Neighbouring Rights 1965 (as amended). The German legislation makes only minimal changes to copyright law. For example, s. 4(1) concerning compilations has been amended to read now:

Collections of works, data or other independent materials which, by reason of their selection or arrangement, constitute personal intellectual creations (collections) shall enjoy protection as independent works without prejudice to any copyright or neighbouring rights subsisting in individual materials.

This definition of collections is complemented by s. 4(2) which defines a database as a type of collection. A database is defined in s. 4(2) as 'a collection of which the materials are arranged in a systematic or methodical way and are individually accessible with the help of electronic or other means'. Presumably the meaning of 'materials' in this context is 'works, data or other independent materials', the wording used in s. 4(1). The word 'independent' appears in a different place to the Directive, such that 'independent' seems to apply to work, data and other materials whereas in the Directive it may only refer to 'works'. However, it is unlikely that there is a material difference created by the slight difference in the order of words.[74]

The standard of originality for databases is therefore ostensibly the same as it is for copyright works generally. Interestingly, Germany had previously inserted specific provisions regarding the required standard of originality for computer programs in response to the EU Directive on the Legal Protection of Computer Software 1993.[75] Yet no specific provisions concerning the required standard for databases have been inserted. The

---

[71] Ibid. 1995 CR 85; 1994 WRP 834; 1994 NJW–CoR 303.
[72] Raubenheimer, 'Germany', p. 123.   [73] Ibid., p. 124.
[74] Section 87a(1) concerning the *sui generis* right adopts precisely the same definition of a database as that contained in the Directive.
[75] OJ No. L290, 24 November 1993. Section 69a of the Law on Copyright and Neighbouring Right 1965 (as amended, 1993) added by Law of 9 June 1993 provided, in s. 69a(3): 'Computer programs shall be protected if they constitute original works in the sense that they are the result of their author's own intellectual creation. No other criteria, particularly of a qualitative or aesthetic nature, shall be applied to determine their eligibility for protection.' Computer programs were also added to the non-exhaustive list of works in s. 2(1).

German Federal Council (*Bundesrat*) has stated[76] that this was unnecessary because the standard of originality concerning computer programs
has already been incorporated into German copyright law[77] and accepted
by German courts.[78] Hertz-Eichenrode has suggested that the standard
of originality in German law is not uniform but is construed according to
the work in question.[79] For example, he states that: 'For literary, artistic
or musical works, a lower creative level may be sufficient; for the shape
of products, a high level of creativity is required.'[80] Given this, it may be
that there is an expectation that German courts will apply the express
test of originality in the modified s. 4, by reference to the objectives and
wording of the Directive. In any event, the issue highlights the difficulties
of actually applying the relevant standard of originality, and the likeli-
hood that *sui generis* protection will usually be relied upon rather than
copyright protection.[81] Nevertheless, a medical lexicon has been held to
be a database protected by copyright due to the effort in structuring the
database.[82]

German copyright law contains a number of exceptions, some of which
have been modified to comply with the Directive's approach to exceptions
to copyright protection of databases. The major relevant provision in this
context is s. 53. It permits private copies of non-electronic databases.[83]

An exception also exists for reproduction for personal scientific use to
the extent that such reproduction is not made for commercial purposes.[84]
Unlike the Belgian provisions, this exception is limited to the right of
reproduction, rather than reproduction and other rights. Exceptions for
teaching purposes are made in a number of different provisions. Section
46 permits reproduction and distribution of limited parts of works if
they are incorporated in a collection of materials by different authors.
The collection must be intended for religious, school or instructional
use. For example, this could include the taking of different contents of a
database where copyright in the individual contents is owned by different
authors. Interestingly, the contemplated reproduction and distribution is
not limited to illustration for the purposes of teaching, and is presumably
justified on the grounds that it is one of the traditional exceptions to

[76] *Bundesrats-Drucksache* 966/96, 45.
[77] Copyright Act s. 69(a) UrhG: s. 69a(3) reads: 'Computer programs shall be protected if
they constitute original works in the sense that they are the result of their author's own
intellectual creation. No other criteria, particularly of a qualitative or aesthetic nature,
shall be applied to determine their eligibility for protection.'
[78] Supreme Court, GRUR 1994, p. 39, Buchhaltungsprogramm.
[79] Hertz-Eichenrode, 'Germany', at Ger-18.   [80] Ibid.
[81] See Leistner, 'Legal Protection of Telephone Directories', at 951–5 for a discussion of
ongoing difficulties with the German standard of originality.
[82] *Medizinisches Lexicon Landgericht* Hamburg 12 July 2000.
[83] Section 53(1), (5).   [84] Section 53(2) (para. 1), (5).

copyright permitted by Article 6 of the Directive. The authors of the parts of the works incorporated into these collections are entitled to equitable remuneration.[85]

Section 53(3) also permits copying of small parts of a printed work or individual articles in newspapers or periodicals, for use in teaching in non-commercial educational institutions or vocational education institutions in a quantity required for one school class, to the extent necessary. The reference to printed work, newspapers or periodicals suggest this exception is aimed at non-electronic material, although its wording leaves open the possibility of encompassing newspapers or periodicals in electronic form. The exceptions created by s. 53(1)–(3) are supported by provisions in s. 54a designed to provide equitable remuneration to the authors of those works reproduced via those exceptions. This is done by payments from manufacturers or importers of photocopiers or similar devices.

There are numerous other general exceptions to copyright. For example, s. 45 provides an exception for the purposes of proceedings before a court, arbitration tribunal or public authority. Other exceptions exist in relation to use of newspaper articles and other articles from journals relating to political, economic or religious issues of the day.[86] It is also permissible to reproduce, distribute and publicly communicate miscellaneous information relating to facts or news of the day which have been publicly disseminated by the press or by broadcasting.[87] It is also permissible to quote passages from a work after its publication.[88]

Finally, s. 55a implements Article 6(1) of the Directive concerning acts by a lawful user that are necessary for the purposes of obtaining access to the database. The provision deals with tangible copies of databases and databases provided on-line. The owner of a copy of a database that has been put into circulation by way of sale by the author or with their consent may take necessary steps to gain access to the database. Similarly, any other person entitled to make use of that copy in some way may also take necessary steps to gain access to the database. Presumably, this would include people who are successors in title to the original purchaser of the database. If the database has only been made available pursuant to a contract with the author or someone who has the author's consent, only those entitled by the contract to gain access may take steps to ensure access to the database. This latter aspect of s. 55a would apply to on-line databases where a licence to gain access is granted but a copy of the database is not sold to the database user.

---

[85] Section 47(4).
[86] Section 49(1) of the Law on Copyright and Neighbouring Rights 1965 (Germany).
[87] Section 49(2).   [88] Section 51(2).

Unfair competition laws

In addition to copyright law, databases could receive protection under the German Act Against Unfair Competition 1909.[89] Section 1 of this law Gesetz gegen den unlauteren Wettbewerb – (UWG) provides that:

> Any person who, in the course of business activity for purposes of competition, commits acts contrary to honest practices, may be enjoined from these acts and held liable for damages.

This provision can confer additional protection on intellectual property provided a breach of 'good morals' has been established.[90] However, unfair competition actions can be pre-empted by intellectual property legislation.[91] Consequently, the plaintiff must be able to identify some element of the defendant's conduct that is not within the scope of, in this case, copyright legislation.[92] Slavish imitation in the form of direct or identical copying will usually meet this requirement as being a breach of good morals and going beyond the scope of copyright, because there is no creative effort on the part of the defendant.[93] If the defendant has created their own database by modifying the plaintiff's database in some significant manner, this would probably obviate an action for unfair competition.

In addition, s. 1 of the Act Against Unfair Competition 1909 will only apply if the plaintiff and defendant are in competition.[94] Hence, gaining access to a database and using it for personal purposes will not be unfair competition. There would need to be some commercial exploitation of the database that competed directly with the plaintiff.

The net result of this requirement is that it is possible but difficult to rely on unfair competition to prevent appropriation of a database. The application of these principles is demonstrated in two cases concerning telephone directories. In a case before the Hamburg District Court[95] the Court found that the defendant had committed unfair competition in creating its own electronic telephone book by downloading from the plaintiff's electronic directory. There had been identical reproduction and the defendant was selling its electronic directory in direct competition with the plaintiff's electronic directory. A similar result was reached

---

[89] Act against Unfair Competition 1909 (*Gesetz gegen den unlauteren Wettbewerb*, (*UWG*)).
[90] Kamperman Sanders, *Unfair Competition Law*, p. 57.   [91] Ibid.
[92] See the discussion in Chapter 5, concerning pre-emption under American law.
[93] Kamperman Sanders, *Unfair Competition Law*, pp. 57–8. See also B. Steckler, 'Unfair Trade Practices under German Law: Slavish Imitation of Commercial and Industrial Activities' (1996) 7 *European Intellectual Property Review* 390.
[94] J. Mehrings, 'Wettbewerbsrechtlicher Schutz von Online-Datenbanken' [1990] *Computer und Recht* 305, 307 at 308.
[95] 1994 CR 476; 1994 NJW-CoR 170. The Court did not express an opinion on the copyright aspects of the claim.

124   Transposition of the Directive

in the Higher Regional Court of Karlsruhe[96] although in that case, the copying had been done manually. In contrast, the Frankfurt Court of Appeal rejected a claim of unfair competition in the same case where it rejected the claim for breach of copyright that was discussed above. The defendant had not engaged in identical reproduction of the plaintiff's directory, as it had added its own information and deleted various parts of the plaintiff's telephone book such as advertisements. This required a considerable investment of time and money on the part of the defendants. In addition, the plaintiff's book was in hardcopy form, whereas the defendant's directory was on a CD. Consequently, it was not in direct competition with the plaintiff's book. For these reasons, the action for unfair competition was not successful. On the other hand, the scanning of a telephone directory onto a CD has been held to constitute unfair competition, as well as a breach of the database right.[97]

Sui generis *protection*

The *sui generis* provisions of the German Law on Copyright and Neighbouring Rights 1965 (as amended) take the form of a new Chapter VI in Part II which deals with neighbouring rights.

The maker of a database is the person who effects the relevant investment in its creation.[98] One German decision has held that a website consisting of a collection of web pages can qualify as a database, subject to *sui generis* protection.[99] However as 'advertisements were published on the web site on commission, the plaintiff was held not to be the entity bearing the commercial risk, [and] therefore could not be considered the database maker'.[100] In contrast, where a plaintiff commissioned another company to develop a database, the plaintiff was held to be a maker because it had effected the relevant investment in creation.[101]

The relevant investment is the qualitative and/or quantatitive investment in the obtaining, verifying or presenting of the database contents.[102] This flows from the definition of a database in s. 87(a)(1) which adopts the definition in Article 7 of the Directive. In the *Baumarkt.de* case,[103] the court held that while a website may constitute a database of the individual web pages, the plaintiff had not demonstrated a substantial investment in the construction, maintenance or display of the data. On the other hand,

---

[96] *OLG Karlsruhe* [1997] NJW 262.
[97] *Tele-Info-Cd* Bundesgerichtshof (Federal Supreme Court) 6 May, 1999.
[98] Section 87a(2).   [99] *Baumarkt.de Oberlandesgericht* Dusseldorf 19 June 1999.
[100] Hugenholtz, 'The New Database Right', at 9.
[101] C Net Kammergetich (Court of Appeal) Berlin 9 June 2000.   [102] Section 87a(1).
[103] *Baumarkt.de Oberlandesgericht*.

the collection of 251 hyperlink texts to various Internet sites relating to childcare in circumstances where the plaintiff had examined the individual sites and made a considered decision as to whether to include the site in its database of web links, has been held to be a substantial investment in a database.[104]

The rights of database makers are described as the rights to 'reproduce, distribute and communicate to the public the database as a whole or a qualitatively or quantitatively substantial part of the database'.[105] The terminology used is therefore identical to the terminology used in s. 15 in respect of the rights of copyright owners. The rights are also subject to exhaustion upon first sale of a database within the EU and the public lending of databases.[106] White pages of a telephone directory have been held to constitute a database, and scanning of the directory onto a CD-ROM as an infringement of the database right.[107]

A number of German decisions have involved search engines that have found on-line databases and automatically forwarded extracts from those databases to users of the search engine. For example, one decision involved a search engine that routinely forwarded real estate advertisements to users. The advertisements were reproduced in full and acknowledged their source. However, the activities of the search engine constituted repeated and systematic re-utilisation of insubstantial parts of the database. The search engine also by-passed advertisements (other than the real estate advertisements) on the original website, and this was the primary cause of the plaintiff's damage.[108]

Right to extract or re-utilise an insubstantial part The reproduction, distribution or communication to the public of insubstantial parts of a database is guaranteed by s. 87e. The right to do this is conferred in the same way that the right to take steps to access a database that would otherwise infringe copyright in a database is conferred by s. 55a. In the case of databases that have been put into circulation with the maker's consent, any owner of such a copy may reproduce, distribute or communicate to the public insubstantial parts. Similarly, a person entitled in any other way to make use of the database may do so. In the case of on-line databases, any person who has access to it pursuant to a contract formed with the maker or the maker's authority may take similar action. Contractual provisions to the contrary are invalid.

[104] *Kidnet/Babynet Landgericht* Koln 25 August 1999.   [105] Section 87b(1).
[106] Section 87b.   [107] *Tele-Info-Cd.*
[108] Hugenholtz, 'The New Database Right', at 9. See also the decision in *Berlin Onlin Landgericht*, Berlin 8 October 1998, a case involving similar facts and *Baumarkt.de Oberlandesgericht* (Court of Appeal) Dusseldorf 29 June 1999.

Exceptions   The exception for private copying of non-electronic databases is contained in s. 87(c)(1).

The equivalent of Article 9(a) of the Directive concerning extraction for scientific research and illustration for teaching is contained in s. 87(c)(1), second and third paragraphs. The exception for scientific research refers to reproduction for personal scientific use. In addition, it is in a self-contained paragraph separated from the reference to reproduction for use for illustration for teaching. This eliminates the possibility that the use for scientific research is limited to illustration for scientific research.

Reproduction, distribution and communication to the public for use in proceedings before a court, arbitration tribunal or authority or for the purposes of public security is permitted by section 87(c)(2).

Term of protection   The fifteen-year term of protection is conferred by s. 87(d). This is supplemented by s. 87(a)(1) which deems a new database to have been created if the contents of an existing database have been substantially amended.

Ireland

Copyright protection before and after transposition

Prior to the implementation of the Directive, copyright protection for databases flowed from the general protection of literary works under the Irish Copyright Act 1963. Article 2 of that legislation defined a literary work as including 'any written table or compilation'. Consequently, the legislative treatment of databases was similar to the approach in the UK, which protected databases as tables or compilations.

The standard of originality for literary works was also similar to that in the UK in that the standard of 'skill, labour and judgement' was applied. While Irish copyright law concerning databases was therefore similar to that of the UK prior to the transposition of the Directive, the transposing legislation operates in a distinctly different manner from that of the UK. A new type of work called an 'original database' has been introduced into the Copyright and Related Rights Act 2000.[109] An original database is defined in Article 2 as a database in any form which, by reason of the selection or arrangement of its contents, constitutes the original intellectual creation of the author. The same article adopts the Directive's definition of a database. Article 17(2)(d) then confers copyright on an

---

[109] See the definition of a work in Article 2.

original database. In this way, original databases are quite clearly delineated from literary works and are a separate work in their own right. A further consequence of this distinction between the two types of works is that general provisions applying to literary works may not apply to original databases. For example, all the fair dealing provisions in Part II, Chapter 6 apply to literary works, but the fair dealing provision in respect of research or private study only applies to non-electronic original databases.

As noted in the previous paragraph, Article 50 permits fair dealing with non-electronic original databases for the purposes of research or private study, but there is no provision at all for fair dealing with electronic databases for research or private study. Article 51 permits fair dealing with works, including original databases, for the purposes of criticism, review or reporting current events.

There is also a generous exception for copying original databases in the course of instruction or of preparation for instruction, although only one copy of the database may be made.[110] Reproduction of 5 per cent of an original database by educational establishments is also permitted, either without charge or pursuant to a statutory licensing scheme.[111] There are also provisions relating to copying by librarians of articles in periodicals and for archiving purposes.[112] There are also various provisions in the legislation permitting copying for the purposes of parliamentary or judicial proceedings,[113] and ensuring access to information that is kept in public registers and records.[114]

The entitlement of a lawful user to undertake steps which are necessary for the purposes of access to, or use of, the contents of the database is contained in Article 83. The person taking those steps is a person 'who has the right to use the database or any part thereof, whether under a licence to undertake any of the acts restricted by the copyright in the original database or otherwise'. The inclusion of the words 'or otherwise' raises the possibility that the provision may apply to a user intending to engage in fair dealing or other conduct falling within the exceptions to copyright protection.

Unfair competition laws

There is no law of unfair competition that would prevent copying in the absence of either confusion or deception being established.

---

[110] Article 53(3), (4). See also Articles 52 and 54 for other exceptions.
[111] Articles 57 and 173.   [112] Articles 59–70.   [113] Article 71.
[114] Articles 72–77.

Sui generis *protection*

The *sui generis* provisions concerning databases are contained in Part V of the legislation. The maker of a database is the person who takes the initiative in obtaining, verifying or presenting the contents of a database and assumes the risk of investing in doing so.[115] The definition of a database is contained in Article 2, and Article 321 confers a database right on a database if there has been a substantial investment in obtaining, verifying or presenting the contents of the database. The acts of extraction and re-utilisation are prohibited without the authority of the database owner, and those terms are defined in accordance with the Directive.[116]

The right to extract or re-utilise an insubstantial part   Article 327 permits lawful users to extract or re-utilise insubstantial parts of the contents of a database. A lawful user means 'any person who, whether under a licence to undertake of the acts restricted by any database right in the database, or otherwise, has a right to use the database'.

Exceptions   Users are not entitled to make a copy of a non-electronic database for private purposes unless the extraction is a fair dealing for the purposes of research or private study.[117] Article 330 permits fair dealing by a lawful user by way of extraction for the purposes of illustration in the course of instruction or of preparation for instruction. For the purposes of that article, educational establishments are included within the meaning of 'lawful user'. However, there is no exception for fair dealing with electronic databases for non-commercial purposes, as permitted by the Directive. Articles 331–336 essentially reproduce the copyright exceptions in respect of administrative and judicial procedures and access to public registers.

Term of protection   Article 325 provides for the required fifteen-year period of protection and the renewal of that period. Retrospective protection from 1 January 1983 for fifteen years from 1 January 1999 is conferred by Schedule 1, Part VI.

Licensing schemes   Many of the provisions concerning licensing schemes for copyright works have been reproduced in respect of the licensing of databases. Where a licensing body establishes a scheme for licensing databases, disputes concerning that scheme can be referred

---

[115] Article 322.   [116] Articles 320 and 324.   [117] Article 329.

to the controller appointed under the legislation to deal with licensing schemes.

Technological protection measures

Ireland is one of the first Member States to implement technological protection measures in accordance with the Copyright Treaty.[118] Those provisions apply to both copyright and the database right,[119] and consequently Ireland is the first Member State to apply technological protection measures to *sui generis* rights, even though it was the penultimate Member State to transpose the Directive.

Article 370 confers rights on rights owners against a person who makes, sells or otherwise commercially deals with, or has in their possession, a protection-defeating device or who offers a service intended to enable persons to circumvent rights protection measures. A protection-defeating device is defined in Article 2 as any device, function or product, the primary purpose or effect of which is to avoid, bypass, remove, deactivate or otherwise circumvent, without authority, any rights protection measure.

Importantly, the provisions concerning circumvention of technological protection measures are clearly subject to the various exceptions to copyright and the database right. Article 374 specifically provides that: 'Nothing in this Chapter shall be construed as operating to prevent any person from undertaking the acts permitted in relation to works protected by copyright', or 'in relation to databases', or from 'undertaking any act of circumvention required to effect such permitted acts'. However, that provision may have to be altered to meet the requirements of the recent EU Copyright Directive.

Article 375 of the legislation also protects rights management information relating to databases.

Italy

Copyright before and after transposition

Article 3 of the Italian Law for the Protection of Copyright and Neighbouring Rights 1961 (as amended) provided specific protection for collections of works:

---

[118] Part VII of the Copyright and Related Rights Act 2000 (Ireland).

[119] Article 2 defines 'rights protection measure' as 'any process, treatment, mechanism or system which is designed to prevent or inhibit the unauthorised exercise of any of the rights conferred by this Act'.

Collective works formed by the assembling of works, or part of works, and possessing the character of a self-contained creation resulting from selection and coordination with a specific literary, scientific, didactic, religious, political or artistic aim, such as encyclopedias, dictionaries, anthologies, magazines and newspapers shall be protected as original works, independently of and without prejudice to any copyright subsisting in the constituent works or parts thereof.

Article 7 still provides that the author of a collective work is deemed to be the person who organises and directs its creation.

Article 2 is supplemented by specific provisions concerning the required standard of originality. Prior to the transposition of the Directive, Italian copyright law protected: 'Works of the mind having a creative character and belonging to literature, music, figurative arts, architecture, theatre or cinematography, whatever their mode or form of expression.'[120]

The requirement of creativity is confirmed by Article 6, that states:

Copyright shall be acquired on the creation of a work that constitutes the particular expression of an intellectual effort.

Databases are now specifically protected under Articles 1 and 2 of the Law on Copyright and Neighbouring Rights 1961 (as amended). Hence, Article 1 now specifically refers to 'databases which by reason of the selection or arrangement of their contents constitute the author's own intellectual creation'. In addition, databases have been added to the inclusive list in Article 2 of subject matter that is protected by copyright. A database is defined as 'collections of independent works, data or other materials arranged in a systematic or methodical way and individually accessible by electronic or other means'.

Ownership of copyright in a database vests in an employer if an employee creates the database in the course of his or her duties.[121] The rights of owners of the copyright in databases are set out in Article 64 *quinquies*. The specific reference to databases without alteration to the provisions concerning collective works may create some difficulties. For example, the owner of the rights in a collective work is the publisher of the work,[122] and authors of individual contributions to a collective work are entitled to reproduce their contribution to a collective work.[123] The relationship between these provisions and the specific provisions concerning databases is not clear, especially as a database would seem to be simply a type of collective work. For example, magazines and newspapers fall within the definition of a collective work and may also fall within the definition of a database.

---

[120] Article 1 of Law for the Protection of Copyright and Neighbouring Rights, Law No. 633 of 22 April 1941 as amended.
[121] Article 12*ter*.   [122] Article 38.   [123] Article 42.

The rights of the author of a database and the exceptions to those rights are included in a new Section VII, Article 64(6). They include access to, or use of, databases for the sole purpose of teaching or scientific research. This exception does not extend to permanent reproduction in another medium, suggesting that it may be limited to the actual act of viewing a database rather than reproducing a substantial part of it in a permanent form. The use of a database for the purposes of public security or an administrative or judicial procedure is permitted by Article 64(6) – 1(b).

The right of a lawful user to take steps to gain access to a database is provided by Article 64(6) (2) and (3). However, no definition of a lawful user is provided in the legislation.

Other general exceptions to copyright also apply to databases. For example, Article 68 permits the reproduction of single works for the reader's personal use when made by hand, or by a means of reproduction unsuitable for marketing or disseminating the work in public. It also permits the photocopying of works available in libraries when made for personal use. It is the equivalent of the exception of reproduction for personal use of non-electronic databases. Article 69 also permits public lending and Article 70 permits reproduction of part of a work for criticism, discussion or for instruction purposes, provided that they do not conflict with the commercial exploitation of the work. In addition, Article 101 permits the reproduction of information and news, 'provided it is not effected by way of acts which are contrary to fair practice in journalism'. That provision is discussed in more detail in the section dealing with unfair competition.

Unfair competition laws

The copyright and neighbouring rights legislation contains a number of provisions that are referred to as 'Prohibitions of Certain Acts of Unfair Competition'. In particular, Article 101 deals with the reproduction of information and news. It provides that:

> The reproduction of information and news shall be lawful, provided it is not effected by way of acts which are contrary to fair practice in journalism, and provided the source is given.

Certain practices are then deemed to constitute unfair practice, including reproducing or broadcasting information bulletins within sixteen hours of their original distribution.[124] Similarly, Article 101(b) deems to be unfair 'the systematic reproduction of published or broadcast information or news, with gainful intent, by newspapers or other periodicals or

---

[124] Article 101(a).

by broadcasting organizations'. These provisions are a quite specific en-
actment of unfair competition principles similar to the American tort of
misappropriation of hot news that is discussed in Chapter 5.

In addition to these provisions, Article 2598 of the Civil Code 1942
contains a general clause prohibiting business conduct that is likely to
damage someone else's goodwill.[125] Kamperman Sanders states that,
while there is a growing body of law concerning this general principle
of unfair competition, its relationship to principles of pre-emption and
intellectual property regimes is not entirely clear.[126] As a general rule,
there must be direct competition between the plaintiff and the defendant
in an unfair competition action, although 'actions for infringement and
unfair competition may be brought concurrently on the basis of the same
facts'.[127] Slavish imitation of products may constitute unfair competition
if the defendant had a clear intention to copy.[128] Most of the case law in
this regard has applied to imitation of designs of products or unregistered
trade marks.[129] However, the law may also apply to the slavish imitation
of databases.[130]

Sui generis *protection*

The *sui generis* protection of databases has been incorporated via the creation of a new Part II *bis*. The maker of a database is defined as someone
who makes a substantial investment in the creation of a database or in
verifying or presenting it. The investment may include the deployment
of financial resources and/or expending time and effort.

No separate definition of a database is provided in the *sui generis* provisions. Consequently, the relevant definition is contained in Article 2(9).
Similarly, the exceptions that are specifically provided for in respect of
databases in section VII would also be exceptions to the *sui generis* rights.

The maker of a database has the right of extraction and re-utilisation,
and those terms are defined in the same way that they are defined in Article 7(2) of the Directive. Public lending is excluded from the definitions
of extraction and re-utilisation.[131]

[125] Kamperman Sanders, *Unfair Competition Law*, p. 49.   [126] Ibid.
[127] Ibid., p. 50.
[128] *Instituto Geografico De Agostini SpA* v. *Gruppo Editorial Bramante Sri*, Court of Milan,
16 February 1995, Riv. dir. ind. 1995, 1009.
[129] M. Franzosi, 'The Legal Protection of Industrial Design: Unfair Competition as a Basis
of Protection' (1990) 5 *European Intellectual Property Review* 154; G. Jacobacci, 'Italian
Trademark Law and Practice and the Protection of Product and Packaging' (1983) 74
Trade Mark Reporter 418.
[130] *BN Marconi Srl* v. *Marchi & Marchi SRL.*, Court of Genoa, 19 June 1993, 1994 Foro
Italiano Part 1, 2559.
[131] Article 102*bis*.

The right to extract or re-utilise an insubstantial part   A lawful user of a database that has been made available to the public may extract or re-utilise insubstantial parts of the database. There is no indication as to who is a lawful user.

Exceptions   There is no express provision concerning copying of non-electronic databases for private purposes. However Article 68, which deals with reproduction of single works for personal use by various means including photocopying, probably applies to the right of extraction and re-utilisation.

Similarly, there is no express exception to the right of extraction and re-utilisation for the purposes of illustration for teaching or research. However, unlike the provisions dealing with reproduction for personal use, Article 64*sexiens* (a) would not appear to be applicable as it is expressed to be an exception to the rights of the author of a database, not the maker of a database. Consequently, the exception is not applicable to the *sui generis* right. The same situation applies in relation to use for purposes of public security, or an administrative or judicial procedure.

The Netherlands

Copyright before and after transposition of databases prior to the Directive

Prior to the implementation of the Directive, Article 10 of the Copyright Act 1912 contained a non-exclusive list of items that received copyright protection. Article 10(12), second paragraph provided protection for 'collections of different works'. The standard of originality has been described as not being very high,[132] namely that the condition of originality is met if it must be considered impossible that the work in question can be created by two persons independently.[133] Dutch copyright law 'has traditionally protected non-original writings' such as compilations of data in alphanumerical form.[134] A database containing the full texts of a large number of laws and treaties did not receive copyright protection in at least one Dutch case, but that was primarily attributable to Article 11 of

---

[132] K. Limperg, 'Netherlands' in Campbell, *World Intellectual Property Rights and Remedies.*
[133] Ibid., p. 10.
[134] Hugenholtz, 'The New Database Right', at 13. See also, B. Hugenholtz, 'Copyright and Databases, Report on the Netherlands' in M. Dellebeke (ed.), *Copyright in Cyberspace, ALAI Study Days 1996* (Amsterdam, 1997), p. 491. See also *KPN* v. *Denda International and Ors.*, District Court Almelo, 6 December 2000, where copyright was held to subsist in a telephone directory prior to the implementation of the Directive and the new database right applied to reproduction after the implementation of the Directive.

the Dutch Copyright Act which provides that laws and regulations are in the public domain.[135]

Article 10 has been amended to implement the Directive's requirements concerning copyright protection of databases. The reference in Article 10 to 'collections of different works' has been deleted and replaced by a reference to 'collections of works, data or other independent elements which are arranged systematically or methodically, and which are accessible through electronic media or other means'. The new provision does not expressly require that the database be an intellectual creation, suggesting that the existing originality stipulations meet this requirement.

Lawful database users may replicate them where it is necessary to gain access to the material or for the normal use of the collection.[136] Private copying of non-electronic databases for private practice, study or use is permitted by Article 16(b), first paragraph. Article 16 provides an exception for use as illustrations for teaching purposes. There is no express exception in respect of use for research purposes. There is an exception in Article 17(1), but it is restricted to works pursuant to Article 10(1) which refers to literary works but does not include databases.

A similar position exists in relation to the exception for public security. An exception already existed in Article 16(b)(5) in respect of reproduction for judicial or administrative proceedings. An exception in respect of the performance of tasks with which institutions serving the general interest have been charged, and for the purposes of the public service, also exists in Article 16(b)(6). However, this is restricted to the works described in Article 10, first paragraph, namely books, pamphlets, newspapers, periodicals and all other writings, and does not seem to apply to databases.

The copyright legislation also provides for a number of other exceptions. These include various provisions for the purposes of news reporting.[137] Public lending is also permissible subject to the payment of equitable remuneration.[138] Even that requirement is waived for educational and research institutes and various other organisations.[139]

Unfair competition laws

Article 6:162(2) in Book 6 on the law of obligations of the Civil Code 1992 makes it a tort to infringe a right by acting contrary to what is,

---

[135] *Koninklijke Vermande BV* v. *Bojkovski*, 98/147 Court Decision of 20 March 1998 (District Court of The Hague).
[136] Article 24a of the Copyright Act.   [137] Articles 15 and 16a of the Copyright Act.
[138] Article 15c of the Copyright Act.   [139] Article 15c(2) and (3) of the Copyright Act.

under unwritten law, proper behaviour in society.[140] This provision prohibits conduct that causes confusion.[141] It can also be relied upon to
prevent the taking of 'inappropriate advantage of the results of the efforts of competitors'.[142] Hence, in some circumstances commercial appropriation of the results of another's labour, skill and money may be
prohibited.[143]

Sui generis *protection*

The *sui generis* provisions are contained in the Database Act 1999. The
maker of a database is the person who bears the risk of the investment
made in the database.[144] The relevant investment is a substantial one,
evaluated qualitatively or quantitatively in the obtaining, verification or
presentation of the contents.[145] There have been conflicting decisions
about the relevant activities that count as the required investment. A
number of decisions have considered the argument that if the database
is simply a by-product or spin-off of the main commercial activities
undertaken by the database owner, then the investment in the database
may not be sufficient to justify *sui generis* protection. For example, in one
case the preparation of radio broadcasting listings was not considered to
constitute the required investment,[146] because the listings were merely a
by-product or spin-off of the running of the broadcasting business and
no substantial investment was made in the listing itself, as opposed to the
programmes that were listed. Consequently, the preparation of a radio
broadcast timetable that combined the listings of several channels did not
infringe the *sui generis* rights of the individual channels.

A similar approach was taken in a case concerning a website providing hyperlinks to the plaintiff's newspaper articles. The defendant's website contained the headlines of individual articles and readers
could click on the headline to take them directly to the article at the
relevant newspaper's website. The court held that the headlines were
a by-product of newspaper publishing and did not reflect a substantial investment by themselves.[147] In addition, the employment of seven

[140] Kamperman Sanders, *Unfair Competition Law*, p. 33.
[141] *Lego v. Oku Hobby Speelgoed BV/Frits de Vrites Agenturen BV Lima Srl*, President District
     Court of Utrecht, 10 September 1998.
[142] Kamperman Sanders, *Unfair Competition Law*, p. 34.
[143] Kamperman Sanders, *Unfair Competition Law*, p. 35.
[144] Article 1(b) of the Database Law.   [145] Article 1(a) of the Database Law.
[146] *NV Holdingmaatschappij de Telegraf v. Nederlandes Omroep Stichting*, The Court of
     Appeal of The Hague 99/165, 30 January 2001.
[147] *Algemeen Dagblad and Others v. Eureka President*, District Court of Rotterdam, 22 August
     2000. The defendant's website of http://www.kranten.com. is still operating.

people by the newspaper in maintaining its website was neglible compared to the total number of employees of the newspaper. Consequently, there was no substantial investment in the collection of the list of headlines.

In another case, the Dutch Court of Appeal held that a database of details of real estate available for sale was not the product of a substantial investment. The database was produced by various real estate agents contributing their listings to the database. The database was created primarily for use by those real estate agents in their work but it was also made publicly available via the Internet. The Court held that the creation of the database was merely a by-product of the principal activities of the relevant real estate agents.[148] On appeal, this decision was reversed by the Dutch Supreme Court.[149] It found that the Court of Appeal had attempted to determine the investment in the database for different purposes and to require a substantial investment for each of those purposes. Consequently, the Court of Appeal disregarded the investment in the creation of the database for the work purposes of the real estate agents in determining whether there had been a substantial investment for the purposes of presenting the information in the database to the public. The Supreme Court rejected that approach on the grounds that neither the Directive nor Dutch legislation justified it and that there would be substantial problems in delineating between the different types of investment. Nevertheless, it did not reject the spin-off argument *per se.*

On the other hand, the argument that a white pages telephone directory was merely a by-product of an existing investment by the telephone company in its general operations was rejected in other case law.[150] The defendant's electronic search engine provided access to an on-line directory but by-passed the advertising placed on the originating site.[151]

The right to extract or re-utilise an insubstantial part   The use of an insubstantial part of a database by a lawful user is permitted by Article 3(1). No definition of a lawful user is given in the legislation, and there have been some conflicting decisions on the meaning of a substantial part. For example, the decision in the case discussed above concerning linking to newspaper websites suggested that the headlines of newspaper articles are not a substantial part of the newspaper database, as they do

---

[148] *NVM* v. *De Telegraaf*, Court of Appeal, The Hague, 21 December 2000.
[149] *NVM* v. *De Telegraaf*, Supreme Court, The Hague, 22nd March 2001.
[150] *KPN* v. *Denda International*, Court of Appeal Arnhem, 15 April 1997.
[151] *KPN* v. *XSO*, President District Court of The Hague, 14 January 2000.

not constitute a substantial part of the investment in the publication of the newspapers. In contrast, in the first instance decision in *NVM* v. *De Telegraaf*, the case concerning real estate listings as discussed above,[152] the court held that 'even the extraction of small amounts of data would qualify as substantial extraction, since just a few data might be of great value to end users'.[153] A similar argument was accepted in a UK decision of *British Horseracing Board* v. *William Hill* which is discussed in the section of this chapter concerning the UK.

Reference to repeated and systematic extraction or re-utilisation of insubstantial parts of a database was also made in *Algemeen Dagblad BV* v. *Eureka*.[154] This case, which involved the reproduction of lists of newspaper headlines and linking to the relevant articles, was discussed in the previous section concerning the necessary investment to acquire the database right. The court held that even if the relevant database were the plaintiff's website consisting of the relevant articles, the defendant had not taken a substantial part of that database by reproducing the headlines. The taking of this insubstantial part on a daily basis did not conflict with the normal exploitation of the database. In the court's view, there was no evidence that the linking to the actual articles, as opposed to the home page of the plaintiff, caused any significant damage. On the contrary, it had a promotional effect, and the plaintiff could avoid any damage by ensuring that advertising was placed on the same page as the actual articles rather than its home page.

Exceptions   Reproduction for private purposes of non-electronic databases is permitted in Article 5(a). Article 5(b) permits extraction for purposes of illustration for teaching or for scientific research. Article 5(c) permits extraction or re-utilisation for administrative or judicial procedures or public security. In addition, a public authority does not have any rights in respect of a database of laws, rulings and provisions enacted by it, or by judicial verdicts and administrative decisions.[155] In addition, public authorities have no rights in databases which they make unless the rights are expressly reserved.

Term of protection   The fifteen-year period of protection is provided for in Article 6. A new database resulting from a new investment in substantial changes gives rise to a new period of protection.

---

[152] President District Court of The Hague, 12 September 2000.
[153] Hugenholtz, 'The New Database Right', at 14.
[154] *Algemeen Dagblad and Others* v. *Eureka President*.   [155] Article 8(1).

Spain

Copyright before and after transposition

Prior to the implementation of the Directive, copyright protection for databases derived from the Spanish Copyright Act 1987 (as amended). Article 12 of the Spanish Copyright Act formerly provided that:

Collections of works of other people, like anthologies, and of other elements or data which by the selection or arrangement of their contents constitute intellectual creations, shall also be the subject of intellectual property within the meaning of this Law.

The requirement of originality is also imposed by Article 10, which provides that the subject matter of intellectual property shall be all original literary, artistic or scientific creations. A modicum of creativity was required in the selection and arrangement of the contents of the compilation.[156]

In order to implement the Directive's provisions concerning copyright protection for databases, Article 12 was amended to provide that:

Intellectual property shall subsist ... in collections of the works of others, or of data or other independent elements, such as anthologies and databases, which, by reason of the selection or arrangement of their contents, constitute intellectual creations, without prejudice to any rights that might subsist in the said contents.
    The protection accorded to such collections under this Article shall relate solely to their structure, meaning the form of expression of the selection or arrangement of their contents, but shall not extend to those contents.

The exceptions to copyright in databases provided for in Article 6(2)(a)–(c) of the Directive concerning private copies of non-electronic databases, use for illustration for teaching and research and use for the purposes of public security or administrative or judicial procedures, are contained within Article 34(2)(a)–(c). The right of a lawful user to take steps to gain access to a database is contained in Article 34(1).

There are a number of other exceptions that apply to copyright generally that may be relevant to copyright in databases, although they may be overriden by the more specific provisions dealing exclusively with databases. For example, Article 31(1) permits the making of private copies, but the limitation of such copying to non-electronic databases in Article 34 suggests that Article 31(1) does not apply to electronic databases.

On the other hand, Article 13 exempts legal and administrative materials from copyright protection, although copyright could still subsist in

---

[156] L. Gimeno, 'Protection of Compilations in Spain and the UK' (1998) 29 IIC 907.

the structure and arrangement of such materials. In addition, Article 35 provides for exceptions in relation to the reporting of current events. In particular, Article 35(1) provides that:

Any work liable to be seen or heard in the reporting of current events may be reproduced, distributed and communicated to the public, but only to the extent justified by the informatory purpose.

Article 37 permits free reproduction and lending in specific establishments. For example, Article 37(1) permits reproduction of works solely for research purposes and without any commercial purpose by 'museums, libraries, record libraries, film libraries, newspaper libraries or archives which are in public ownership or form part of institutions of a cultural or scientific character'. Similarly, Article 37(2) permits the public lending of works.

The extent to which these provisions apply to databases is not entirely clear from the wording of the legislation. A strict reading of the legislation would suggest that the exceptions to copyright in databases extend only to those provided for in Article 34, that reflect the specific exceptions provided for in the Directive. However, this would exclude the general application of any of the other traditional exceptions to copyright that are permitted by Article 6(2)(d) of the Directive.

Unfair competition laws

Spain passed an Unfair Competition Act in 1991. Prior to that there was no tradition of unfair competition.[157] Article 11 of the legislation provides that imitation is free subject to the existence of exclusive rights and two other exceptions. In particular, Article 11(3) provides an action where there is systematic imitation of the products or services of a competitor. Article 11(2) also confers a cause of action when imitation represents the wrongful misappropriation of the reputation or effort of a competitor. The inclusion of the reference to effort in the legislation raises the possibility of its application to the extraction and re-utilisation of the contents of databases.[158]

An example of the application of Article 11 is a decision of the Appeal Court of Barcelona in 1994 where the defendant was prohibited from slavishly copying the plaintiff's self-adhesive tags. This was despite the fact that the plaintiff's patent and design rights had lapsed. The basis of the Court's decision was that consumer confusion may arise due

[157] L. Gimeno, 'News Section: National Reports' (1996) 2 *European Intellectual Property Review* D-49.
[158] Ibid.

to the defendant's tags having the same dimensions and shape but it is unclear whether confusion was a necessary part of the finding of unfair competition.[159]

Sui generis *protection*

The *sui generis* provisions concerning databases have been incorporated in a new Title VIII of Book II concerning 'Other Intellectual Property Rights and Sui Generis Protection of Databases'. The maker of a database is defined as the person who takes the initiative and risk of making the substantial investments for the obtaining, verification or presentation of the contents of the database.[160]

The relevant investment includes investment in the form of finance, time, effort or energy or other means of similar nature expended in either the obtaining, the verification or the presentation of its contents.[161] The formal definition of a database contained in Article 12 also applies to the *sui generis* provisions.[162] A database of case law and legislation has been held to be a database due to the time and effort put into compiling and systematising the material.[163] The rights of extraction and re-utilisation are defined in Articles 133(3)(b) and (c) in the same words used in the Directive.

The right to extract or re-utilise an insubstantial part   Article 134(1) prohibits a database maker from preventing a lawful user from extracting and/or re-utilising insubstantial parts of their database. No definition of a lawful user is provided.

Exceptions   Article 135(a) permits extraction for private purposes of non-electronic databases. Article 135(b) implements the exceptions concerning illustration for teaching and scientific research. Article 135(a) provides the exception in relation to use for public security or an administrative or judicial procedure.

Term of protection   The relevant provisions concerning the term of protection and the renewal of that protection as a consequence of any

---

[159] Ibid.
[160] Article 133(3)(a) of the Consolidated Text of the Law on Intellectual Property, Law No. 22/1987 of 11 November 1987.
[161] Article 133(1).   [162] Ibid.
[163] *Editorial Aranzadi*, Court of First Instance Elda 2 July 1999.

substantial change to the contents of the database are contained in Article 136. The retrospective effect of protection is provided by paragraph 16 of the transitional provisions of the legislation.

Sweden

Copyright before and after transposition

Prior to the Directive, some compilations, including some databases, received copyright protection as a literary work.[164] In addition, Sweden provided specific protection for 'A catalogue, a table or another similar production in which a large number of information items have been compiled' for a period of ten years. Such catalogues were subject to relevant copyright exceptions.[165]

While there are no specific provisions concerning originality, the Swedish copyright legislation gives protection to anyone who has 'created a literary or artistic work'.[166] The existence of the catalogue protection provision in itself indicates that mere sweat of the brow was and is not sufficient to meet the requirements of originality.

There have been almost no changes to Swedish copyright law, reflecting a belief that the existing law already met the Directive's requirements in relation to databases. Section 26(b) has been amended to provide that 'copyright does not prevent a work from being used in the interests of the administration of justice or public safety'. In addition, s. 21 has been amended to provide that, while published works may be reproduced for teaching or for a religious service, that exception no longer applies to teaching for a commercial purpose.

Swedish copyright law contains generous exceptions and these exceptions have been maintained, presumably on the basis that they constitute traditional exceptions to copyright. For example, reproduction is permitted for private purposes[167] and reprographic reproduction for educational purposes is permitted.[168] So too is reproduction by libraries and archives for certain purposes,[169] as is use of documents presented to public authorities and in public debates on public matters.[170] Various other provisions permit copying of documents prepared by Swedish public authorities.[171]

---

[164] Article 1, Act on Copyright in Literary and Artistic Works (Sweden), Law No. 729 of 1960 (as amended).
[165] Article 49.   [166] Article 1.   [167] Article 12.   [168] Articles 13 and 18.
[169] Article 16.   [170] Article 26.   [171] E.g. Article 26a.

Unfair competition laws

The Market Practices Act 1996 prohibits acts of improper marketing but the emphasis of that legislation is on the prevention of confusion rather than parasitic behaviour.[172]

Sui generis protection

The *sui generis* provisions in the Swedish legislation are undoubtedly the most minimalist provisions of any Member State. Sweden made a small amendment of Article 49 to provide now that 'a catalogue, table or other such work in which a large amount of data has been compiled or which is the result of a substantial investment has the exclusive right to produce copies of the work and make it accessible to the public'. In addition, the period of protection has been extended from ten years to fifteen years.

No other changes have been made. In particular, the broad exceptions to copyright also apply to this amended version of the catalogue protection rules. This approach is apparently justified by Recital 52 of the Directive which permits those Members States which have specific rules providing for a right comparable to the *sui generis* right to retain their traditional exceptions to that right. As the catalogue rules certainly constitute such a comparable right, there is an argument that the exceptions in the Swedish copyright legislation may therefore apply to the slightly amended catalogue rules. However, some EU officials have questioned whether Recital 52 provides a basis for the broad exceptions that are contained in the Swedish legislation and the legislation of other Nordic states.[173]

Partly as a consequence of this approach to transposition, Swedish courts have adopted the same approach to the interpretation of the amended catalogue laws as they did to the original catalogue laws. For example, in *Fixtures Marketing Ltd* v. *AB Svenska Spel*,[174] the Gotland City Court declined to find infringement of the plaintiff's football fixture lists, despite the fact that a very large amount of information had been taken from that list. The defendant was a gambling house that used about

---

[172] Kamperman Sanders, *Unfair Competition Law*, p. 68.

[173] C. Auinger, 'Implementation of the Database Legislation in the EU and Plans for Review', paper presented at a workshop conducted by the ICSU, Baveno, 14 October 2000.

[174] T 99–99, 11 April 2001. See the discussion of this case in C. Colston, 'Sui Generis Database Right: Ripe for Review?' (2001) 3 *Journal of Information, Law and Technology*; and J. Gaster, 'European Sui Generis Right for Databases' (2001) 3 *Computer Und Recht International* 74.

90 per cent of the games stated in the plaintiff's list for the purposes of its gambling activities.

The defendant put forward two defences. The first was the by-product or spin-off argument that has been accepted in the Netherlands. It argued that the major investment of the plaintiff was in planning and organising a football competition. Consequently, the compilation of a fixture list was merely a by-product of that activity. This argument was rejected on the grounds that there had still been a substantial investment in creating the fixture list.

The defendant's second argument was that protection under the amended catalogue laws did not extend to the underlying information, but was restricted to reprinting or copying the information in the same or similar compilation. This argument was accepted and, as the defendant had not engaged in literal copying, the plaintiff's case failed even though the defendant had obtained the information about the football matches from the plaintiff's database.

United Kingdom

Copyright before and after transposition

Prior to the implementation of the Directive, protection was given to databases as compilations, a type of literary work.[175] The standard of originality for copyright protection under UK law prior to the transposition of the Directive was low, and it remains so, except for databases. The standard of originality has only been altered in respect of databases.[176] It is not entirely clear how low the requisite standard for copyright works generally is, and whether it embraces mere sweat of the brow without any trace of intellectual creativity. The legislation, both past and present, is not clear. It merely refers to works being original without providing a definition of originality. The case law applying that requirement is ambiguous. Many judgments refer to the need for an author to exercise skill, labour and/or judgement. No case law makes reference to the more American term of 'sweat of the brow'. There is no clear authoritative statement that the exercise of considerable labour is sufficient in itself to confer copyright protection, and that therefore the sweat of the brow doctrine is part of UK copyright law. However, the statement below from Lord Devlin in the House of Lords comes close to stating such a proposition.

---

[175] Section 3 of the Copyright, Designs and Patents Act 1988.
[176] Arguably only for literary databases, not databases that are not literary works, e.g. compilations of sound recordings.

There is copyright in every original literary work, which by definition includes compilations, so that there can be copyright in such productions as timetables and directories, provided always they are 'original'. The requirement of originality means that the product must originate from the author in the sense that it is the result of a substantial degree of skill, *industry* or experience employed by him. [emphasis added][177]

In contrast, there is authority that there is no copyright in information and other formulations of originality refer to both skill and labour:

Copyright can only be claimed in the composition or language which is chosen to express the information or the opinion ... where the facts are presented in some special way, it then becomes a question of fact and degree as to whether the skill and labour involved in such special representation of the information is entitled to copyright.[178]

The consensus of opinion amongst academic writers is that the standard of originality under UK copyright law is either a sweat of the brow standard, or one very close to it in which sweat of the brow, coupled with a very small amount of creativity, will be sufficient.[179]

The Directive has been implemented by The Copyright and Rights in Databases Regulations 1997 (the UK Regulations).[180] The UK Regulations are regulations associated with the Copyright, Designs and Patents Act 1988 and they amend various provisions of the legislation dealing with copyright. They also provide for various regulations concerning *sui generis* protection of databases. Regulation 6 inserts a new section 3A that contains a definition of a database adopting the Directive's definition.

One difficulty with the provision of copyright protection to a compilation was that its inclusion within the definition of a literary work presented, and still presents, the difficulty that compilations that do not qualify as literary works do not receive copyright protection.[181] For example, a compilation of dramatic or musical works would not be a literary work and hence would be unprotected, as would a collection of three-dimensional items that are not written or represented in written form.[182]

---

[177] *Ladbroke (Football) Ltd* v. *William Hill (Football) Ltd* [1964] 1 WLR 273.

[178] *Football League Ltd* v. *Littlewoods Pools Ltd* [1959] 1 Ch 637 at 651–2.

[179] See Chapter 2 for more case law concerning the sweat of the brow standard for originality.

[180] SI 1997, No. 3032.

[181] C. Rees and S. Chalton (eds.), *Database Law* (Jordans, Bristol, 1998), p. 44. A similar problem exists under Australian copyright law in which only compilations that can be described as literary works receive copyright protection. See A. Monotti, 'The Extent of Copyright Protection for Compilations of Artistic Works' (1993) 15 *European Intellectual Property Review* 156.

[182] Rees and Chalton, *Database Law*, p. 45.

This anomaly does not seem to have been addressed by the UK database regulations when conferring specific protection on databases.

The new s. 3A still refers to a database as a type of literary work, suggesting that databases that cannot be considered to be literary works are not protected. Hence the requirement in the Directive to confer copyright protection on all databases that manifest intellectual creativity in the selection or arrangement of their contents has not been complied with.

Section 3A(2) of the Copyright, Designs and Patents Act 1988 prescribes the level of originality required of literary works consisting of databases in the following terms:

For the purposes of this Part a literary work consisting of a database is original if, and only if, by reason of the selection or arrangement of the contents of the database the database constitutes the author's own intellectual creation.

While adopting the Directive's standard of originality for databases, the Copyright, Designs and Patents Act 1988 and the UK database regulations leave untouched the standard of originality for all other copyright works. In addition, copyright protection is retained for compilations although it is certainly arguable that few, if any, compilations would not be databases given the wide definition of a database in the Directive that has been adopted by s. 3A(1) of the Copyright, Designs and Patents Act 1988.[183] If there are compilations that are not databases, the test for whether copyright subsists in them is the same as it was prior to 1 January 1998.

The general provisions of the legislation concerning exceptions to copyright apply to databases although there are some specific provisions concerning databases. For example, ss. 50D and 296B combine to prohibit the owner of the copyright in a database from preventing a user who has a right to use the database from doing anything necessary for the purposes of access to, and use of, the contents. In this context, a person who has a right to use the database is a person who has such a right 'under a licence to do any of the acts restricted by the copyright in the database or otherwise'.[184] The use of the words 'or otherwise' introduces some ambiguity into the provision as it necessarily includes some other users who do not have a licence to use the database. Those other users may be limited to users of a tangible copy who obtain it from the original purchaser. Alternatively, they may include those who are gaining access for the purposes of fair dealing.

---

[183] One example may be a crossword puzzle.   [184] Section 50D.

The fair dealing provisions have been amended so that fair dealing with databases is permitted for research purposes provided it is not for a commercial purpose.[185] The general fair dealing provisions concerning other works do not require a non-commercial purpose, although that would be relevant to a decision as to whether the use was a fair dealing. There is no specific exception for illustration for teaching. However, there are a number of provisions concerning copying by educational establishments in ss. 32–36. There are also a number of provisions regulating licensing schemes in Chapter VII. Sections 45–50 contain exceptions for the purposes of public administration that equate with the Directive's reference to exceptions for the purposes of public security and administrative and judicial procedures.

There is no general exception in UK copyright law for private copying for personal purposes, and no such exception has been made for non-electronic databases. Numerous other general exceptions are contained throughout the legislation. These include a provision permitting fair dealing for the purposes of criticism, review and news reporting.[186] There are also a number of provisions concerning copying by libraries and archives in ss. 37–44 that may be relevant to databases. For example, s. 38 permits librarians to copy and supply an article in a periodical if they are satisfied that they are supplying a person who requires it for the purposes of research or private study. The specific alterations to the fair dealing provisions concerning databases places an onus on librarians to ensure that fair dealing with a database for research is for non-commercial purposes.

Unfair competition laws

The UK has no law of unfair competition that would be relevant to the issue of protection of databases by either prohibiting the appropriation of the contents of a database or requiring payment of remuneration for the appropriation.[187] This gap in the UK law was offset to a large extent by the low standard of originality that was previously required for copyright protection. While other members of the EU have, or had, high originality standards for copyright, unfair competition law had the potential to deal

---

[185] Section 29(1A)(5).   [186] Section 30.

[187] See, e.g. *Hodgkinson & Corby Ltd and Roho Inc.* v. *Wards Mobility Services Ltd* [1995] FSR 169, *per* Jacob J: 'I turn to consider the law and begin by identifying what is not the law. There is no tort of copying. There is no tort of taking a man's market or customers . . . There is no tort of making use of another's goodwill as such. There is no tort of competition.' See generally, Kamperman Sanders *Unfair Competition Law.*

with some of the difficulties that may have arisen as a consequence of those high standards.

Sui generis *protection*

The maker of a database is defined in Regulation 14. In particular, Regulation 14(1) defines the maker as the person who takes the initiative in obtaining, verifying or presenting the contents of a database and assumes the risk of investing in that obtaining, verification or presentation. This definition introduces the possibility of more than one maker, as one person may initiate the obtaining, verifying or presenting whereas another may assume the risk of the investment.[188] Ownership of the *sui generis* rights vests in an employer, the Crown or the UK Parliament in the same circumstances that copyright vests in employers, the Crown or the UK Parliament.[189]

The definition of a database contained in s. 3A(1) applies for the purposes of both copyright and *sui generis* protection. Regulation 13(1) goes on to provide that *sui generis* protection, described as 'database right' is conferred if a substantial investment has been made in obtaining, verifying or presenting the contents of the database. The decision of Mr Justice Laddie in the *British Horseracing Board Ltd* v. *William Hill Ltd*[190] casts some light on what will constitute a substantial investment and a database for these purposes. In that case, the British Horseracing Board (the Board) objected to William Hill, a bookmaking company, using information about race meetings conducted by the Board in its Internet betting service. William Hill obtained the information from Satellite Information Services Ltd, which held a licence from the Board to transmit much of the Board's data to its subscribers. William Hill then used the information on its Internet betting site to provide punters with details of races and provide an Internet betting service.

Mr Justice Laddie held that the expression 'database had a very wide meaning covering virtually all collections of data in searchable form'[191] which probably includes any collection of data stored in computer memory as software can access and search such collections.[192] In addition, 'the qualifying level of investment is fairly low'[193] although a number of comments were offered about the type of relevant investment. For

---

[188] Regulation 14(5).
[189] Regulation 14(2)–(4); ss. 11, 163 and 165 of the Copyright, Designs and Patents Act of 1988.
[190] HC 2000 1335, judgment of 9 February 2001.   [191] Ibid., at para. 30.
[192] Ibid., at para. 49.   [193] Ibid., at para. 32.

example, 'the effort put into creating the actual data which is subsequently collected together in the database is irrelevant',[194] although it may be difficult to distinguish between that effort and the effort of obtaining or gathering data together.[195] Consequently, the Board's investment in arranging a racing fixture did not constitute relevant investment although gathering all the data concerning races together did. Similarly, investment in verification was relevant to both the initial creation of the right and renewal of the term of protection.[196] As for the relevance of presentation, Mr Justice Laddie noted that it appears that this must cover 'at least the effort and resources put into making the data more readily accessible by the user'.[197] This would include the effort put into the design of the layout of the information and may also include investment in designing computer programs which make the data more readily accessible.[198]

Regulation 16 provides that extraction or re-utilisation of a substantial part of a database constitutes infringement of the database right, and extraction and re-utilisation are defined in Regulation 12(1) in accordance with the wording of the Directive. Extraction includes extracting the information from a source other than the database owner. For example, in the *British Horseracing Board* decision, the defendant obtained the data from a third party that had legitimately obtained it from the Board. Yet the defendant still infringed the right of extraction. The effect of this might be that a defendant may be liable for infringement, even though they are not aware that it is extracting or re-utilising information originally taken from a database protected by the database right. On the other hand, any finding to the contrary would severely limit the usefulness of the *sui generis* protection as it would not, in effect, extend beyond the protection that could be obtained via contract.

In addition, extraction does not require a taking from the database owner so that the information is no longer held by the database owner after the taking.[199] In this instance the information was, of course, still contained within the Horseracing Board's database after being re-utilised by the defendant. However, it was noted that there must be a transfer to another medium, which led to the interesting comment that:

A hacker who accesses a database without a licence, looks at the data and memorises it may well not be guilty of extraction if his actions do not involve the making of a copy of the data in material form.[200]

---

[194] Ibid., at para. 33.   [195] Ibid., at para. 34.   [196] Ibid., at paras. 35–36.
[197] Ibid., at para. 37.   [198] Ibid.   [199] Ibid., at para. 57.   [200] Ibid.

Some doubt must exist about that *obiter* statement, given that the data would be in the RAM of the hacker and that extraction includes temporary transfers.

The main submission of the defendant, was that it would not be liable for infringement of the database right unless its actions involved extraction or re-utilisation relating to the nature of the database as a database. This argument relied on the concept described by counsel for the defendant as the 'database-ness' of the database. This concept relied on the principle that the Directive and its *sui generis* protection was aimed primarily at protecting a database as a collection of information, rather than individual items of information that happened to be contained within a database. Consequently, any extraction or re-utilisation would have had to be in relation to a significant amount of data that could be recognised as being, as a whole, a substantial part of the relevant database.

Mr Justice Laddie firmly rejected this argument by the defendant. While the database must be in a particular form to achieve *sui generis* protection, namely that it is searchable, the *sui generis* right does not protect that form but rather the investment in obtaining, verifying and presenting the contents. Consequently, taking the contents and re-arranging them does not avoid infringement, if the part taken is a substantial part of the contents of the database.[201]

Some light was cast on the meaning of a substantial part in this context. According to Mr Justice Laddie, Article 7(1) of the Directive contemplates looking at the quantity and quality of what was taken in combination and does not require separate consideration of those two issues.[202] In the context of the decision in *British Horseracing Board*, Mr Justice Laddie acknowledged that the quantity of information taken from the Board's database was not large, especially given the enormous size of the database. However a number of factors combined, leading to the conclusion that the part taken was a substantial part. While the part taken should be compared with the plaintiff's database, the importance of the part taken to the infringer is still relevant.

[T]he significance of the information to the alleged infringer may throw light on whether it is an important or significant part of the database. If one of the purposes of the database is to service businesses of the same general type as that run by the alleged infringer with the same type of information taken by him, then the collection, verification and presentation of that type of information within the database is likely to be an important or substantial part of its contents.[203]

In addition, it was the data relating to the races themselves which was the ultimate and crucial information, and it was this that was taken rather

---

[201] Ibid., at paras. 47–48.   [202] Ibid., at para. 53.   [203] Ibid., at para. 52.

than other information such as details about registered trainers, racing colours and jockeys. In particular, the defendant was taking advantage of the currency and reliability of the information about impending races. These aspects of the information lent qualitative substantiality to it.

The defendant also claimed that it had not taken a substantial part of the plaintiff's database because it had taken insubstantial parts of a number of the plaintiff's different databases rather than a substantial part of one database. It contended that as the Board's database was being continually updated with new information, a new database was being created regularly, at least every few days. Therefore, it had taken insubstantial parts of each of these individual databases. Such conduct may not have been caught by Regulation 16(2), which prohibited the repeated and systematic extraction or re-utilisation of insubstantial parts of the contents of a database, as that provision arguably only applied to systematic and repeated extraction or re-utilisation from the one database. Mr Justice Laddie dealt with this argument by holding that the Board had only one database that was in a constant state of refinement.[204] The defendant was therefore taking a substantial part of that database.

In addition, the right of extraction and re-utilisation was held to apply to the use and publication of modifications of the original data. The defendant proposed substituting the time of each race with the number of each race and to identify horses by their number rather than their name in order to avoid infringement. The Court's response to this proposal was that:

Infringement of the [Board's] database right in this respect would be unaffected. Furthermore, I do not see how the modified method of presenting substantially the same data could avoid infringement by re-utilisation. If a database happened to be written in English, an unlicensed third party who displayed a substantial part of it would not avoid infringement by doing so in French, German or Chinese ideograms, nor would he avoid infringement if he translated information in denary code to its binary equivalent.

The defendant appealed to the Court of Appeal which subsequently referred the matter to the European Court of Justice.[205] While the Court of Appeal indicated its preference for the opinions of Mr Justice Laddie at first instance, it considered that the decisions in other members of the EU such as those in Sweden and the Netherlands required resolution of disputed issues by the European Court of Justice.

---

[204] Ibid., at para. 72.
[205] *British Horseracing Board Ltd* v. *William Hill Ltd* [2001] EWCA Civ 1268, 31 July 2001.

Right to extract or re-utilise an insubstantial part   Regulation 19 confers a right on a lawful user to extract or re-utilise insubstantial parts of the contents of the database for any purpose. A lawful user is defined in Regulation 12 as:

Any person who (whether under a licence to do any of the acts restricted by any database right in the database or otherwise) has a right to use the database.

The use of the words 'or otherwise' is ambiguous. It suggests that a lawful user includes a person who is availing themselves of the exceptions to the *sui generis* right.

Exceptions   There is no exception in relation to reproduction of non-electronic databases for private purposes. A lawful user is entitled to extract a substantial part for the purpose of illustration for teaching or research and not for any commercial purpose, if such use is fair dealing.[206] In this context, fair dealing can probably be equated with the Directive's requirements that the extraction be justified by the non-commercial purpose to be achieved and that the lawful user's actions do not conflict with the normal exploitation of the database or unreasonably prejudice the legitimate interests of the maker.[207] Consequently, the application of the exception will presumably draw upon existing copyright principles concerning fair dealing.

Schedule 1 of the Regulations provides for various circumstances relating to public administration in which the database right is not infringed. For example, actions taken for the purposes of parliamentary or judicial proceedings do not infringe the database right. Nor does reporting of such proceedings.[208] Various other provisions relate to databases open to public inspection pursuant to a statutory authority and material communicated to the Crown in the course of public business.[209]

Term of protection   The term of protection is defined in Regulation 17, as are the circumstances under which the period of protection may be renewed. In *British Horseracing Board*, Mr Justice Laddie held that the renewed period of protection only applies to that part of the database that is new, and dynamic on-line databases are to be treated as one single database. Consequently, the information which has been available for more than fifteen years could be extracted and re-utilised, even if the database has been substantially amended during that time. However, there are no provisions that require a maker to identify material that has

---

[206] Regulation 20.   [207] Articles 8 and 9 of the Directive.
[208] Schedule 1, reg. 20(2)1.   [209] See schedule 1 generally.

been available for less or more than fifteen years. A user would have to take the risk that material had been available for more than fifteen years, although it could possibly rely on the defence contained in Regulation 21 that infringement is justified if it is reasonable to assume that the database right has expired.

Licensing schemes   Many of the provisions concerning licensing schemes for copyright works have also been reproduced in relation to databases. Under the Copyright, Designs and Patents Act 1988, schemes for licensing copyright works owned by more than one author are subject to the jurisdiction of the Copyright Tribunal. In the event of a dispute, the Copyright Tribunal has the authority to vary the scheme in accordance with what it sees as reasonable.[210] Similarly, a dispute concerning a licensing scheme for databases may be referred to the Copyright Tribunal.[211] The copyright provisions of the Copyright, Designs and Patents Act 1988 also provide for circumstances in which one owner of copyright in a work or works may be subjected to compulsory licensing, even though it is not part of a licensing scheme.[212] This may occur where there has been a report of the Monopolies and Mergers Commission to the effect that the conditions in licences or a refusal to grant a licence on reasonable terms operates against the public interest. Mirror provisions exist in relation to the database right.[213]

Summary of the transposition of the Directive

There are a number of general observations that can be made as a consequence of the above examination of implementing legislation. The first of these is that there must be some debate as to whether the Directive, as yet, has achieved its goal of harmonising the law concerning the protection of databases.

Harmonisation of copyright   There are several reasons for questioning the degree of harmonisation. The first is that while the standard of originality required for copyright protection of databases has been harmonised, there are considerable differences in the exceptions to copyright in databases. These differences are primarily due to the traditional exceptions to copyright that have been preserved by a number of countries, as permitted by the Directive. A major example of this is the fair dealing

---

[210] Section 121, Copyright, Designs and Patents Act 1988.   [211] Regulation 4.
[212] Section 44 of the Copyright, Designs and Patents Act 1988.   [213] Regulation 15.

or similar exceptions in relation to reporting of current events,[214] and the right to make private copies of non-electronic databases. Other examples include uses in schools and for religious purposes. In addition, the lack of mandatory requirements in relation to exceptions has meant an inconsistent approach to copyright exceptions. This situation has not been assisted by the Copyright Directive, which has left open the possibility of individual members retaining or adopting more than twenty different exceptions to copyright.

On the other hand, the limited exceptions to *sui generis* protection have prompted some countries also to limit the exceptions to copyright, at least as they apply to databases. An example of this is the UK, where fair dealing with databases for research has been limited to non-commercial purposes in order to make the copyright exceptions consistent with the exceptions for the *sui generis* right.

In many respects, these differences in copyright protection of databases will cease to be relevant. One effect of the Directive's implementation is to make copyright protection for databases largely irrelevant. The *sui generis* protection is easier to obtain, more easily proven, probably provides rights over the content of databases and the exceptions to those rights are either narrower, or no wider, than they are under copyright. The *British Horseracing Board* decision is an example of the increasing irrelevance of copyright, as the plaintiff in that case did not plead any infringement of copyright and chose to rely solely on the *sui generis* protection. One possible exception to this situation may develop as a consequence of the EU's refusal to accord national treatment to foreign databases. Users may be more inclined to deal with and use the databases of foreigners, as those databases will be subject to the more familiar and slightly less restrictive copyright provisions. Whether that will in fact occur is still unknown.

Yet even in relation to the *sui generis* right, there is still a lack of harmonisation. A number of issues have arisen as a consequence of the different pieces of transposing legislation and resulting case law. They include the following.

The investment necessary to qualify for sui generis *protection*   There seems to be considerable debate about the nature and extent of the investment necessary to obtain *sui generis* protection. There are some cases that suggest an investment in the form of selecting material to be included in a database may constitute a necessary qualitative investment. Consequently, a list of about 100 websites providing information about

---

[214] E.g. Article 22(1) of the Belgian Copyright Law, and Article 101 of the Italian Copyright Law.

childcare received protection as did a pamphlet identifying self-help organisations. These decisions are consistent with the view expressed in Chapter 3 that the act of selection which confers copyright protection on a database may simultaneously be the qualitative investment necessary to confer *sui generis* protection.

The other issue in this regard is the extent to which a database is the by-product or spin-off of an underlying business activity. Some cases, such as the Dutch cases dealing with broadcast listings[215] and newspaper headlines[216] and the *British Horseracing Board* case, have held that the investment in the business activity that generates the contents of the database is not relevant for the purposes of acquiring the *sui generis* protection. In some of the Dutch cases, this has led to a finding that the databases in question did not qualify for protection. This approach, if it were accepted in its broadest possible interpretation, would erode the intended effect of the Directive.

Yet a broad approach to the spin-off argument is unlikely to survive close scrutiny by the European Court of Justice for a number of reasons. First, it has not been universally accepted, even in those countries such as the Netherlands where it has gained some credence. Second, some of the decisions taking this approach have attempted to compare the plaintiff's major business activities with its database creating activities. Hence in *Algemeen Dagblad and Others* v. *Eureka* the court compared the plaintiff's investment in running a newspaper with the plaintiff's investment in maintaining its website. This comparative approach is not justified by the Directive's requirement to focus on whether the investment in obtaining, verifying and presenting the contents of the database has been substantial. The fact that the database owner may have made a far bigger investment in another activity is not the point. At best, the spin-off argument may be used to disregard the investment in creating information during the course of business activities, and to require the database owner then to point to a substantial investment in collecting (obtaining) that information, verifying and presenting it in its database. Consequently, it may be successful in cases involving television and broadcasting programme listings. In those cases, the investment in the programmes themselves would not be relevant. Arguably, the resources invested in deciding when to schedule a particular programme due to its content or demographic appeal may also be disregarded as part of the business of maximising the programme's profitability. Once those decisions are made and their

---

[215] *NV Holdingmaatschappij de Telegraaf* v. *Nederlandes Omreope Stichting* The Court of Appeal of The Hague, 99/165, 30 January 2001.
[216] *Algemeen Dagblad and Others* v. *Eureka President*.

relevance disregarded, the investment in actually verifying and presenting the listings may be quite slight. On the other hand, businesses such as telephone companies would have little difficulty establishing that they have made a substantial investment in bringing together their telephone listings, verifying and presenting them. The investment in presentation of such a large mass of information would alone qualify the directory for protection.

Nature of the right and the test of infringement   Differences have also emerged in relation to the nature of the rights conferred and, consequently, what constitutes infringement of those rights. The UK decision in the *British Horseracing Board* case clearly suggests that protection is provided for the contents of a database, rather than, as the defendant claimed, the 'database-ness' of the database. On the other hand, the Swedish courts have taken a far more restrictive approach,[217] primarily as a consequence of their previous catalogue laws and the minimalist approach to the transposition of the Directive. In their approach, there must be a direct taking of the data in the form in which it appears in the database; they have in effect adopted the approach argued by the defendant in *British Horseracing Board* that what must be taken is the 'database-ness' of the database, not just a large amount of its contents. This approach has been the subject of some criticism and it is questionable whether it will survive scrutiny by the European Court of Justice. Article 7(1) provides for an exclusive right to prevent 'extraction and/or re-utilisation of the whole or a substantial part of . . . the *contents*' (emphasis added) of a database, not a substantial part of a database. However, if such a restrictive approach were adopted, it would certainly significantly limit the effect of the Directive. The English Court of Appeal has referred the *British Horseracing Board* case to the European Court of Justice to resolve that issue and others.[218]

A related aspect of infringement that has received some attention is the issue of what constitutes 'a substantial part' of the contents of a database. Again, this is an area where there is likely to be an overlap with copyright law as this term is borrowed from that area of law. A couple of cases have suggested that one of the criteria for determining substantiality is the value of the part taken to the end user. This is an approach that runs the risk of creating circular thinking, where the mere use of data will in itself be evidence that the data used are a substantial part of a database. At that point the concept of an insubstantial part may become meaningless,

---

[217] *Fixtures Marketing Ltd* v. *AB Svenska Spel* T99-99 11 April 2001.
[218] *British Horseracing Board Ltd* v. *William Hill Ltd* [2001] EWCA Civ 1268, 31 July 2001.

as might the right provided in the Directive and transposing legislation to extract or re-utilise an insubstantial part.

On the other hand, these approaches may be the manifestation of an unfair competition based approach to the issue. For example, a number of the decisions suggest that a finding that a 'substantial part' has been extracted or re-utilised have been influenced by the impact of the defendant's actions on the plaintiff's market for the information in question.[219]

As with the issue of the relevant investment, the discussion of what constitutes a 'substantial part' in the context of the infringement of the *sui generis* right is unnecessarily complicated by the introduction of the same qualitative test as that used for copyright infringement. Consequently, there are cases in which the selection of a relatively small amount of information constitutes the necessary qualitative investment for protection, and the taking of that selection infringes the *sui generis* right.

Definition of a lawful user   Related to the right of lawful users to extract or re-utilise an insubstantial part of a database is the definition of a lawful user. Some countries, such as France, clearly envisage that a lawful user is someone in a contractual relationship with the database owner. Others, such as Germany, envisage that it is any person availing themselves of the exceptions; and still others such as the UK have drafted their transposing legislation so as to leave either interpretation open.

Lack of harmonisation of the exceptions   There is also a lack of harmonisation in relation to the exceptions to the *sui generis* right, although this is not as marked as with copyright protection. For example, there is no uniform approach to the private copying of non-electronic databases. In addition, some countries have chosen not to provide even those very limited exceptions contained within the Directive.

The period of protection   The decision of Mr Justice Laddie in *British Horseracing Board* suggests that individual items of information within a database would fall into the public domain after fifteen years. The wording of the Directive and most of the transposing legislation would suggest otherwise: that the entire contents of a database obtain the extended period of protection in the event of there being a further substantial investment in updating the database. This latter approach generates a number of difficulties relating to the public domain that have already been addressed in Chapter 3, but it may also generate difficulty

---

[219] E.g. *Cadremploi* v. *Keljob and Colt Telecommunications*, and *Algemeen Dagblad and Others* v. *Eureka President*.

for a plaintiff. If the defendant can allege that there is a series of different databases being created, it may be able to allege that it is taking insubstantial parts from different databases. Consequently, it can rely on the right to extract or re-utilise insubstantial parts, and avoid the restriction on repeated and systematic extraction or re-utilisation on the grounds that it is not engaging in that conduct in relation to the same database. The effect may be that a provision designed to provide extensive protection may actually limited the extent of protection. This is one of the issues to be addressed by the European Court of Justice. One possible response to this, other than taking the approach in the *British Horseracing Board* case, may be to rely on Article 8(2) which prevents a lawful user of a database performing acts which conflict with normal exploitation of the database or unreasonably prejudice the legitimate interests of the maker of the database. If in fact circumstances such as those in the *British Horseracing Board* case involve the creation of a series of new but closely related databases in a short period of time, the extraction of insubstantial parts from each on a systematic basis may well contravene Article 8(2).

Relationship to unfair competition laws One of the interesting issues to emerge is the ongoing use of pre-existing unfair competition principles, either in their own right or as an influence on the application of *sui generis* protection. At least one French decision has been based on unfair competition even though the claim based on the *sui generis* right was unsuccessful on the grounds that insufficient investment had been made in the database.[220] In addition, as pointed out above, unfair competition principles have had a significant influence on the application of the *sui generis* right in a number of circumstances. For example, it has had an impact on findings of what constitutes a substantial part of a database.

All of the case law has involved the extraction or re-utilisation for commercial purposes. This suggests that if the EU had adhered to its original approach of relying on unfair competition principles, a satisfactory result could have been achieved that met the needs of owners to prevent commercial copying of their databases.

Single source databases Further, much of the case law involves what has been described as 'synthetic' information, that is, information generated by the database makers themselves.[221] Telephone directories

---

[220] *Groupe Moniteur and Ors. v. Observatoire des Marches.*
[221] S. Maurer, B. Hugenholtz and H. Onsrud, 'Europe's Database Experiment' (2001) 294 *Science's Compass* 789–90.

are classic examples of databases containing synthetic information as the telephone companies create the telephone numbers. This synthetic information is often made as a by-product of an underlying business activity and, by definition, it comes from a single source. Consequently, extensive *sui generis* protection has often been conferred on this single source information. This situation does not appear to be consistent with the Directive's intention of increasing the incentive to create databases, as these databases would almost certainly have been created without the adoption of the Directive.

In addition, a number of the difficulties associated with single source databases created as a by-product of existing commercial activities could have been dealt with by principles that were jettisoned during the formulation of the Directive. For example, compulsory licensing provisions were deleted from the first versions, as were unfair competition principles relating to infringement.

Conclusion

There are still a number of differences in the approach of Member States to various issues that can only be finally resolved by the European Court of Justice. The primary issue that is yet to be finally resolved is the one raised in the *British Horseracing Board* case, as to whether the *sui generis* right protects the contents of the database or the database itself. If that issue is determined by essentially adopting the first instance decision in that case, this will have significant implications for the Nordic countries that have adopted a minimalist approach to the transposition of the Directive, both in their transposing legislation and in associated case law. It will also result in a definitive statement that the Directive has very significantly increased the protection for databases over and above that previously existing under unfair competition laws and copyright.

Other issues to be determined by the European Court of Justice include the following:
• The necessary investment to constitute a substantial investment, especially in light of the arguments based on spin-off databases.
• The tests for determining a substantial part of a database.
• The definition of the relevant database for the purposes of both duration of protection and infringement where a database is the subject of constant updating.
• The extent to which extraction or re-utilisation by a defendant that acquires the information via a third party rather than the database constitutes infringement.

Until the decision of the European Court of Justice is finally handed down in *British Horseracing Board*, the determination of these issues remains unresolved. However, an examination of the history of the Directive and the Directive itself and the preponderance of case law to date suggest that there are reasons to believe these issues are likely to be resolved in ways favourable to database owners.

5 Protection of databases in the United States of America

This chapter deals with two basic issues. First, it examines the application of American copyright law and the tort of misappropriation, part of the wider law of unfair competition, to databases. The discussion of copyright is relatively straightforward and brief (this is because the American standard of originality was discussed in some detail in Chapter 2). However, the American copyright provisions on circumvention of technological measures are also discussed as they provide a means of obtaining de facto protection for the contents of databases, even in circumstances where the copyright protection for a database is minimal. This section on copyright also deals with the American defence of fair use, because the latest legislative proposals for *sui generis* protection have included a defence that is analogous to fair use. Consequently, an appreciation of the defence of fair use in copyright is necessary to an understanding of the proposed analogous defence to *sui generis* claims. In addition, the broad, discretionary defence of fair use needs to be compared with the far more restrictive exceptions contained within the Directive.

The discussion concerning the tort of misappropriation is considerably longer than the treatment of copyright for a number of reasons. It deals with the history of the tort, including its chequered history since its initial acceptance in 1918 by the American Supreme Court,[1] the subsequent judicial reluctance to apply it[2] and the more recent application of it to provide protection separate from that provided by copyright.[3] The history of the tort also reveals changes in the justification for the tort. The initial justification for the tort, that the misappropriation complained of was contrary to good conscience, seemed to be based on a natural right theory that appeared to place no easily recognised limitations upon its application.[4] Partly for this reason, a number of American states declined

---

[1] *International News Service* v. *Associated Press*, 248 US 215 (1918).
[2] E.g. *Cheney Bros.* v. *Doris Silk Corp.*, 35 F 2d 279 (2nd Cir. 1929).
[3] E.g. *National Basketball Association* v. *Motorola Inc.*, 105 F 3d 841 (2nd Cir. 1997).
[4] *International News Service* v. *Associated Press*, at 241.

to adopt the tort.[5] More recent justifications of the tort have been more clearly based on economic considerations, reflecting a desire to achieve a balance between protection of a plaintiff's labour and investment in intangible trade values and the need for access to information.[6]

In addition, the relationship between the tort and intellectual property regimes was not clear. For example, to what extent should the tort operate in the same area as those intellectual property regimes? More recent iterations of the tort have delineated between the tort and copyright protection, partly as a consequence of legislative pre-emption of common law remedies that intrude into the scope of copyright protection.[7] Consequently, with clarification of the justification for the tort and a clearer delineation between tort and intellectual property regimes, its operation has been more clearly circumscribed.

After dealing with the copyright position and tort of misappropriation, the second part of this chapter examines various legislative proposals for *sui generis* protection that have been put forward in the United States. These proposals have combined copyright principles with misappropriation principles. Not surprisingly, as the tort of misappropriation has been a movable feast since its first acceptance, the legislative proposals based on the tort have also varied widely in the nature and extent of protection proposed to be conferred on databases. The initial proposed legislation in 1996[8] was framed so broadly that it was difficult to see any practical difference between the rights conferred and the exclusive property rights conferred by the Directive. In addition, the exceptions to the rights conferred were narrower than the exceptions provided by copyright law. Later proposals have provided more restricted protection by imposing limits such as a requirement that a plaintiff demonstrate material harm to its market from the defendant's activities.[9] In addition, exceptions have been included that are as broad as and, in some cases, broader than the exceptions for copyright.[10]

In the course of analysing the various legislative proposals for *sui generis* protection, a comparison will be made between those proposals on the

---

[5] See the discussion below concerning the chequered history of the tort and D. Baird, 'Common Law Intellectual Property and the Legacy of *International News Service* v. *Associated Press*' (1983) *University of Chicago Law Review* 411.

[6] See, e.g. s. 38 of the Restatement of the Law, Third, Unfair Competition 1995, The American Law Institute in Comments and Illustrations, (b) and *National Basketball Association* v. *Motorola Inc.*

[7] *National Basketball Association* v. *Motorola Inc.*

[8] The Database Investment and Intellectual Property Antipiracy Bill of 1996, HR 3531 of 1996.

[9] The Collections of Information Antipiracy Act of 1999, HR 354 of 1999.

[10] See the discussion of The Collections of Information Antipiracy Act of 1999, HR 354 of 1999 below.

one hand and the Directive and the tort of misappropriation on the other. This comparison shows that the latest proposals for *sui generis* protection differ from the Directive in a number of important aspects. In particular, those proposals have avoided a number of the difficulties associated with the Directive that were identified in Chapter 3. On the other hand, the legislative proposals provide considerably greater protection than the common law protection provided by misappropriation. While they draw upon some of the general principles of misappropriation, they have extended that protection beyond the scope provided by the courts. For example, the latest cases on misappropriation require proof that the owner of information has suffered substantial harm as a consequence of the defendant's actions,[11] whereas legislative proposals have adopted a far lower threshold of harm to the plaintiff.[12]

Copyright

The US Supreme Court unequivocally clarified the standard of originality through its decision in the *Feist* case.[13] Chapter 2 discussed that case and the standard under American law. There have been a number of cases decided since the decision in *Feist* that confirm that the level of originality required in order to obtain copyright protection is quite low, but mere sweat of the brow will not suffice to confer protection.

Some decisions since Feist

These cases included other cases relating to telephone directories.[14] For example, in *Bellsouth Advertising & Publishing Corporation* v. *Donnelly Information Publishing Inc.*,[15] copyright protection was denied to yellow pages advertising directories.[16]

A number of other cases related to the compilations of what could be loosely described as government information. The best known of these examples are those relating to the appropriation of copies of court opinions compiled by Westlaw.[17] Westlaw publishes reports of court decisions in

---

[11] *National Basketball Association* v. *Motorola Inc.*
[12] See the discussion of The Collections of Information Antipiracy Act of 1999, HR 354 of 1999 below.
[13] *Feist*, 499 US 340 (1991).
[14] See, for example, *Illinois Bell Telephone Company* v. *Haines and Co. Inc.*, 932 F 2d 610, where the facts were very similar to the decision in *Feist*.
[15] 999 F 2d 1436 (1993).
[16] Canadian courts have taken a similar approach. See *Tele-Direct (Publication) Inc.* v. *American Business Information Inc.* (1996) 74 CPR (3d) 72.
[17] *West Publishing Co.* v. *Mead Data Central Inc.*, 616 F Supp. 1571 (D. Minn. 1985); 799 F 2d 1219 (8th Cir. 1986); 479 US 1070 S. Ct (1987), *Oasis Publishing Co.* v. *West*

a number of jurisdictions. In a series of cases asserting copyright in its reports, Westlaw claimed copyright in the reports on the basis of its star pagination[18] and its editing of the judgments. Initial decisions favoured Westlaw[19] but later decisions of the Second Circuit, affirmed by the Supreme Court,[20] held that copyright did not subsist in the pagination system and was not conferred by the editing that Westlaw provided. As Westlaw held no copyright in the judgments itself, it was unable to prevent copying of the judgments, editing and pagination.

A similar decision involving a database of public information was made in *National Council on Compensation Insurance Inc. (NCCI)* v. *Insurance Data Resources Inc.*[21] The plaintiff, NCCI, had been appointed by the Florida Department of Insurance to compile information concerning workers' compensation experiences in Florida. All insurance companies were required by statute to provide the data in question and the Department of Insurance approved the system of organising the information by reference to job codes and other criteria. Manuals containing the information were made available for sale to the public by NCCI. The defendant copied the job classifications contained in the manuals. But the court concluded they were:

[A] straightforward alphabetical listing of classifications of workers, a descriptive and non-creative identification of the type of workers to be included in each class, and a numerical code assigned to each class ... Thus, this Court finds that the codes and formulas do not possess the creativity, and are not the product of an original selection and arrangement.[22]

Other types of compilations have also failed the test of originality. A compilation of lucky numbers used in gambling could not be copyrighted.[23] The numbers in question were generated pursuant to two standard formulae used within the 'industry' and, although calculating them involved a great deal of labour, there was insufficient creativity to constitute a literary work. Similarly, a directory of attorneys for Massachusetts did

---

Publishing Co., 924 F Supp. 918 (D. Minn. 1996) and *Matthew Bender Co. Inc.* v. *West Publishing Co.*, 158 F 3d 693 (1988), cert. denied, S. Ct, *West Publishing Co.* v. *Matthew Bender & Co.*, 522 US 3732 (1999), *Matthew Bender & Co.* v. *West Publishing Co.*, 158 F 3d 674 (2nd Cir. NY, 1998).

[18] Star pagination enables the reader of an electronic version of a case to identify precisely where a page break occurs in the body of a printed version. This permits the use of the electronic version to identify correct citations for a court without having access to Westlaw's hardcopy of the report.

[19] *West Publishing Co.* v. *Mead Data Central Inc.*, *Oasis Publishing Co.* v. *West Publishing Co.*

[20] *Matthew Bender & Co.* v. *West Publishing Co.* (1998), cert. denied, S. Ct, *West Publishing Co.* v. *Matthew Bender & Co.*, *Matthew Bender & Co.* v. *West Publishing Co.* (1998). *West Publishing* v. *Hyperlaw Inc.*, cert. denied, S. Ct, 526 US 1154 (1999).

[21] 40 USPQ 2d 1362 (SD Fla. 1996).   [22] Ibid., p. 1364.

[23] *Victor Lalli Enterprises Inc.* v. *Big Red Apple Inc.*, 936 F 2d 671 (2nd Cir. 1991).

not derive originality on the basis that the attorneys selected for inclusion were those in the Massachusetts area, who were actively practising law as opposed to those who may have retired or been suspended from practice.[24]

On the other hand, a number of cases have demonstrated that the requirement of originality can be met quite easily. In *Key Publications Inc.* v. *Chinatown Today Publishing Enterprises Inc.*,[25] copyright protection was conferred on a telephone directory of New York City's Chinese-American community, consisting of businesses that the publisher considered were associated with that community. The manner of selection and arrangement of the directory conferred copyright. Some businesses were excluded from the directory on the grounds that the publisher did not think they would remain open for very long.[26] In addition, a number of new categories such as 'Bean Curd & Bean Sprout Shops' were included that are not found in standard yellow pages directories. In *Kregos* v. *Associated Press*,[27] a table of nine statistics concerning the performance of baseball pitchers was held to be subject to copyright. The court found that there was sufficient creativity involved in choosing the nine criteria for the statistics, since it was possible to choose a myriad of different criteria for statistical measurement of a pitcher's performance.[28] A more obvious case in which originality was found to exist in a compilation was *Montgomery County Association of Realtors Inc.* v. *Realty Photo Master Corporation*.[29] The compilation in that case was a computerised directory of real estate available for purchase in Montgomery County, MD. In addition to purely factual information such as the address, list price and other details concerning each property, there was original expression in the form of marketing puffery describing each house in an advantageous manner as well as a 'unique and elaborate system of abbreviations'.[30] Consequently, copyright protection was obtained by adding an expressive element to the basic factual information concerning the listed houses.

Circumvention of technological measures

A further means of protecting basic factual information after adding an expressive element is by the use of technological measures that prevent

---

[24] *Skinder-Strauss Associates* v. *Massachusetts Continuing Legal Education*, 914 F Supp. 665 (D. Mass. 1995).
[25] 945 F 2d 509 (2nd Cir. 1991).   [26] Ibid., p. 513.   [27] 3 F 3d 656 (2nd Cir. 1993).
[28] See also the decision in *Armond Budish* v. *Harley Gordon*, 784 F Supp. 1320 (1992) where the plaintiff selected information from existing sources providing information about aged care in a creative manner.
[29] 878 F Supp. 804 (1995).   [30] Ibid., p. 810.

access to such material. These measures are supported by prohibitions on circumvention of such measures. The American provisions on circumvention of copyright protection devices were incorporated into the Digital Millennium Copyright Act of 1998.

This Act came into effect in October 1998, although the circumvention provisions were expressed to take effect in October 2000.[31] Section 1201 provides a basic prohibition against unauthorised circumvention of technological measures. In addition to this basic prohibition, there is a further prohibition on the manufacture of or commercial dealing with circumvention devices. This additional prohibition is apparently somewhat broader in that it refers to devices primarily designed or produced for the purpose of circumventing protection afforded by a technological measure that 'effectively protects a right of a copyright owner'. Hence, it would cover the situation where a user has lawfully obtained access to a work but some technological measure prevents a particular act that is within the scope of the copyright owner's rights, such as printing the work or retaining a digital copy. Devices primarily designed to circumvent those technological measures would be caught by the additional prohibition but not by the basic prohibition. In addition, the actual act of circumvention by a user who has lawfully obtained access to a work would not constitute an infringement of the circumvention provisions, although it may infringe the copyright in the work. Nevertheless, a user who has lawfully obtained access to a work would, in theory, be permitted to circumvent protection measures for the purpose of engaging in fair use. Actually doing so would be difficult, as the additional prohibitions place great restraints on the manufacture and distribution of devices that would enable such circumvention.

A number of specific exceptions to the prohibitions have been crafted. For example, there is an exception for the purposes of reverse engineering a computer program.[32] Non-profit libraries, archives and educational institutions may gain access to a copyrighted work 'solely in order to make a good faith determination of whether to acquire a copy of that work for the sole purpose of engaging in conduct permitted under this title'.[33] Even that exception is not applicable unless 'an identical copy of that work is not reasonably available in another form'.[34] There is no general right to engage in circumvention for the purposes of taking advantage of the exceptions to copyright, particularly the defence of fair use.

In addition, Section 1201(a)(1)(B) and (C) empowered the Librarian of Congress to determine that the circumvention provisions do not

---

[31] Section 1201(a)(1)(A).   [32] Section 1201(f).
[33] Section 1201(d).   [34] Section 1201(d)(2).

apply to 'persons who are users of a copyrighted work which is in a particular class of works if such persons are... adversely affected by virtue of such prohibition in their ability to make noninfringing uses of that particular class of works'. The Librarian of Congress had the power to make such determinations in the two years after the legislation was passed, and has the power in respect of each succeeding three-year period. The power requires the Librarian to act on the recommendation of the Register of Copyrights, who in turn is required to consult the Assistant Secretary for Communications and Information of the Department of Commerce.

After the first investigation of the issue, the Librarian of Congress announced that two classes of works would be exempted from the circumvention provisions. These are:

1. compilations consisting of lists of websites blocked by filtering software applications; and
2. literary works, including computer programs and databases, protected by access control mechanisms that fail to permit access because of malfunction, damage or obsolescence.

The first of these exemptions relate to filtering software that prevents access to websites that may contain pornographic material. However, some websites may be caught by that software even though their content is not pornographic. Circumvention is permitted in order to ascertain if a particular website is being filtered out by the software in question. The second provision is aimed mainly at malfunctioning or obsolescent technology. For example, the Librarian received a number of submissions concerning malfunctioning 'dongles' (locks on computer hardware that interact with computer software). These submissions showed that many dongles malfunctioned and that vendors either demanded purchase of new software as well as a new dongle, or the vendors were out of business and new dongles were unavailable.

The Librarian of Congress also considered other exemptions that were called for by various groups and individuals. One possible exemption particularly related to the database debate. A number of commentators claimed that copyright owners were attaching public domain material to minimal copyright material such as a brief introduction. They were then bootstrapping these public domain documents to the minimal copyright additions and effectively acquiring protection for non-copyright material.[35] In particular, they urged that compilations of works or materials in the public domain be exempted unless the public domain components of the compilation are marked, thus permitting circumvention

---

[35] Letter of Professor Jane Ginsburg to US Copyright Office, 11 June 2000.

of any technological measure that controls access to the public domain components.[36]

The Librarian of Congress took the view that the need for such an exemption had not been demonstrated. He also took the view that:

In general, it appears that the advent of access control protections has increased the availability of databases and compilations. Access controls provide an increased incentive for database producers to create and maintain databases... If a database producer could not control access, it would be difficult to profit from exploitation of the database. Fewer databases would be created, resulting in diminished availability for use.[37]

In addition, the Librarian took the view that most of the uncopyrighted material could be obtained from other sources.[38] Consequently, no exemption was provided in respect of circumvention for the purposes of obtaining public domain information. The effect of this decision, in conjunction with the anti-circumvention provisions, is to increase substantially the protection for databases that qualify for copyright protection. Technological measures can be used to prevent access to the information that is contained in databases, even if that information is not in a form that confers copyright protection. On the other hand, once access is obtained, the anti-circumvention provisions would not prevent fair use of information within a database which would include reproduction of large amounts of information, but not their selection or arrangement. However, while the anti-circumvention provisions would not prevent this, the contract providing for access to the material in the first place may do so. In other words, the contractual terms upon which access is granted could preclude subsequent unauthorised use of the non-copyright information within the database.

The end result is that considerable protection can be conferred on non-copyright material within databases by a combination of contract, technological protection devices and the anti-circumvention provisions of the Digital Millenium Copyright Act of 1998. This combination confers de facto protection of such strength that it may have an impact on the need for *sui generis* protection.

The fair use defence

If the difficulties posed from a user's perspective by technological measures can be overcome, the defence of fair use can be used to justify what

---

[36] Ibid.
[37] P. 64,567 of the Rules and Regulations of the Library of Congress 27 October 2000 (Vol. 65, No. 209).
[38] Ibid.

would otherwise be an infringement of copyright. The defence may have particular relevance to databases and the use of information contained within them. In addition, as an equivalent defence to the *sui generis* rights has been suggested in the more recent proposals for *sui generis* legislation, an examination of that defence is necessary in order to gain an understanding of the proposed equivalent defence. Section 107 of the Copyright Act of 1976 contains the defence of fair use, a defence that was recognised by the courts prior to that legislation.[39] It 'permits courts to avoid rigid application of the copyright statute when, on occasion, it would stifle the very creativity which that law is designed to foster.'[40] Section 107 reads, in part, as follows:

[T]he fair use of a copyrighted work . . . For purposes such as criticism, comment, news reporting, teaching, scholarship or research, is not an infringement of copyright. In determining whether the use made of a work in any particular case is a fair use the factors to be considered shall include –
1. the purpose and character of the use, including whether such use is of a commercial nature or is for nonprofit educational purposes;
2. the nature of the copyrighted work;
3. the amount and substantiality of the portion used in relation to the copyrighted work as a whole; and
4. the effect of the use upon the potential market for or value of the copyrighted work.

A few points can be made about the defence and the four criteria as they may apply to databases. The first is that American courts have recognised the difficulty in making a sharp distinction between commercial and nonprofit uses, such as educational uses.[41] In reality, any particular use will lie somewhere on the continuum between commercial and non-profit use.[42] The focus should be on where the use lies on that continuum rather than attempting a black and white analysis that defines the use as either commercial or non-profit. Consequently, while the commercial or non-commercial purpose of the user is relevant, it is not determinative of the issue of fair use.[43] In contrast, the Directive requires the use of the database to be for non-commercial purposes of illustration for teaching or research in order to justify the use in question.

---

[39] *Harper & Row, Publishers, Inc.* v. *National Enterprises*, 471 US 539 (1985) at 549.
[40] *Iowa State University Research Foundation Inc.* v. *American Broadcasting Co.*, 621 F 2d 57 (2nd Cir. 1980); *Stewarts* v. *Abend*, 495 US 207 (1990) at 236.
[41] '[A] serious scholar should not be despised and denied the law's protection because he hopes to earn a living through his scholarship.' *Salinger* v. *Random House Inc.*, 650 F Supp. 413 at 425 (SDNY 1986).
[42] This point is acknowledged in the Report of the Judiciary Committee on The Collections of Information Antipiracy Bill, 30 September 1999 at p. 6.
[43] See M. Nimmer and D. Nimmer, *Nimmer on Copyright* (Lexis, New York, 1963), at p. 13.05[A][1][c].

In addition to the commercial or non-commercial purpose of the user, an issue of critical importance in considering the first criterion is the extent to which the user adds value to the original copyrighted work. The extent to which the user creates a new productive or transformative use of the material in the original work will be a relevant factor in determining whether fair use has occurred. Hence, simply reproducing the material and using it for its original, intended purpose is highly unlikely to be fair use[44] whereas creating something new with a different purpose or different character is more likely to be fair use.[45] In a more general context, Cooter and Ulen[46] make this point by differentiating between productive facts and redistributive facts. Productive facts, such as the formula for a vaccine against polio, create more wealth. Redistributive facts can be used to redistribute wealth in favour of the party who obtains or uses existing information, but do not lead to the creation of new wealth. In the context of databases, this has particular relevance to transformative uses of databases in which information from one database is used as part of a bigger, better database designed to provide information concerning other issues. (Such transformative possibilities are discussed in more detail in Chapter 7.) The second criterion also has particular relevance to databases. In keeping with the general approach to the requirement of originality, the more informational the work, the broader is the scope for fair use.[47] In this sense, this aspect of the defence of fair use reflects the approach to protection of facts in the *Feist* decision.

The other two criteria are relatively obvious although, again, they have particular relevance in the context of databases. The first is that the reproduction of the entire work is unlikely to constitute fair use.[48] This is often the plaintiff's complaint in the context of databases, although it is not a complaint that is of any use if the work lacks sufficient originality to have copyright. However, if a database does meet the minimal originality requirement, a fair use defence is unlikely ever to justify taking the entire database. The criterion of effect on the plaintiff's potential market is also relevant, because American courts have found that such effects need 'not take into account the adverse impact on the potential market for plaintiff's work by reason of defendant having copied from plaintiff

---

[44] See Nimmer and Nimmer, *Nimmer on Copyright*, at 13.05[A][1][b]. *Campbell* v. *Acuff-Rose Music Inc.*, 114 S Ct 1164, 1170 (1994).

[45] *Campbell* v. *Acuff-Rose Music Inc.*, at 1171.

[46] R. Cooter and T. Ulen, *Law and Economics* (Forseman, Glenview, 1986), p. 259.

[47] *Diamond* v. *Am-Law Corp.*, 745 F 2d 142 (2nd Cir. 1984), *Maxtone-Graham* v. *Burtchaell*, 631 F Supp. 1432 (SDNY 1986). Nimmer and Nimmer, *Nimmer on Copyright*, at p. 13.05[A][2][a].

[48] *Infinity Broadcast Corp.* v. *Kirkwood*, 150 F 3d 104, 109 (2nd Cir. 1998), *American Geophysical Union* v. *Texaco Inc.*, 802 F Supp. 1, 17 (SDNY 1992).

noncopyrightable factual material'.[49] Again, in the context of databases, this means that taking large amounts of factual material will not constitute infringement. Whether one explains that proposition in terms of infringement or a defence to infringement via fair use, the end result is the same.

A more general observation about the nature of the fair use defence can be made that has significant relevance to the debate concerning *sui generis* protection. The fair use defence can be regarded as a standard rather than a rule. This is because it prescribes the kinds of circumstances relevant to determining the legality of a particular use of copyright material, but it does not prescribe with precision what is lawful and what is not. It can be contrasted with rules which are far more precise.[50] Theoretical writing on rules and standards suggests that standards are more appropriate than rules when it is difficult to predict with some precision the circumstances in which the standard or rule will be applied.[51] In the context of copyright, one can readily see that there is a potential for many different uses of many different types of copyright material. Consequently, the general standard of the fair use rule is preferable to more precise rules. The same reasoning applies in relation to *sui generis* protection of sweat of the brow. The heterogeneity of information contained within databases and the myriad of different potential uses lend themselves to less precise rules and reliance on a general standard such as fair use. (This issue is discussed further in Chapter 6.)

Summary of the copyright position

From the perspective of database owners, there are three significant problems posed by the American copyright law. The first of these is that many databases derive their value to users from their comprehensiveness. Often, it is the lack of selection that makes a database most useful, as selection implies excluding some material from a large field of information. Hence, a telephone directory should contain the names of all the subscribers to that telephone company, and a directory of attorneys should contain the names of all those who are actively practising law.[52] The second difficulty is that the information within many databases does not lend itself to any innovative means of arranging it. Consumers want telephone directories

---

[49] See Nimmer and Nimmer, *Nimmer on Copyright*, at p. 13.05[A][4].
[50] I. Ehrlich and R. Posner, 'An Economic Analysis of Legal Rulemaking' (1974) 3 *Journal of Legal Studies* 258 at 259.
[51] Ibid. See also L. Kaplow, 'Rules versus Standards: An Economic Analysis' (1992) 42 *Duke Law Journal* 557.
[52] *Skinder-Strauss Associates* v. *Massachusetts Continuing Legal Education*.

to be arranged in alphabetical order. They would be dismayed by any other arrangement. Third, is the defence of fair use. In particular, the emphasis upon not protecting factual material within copyright works (and discounting the impact on a potential market of taking that factual material) dilutes the protection provided, even if the database does meet the necessary standard of originality.

Consequently, the investment associated with any particular database may not lend itself to copyright protection. Indeed, attempting to obtain copyright protection by providing the necessary level of creativity via selection or arrangement may render the database useless. On the other hand, the US Supreme Court made it clear in the *Feist* decision that 'only the compiler's selection and arrangement may be protected; the raw facts may be copied at will. This result is neither unfair nor unfortunate. It is the means by which copyright advances the progress of science and art.'[53] It was clearly concerned that copyright could be used to protect raw facts and its concern was motivated, in part, by the constitutional justification for copyright. Article I, clause 8 of the American Constitution permits Congress to pass laws 'to promote the Progress of Science and useful Arts'.

Part of the difficulty with this all or nothing approach to protection of the labour involved in compiling databases is that it leaves open the possibility of free riding on that labour. This free riding may reduce the incentive to compile and make databases available, something that in turn may have a negative effect on the progress of science and the arts. The tort of misappropriation has been used to ameliorate this difficulty. However, an overly broad application of the tort can lead to excessive protection and the problems that the US Supreme Court sought to avoid when deciding *Feist*. On the other hand, an application of the tort, or a statutory variant of it with due regard to the need to balance the interests of database owners and users, has the potential to overcome the difficulties associated with the all or nothing consequences of the *Feist* decision.

Nature and history of the American tort of misappropriation

While the copyright position of databases is quite clear, the protection provided by other legal regimes is not. The tort of misappropriation, which is part of a larger area of unfair competition law in a number of American states, has had a pivotal role in the debate concerning the protection of databases. All American legislative proposals for *sui generis*

[53] *Feist*, at 349–50.

protection have been based on the concepts underlying this tort or, at the least, the proposers of the legislation have claimed that their legislation is based on the tort. Yet, as will be seen below in the section of this chapter dealing with the various pieces of proposed legislation, the proposed legislation itself has differed in a number of critical respects. This in turn leads to the conclusion that the elements of the tort of misappropriation are themselves open to a number of different interpretations and, indeed, this is the case. What actually constitutes misappropriation leading to court intervention on behalf of a plaintiff claiming to be a victim of it has been a matter of debate in the American courts since the seminal decision of the US Supreme Court in *International News Service v. Associated Press* in 1918.[54] Consequently, a claim that a piece of legislation is based on the tort of misappropriation has little or no meaning unless some relatively specific meaning is given to the concept of misappropriation. Due to the pivotal role of the tort in the debate about possible *sui generis* protection in America and the controversy about what it actually entails, a discussion of its treatment in American cases appears below.

International News Service v. Associated Press

The logical and probably necessary starting point for any consideration of the tort of misappropriation is the decision of the American Supreme Court in *International News Service v. Associated Press*[55] in 1918. In that case, Associated Press sued International News Service when the latter used some news that had been gathered by the former in the course of its news service business. Details of the news were obtained via a number of means. These included obtaining the news from newspapers that were part of the Associated Press news service prior to the publication of those newspapers and copying news from bulletin boards and from early editions of Associated Press's newspapers that were published on the US eastern seaboard. They then took advantage of time differentials in America to telegraph the news, either bodily or after rewriting it, to papers on the western seaboard. The stories then appeared in newspapers that obtained their news from International News Service at about the same time as some other newspapers aligned with Associated Press.

Importantly, for various reasons – including the fact that many of the stories were rewritten so as only to incorporate the information obtained rather than the expression of that information – an action for breach of copyright was not available. Nevertheless, the US Supreme Court granted Associated Press relief on the basis of a common law action for

[54] 248 US 215 (1918).   [55] Ibid.

unfair competition. The decision of the majority was clearly based on the appropriation of the plaintiff's labour expended in collecting the news, rather than any claim based on misrepresentation as is the case in the majority of case law referring to unfair competition.[56] This is emphasised by the fact that two of the justices of the court wrote a separate judgment concurring with the outcome but not the reasoning.[57] They took the view that International News Service had impliedly misrepresented that the material in its newspapers had been gathered by itself, when, in fact, Associated Press had gathered it.

The majority had to grapple with a number of issues in reaching their conclusion that International News Service's actions constituted a misappropriation of the news and actionable unfair competition. In particular, there was the difficulty that there is no common law property in news, and no copyright protection in the news *per se* as opposed to the expression of the news.

The majority of the Supreme Court stated that:

[I]n a court of equity, where the question is one of unfair competition, if that which complainant has acquired fairly at substantial cost may be sold fairly at substantial profit, a competitor who is misappropriating it for the purpose of disposing of it to his own profit and to the disadvantage of the complainant cannot be heard to say that it is too fugitive or evanescent to be regarded as property. It has all the attributes of property necessary for determining that a misappropriation of it by a competitor is unfair competition because contrary to good conscience.[58]

Subject matter of protection   This broad statement of the position had a number of difficulties associated with it. For example, what is the 'that' acquired by the complainant? Clearly, it was not any tangible items of property such as goods, as protection of misappropriation of such property is provided under laws concerning conversion, trespass and other related laws. Is it any intangible item, such as news or an idea about how to market various products? It seems that the court was suggesting that any intangible concept could be regarded as property, provided that its misappropriation was unfair competition because it was contrary to good conscience. On what basis then would it be decided that the defendant's use of the intangible was contrary to good conscience and, therefore, unfair competition? The answers to these questions come from a reading of the full judgment. First, the intangible in question, in this case news, had to have been acquired through the investment of considerable resources:

---

[56] Ibid., p. 242.
[57] See the judgment of Mr Justice Holmes. Mr Justice McKenna concurred with his opinion.
[58] Ibid., p. 240.

[N]ews matter, however little susceptible of ownership or dominion in the absolute sense, is stock in trade, to be gathered at the cost of enterprise, organization, skill, labor, and money, and to be distributed and sold to those who will pay money for it, as for any other merchandise. Regarding the news, therefore, as but the material out of which both parties are seeking to make profits at the same time and in the same field, we hardly can fail to recognize that for this purpose, and as between them, it must be regarded as quasi property, irrespective of the rights of either as against the public.[59]

Protection against whom   Clearly then, any plaintiff had to prove a considerable investment by it in the acquisition of 'that' for which protection was being sought. However, simply defining what was being protected was not sufficient. The 'that' being protected only received protection against the appropriation of it by some legal persons, specifically direct competitors. This is exemplified by a number of statements by the majority including the following:

The fault in the reasoning lies in applying as a test the right of the complainant as against the public, instead of considering the rights of complainant and defendant, competitors in business, as between themselves. The right of the purchaser of a single newspaper to spread knowledge of its contents gratuitously, for any legitimate purpose not unreasonably interfering with complainant's right to make merchandise of it, may be admitted; but to transmit that news for commercial use, in competition with complainant – which is what defendant had done and seeks to justify – is a very different matter. In doing this defendant, by its very act, admits that it is taking material that has been acquired by complainant as the result of organization and the expenditure of labor, skill, and money, and which is saleable by complainant for money, and that defendant in appropriating it and selling it as its own is endeavoring to reap where it has not sown, and by disposing of it to newspapers that are competitors of complainant's members is appropriating to itself the harvest of those who have sown.[60]

Numerous other references were made to the fact that Associated Press and International News Service were direct competitors[61] and the principle being espoused applied between direct competitors only.[62]

Nature of the protection   A further, important restriction on the tort of misappropriation established in that case was the nature and extent of the protection provided to Associated Press. An acknowledgment that it had 'quasi-property' in its news did not lead to the conclusion that its competitors were excluded completely from using the news that it had gathered.

---

[59] Ibid., p. 236.   [60] Ibid., p. 239.
[61] Ibid., pp. 229 and 235.   [62] Ibid., pp. 240 and 235.

It is to be observed that the view we adopt... only postpones participation by complainants' competitors in the processes of distribution and reproduction of news that it has not gathered, and only to the extent necessary to prevent that competitor from reaping the fruits of complainant's efforts and expenditure.[63]

While the Supreme Court was not responsible for shaping the final form of the injunction against International News Service, it also noted that any injunction against International News Service should be framed so 'as to confine the restraint to an extent consistent with the reasonable protection of complainant's newspapers, each in its own area and for a specified time after its publication'.[64]

The nature of the protection provided was also intimately connected with the question of 'that' which was protected. The judgment suggested that the news was only protected while it was still 'hot' or time sensitive. A number of comments in the judgment emphasised the importance of the fact that the news was 'fresh':

The value of the service, and of the news furnished, depends upon the promptness of transmission... it being essential that the news be transmitted to members or subscribers as early or earlier than similar information can be furnished to competing newspapers.[65]

The peculiar value of news is in the spreading of it while it is fresh.[66] [...]

The peculiar features of the case arise from the fact that, while novelty and freshness form so important an element in the success of the business, the very processes of distribution and publication necessarily occupy a good deal of time.[67]

The issues raised by the majority judgment have echoed down to today's debates concerning the protection of databases. The judgment raised a number of issues that have become even more relevant in the context of the decision in *Feist* to refuse protection for sweat of the brow, and the possibility of cheap and quick appropriation of large amounts of information, particularly if it is in digital form. The principles espoused in the judgment have been relied upon by a number of those who have proposed legislation for *sui generis* protection of databases.

The dissenting judgment in International News Service *v.* Associated Press   Mr Justice Brandeis addressed the same issues in his dissenting judgment but reached different conclusions in relation to them. In particular, he expressed the view that the particular problems raised by the case were not suitably resolved by the development of new common law principles:

---

[63] Ibid., p. 241.   [64] Ibid., pp. 245–6.
[65] Ibid., p. 230.   [66] Ibid., p. 235.   [67] Ibid., p. 238.

[W]ith the increasing complexity of society, the public interest tends to become omnipresent; and the problems presented by new demands for justice cease to be simple. Then the creation or recognition by courts of a new private right may work serious injury to the general public, unless the boundaries of the right are definitely established and wisely guarded. In order to reconcile the new private right with the public interest, it may be necessary to prescribe limitations and rules for its enjoyment.[68]

This view that the dispute inevitably involved public interest as well as the interests of the two parties involved, contrasts with the view expressed by the majority that the news was to be considered property or quasi-property as between the two parties.

Mr Justice Brandeis went on to identify some of the public interest issues that may have to be considered. For example, he noted that it appeared that International News Service had been unable to gather news from foreign countries itself, not because of its unwillingness to pay for it, but because of undeserved prohibitions imposed by foreign governments on the transmission of news to International News Service.[69] This raised the possibility that Associated Press was effectively the sole supplier of foreign news in the United States, unless International News Service was permitted to do what it had in fact done. This point about the market power conferred on Associated Press by the decision was emphasised by a later decision of the Supreme Court.[70] It found that Associated Press was operating as a monopoly in restraint of trade due to rules of the newspaper association that placed unlawful limits on who could join it. In effect, existing members could veto new membership of any potential competitor. In addition, those competitors were unable to obtain Associated Press's news as there were other rules of the newspaper association forbidding the dissemination of the Association's news to non-members. The legislative debates concerning *sui generis* protection have confirmed Mr Justice Brandeis's view that it is necessary to prescribe limits and rules for any new rights that are created. The section below concerning legislative proposals demonstrates the complexity of the issue, and the difficulties with providing a new form of protection without giving serious consideration to the need for exceptions to that protection.

Summary of the position in International News Service *v.* Associated Press   The difficulty with the decision in this case is determining the general principle or principles that were adopted and that

[68] Ibid., pp. 262–3.
[69] Ibid., p. 264. These prohibitions may have been imposed because of International News Service's editorial opposition to the war.
[70] *Associated Press v. United States*, 326 US 1, 65 S. Ct 1416 (1945).

should be applied in future cases. While the analysis above indicates some of the significant restrictions on a tort of misappropriation within the ambit of the law of unfair competition, it is possible to take a far broader view of what the Supreme Court decided. Some courts did. For example, the Supreme Court of Wisconsin in *Mercury Record Productions Inc.* v. *Economic Consultants Inc.* summarised the decision as holding that:

The elements of the misappropriation clause of action developed in International News Service are (1) time, labor and money expended in the creation of the thing appropriated; (2) competition; and (3) commercial damage to the plaintiff.[71]

Such an interpretation of the decision would lead to an extraordinary degree of protection being conferred on ideas and information by a tort of misappropriation.[72] For example, the protection would be virtually perpetual and would take no account of any efforts by a potential defendant to refine and improve on the ideas or information that it appropriated. The first person to invest substantial resources in the development of a particular product or to exploit a particular idea, such as a marketing scheme, would have exclusive rights in relation to them until all commercial value was extracted. It would lead to a form of infinitely expandable, perpetual intellectual property rights. As noted in *Synercom Technology Inc.* v. *University Computing Company and Engineering Dynamics Inc.*:

Even casual analysis will reveal, however, that the doctrine's reach cannot be as broad as is indicated by this formulation of elements. Literally applied, for instance, the doctrine as set out would encompass the manufacture by a non-patentee of a product upon which a patent had expired. Obviously, then, the doctrine of misappropriation has limits, both inherent to the doctrine itself and externally imposed by the United States Constitution and the federal patent and copyright laws.[73]

The inherent limitations on the doctrine are our primary concern at this point. The external limitations imposed by federal law are discussed below in the section dealing with pre-emption.

Far narrower interpretations of the decision were possible and, for many years, were made by a number of courts considering the decision. For example, in *Cheney Bros.* v. *Doris Silk Corp.*,[74] Mr Justice Learned Hand said about the decision:

---

[71] 218 NW 2d 705 (Wis. 1974) at 709.
[72] E. Sease, 'Misappropriation is Seventy-five Years Old; Should We Bury it or Revive it' (1994) 70 *North Dakota Law Review* 781.
[73] 474 F Supp. 37 (1979) at p. 40.   [74] 35 F 2d 279 (2nd Cir. 1929).

There are cases where the occasion is at once the justification for, and the limit of, what is decided. This appears to us such an instance; we think that no more was covered than the situation substantially similar to those then at bar. The difficulties of understanding it otherwise are insuperable.[75]

The decisions in the *Mercury Records* case and *Cheney Bros* represent two extremes of a wide spectrum of possible interpretations of the decision in *International News Service* v. *Associated Press* and the tort of misappropriation. They also demonstrate the point that justifying legislation on the basis that it reflects the principles underlying a tort of misappropriation is meaningless, unless content is given to that tort. Equally, the references to 'property' rights in the decision were unhelpful. The news was considered property if it was contrary to good conscience to appropriate it, and not property if it was not contrary to good conscience to appropriate it. Such reasoning is tautological.

The chequered history of the decision in International News Service v. Associated Press

Since the decision in *International News Service*, the tort has had what has been described as a chequered history. For a very long time, it was ignored, distinguished on the most specious of grounds[76] or simply not followed by many courts. The situation was complicated even more by the federal nature of the legal system in the United States. Different approaches to the tort were taken at federal and state levels. This dichotomy between the federal common law tort of misappropriation and different state common law approaches to a tort of misappropriation became an even more important issue when federal common law was abolished. In *Erie Railroad* v. *Tompkins*,[77] the US Supreme Court decided that there is no independent federal common law in the US and that the common law is a separate entity in each of the states. As the original decision in *International News Service* was expressed to be a federal decision, in theory, courts could ignore it on that basis as it was therefore no longer of any authority.[78]

---

[75] Ibid., p. 280.
[76] E.g. *Cheney Bros* v. *Doris Silk Corp.*, *De Costa* v. *Viacom Int. Inc.*, 981 F 2d 602 (1st Cir. 1992) which held that the decision was based on misrepresentation, *PIC Design Corp.* v. *Sterling Precision Corp.*, 231 F Supp. 106 (2nd Cir. US Dist. Ct, SD NY, 1964) at 113, 'the International News Service case has not been given the scope and effect such language would seem to demand. Subsequent cases exhibit a lack of judicial enthusiasm for a full extension of this doctrine.' *Neal* v. *Thomas Organ Co.*, 241 F Supp. 1020 (US Dist. Ct SD Cal. 1965).
[77] 304 US 64 (1938).
[78] *Columbia Broadcasting System Inc.* v. *De Costa*, 377 F 2d 315 (Ct App., 1st Cir. 1967).

Hence, the tort was refined and adopted or rejected on a state-by-state basis. New York, California and Florida embraced it relatively quickly, while a number of other states held that the decision was a US federal law decision and that it was not part of the law of their state. New York law adopted an extremely broad interpretation of misappropriation, as standing for the 'broader principle that property rights of commercial value are to be and will be protected from any form of commercial immorality',[79] and that misappropriation law developed 'to deal with business malpractices offensive to the ethics of society' and that the doctrine is 'broad and flexible'.[80]

In contrast, the courts applying the law of Massachusetts held that 'it is not unfair competition in Massachusetts to use information assembled by a competitor'.[81] The tort is yet to be accepted in Massachusetts.[82] Other states have altered their position over time, perhaps in response to technological developments that have increased the ease with which information can be appropriated, but perhaps as a consequence of a change in prevailing views about what constitutes free riding. For example, the state of Illinois initially rejected the tort[83] but later accepted it.[84]

Limitations on the scope of the tort of misappropriation

An analysis of the cases in which the tort was acknowledged to exist at all reveals the nature of the inherent and externally imposed limitations on its scope that were referred to in *Synercom Technology Inc. v. University Computing Company and Engineering Dynamics Inc.*[85] These are best expressed in one of the doctrine's most recent authoritative iterations which appeared in the decision of the US Court of Appeal, Second Circuit decision in *National Basketball Association v. Motorola Inc.*[86] (the *Motorola* case). The plaintiff, the National Basketball Association (NBA), was responsible for organising basketball matches. The defendant made arrangements whereby results and various details concerning these games

---

[79] *National Basketball Association* v. *Motorola*, at 851.

[80] *Metropolitan Opera Association* v. *Wagner-Nichols Recorder Corp.*, 199 Misc 786, 101 NYS 2d 483 (NY S. Ct, 1950) at 492, 488–9.

[81] *Triangle Publications Inc.* v. *New England Newspaper*, 46 F Supp. 198 (D. Mass., 1942) *per* Wyzanski J at 203.

[82] D. Robins, 'Will Massachusetts Adopt the Misappropriation Doctrine?' (1999) 43 *Boston Bar Association Boston Bar Journal* 4.

[83] *Addressograph-Multigraph Corp.* v. *American Expansion Bolt and Manufacturing Co.* (124 F 2d 706 7th Cir. 1942), *Continental Casualty Co.* v. *Beardsley* US Dist. Ct SD NY 151 F Supp. 28 (1957) (commenting on Illinois law).

[84] *Capitol Records Inc.* v. *Spies* 130 Ill. App. 2d 429 (1970), 264 NE 874 (1970), *Board of Trade* v. *Dow Jones and Co.*, 456 NE 2d 84 (S. Ct Ill. 1983).

[85] 474 F Supp. 37 (ND Tex. 1979) at 40.   [86] 105 F 3d 841 (2nd Cir. 1997).

were relayed to subscribers via its paging service while the games were in progress. These details were derived from reporters who watched the games on television or listened to them on the radio.

The plaintiff objected to this use of what it claimed to be information that had been created (the scores and other details) by its efforts. The Second Circuit held that a cause of action in misappropriation exists when the following conditions are met:

(i) a plaintiff generates or gathers information at a cost; (ii) the information is time-sensitive; (iii) a defendant's use of the information constitutes free-riding on the plaintiff's efforts; (iv) the defendant is in direct competition with a product or service offered by the plaintiff; and (v) the ability of other parties to free-ride on the efforts of the plaintiff or others would so reduce the incentive to produce the product or service that its existence or quality would be substantially threatened.[87]

However, the action failed in that case because of the Court's finding that the defendant was not taking a free ride on the plaintiff's efforts. The statistics were compiled by people in the employ of the defendant and were not obtained directly from the plaintiff. The mere fact that the plaintiff organised the basketball games which were then statistically analysed by the defendant did not mean that the defendant was taking a free ride on the plaintiff's efforts. It engaged in its own analysis of the games and generated its own information to be distributed through its telephone network.

There are three critical restraints on the tort of misappropriation imposed by the decision: time-sensitivity; that the parties are in direct competition; and that the defendant be shown to be taking a free ride on the plaintiff's efforts. This third restraint is a potentially broad one as the free ride in question must be of such a nature as to provide a substantial disincentive to the production or quality of the product, unless the free riding is prevented. Hence, the emphasis is not so much on whether the defendant has obtained an advantage from using the plaintiff's product, but whether such harm has been done to the plaintiff that it will be discouraged from continuing to produce its product. Arguably, these limitations were also part of the decision in *International News Service* as the facts of that case met all of the five requirements set out in *Motorola*. However, the wording of the decision left open a far wider interpretation of the tort which was part of the reason for its unpopularity in the wake of *International News Service*.

Pre-emption by the Federal Constitution and intellectual property legislation   The criteria set out in the *Motorola* case are a reflection of not

[87] Ibid., p. 845.

only inherent limitations on the doctrine, but also the effect of federal copyright legislation on misappropriation claims that are no more than failed copyright infringement actions in a different form. 'Pre-emption' refers to the pre-eminence of federal intellectual property legislation over misappropriation, and the relationship between the two. That relationship has been almost as complex as the history of the tort of misappropriation itself. Basically, pre-emption means that the tort of misappropriation cannot be relied upon by a plaintiff if it is seeking protection for subject matter that is dealt with by intellectual property legislation, unless its claim of unlawful conduct by the defendant involves an allegation of some additional element over and above that required to establish an infringement of the intellectual property legislation in question.[88] These two requirements are usually referred to as the subject matter tests and the additional element or general scope test of pre-emption.[89]

The issue of pre-emption was addressed directly by the US Supreme Court in two cases in 1964.[90] In *Sears, Roebuck & Co. v. Stiffel Co.*, the plaintiff sued in respect of the sale by the defendant of 'pole lamps' similar to those made by the plaintiff. The plaintiff had obtained mechanical and design patents in respect of its pole lamps. However, those patents were held invalid for want of invention. At first instance and on appeal to the Court of Appeals, the plaintiff succeeded under unfair competition law. In the words of the Supreme Court, 'the Court of Appeals... held Sears liable under Illinois law for doing no more than copying and marketing an unpatented article'.[91]

It went on to hold that state unfair competition law could not be applied in such a way as to frustrate the objectives of federal patent law to permit copying of non-inventive articles:

[T]he patent system is one in which uniform federal standards are carefully used to promote invention while at the same time preserving free competition ... Just as a State cannot encroach upon the federal patent laws directly, it cannot, under some other law, such as that forbidding unfair competition, give protection of a kind that clashes with the objectives of the federal patent laws.[92]

The full extent of the operation of pre-emption has been a matter for debate for a number of years, particularly as the Supreme Court seemed

---

[88] *Information Handling Service Inc. v. LRP Publications Inc.*, 54 USPQ 2d (BNA) 1571 (2000), *CD Law Inc. v. Lawworks Inc.*, 35 USPQ 2d (BNA) 1352 (1994), *Skinder-Strauss Associates v. Massachusetts Continuing Legal Education Inc.*

[89] *Del Madera Properties v. Rhodes and Gardner Inc.*, 820 F 2d 973, 976 (9th Cir. 1987).

[90] *Sears, Roebuck & Co. v. Stiffel Co.*, 376 US 225, 84 S. Ct 784 (1964) and *Compco Corp. v. Day-Brite Lighting Inc.*, 376 US 234, 84 S. Ct 779 (1964).

[91] *Sears, Roebuck & Co. v. Stiffel Co.*, at 228.   [92] Ibid., at 230–1.

to limit the extent of pre-emption in later decisions.[93] However, the pre-emptive effect of copyright legislation on unfair competition cases was made explicit in s. 301, Title 17 of the United States Code in 1976 when copyright legislation was amended to provide that:

On and after January 1, 1978, all legal or equitable rights that are equivalent to any of the exclusive rights within the general scope of copyright as specified by section 106 in works of authorship that are fixed in tangible medium of expression and come within the subject matter of copyright as specified by sections 102 and 103, whether created before or after that date and whether published or unpublished, are governed exclusively by this title. Thereafter, no person is entitled to any such right or equivalent right in any such work under the common law or statutes of any State.

However, the legislation did not pre-empt claims where the cause of action involved more than an allegation of a breach of copyright.[94] Consequently, in the *Motorola* case, the Second Circuit of the Court of Appeals found that the unfair competition claim was not pre-empted by copyright legislation. While the broadcast by the NBA and the underlying facts were within the scope of copyright legislation, the NBA was alleging additional acts beyond the exclusive rights of a copyright owner. In that case, the NBA was alleging that the information being disseminated by Motorola was time-sensitive and this gave the unfair competition action an element not found in a copyright infringement action.

However, copyright pre-emption has had a very significant impact on the operation of state misappropriation law and its application to the appropriation of large amounts of information that is not time-sensitive. This is demonstrated by the *Feist* decision itself and a number of decisions both pre- and post-*Feist*. All these decisions effectively prevented the application of the tort to mere sweat of the brow compilations, on the grounds that the claims based on the tort were no more than copyright infringement actions under another name.[95] The particular difficulty that is confronted in cases claiming misappropriation of material brought together and organised through industrious collection or sweat of the brow, is that the material clearly comes within the scope of the copyright legislation but not its protection.[96] With these inherent and external limitations

[93] *Goldstein* v. *California*, 412 US 546 (1973) and *Kewanee Oil Co.* v. *Bicron Corp.*, 416 US 470 (1974). See also the discussion in Sease, 'Misappropriation' at 781.
[94] *National Basketball Association* v. *Motorola* Inc., at 27.
[95] *Kregos* v. *Associated Press*, 3 F 3d 656 (2nd Cir. 1993) at 665–6, *Information Handling Service Inc.* v. *LRP Publications Inc.*, *CD Law Inc.* v. *Lawworks Inc.*, *Skinder-Strauss Associates* v. *Massachusetts Continuing Legal Education Inc.*, *RR Donnelly & Sons Co.* v. *Haber*, 43 F Supp. 456 (1942).
[96] See *US Ex Rel Berge* v. *Board of Trustees of University of Alabama*, 104 F 3d 1453 (4th Cir. 1997) at 1463 where the Fourth Circuit Court of Appeals noted 'scope and protection

in mind, we can analyse a number of cases concerning the individual elements of the tort and some of the difficulties associated with applying those elements to particular facts.

Direct competition between the parties   One area of difficulty has been in determining whether the parties are in direct competition and, if not, whether the tort should apply in any event. For instance, in *KVOS v. Associated Press*,[97] Associated Press sued a radio station. The radio station had taken news assembled by Associated Press and used that news as the basis of radio news broadcasts that were made either prior to, or shortly after, the publication of newspapers in the broadcast area that used the news supplied by Associated Press. Associated Press sued on the same grounds that it had sued in the *International News Service* decision. At first instance, the claim was dismissed on the basis that the radio station and Associated Press's newspapers were not in direct competition, due to the different media used to disseminate the news. This finding was reversed on appeal by the Ninth Circuit which found that the radio station and Associated Press's newspapers were clearly in competition.[98]

A number of other cases have dealt with the alleged misappropriation of information from sporting events organised by the plaintiff in circumstances where the plaintiff wished to exploit that information itself, or had licensed others to exploit that information. This was, in part, due to a lack of copyright protection for broadcasts of sporting events. Such protection was afforded by amendments to copyright legislation that came into effect in 1978 but, prior to that, plaintiffs had to rely on misappropriation. For example in *Pittsburgh Athletic Co. v. KQV Broadcasting Co.*,[99] the organiser of a baseball game was able to prevent a live broadcast of the game based on observations of the game by a commentator who was outside the stadium but overlooking it.[100] In contrast, in *Loeb v. Turner*,[101] the plaintiff was a radio station that had been given exclusive rights to

---

are not synonymous. Moreover, the shadow actually cast by the Act's preemption is notably broader than the wing of its protection.'

[97] 299 US 269 (1936), 80 F 2d 575 (9th Cir. 1935), 9 F Supp. 279 (1934).

[98] The action finally failed in the Supreme Court on the grounds that the plaintiff had not proved that its damages exceeded $3,000, a prerequisite to the Court of First Instance having jurisdiction in the matter. Although the Supreme Court made no comment on the decision in *INS*, its reluctance to find that the damage in question exceeded $3,000, was indicative of the somewhat antagonistic attitude towards the tort at the time.

[99] 24 F Supp. 490 (D. Pa. 1934).

[100] Cf. *National Exhibition Co. v. Tele-Flash Inc.*, Dist. Ct SD NY 24 F Supp. 810 (1936) where the facts were virtually identical but the opposite finding was made. See also the decision in *NFL v. Governor of Delaware*, US Dist. Ct, 435 F Supp. 1372 (1977).

[101] 257 SW 2d 800 (1953).

broadcast stock car races being conducted in Phoenix. It did so and the defendant arranged for its agents to listen to the broadcast and telephone information concerning the races to its radio station in Dallas. In Dallas, a recreated broadcast of the races was made based on the news being telephoned through to the station. The Court of Civil Appeals, Texas, held that the decision in *International News Service* did not apply as the radio station in Phoenix was not in competition with the radio station in Dallas, and neither party had attempted to compete with the other in their respective territories.

Apart from general news and sports information, commercial information concerning stock markets, the credit ratings of companies or other commercially valuable information has been one of the main sources of litigation based on the tort of misappropriation. In *McCord Co.* v. *Plotnick* in 1951,[102] the Court of Appeal of California affirmed a first instance decision in favour of the publisher of a newspaper that contained credit items of interest to banks and other commercial enterprises. The plaintiff also published a textile edition of its newspaper, containing information from the general edition that was particularly relevant to the textile industry. Both the general edition and the textile edition were published five times a week. This edition was the subject of the litigation in question. The defendant published a newsletter three times a week entitled 'Credit Briefs' that pirated information from the plaintiff's textile edition. The plaintiff's plea of misappropriation was successful.[103] The court rejected a claim by the defendant that it was not in direct competition with the plaintiff because the plaintiff's textile edition carried ten times as many items as the defendant's newsletter, and the defendant offered other services such as collecting accounts and checking credits while the plaintiff merely supplied information. In particular, the Court noted the evidence that several hundred textile companies had declined an offer to subscribe to the plaintiff's textile edition on the grounds that they obtained necessary information from the defendant's newsletter.[104]

More recent examples of cases involving the appropriation of information based on the tort of misappropriation are also worthy of mention at this point. In *Standard & Poor's Corporation Inc.* v. *Commodity Exchange Inc.*,[105] the Court of Appeals for the Second Circuit upheld a first instance decision to grant an injunction against the defendant. The defendant wished to use the plaintiff's stock market index as the basis for calculating the prices in its stock index futures contract. The plaintiff

---

[102] 108 Cal. App. 2d 392, 239 P 2d 32 (1951).
[103] Ibid., at 395. This was despite the fact that it seemed that the plaintiff could have brought an action for breach of copyright if it had registered the copyright in its edition.
[104] Ibid., at 394.   [105] 683 F 2d 704 (2nd Cir. 1982).

objected on the grounds that it invested considerable resources in the day-to-day and minute-to-minute calculation of its index.[106] It had also licensed the use of its index to another party for the same purpose but the defendant was using it without payment. Obviously, if the defendant could have used the index for the same purpose without payment, the license would have conferred no value on that other party. While the nature of the litigation, an action for a restraining order pending the final trial, did not require the Court finally to resolve the issue, the Court did note that:

[A]t a minimum S&P's claim of misappropriation presents sufficiently serious questions going to the merits to make them a fair ground for litigation.[107]

It also noted that the tort of misappropriation is both 'adaptable and capacious'.[108]

A very similar set of facts arose for consideration in *The Board of Trade of the City of Chicago* v. *Dow Jones & Company*.[109] Dow Jones sought to restrain the Chicago city Board of Trade from utilising the Dow Jones Industrial Average in its commodity futures contracts. Unlike the situation in the *Standard & Poor's* case, Dow Jones did not have any licensing arrangement with any other party to use its average. Nor did it have any immediate plans to enter into such an arrangement. Consequently the Board was not in competition with the current uses of the index by Dow Jones. Yet the Supreme Court of Illinois was still prepared to prevent the Board utilising the average in the way that it wished. This was in the face of a strong dissenting opinion that the tort of misappropriation only applied in cases where the plaintiff and the defendant were in direct competition.[110] It also contradicts the views expressed in the *Motorola* case and other cases[111] and the Re-Statement (Third) of Unfair Competition.[112]

Time-sensitivity   In both cases, there must also be a question mark over the time-sensitivity of the information in question. The defendant's contracts used the indexes as at the close of business on the day of settlement for those contracts. The index was published and generally available to the public at the time, and while it was clearly still of commercial value in that it could be utilised as the basis for calculating

---

[106] Ibid., at 710.   [107] Ibid., at 711.   [108] Ibid., at 710.
[109] 98 Ill. 2d 109, 456 NE 2d 84 (1983).   [110] Ibid., Justice Simon (dissenting) at 124.
[111] *Loeb* v. *Turner et al.*, 257 SW 2d 800 (Ct Civ. App. Tex. 1953); *NFL* v. *Governor of Delaware*, 435 F Supp. 1372 (1977).
[112] Restatement of the Law, Third, Unfair Competition, 1995, The American Law Institute. See Comments and Illustrations.

contract costs, the time-sensitivity of the information had clearly diminished by the time it was so utilised.

An even more questionable situation arose in the 1925 Texas case of *Gilmore* v. *Sammons*.[113] The plaintiff, Gilmore, compiled information concerning building and construction work in the Dallas area. This was published in two documents entitled 'Texas Contractor' and 'Advance Construction Reports'. The plaintiff claimed that this news was valuable to it for up to six months, as the documents in question were published every six months and it was on sale during that entire six-month period. The defendant appropriated the information contained in the plaintiff's publications and published its own version. Since the news was assembled by the investment of significant resources, and the defendant had used the information for essentially the same purpose and in order to compete directly for essentially the same readership, the Texas courts were prepared to injunct the use of the news by the defendant for six months after its initial publication. When compared with the criteria later set out in the *Motorola* case, there was an obvious issue as to whether the information in question was time-sensitive for the entire six-month period between publications. If 'time-sensitivity' is to be measured by reference to the period for which the material is made available for sale before being updated or replaced, then the concept becomes identical with 'commercial value'. It therefore ceases to be a separate and relevant criterion of misappropriation and is replaced by a far broader test of whether anything of commercial value to the plaintiff has been taken. The decision also contrasts with another Second Circuit Court of Appeals decision in *Financial Information Inc.* v. *Moody's Investors Service Inc.*[114] In that case, the plaintiff published daily reports and an annual cumulative volume of information concerning municipal or other government redemptions of bonds. The defendant published a bi-weekly supplement to a yearly publication that contained much of the information in the plaintiff's daily reports, although the defendant's publication was more selective and contained additional information. Actions based on copyright and misappropriation failed. The misappropriation action was dismissed, in part, because the plaintiff failed to prove that there was a 'hot news' element to its claim:

Because of lead times, to the extent that Moody's did copy from FII, the information it published would have been at least ten days old. The hot news doctrine is concerned with the copying and publication of information gathered by another before he has been able to utilise his competitive edge.[115]

---

[113] 269 SW 861 (1925) at 863.   [114] 808 F 2d 204 (1986).   [115] Ibid., at 209.

This reference to the hot news requirement appears to suggest a distinction between time-sensitivity and commercial value. While the defendant published its cards daily, the previous cards still retained valuable information that was not replaced or rendered obsolete by new information concerning new redemptions. Presumably, there was still some commercial value obtained by the defendant in publishing the information ten days after its initial publication by the plaintiff, but this did not alter the fact that it had lost much of its 'heat'.[116]

Reducing the plaintiff's incentive   The other key issue is whether the defendant has taken such a free ride that its actions would substantially detract from the incentive for the plaintiff to create the product or a product of the same or higher quality. This was considered to be a critical issue in *Fred Wehrenberge Circuit of Theatres Inc.* v. *Moviefone Inc.*[117] In that case, the plaintiff movie theatre sued a telephone information line that provided data about movie theatre schedules, including the plaintiff's schedules. Judge Perry of the District Court for the Eastern District of Missouri held that the plaintiff had failed to meet the fifth criteria identified in the *Motorola* case:

Plaintiff is in the business of exhibiting movies. In order for plaintiff to conduct its business, it is necessary for it to generate movie show time schedules and publicize those schedules to the public . . . The core of plaintiff's business and the source of the majority of its profits is not the publication of movie schedules, even though plaintiff contends it receives some revenue in exchange for its movie schedules. The core of plaintiff's business is exhibiting movies and the profit it makes from ticket and concession sales . . . defendant's actions will not reduce plaintiff's incentive to generate movie schedules or publicize them to the point that the existence or quality would be threatened.[118]

The decision raised some interesting points about the nature of the plaintiff's business which have direct relevance in a number of similar scenarios. In particular, it referred to the production of information as a necessary part of the plaintiff's core business. It suggested that even though a business may be able to derive revenue from information concerning its business, the appropriation of that information will not be unlawful unless the plaintiff's business can demonstrate that its incentive to create information of the same quality is thereby diminished. Some examples of this would be television programme schedules and telephone directories,

---

[116] Other cases more obviously meet the requirement of time-sensitivity. For example, *Lynch, Jones & Ryan Inc.* v. *Standard & Poor's*, 47 USPQ 2d BNA 1759 (S. Ct, NY, 1998), where the defendant breached a 35-minute embargo on the release of commercial information.

[117] 73 F Supp. 2d 1044 (1999).   [118] Ibid, at 1050.

as television stations and telephone companies would still have a very significant incentive to create directories for their customers and those wishing to telephone their customers. In other words, they would still be receiving a sufficient return on their investment to encourage them to continue to compile the information in question, although their market would be harmed in the sense that they would be deprived of the opportunity to maximise their return from the investment in the production and distribution of the information in question.

While the general approach seems to be consistent with the criteria expressed in the *Motorola* case, there are a few difficulties with this approach. In particular, there are questions of degree that need to be addressed. For example, telephone directories can generate considerable advertising revenue over and above the revenue from a telephone company's core business of telephone services. Some companies also hive off these related businesses to separate corporate entities, thus making them the core activity of that separate corporate entity. Hence, while the issue of whether the provision of the information is part of the core business is important, it cannot be determinative of the issue of whether the defendant's actions have a substantial effect on the incentive to create the product in question or on the quality of the product. Whether or not the related business is separated from the core activity, once significant amounts of revenue are generated from information associated with the core business, there must be some negative incentive effects of permitting a competitor to copy the directory. Therefore, there must be a question of degree involved and a decision made as to whether the impact on the incentive to produce the product (or a product of the same or a higher quality) is sufficiently substantial to justify protection against copying. Once that issue of questions of degree is acknowledged, it becomes intimately connected with the nature and extent of protection to be given.

The issue arose, but was not dealt with comprehensively, in the cases concerning stock market indexes where the core business was the provision of minute-by-minute information about stock market developments. Yet, the owners of the indexes argued that their incentive to continue to provide the indexes would be diminished if protection was not provided against copying as they would lose the opportunity to licence the use of the indexes for futures contracts.[119] However, if the plaintiff only has to demonstrate that it will lose some revenue as a consequence of the defendant's actions, the nature and extent of the protection conferred will be quite extraordinary.[120]

---

[119] *The Board of Trade of the City of Chicago* v. *Dow Jones & Co.*, 98 Ill. 2d 109; 456 NE 2d 84 (1983) at 117.

[120] This issue is similar to the 'spin-off' argument that has been addressed in various European cases and which was discussed in Chapter 4.

Summary of American unfair competition law

As the above analysis demonstrates, the tort is an amorphous one that has developed differently in different states. Yet, there are some general principles underlying it that can be divined from an examination of case law involving the tort. One of these is the clear separation of the application of the tort from copyright. All the jurisdictions applying the tort imposed some sort of pre-emptive application of copyright law, such that the tort had either to apply to subject matter outside of the scope of copyright or involve an additional element over and above that required to demonstrate a copyright infringement. While there was some disagreement over the nature and degree of that pre-emption, there was no disagreement over the need for some distinction between the tort and copyright. The tort has rarely, if ever, been used to confer protection on mere sweat of the brow. An action for misappropriation has had to demonstrate more than just a free ride on the efforts of the person expending time and resources.

These distinguishing features have varied from state to state, but may include the following.
1. A requirement that the information taken is time-sensitive.
2. A requirement that the plaintiff and the defendant be in direct competition with each other. Alternatively, a lesser requirement that the plaintiff demonstrate it had some commercial interest that was affected by the manner in which the defendant had used the information.
3. A requirement that the defendant's actions inhibited or would inhibit the activities of the plaintiff.

These requirements are also connected with the underlying policy of the tort which, in itself, has also been a matter of considerable debate since the decision in *International News Service*. Some decisions, such as *International News Service* itself, suggest that the tort is based on the immorality of reaping where one has not sown. The breadth of that proposition leaves open the possibility of ignoring the requirements that restrict the operation of the tort. However, later decisions embracing these requirements have clearly based the tort on economic considerations of balance between the need to provide an incentive to invest in the product in question, and the countervailing need for freedom of use of information and the importance of such freedom to economic and social progress.

In addition, none of the cases has restricted the use of information for personal, non-commercial use. Even those that protected potential or related markets did not impose liability on individual users of information for these purposes and, at the least, the potential market affected by the defendant's actions was easily discernable, even if the need to protect it was a matter of conjecture.

The net effect of this is that while the tort of misappropriation, as a basis for *sui generis* protection of databases, is not defined with complete precision, there are some basic principles that underlie the tort and thus, in theory, should underlie any legislation based on it. With these principles in mind, an examination of the various pieces of legislation that have been proposed can be undertaken.

Legislative proposals for *sui generis* protection

The history of the proposals for American legislation concerning *sui generis* protection for databases or collections of information is a complicated one. Between 1996 and 1999 a number of different bills were introduced into Congress. A number of amendments were made to some of those bills during their consideration at committee stages, and in 1997 legislation was passed by the House of Representatives on two separate occasions.

The earliest proposal for *sui generis* protection adopted some of the language of misappropriation. However, it took such a broad view of what constituted misappropriation that it was, in effect, an exclusive property-based model. Its similarity to the Directive was striking. New proposals since then have moved closer towards adopting the more recent common law approaches to misappropriation, apart from the requirement that the information in question be time-sensitive. In addition, exceptions have been incorporated into the proposals that are, except in the case of fair use, at least as broad as the exceptions to copyright. In terms of a comparison between the Directive and the legislative proposals, the most striking feature of these developments is that the starting point of the legislative process was the endpoint of the EU process and the endpoint, to date, of the process was the starting point of the EU process. America started with a proposal for what was, in effect, an exclusive property right that was almost identical to the EU *sui generis* right and, in the last proposed legislation, ended with a misappropriation approach that is similar to the unfair competition approach originally suggested by the EU.

The Database Investment and Intellectual Property Antipiracy Bill of 1996

The first proposed legislation was the Database Investment and Intellectual Property Antipiracy Bill of 1996 (the 1996 Bill).[121] It was introduced into the House of Representatives on 23 May 1996, a little over

---

[121] HR 3531 of 1996.

two months after the adoption of the Directive. Its resemblance to the final form of the Directive is noteworthy.

Definition of a database   The proposed definition of a database was almost identical to the definition in the Directive being 'a collection, assembly or compilation in any form . . . of works, data or other materials, arranged in a systematic or methodical way'.[122] As with the Directive, there was an attempt to distinguish between the computer program that may be used to create and operate a database and the contents of the database.[123]

The sui generis *right*   The proposed *sui generis* protection would have been conferred on databases that were the result of 'a qualitatively or quantitatively substantial investment of human, technical, financial or other resources in the collection, verification, organization or presentation of the database contents'.[124] This constituted a slight departure from equivalent wording in the Directive. For example, in the reference to 'collection' rather than 'obtaining' the contents would seem to have definitely ruled out the investment in generating or creating the contents of the database.

The proposed *sui generis* rights granted to database makers were rights of extraction, use and re-use that were defined in such a way as to include performing the same acts as those included in the Directive's right of extraction and re-utilisation.[125] These acts were prohibited if they conflicted with 'the database owner's normal exploitation of the database or adversely [affected] the actual or potential market for the database'.[126] Also prohibited was the repeated or systematic extraction, use or re-use of insubstantial parts of the database that cumulatively conflicted with the database owner's normal exploitation of the database, or adversely affected its actual or potential market.[127] An inclusive definition of conduct that would conflict with the normal exploitation of the database or adversely affect the actual or potential market for the database was provided in section 4(b). This inclusive definition related to commercial uses of the information. However, as the definition was only inclusive it very arguably included personal use of a database by accessing that database without the permission of the database owner, as such a use would conflict with the database owner's normal exploitation of the database.

---

[122] Section 2 of the 1996 Bill.
[123] Section 3(d) of the 1996 Bill provided that 'Computer programs are not subject to this Act, including without limitation any computer programs used in the manufacture, production, operation or maintenance of a database.'
[124] Section 3(a) of the 1996 Bill.   [125] Section 2 of the 1996 Bill.
[126] Section 4(a)(1) of the 1996 Bill.   [127] Section 4(a)(2) of the 1996 Bill.

Comparisons with misappropriation While the wording of the prohibition adopted the terminology of misappropriation, the breadth of that wording would have been such as effectively to confer exclusive property rights upon the database owner. The database owner would simply have had to demonstrate a conflict between the defendant's actions and the owner's normal exploitation of the database. Any unauthorised use of the database could have met this criterion. This in turn would have converted what was, in form, a type of misappropriation into what was, in substance, an exclusive property model in which any unauthorised use of a database would be illegal.

Comparisons with the Directive In addition to being, in effect, an exclusive property model, it contained the same flaws as those in the Directive that are described in Chapter 3. An example of this is its definition of a database and the potential for perpetual protection. A database became subject to the legislation once the relevant investment had been made but it was easy to renew the period of protection. Section 6(b) provided that a new term commenced for a database resulting from any change of commercial significance, qualitatively or quantitatively, to a database. Those changes included change through 'the accumulation of successive additions, deletions, reverifications, alterations, modifications in organization or presentation, or other modifications'.[128] Hence, like the Directive, it provided the potential for perpetual protection of a database. The reference to modifications to organisation and presentation also reinforced the difficulties associated with distinguishing between copyright in the structure of the database and the *sui generis* right.

In other respects, the 1996 Bill would have provided even more protection than the Directive. For example, the proposed period of protection was twenty-five years,[129] rather than fifteen years, and there were no exceptions whatsoever for fair use or fair dealing. Unlike the Directive, the 1996 Bill also dealt directly with the issues of circumvention of database protection systems and the preservation of the integrity of database management information. Hence, s. 10 prohibited the importation, manufacture or distribution of any device that had as its primary purpose or effect the circumvention of any database protection systems. The provision of any service to circumvent database protection systems was also prohibited. Section 11 also prohibited the distribution of false database management information or removal or alteration of database management information. Both of these provisions were analogous to the provisions in the Copyright Treaty concerning circumvention of

---

[128] Section 6(b) of the 1996 Bill.   [129] Section 6(a) of the 1996 Bill.

copyright protection devices and protection of copyright management information, that was adopted seven months after the 1996 Bill was introduced.

In addition, the proposed legislation did not derogate from contract law in any way. Consequently, even the legislative permission to extract, use or re-use insubstantial parts of a database would have been subject to contractual provisions that may have prevented even that limited use of the database. In addition, other legal regimes that may have had an impact on the protection of databases were preserved,[130] which included the tort of misappropriation.

There was considerable criticism of the 1996 Bill, particularly from scientific and educational organisations.[131] Partly in response to this criticism, subsequent bills ostensibly moved away from the exclusive property model of the Directive and were based more firmly on the tort of misappropriation. Consequently, the focus of the subsequent legislative proposals was protection of the database maker's market for its database rather than exclusive rights in relation to it. This focus manifested itself in the inclusion of a requirement that the owner of a collection of information must demonstrate harm to either its actual or potential market as a consequence of the defendant's actions.[132] It was not sufficient to merely demonstrate that unauthorised use of the collection of information had occurred.

The Collections of Information Antipiracy Bill 1997

This approach was clearly taken in the 1997 Bill (the 1997 Bill) that was introduced into the House of Representatives on 9 October 1997.[133] The 1997 Bill underwent a number of changes between its original introduction to the House of Representatives and being finally passed by that chamber after consideration by the Committee on the Judiciary and its Subcommittee on Courts and Intellectual Property.[134] The final version of the 1997 Bill departed considerably from the Directive. Liability was based upon misappropriation and a number of the difficulties addressed in Chapter 3 concerning the wording of the Directive were avoided.

---

[130] Section 9(c) of the 1996 Bill.
[131] See, e.g. National Research Council, *Bits of Power: Issues in Global Access to Scientific Data* (National Academy Press, Washington, DC, 1997), pp. 157–60.
[132] These terms were eventually replaced by a reference to the 'primary or related' markets. See s. 1402, HR 354 of 1999.
[133] HR 2652 of 1997.
[134] See HR 2652 IH1S of the 105th Congress for the version that entered the House, and HR 2652 RFS of the 105th Congress as it was referred to the Senate: http://thomas.loc.gov.

Definition of a Database   The term 'database' was actually abandoned in the 1997 Bill and replaced by the term 'Collection of Information'. 'Information' was defined as 'facts, data, works of authorship or any other intangible material capable of being collected and organized in a systematic way'. Even more importantly, the definition of 'Collection of Information' in the final draft of the 1997 Bill that was passed by the House of Representatives referred to 'information that has been collected and has been organized for the purpose of bringing discrete items of information together in one place or through one source so that users may access them.' This definition introduced a purposive element that narrowed the definition of a database and avoided the difficulties with the Directive's definition (as discussed in Chapter 3). For example, it would have excluded the application of the legislation to the facts in *Mars UK Ltd* v. *Teknowledge Ltd*[135] as the information there was not 'organized for the purpose of bringing discrete items of information together in one place or through one source so that users may access them'.

Prerequisite for sui generis *protection*   For the purposes of defining what activities would have attracted the protection of the 1997 Bill, the wording adopted in the 1997 Bill referred to an investment of substantial monetary or other resources in gathering, organising or maintaining a collection of information.[136] Again, the reference to gathering information seemed to rule out the possibility of any investment in the creation of information being considered relevant. However, the concepts of gathering and organising a collection of information continued to incorporate the copyright concept of creative selection and arrangement, as well as the sweat of the brow that may be associated with that selection and arrangement.

The introduction of the concept of an investment in maintaining a database raised the prospect of ongoing maintenance costs of a database as being a relevant factor in measuring the required substantial investment. As maintenance was undefined in the 1997 Bill, this could have included the costs associated with maintaining the availability of a database via a computer network rather than any costs associated with updating its contents. This in turn could have effectively led to perpetual protection. In the context of the 1997 Bill, this was not initially a large issue; the legislation (as it entered the House of Representatives) did not place any time restriction on the protection period of any collection of information. However, the period of protection was subsequently limited to

---

[135] [2000] FSR 138, [1999] AU ER 600 (QB).   [136] Section 1202 of the 1997 Bill.

fifteen years,[137] thus making it a 'live' issue. In addition, the reference to investment in maintenance had the potential to affect what would constitute harm to the database owner's market, a necessary component of any action and an issue that is discussed below. In addition to having to demonstrate the necessary investment, protection was only provided if the collection of information was part of a product or service offered in commerce or intended to be offered in commerce.[138]

Nature of the sui generis *right*   While the 1996 Bill contained some overtones of misappropriation law in its standard of liability, it also used the more traditional copyright formulation of use of the database 'in a manner that conflicts with the database owner's normal exploitation of the database'. The 1997 Bill omitted that wording, and focused exclusively on the harm caused to the actual or potential market of the owner of the collection of information.[139] This harm would have had to be caused by extracting or using in commerce, 'a substantial part, measured either quantitatively or qualitatively' of a collection of information. Surprisingly, no definition of extraction or use in commerce was provided and the term 'use' arguably encapsulated any kind of use, provided it was in commerce. In this sense there would have been an expansion of the rights of owners, as compared with the 1996 Bill, that contained definitions of extraction, use and re-use. Nevertheless, the limitation of protection to the prevention of harm to actual or potential markets was a significant change, depending upon how those markets were defined.

Potential market   A critical issue then became the definition of 'the potential market', something that was not provided in the original draft of the 1997 Bill but which was inserted in the final draft passed by the House of Representatives. It was defined as 'any market that a person claiming protection under Section 1202 has current and demonstrable plans to exploit or that is commonly exploited by persons offering similar products or services incorporating collections of information'. The distinction between actual and potential markets may reduce the scope of the rights of an owner of a collection of information although this will depend on how generously the courts interpret the notion of a potential market. The point can probably best be explained by reference to the two cases of *Standard & Poor's Corporation Inc.* v. *Commodity Exchange Inc.*,[140] and *The Board of Trade of the City of Chicago* v. *Dow Jones &*

---

[137] Section 1208(c) of the 1997 Bill.   [138] Section 1202 of the 1997 Bill.
[139] Ibid.   [140] 683 F 2d 704 (1981).

Company Inc.,[141] which were discussed previously in the context of the tort of misappropriation. Each case involved the use of information contained in stock market indexes that were prepared and commercially distributed by private companies. In each case, another entity intended to use the information contained within the indexes as the basis for the settlement prices for futures contracts regulated by those other entities. In each case, the creators of the indexes objected to this use of their indexes on the basis that this constituted misappropriation of the money, labour and expertise expended in calculating them. Despite these similarities in each case, there was a significant difference in the position of the respective producers of the indexes. Standard & Poor's had already licensed another entity to use its index for the purposes of settlement prices for futures contracts, while Dow Jones had not and did not have any plans at the time of litigation to do so. Standard & Poor's therefore had a significant interest in the futures contracts business by virtue of its licensing agreement,[142] whereas there was no direct effect on Dow Jones's existing business.[143] While both index producers were successful in their misappropriation claims, the position in the *Dow Jones* case may have been different if it had been decided by reference to the 1997 Bill rather than the common law tort of misappropriation.[144] This would have been the case if a court had decided that no potential market of Dow Jones had been harmed, because Dow Jones had no existing plans to enter the futures contracts business.

On the other hand, Dow Jones may have succeeded on the basis of the second limb in the definition of a potential market, namely that the futures contracts business was a market 'commonly exploited by persons offering similar products or services incorporating collections of information'. The question would then have become at what point such a market would be considered to be 'commonly exploited'. This is obviously a question of degree that would have had to be assessed by the individual court in each case. In any event, the distinction between harm to actual markets,

---

[141] 456 NE 2d 84 (1983). See also *National Business Lists Inc.* v. *Dun & Bradstreet*, 552 F Supp. 89 (1982) for another case that would have involved the concept of a potential market. Dun & Bradstreet published credit information concerning businesses and obtained its income from supplying this information. The defendant used this information to help it to create mailing lists. Dun & Bradstreet decided to become involved in the provision of mailing lists many years after the defendant's initial involvement in, and use of, the credit information for that purpose. The plaintiff was held to have been estopped on the basis of its acquiescence to the defendant's conduct over many years. The action was based on copyright and is overruled by the decision in *Feist*, as it applied a sweat of the brow test for copyright protection.

[142] 683 F 2d 704 (2nd Cir. 1982) at 710.   [143] 456 NE 2d 84 (1983) at 89–90.

[144] Actions based on misappropriation would been pre-empted by the 1997 Bill. See s. 1205(b).

as opposed to potential markets, would have created an incentive for owners of collections of information to use and exploit that information in as many ways as possible in order to maximise their protection.

Circumvention of database protection systems and protection of database management information   The provisions concerning circumvention of database protection systems and protection of database management information that appeared in the 1996 Bill were not replicated in the 1997 Bill. The effect of this was to increase the relevance of equivalent provisions concerning copyright material in American legislation passed to implement the Copyright Treaty.[145]

Permitted acts   The 1997 Bill would have provided for a number of permitted acts and exceptions to the *sui generis* right that did not appear in the 1996 Bill, although both the 1996 and 1997 Bills would have permitted the extraction or use of an insubstantial part of a collection of information. The 1997 Bill specifically provided that 'an individual item of information, including a work of authorship, shall not itself be considered a substantial part of a collection of information'.[146] This raised the possibility that the extraction or use of two items of information may have constituted a substantial part of a collection of information. In addition, this exception could not have been relied upon to permit repeated extractions of insubstantial parts that in total constituted an extraction of a substantial part.[147] The end result was that the provision provided some support for the proposition that as little as two pieces of information may have constituted a substantial part of a collection of information. It also merely confirmed that extraction or use of an insubstantial part did not infringe the legislation. This was already the case, as there was never any prohibition on extracting and using an insubstantial part. Unlike the Directive, there was no positive right conferred to use an insubstantial part and contract could have been used to override the entitlement to use an insubstantial part.

A number of other permitted acts were described in the 1997 Bill. For example, use and extraction for non-profit educational, scientific or research purposes would have been permitted, provided that it did not harm the actual or potential market for the product or service incorporating the collection of information. Again, this was no more than the description of an act that was already permitted, as it merely reiterated

---

[145] Section 1201 of the US Copyright Act of 1976. See the discussion of this issue earlier in this chapter in the section dealing with copyright.
[146] Section 1203(b) of the 1997 Bill.   [147] Ibid.

the point that an owner of a collection of information had no cause of action unless its market or potential market had been harmed. The only real concession made to educational, scientific and research institutions was in relation to the remedies for infringement. Under s. 1206(e), the court would have been directed to reduce or entirely remit any monetary relief if the database owner's rights were infringed by an employee of such an institution who reasonably believed that their conduct was permissible. Given the lack of concessions concerning the use of a database made in the legislation, it is difficult to envisage how an employee would have been able to demonstrate that they had such a reasonable belief.

Similarly, s. 1203(b) specifically provided that any person could independently gather information by any means other than extracting it from another person's collection of information. Again, this was simply a reiteration of what was never prohibited in the first place.

Other permitted acts were more relevant in the sense that they would have permitted what was otherwise prohibited by s. 1202. Where a person had independently gathered a collection of information but now wished to verify its accuracy, s. 1203(c) permitted that person to extract or use information from a database for that verification process. A specific exception was made for extracting or using information for the purposes of news reporting although a number of restrictions were placed on this. Those restrictions are a reflection of the elements of the action for misappropriation espoused in the *International News Service* and *Motorola* cases. Consequently, the news reporting defence was not available in respect of a consistent pattern of using time-sensitive information gathered by another news reporting entity for a particular market, if that information had not yet been distributed to that market. Finally, the owner of a lawfully made copy of a collection of information was entitled to sell or dispose of the possession of that copy.

Exclusions   A specific exclusion was made in respect of collections of information gathered, organized or maintained by or for a government entity.[148] This exclusion was in turn subject to an exception in relation to information that must be collected and disseminated under legislation relating to securities exchanges and commodity exchanges.[149]

As with the Directive, protection under the proposed legislation was expressed not to extend to computer programs. This was coupled with a further statement that a collection of information was not disqualified from protection solely because it was incorporated into a computer program. This had the potential to reopen some of the difficulties discussed

[148] Section 1204(a) of the 1997 Bill.   [149] Section 1204(a)(2) of the 1997 Bill.

in Chapter 3, although they were avoided to some extent by the purposive aspect of the definition of a collection of information (as discussed above).

Preservation of contract law and other legal regimes   Unlike the Directive, but as with the 1996 Bill and all proposed legislation on the topic, the 1997 Bill would not have derogated from contract law in any way. The law of contract therefore takes on an increasing importance in the protection of databases, as do other legal means of derogating from contract law and any other legislative provisions that strengthen the role of contract law in access to, and use of, databases. For example, anti-trust provisions that may have the effect of requiring the licensing of information by a sole supplier take on an increasingly important role in restricting any abuse of a database owner's market power.

Pre-emption of state law   While the 1997 Bill would not have derogated from any contractual provisions concerning access to and use of databases, it did provide for pre-emption of any state laws that provided rights equivalent to the *sui generis* right. This would have pre-empted the application of the tort of misappropriation.

Comparisons with the Directive   The 1997 Bill differed from the Directive in a number of respects, although arguably many of these differences were more of form than substance. One clear substantive difference was in the definition of a collection of information with its introduction of a purposive element. Other differences related to the test of infringement of a plaintiff's rights. There was clearly a shift away from a purely exclusive rights model to a requirement that the plaintiff demonstrate harm to its actual or potential market. Whether that would have imposed any real limitation on an owner of a collection is a matter of debate. As with the 1996 Bill, any unauthorised use of a collection of information could have constituted harm, thus effectively eliminating it as an obstacle to successful litigation. In addition, the actual or potential markets for the collection of information were defined in such a way that they could have incorporated almost any actual or possible use of the collection. A broad concept of harm, coupled with equally broad concepts of actual and potential markets, would have placed no real limit on the control of an owner over its collection of information. In addition, the undefined reference to 'use' of the collection went beyond the more clearly delineated right of extraction and re-utilisation defined in the Directive.

On the other hand, there was some attempt to distinguish between the rights in the individual contents of the collection and the protection of the investment in the collection. This was manifested by the provision that the use of an individual item of information would not constitute a breach of the *sui generis* right.

Comparisons with misappropriation   There were also significant differences between the 1997 Bill and the tort of misappropriation. While the 1997 Bill more closely approximated the protection provided by the tort than the 1996 Bill, it still provided vastly greater protection than the tort. The major differences were:

- protection for potential, as well as actual markets;
- protection against any harm, not substantial harm as envisaged in the *Motorola* case; and
- protection for fifteen years, not just during the period of time-sensitivity.

The Collections of Information Antipiracy Bill of 1999

The 1997 Bill was passed by the House of Representatives in 1998 but subsequently deleted from other intellectual property legislation that was passed by the American Senate.[150] Its successor, the Collections of Information Antipiracy Bill of 1999 ('the 1999 Bill'),[151] was introduced into the American House of Representatives on 19 January 1999.[152] The 1999 Bill, as introduced in the House of Representatives, was very similar to the 1997 Bill. Nevertheless, there were some significant differences between the 1997 and 1999 Bills. In introducing the 1999 Bill, Howard Coble stated that the main changes to the 1997 Bill clarified and embodied fair use and addressed the issue of perpetual protection in response to the concerns expressed by non-profit scientific, educational and research communities during the consideration of the 1997 Bill.[153]

---

[150] HR 2652, which was passed by the House of Representatives on 19 May 1998, was subsequently incorporated into the Digital Millennium Copyright Act, 1998, 12 Stat. 2860 (1998), which was passed by the House on 4 August 1998. The aspects of that legislation dealing with the protection of collections of information were subsequently deleted in the Senate pursuant to a Conference Report to the Senate on 8 October 1998.

[151] HR 354, 106th Congress.

[152] On the same date, Senator Hatch introduced two other pieces of legislation into the Congressional Record as a basis for discussion and negotiation. These were the Database Antipiracy Bill of 1999 and the Database Fair Competition and Research Promotion Bill of 1999. The first represented the position of database owners, and the second represented the position of users such as scientific organisations and libraries. Some aspects of these bills were incorporated into amendments to the Collections of Information Antipiracy Bill. See the Congressional Record for 19 January 1999 at http//thomas.loc.gov.

[153] Speech of the Honourable Howard Coble in the House of Representatives, 19 January 1999.

Further amendments were made during the consideration of the 1999 Bill at the Committee stage.[154]

Definition of a collection of information   The 1999 Bill as it was reported in the House of Representatives made some significant changes to the prerequisite for obtaining *sui generis* protection and the nature of that protection. The definition of a collection of information was similar to that in the 1997 Bill but a further clause was added, providing that 'the term does not include an individual work which, taken as a whole, is a work of narrative literary prose'.[155] In addition, a definition of maintaining a collection of information was provided, which did not appear in previous legislation.[156] It provided that 'maintain' meant to 'update, verify or supplement the information the collection contains'. This would suggest that it did not include the costs of maintaining or upgrading hardware or software used to store and present a database, although arguably this might be part of the process of verifying that the collection still contains the information it is intended to contain.

Material harm   In previous bills, the owner of a collection of information merely had to prove harm to its market. This could have included any harm, including the loss of licence fees from any unauthorised use for personal use.[157] The effect of such a minimal test of harm would have been severely to dilute the misappropriation basis for such legislation and potentially to convert the legislation into an exclusive property-based legislation. Consequently, the references to harm in previous bills were the subject of some criticism.[158] Consequently, a test of 'material harm' was adopted and aimed at injury that is 'so isolated, minor or speculative that the defendant's conduct, even if it were to become widespread...would not be considered by a reasonable person in deciding whether to invest in gathering, organizing or maintaining collections of information'.[159] The test of substantial harm adopted in the *Motorola*

---

[154] HR 354 RH of the 106th Congress.   [155] Section 1401(1) of the 1999 Bill.
[156] Section 1401(6) of the 1999 Bill.
[157] Statement of Charles Phelps on behalf of the Association of American Universities, the American Council on Education and the National Association of State Universities and Land-Grant Colleges to the Subcommittee on Courts and Intellectual Property of the Judiciary Committee concerning the 1999 Bill, 18 March 1999 at 8.
[158] Ibid.; statements of Joshua Lederberg and Andrew Pincus (General Counsel US Department of Commerce) before the Subcommittee on Courts and Intellectual Property of the Judiciary Committee concerning the 1999 Bill, 18 March 1999 at 4.
[159] Report of the Committee on the Judiciary, No. 106–349 on the Collections of Information Antipiracy Act, 30 September 1999 Section-by-Section Analysis and Discussion.

case was specifically rejected as being too burdensome for owners of collections of information.[160]

The market protected A number of very significant changes were made to the nature of the *sui generis* protection conferred as compared with the 1997 Bill. A starting point for these changes was the introduction of a new dichotomy to replace the distinction between an actual market and a potential market. These terms were replaced by references to the primary and related market of the owner of the collection of information.[161] Primary markets were defined as markets in which the owner of the collection of information is already offering a product or service incorporating the collection of information, and the owner derives, or reasonably expects to derive, revenue from that market.[162] The term was considered to be more in keeping with the tort of misappropriation than the term 'actual market'.[163]

Related markets were defined as markets in which the owner of a collection of information has taken demonstrable steps to offer products in commerce within a short period of time. The reference to demonstrable *steps* in s. 1401(4) of the final version of the 1999 Bill contrasted with the original reference to demonstrable *plans* in the definition of potential market, as that definition appeared in the 1997 Bill and the original version of the 1999 Bill as it entered the House of Representatives. A related market was also defined as one in which other people offer products or services incorporating collections of information similar to a product or service offered by an owner of a collection of information, and from which those other people derive, or expect to derive, revenue.

This dichotomy was then the basis for different prohibitions imposed in respect of conduct relating to primary markets and related markets. The reference in the 1997 Bill to a general test of extracting or using in such a way as to harm the actual or potential market of the owner was replaced by two separate prohibitions. The first was a prohibition on the making available or the extraction for the purpose of making available the collection of information, or a substantial part of it, to others so as to cause material harm to either the primary or related market of the owner. Consequently, it was effectively restricted to commercial use of the collection of the information by resale, rent, transmission or making available on-line. In this regard it was similar to the right of re-utilisation under the Directive, except that it is subject to a requirement of material

---

[160] Ibid.   [161] Section 1402 of the 1999 Bill.   [162] Section 1401(3) of the 1999 Bill.
[163] Statement of Charles Phelps concerning HR 354, 18 March 1999 at 8.

harm to the primary or related market. Extraction for personal use would not be caught by this prohibition.

The second prohibition related to other acts of extraction that caused material harm to the primary market. There was no prohibition in respect of other acts of extraction that affected related markets.

A substantial part   Finally, there was a significant change to what part of the collection of information could not be extracted or made available to others. Previous bills had adopted the Directive's approach in referring to either a quantitative or a qualitative test to determine a substantial part of the collection of information. The reference to both these measures of a substantial part of a collection of information was absent from the final version of the 1999 Bill. Instead, it referred only to the making available or extraction of all or a substantial part of a collection of information.[164]

The test of what constituted a substantial part then seemed to be connected with the investment in gathering, organising or maintaining the part taken. The relevant part of s. 1402 read:

Any person who [extracts or re-utilises] . . . all or a substantial part of a collection of information gathered, organized or maintained by another person through the investment of substantial monetary or other resources . . . so as to cause material harm to the primary market.

This wording suggested that in order for a part to be substantial the gathering, organising or maintaining of that part must have involved a substantial investment. Therefore, the wording achieved congruence between the subject matter of protection, namely the investment, and rights granted in respect of that subject matter.[165] The taking that constitutes infringement must involve a taking of a part that is substantial by reference to the investment in it and the effect of the taking must be to cause material harm to the investment by harming the market of the owner. The wording still leaves open the possibility that the investment in question may have been qualitatively significant by, for example, being a large investment in obtaining a small amount of material. Correspondingly, taking a small amount of material may constitute taking a substantial part as well as harming the owner's market.[166] One complicating factor

---

[164] Section 1402 of the 1999 Bill.

[165] This is confirmed by Report No. 106–349 of the Judiciary Committee on the 1999 Bill, which states: 'The intent is to prohibit piratical takings that misappropriate the value of the collection itself, rather than particular items of information it contains.' See the section-by-section analysis and discussion at http://thomas.loc.gov.

[166] This is also confirmed by Report No. 106–349. See the section-by-section analysis and discussion at http://thomas.loc.gov.

in this regard was the retention in the 1999 Bill of a similar provision to that in the 1997 Bill which provided that the extracting or making available of an individual item of information would not, in itself, have violated s. 1402.[167] This continued to suggest that two items of information could constitute a substantial part of a collection of information, provided that a substantial investment had been made in the gathering, organising or maintaining of those two items of information.

Opponents of the 1999 Bill had suggested that the test of a substantial part should require both quantitative and qualitative substantiality as well as appropriation of content embodying substantial investment by the creator.[168] This was based on the argument that the purpose of the legislation was to protect the investment in gathering large quantities of database from disparate sources, and that small quantities are 'precisely the individual items of data or information that should not be the subject of protection'.[169] 'Likewise, there is no justification for prohibiting the appropriation of even a large quantity of material that is qualitatively insubstantial.'[170] Nevertheless, while that argument was not accepted, the introduction of a requirement of material harm to the collection of information owner's market, the differentiation of what constitutes infringing activity according to the type of market in question and the linking of the meaning of a substantial part to the investment in that part, all contributed to legislation that had a better symmetry between what was being protected and the means adopted to provide that protection. In addition, while drawing upon some copyright principles, the legislation was clearly based on principles of misappropriation.

Fair use The 1999 Bill also contained more exceptions to the prohibitions contained in s. 1402. In particular, a form of fair use very similar to that in American copyright law was introduced in respect of collections of information.[171] Five factors were defined as being relevant to the reasonableness of the act in relation to a collection of information.
1. The extent to which the making available or extraction is commercial or non-profit.
2. Whether the amount of information made available or extracted is appropriate for the purpose.
3. The good faith of the person making available or extracting the information.

---

[167] Section 1403(c) of the 1999 Bill.
[168] Statement of Charles Phelps, at 7.   [169] Ibid.   [170] Ibid.
[171] Section 1401(a). The fair use provisions for copyright are contained in s. 107 of the Copyright Act of 1976.

4. The extent to which and the manner in which the portion made available or extracted is incorporated into an independent work or collection, and the degree of difference between the collection from which the information is made available or extracted and the independent work or collection.

5. The effect of the making available or extraction on the primary or related market for a protected collection of information.[172]

A number of these factors were similar to the four factors in the copyright defence of fair use but there were also significant differences worthy of note. These are an inevitable consequence of the difference in the nature of the subject matter. The similarities related to three of the copyright factors, namely purpose and character of the use, the amount and substantiality of the part used and the effect of the use upon the market for the copyrighted work. In particular, the commercial or non-profit purpose of the user is relevant to both defences. In addition, the transformative nature of the use is important both in copyright and in the context of *sui generis* rights. However, inevitable differences arise as a consequence of the criterion of assessing the amount of information that has been taken. With copyright, the amount of information taken is irrelevant as information is not the subject of protection. With the *sui generis* right, the protection of the information as it is contained in the database is the very purpose of the right. Similarly, when considering the effect of the defendant's actions on the plaintiff's market, the taking of non-copyrightable information must be taken into account, whereas it would not be with the copyright defence of fair use.[173]

Reasonable uses for educational, scientific or research purposes An important alteration that favoured database users was inserted in ss. 1403(a)(1) and (2) relating to educational and research activities. Section 1403(a)(1) states in part that 'no person shall be restricted from extracting or using information for nonprofit educational, scientific, or research purposes in a manner that does not harm directly the primary market for the product or service referred to in section 1402'.

This is a considerable change to s. 1203(d) of the 1997 Bill which purported to provide an exemption for such uses which did not harm the actual or *potential* market. As indicated in the previous discussion concerning the 1997 Bill, the effect of such wording was to provide for

---

[172] Section 1403(a) of the 1999 Bill.

[173] The criterion of good faith is incorporated within the criterion of the character of the use in the copyright defence. See Nimmer and Nimmer, *Nimmer on Copyright*, at p. 13.05[A][1][d].

no exemption at all from the liabilities created by s. 1202. The new provision provides some protection by permitting the educational, scientific or research uses unless they directly harm the database owner's primary market. Indirect harm to the primary market and any harm to any related market were excluded.

In addition to the defences provided for non-profit educational, scientific or research institutions, libraries or archives, the remedies available against these institutions were significantly less than those available against others who violated s. 1402. Under s. 1406(e) the court was directed to reduce, or entirely remit, monetary relief if the defendant reasonably believed that its conduct was permissible. In addition, criminal sanctions were not applicable to such institutions or their employees or agents acting within the scope of their employment.[174]

Other reasonable uses   The 1997 Bill had an exception for news reporting[175] but the scope of that exception was further limited in s. 1403(e) of the 1999 Bill. Section 1403(e) permitted use or extraction of information for the sole purpose of news reporting, dissemination of news and comment but not if the information in question is time-sensitive, the information has been gathered by a news reporting entity and the extraction or use is part of a consistent pattern engaged in for the purpose of direct competition. Section 1203(e) of the 1997 Bill was similar, except that protection pursuant to s. 1202 only existed if the news was gathered for distribution for a particular market and had not yet been distributed to that market. The new provision in the 1999 Bill did not require that the news be gathered for a particular market and protection extended to all markets for as long as the information was time-sensitive, regardless of whether it had yet been distributed to any particular market. Arguably, it went beyond the scope of protection provided by the principle in *International News Service* v. *Associated Press*. In that case, the information had not been published in the plaintiff's market at the time of its publication by the defendant. A strict reading of the case would lead to a conclusion that a finding of misappropriation would not have been made if the plaintiff had had the first opportunity to publish the material in its market. According to the more recent formulation of the tort of misappropriation in the *Motorola* case, misappropriation only occurs if the defendant is in direct competition with a product or service offered by the plaintiff, and the defendant's actions would so reduce the incentive to produce the product or service that its existence or quality would be substantially threatened. That would not be the case if the

---

[174] Section 1407(a)(2) of the 1999 Bill.   [175] Section 1203(e).

defendant were making the information available in a market other than the plaintiff's market. On the other hand, the problem may have been resolved by considering the time-sensitivity of the material and a finding that once published in the plaintiff's market, it would quickly have lost its time-sensitivity. Either way, the information would have been available relatively soon after its initial publication.

Special provisions for securities and commodities market information and digital on-line communications   All of the reasonable use defences contained in s. 1403 were, however, subject to special protective provisions contained in s. 1405(g) which provided specific protection for real-time market information concerning 'quotations and transactions that are collected, processed, distributed, or published pursuant to the provisions of the Securities Exchange Act of 1934 or by a contract market that is designated by the Commodity Futures Trading Commission pursuant to the Commodity Exchange Act and the rules and regulations thereunder'.

Real-time market information could not have been extracted, used, resold or otherwise disposed of except pursuant to legislation which already regulates such activities and ss. 1403(a), (b), (c), (d) and (f) were not available as defences to such conduct. In addition, s. 1403(e), the reasonable use provision concerning the reporting of news, did not permit the extraction or use of real-time market information in a manner that constituted a market substitute for a real-time market information service. This protection for this particular type of information went beyond that provided in the 1997 Bill.[176]

Special provisions regarding genealogical information   The trend towards creating specific provisions to deal with specific informational activities was continued by the inclusion of provisions concerning genealogical information. Section 1403(h) permitted the making available or extracting of genealogical information for non-profit, religious purposes or making available or extracting information for private, non-commercial purposes such information that has been gathered, organized, or maintained for non-profit, religious purposes.

Investigative, protective or intelligence activities   In a similar vein, s. 1403(i) preserved the right of government officials to make information available and extract it as part of their investigative, protective or intelligence duties.

---

[176] See s. 1205 and s. 1204(a)(2) of the 1997 Bill.

Computer programs and digital on-line communications   As with all the previous bills, an express provision was included stating that the legislation did not extend protection to computer programs used in the manufacture, production, operation or maintenance of a collection of information.[177]

The 1999 Bill went further and addressed some computing issues associated with on-line communications and their relationship with the protection provided for collections of information. Section 1201(5) of the 1997 Bill had effectively excluded protection for 'a collection of information gathered, organized, or maintained to address, route, forward, transmit, or store digital online communications or provide or receive access to connections for digital online communications'. A similar provision appeared in s. 1404(c) of the 1999 Bill. The purpose of these provisions was to ensure protection was not extended to 'functional network elements such as domain name tables and interface specifications, and thereby unintentionally impede the development and functioning of the Internet'.[178]

These provisions concerning computer programs and on-line communications, coupled with the more precise definition of a collection of information that focused on the purpose for a protected collection of information, would have been far more effective than equivalent provisions in the Directive. They effectively segregated issues of protection of computer programs via copyright and other issues concerning the operation of the Internet from the issue of protection of collections of information.

Government collections of information   The 1999 Bill also demonstrated a considerable concern with access to government information. It did this by excluding most government collections of information from the operation of the Bill.[179] It also contained generous provisions ensuring access for non-profit educational, scientific or research institutions, libraries and archives to collections of government information contained within private collections of information.[180] This was done by providing for what was, in reality, a compulsory licence in respect of government information contained in collections of information that were created prior to what would have been the effective date of the legislation.

---

[177] Section 1404(b) of the 1999 Bill.
[178] Statement of Marybeth Peters, Register of Copyrights before the House Subcommittee on Courts and Intellectual Property of the Judiciary Committee, 18 March 1999 at 4.
[179] Section 1404(a) of the 1999 Bill.
[180] Sections 1408(b) and (c) of the 1999 Bill.

Hence, protection was not extended to collections of information created to achieve a government purpose or fulfil a government obligation imposed by law or regulation.[181] This was so whether the collection was created by government employees or contractors engaged by a government entity.

In the case of collections of information created after the date that the legislation would have come into effect, if a collection of information incorporated all or a substantial part of a government collection, the owner of the collection would have been effectively required to provide a notice identifying the government collection and the government entity from which it was obtained. If this notice had not been provided in a reasonable manner, no monetary relief would have been available for violation of the prohibitions in s. 1402.[182]

In the case of collections of information created prior to the date that the legislation would have come into effect, in certain circumstances, the owner of the collection of information incorporating the government information would have been required to provide the information at the cost of its identification, extraction and delivery. If the owner had failed to do so, there would have been no action available for a breach of s. 1402. The defence would have been available to non-profit educational, scientific and research organisations and libraries and archives that used the information for non-profit purposes. It was conditional upon the government information not being publicly available or reasonably available from any other source. In addition, the organisation seeking the information would have had to provide a notice to the owner of the collection of information, stating the efforts they had taken to obtain it elsewhere and clearly identifying the information. Thereafter, the owner of the collection of information would have been obligated to provide it at the cost of identifying, extracting and delivering it.

Duration of protection   The 1999 Bill limited the period of protection for particular information contained within a collection of information to fifteen years after the time at which that information was first offered in commerce after the investment of resources that qualified the information to protection.[183] Consequently, the owner of a collection of information had a fifteen-year period of protection, and once particular items had been commercially available for more than fifteen years, they could be extracted or used in commerce. However, other items of information within the collection which had been available for less than fifteen

---

[181] Section 1404(a).   [182] Section 1408(b).   [183] Section 1408(c).

years would continue to be protected until they had been commercially available for fifteen years. Under the 1997 Bill, the fifteen-year period ran from the time of the investment that qualified the portion of the collection of information for protection.[184] Hence, under the 1997 Bill, the fifteen-year period started to run at an earlier point in time than under the 1999 Bill and so, in effect, the period of protection under the 1999 Bill was slightly increased.

However, the 1999 Bill would have had the effect of ensuring that perpetual protection could not be conferred upon the entirety of a collection of information, even if further investment were made in updating that collection of information. Only the new information contained within the collection would have been protected as older information only qualified for a fifteen-year period of protection from the first time it was made commercially available after the relevant investment in gathering, organising or maintaining it. This contrasts with the Directive, which effectively confers perpetual protection on the entire contents of databases for as long as they are updated by their owner. The only caveat to this proposition was the inclusion of investment in 'maintaining' as one of the criteria for obtaining protection. Some of the issues concerning the meaning of 'maintaining' have already been discussed above. In this context, there is a further issue associated with the fact that 'maintain' included verifying the information that the collection contains.[185] Arguably, verification of the information's ongoing accuracy after it had first been made commercially available may have constituted a new investment in that information. Consequently, a new fifteen-year period of protection may have commenced upon the making of the new investment in verification, even though no actual updating or supplementation of information may have occurred.

In addition, the 1999 Bill added a specific requirement that the owner of the collection of information had the onus of proving that any information that was extracted or used without its consent had been commercially available for less than fifteen years.[186] In addition, monetary damages were not available against a user who could not reasonably determine whether the information made available or extracted had been commercially available for less than fifteen years.[187] These provisions would have had the practical effect of requiring the owner of a collection of information to indicate clearly what items of information within its collection were protected and the date from which that protection began.

---

[184] Section 1208(c) of the 1997 Bill.   [185] Section 1401(6) of the 1999 Bill.
[186] Section 1409.   [187] Section 1408.

Retrospectivity The 1999 Bill would not have applied to conduct prior to the legislation coming into effect but, after coming into effect, it would have protected collections of information for fifteen years after they had been first made commercially available. This retrospective element to the legislation was considerably different from the Directive, which conferred the greatest possible retrospective protection on databases.

Remedies Section 1406 of the 1999 Bill provided for the usual range of remedies in intellectual property cases. These included damages, an account of profits, injunctions and impoundment of all copies of contents of a collection of information and all articles by means of which such copies may have been reproduced. It also gave the court the discretion to award triple damages. In addition, the 1999 Bill provided for criminal sanctions consisting of fines up to $500,000 and imprisonment for up to ten years for repeat offenders.[188]

Study and report The final point to make concerning the 1999 Bill is that it provided for the Copyright Office and the Antitrust Division of the Department of Justice to provide a report on whether the defence in s. 1408 should be extended to all collections of information that are not publicly available from any other source, not just government collections of information.

Comparisons with the Directive The final version of the 1999 Bill was quite distinct from the Directive. The requirement to prove material harm and the references to primary and related markets firmly shifted the legislation into a misappropriation model and further away from the exclusive rights model of the Directive. The prohibitions also reflected a clearer relationship between protection for the investment in creating the collection and the infringing uses of the collection. In addition, changes to the provisions concerning the renewal of the period of protection eliminated the possibility of perpetual protection for the entire collection of information.

The proposed exceptions also reflected a more sophisticated approach to the differences in types of information.[189] The general defence of fair use provided a defence based on a number of criteria that took account of varying uses of different types of information. Other exceptions from those for genealogical information to information gathered for intelligence and security purposes exemplified the difficulties in thinking of

---

[188] Section 1407.
[189] This issue is addressed in more detail in Chapter 6.

information as a homogenous item. In addition, these exceptions would have ensured that the *sui generis* right did not unnecessarily cut across copyright law and they would have tailored the rights conferred so that the legislation was targeted at protection of the investment.

The one area in which, by comparison with the Directive, the 1999 Bill can be considered to have favoured the owners of databases over users was in relation to the derogation from contractual arrangements concerning access to, and use of, databases. The Directive provides a positive right to lawful users of databases to extract and re-utilise insubstantial parts of a database. The 1999 Bill did not prevent contractual restrictions on extracting and making available insubstantial parts of a collection of information. The only conceivable derogation from contract law provided for under the 1999 Bill was in relation to collections of government information pursuant to s. 1408(c). Even this provision only indirectly dealt with contract law, as it effectively conferred a positive right on a user to extract and make information available in certain prescribed circumstances by exempting them from any liability for violating the prohibitions in s. 1402. However, it did not confer a positive obligation on the owner of the collection of information to supply the information in question. So while the legal basis for preventing access to the information was removed, there was no restriction on the use of technological devices by the owner of the collection to prevent or restrict access to the information. In any event, both the Directive and the American legislation shied away from compulsory licences and left that issue for later consideration.

Comparisons with misappropriation   Despite the changes that moved the proposed legislation further away from the Directive, the protection was still clearly greater than that conferred by the tort of misappropriation. The reluctance to embrace a test of substantial harm as opposed to material harm was the most important manifestation of this. Consequently, while the proposed legislation clearly moved closer to a misappropriation model, there were still significant differences between the two and a view that the common law tort of misappropriation does not provide sufficient protection for collections of information.

Nevertheless, it did move towards a model of protection designed to ensure some return on the investment of an owner without attempting to capture for the owner the entire commercial value of the collection. The adoption of the standard of material harm, the introduction of the concepts of primary and related markets and the exceptions were examples of this. Another important example was the introduction of provisions that would have ensured that particular information went into the public domain fifteen years after it was first made commercially available.

The Consumer and Investor Access to Information Bill of 1999

There has been one other piece of legislation introduced to Congress concerning this issue. On 20 May 1999, the Honorable Tom Bliley introduced the Consumer and Investor Access to Information Bill of 1999 (the Alternative Bill).[190] The Alternative Bill was a counterpoint to the 1999 Bill. In many ways, it could be considered to be an ambit claim by those opposed to the 1999 Bill. It proposed a considerably narrower *sui generis* right than that proposed in previous Bills. The *sui generis* right proposed was a right to prevent the sale or distribution to the public of a duplicate of a database in circumstances where the sale or distribution was in competition with that other database.[191] There was no prohibition on the duplication of any part of the database less than the entirety. Even with this very minimalist protection, there were also a number of broad exclusions and permitted acts. For example, s. 103(d) permitted duplication for scientific, educational or research purposes provided it was not part of a consistent pattern engaged in for the purpose of direct commercial competition. The Alternative Bill also excluded government databases altogether from protection.[192]

Summary of the American position

Ultimately, both the 1999 Bill and the Alternative Bill lapsed at the end of the 106th Congress. Consequently, the United States is still to pass any *sui generis* legislation[193] and protection for databases is derived principally from copyright, misappropriation and contract. Nevertheless, the various bills that have been proposed demonstrate the considerable range of possible models of protection. Apart from the quasi-copyright model adopted in the Directive, any number of variations of a misappropriation-based model could be adopted. As indicated at the outset of the discussion of the history of the American legislative proposals, the starting point for proposals in the United States was the finishing point for the EU and the finishing point, at least at the time of writing, is very similar to the EU's

---

[190] HR 1858 of the 106th Congress.   [191] Section 102 of the Alternative Bill.
[192] Section 104 of the Alternative Bill.
[193] During 2001 joint meetings of the Judiciary Committee and the Commerce Committee were held in an attempt to produce legislation based on a consensus of the opposing viewpoints. At the time of writing, no new legislation had been proposed.

starting point. The United States has eschewed an exclusive property approach. Instead, it has opted for a misappropriation-based approach which focuses on the effect of the defendant's actions on the plaintiff and the plaintiff's capacity to obtain a reasonable return on its investment in the production of the database or collection of information.

There is some question about the extent to which the early draft legislation such as the 1996 and 1997 Bills did in fact adopt an unfair competition approach. The necessary harm would have been caused by any person using a collection of information without authorisation. It would have been an irrelevant requirement in that every plaintiff would have been able to satisfy it without the slightest difficulty. The concepts of actual and potential markets were sufficiently broad to suggest that almost any use of a substantial part of the database by anyone would have constituted the necessary harm. Their replacement with the terms 'primary' and 'related' and the introduction of a requirement of material harm are more in keeping with the tort of misappropriation, although they still depart significantly from the most recent iterations of the elements of that tort. The wide scope of the prohibited acts with their reference to use of a collection of information, a term that has been described as having 'no meaningful bound',[194] also raised doubts about the extent to which the proposed legislation did anything other than provide exclusive property rights similar to those granted by the Directive.

The final drafts of legislation that were considered by Congress went a long way to moving from the original draft in the 1996 Bill that was based on the Directive to an approach more firmly based on the more modern concept of misappropriation as described in the *Motorola* case. Nevertheless, considerable differences between this draft legislation and the tort of misappropriation still exist. There are some obvious reasons for the differences between the legislative approach and the tort of misappropriation. In particular, the latter is the product of American common law and, by its nature, has progressed, regressed, expanded and contracted in response to individual court decisions. These decisions, in turn, have arguably been influenced by prevailing judicial views about the nature of competition and the role of courts in shaping it. The tort of misappropriation is also more general in nature and, in keeping with a tort that had its origin during the First World War, is not specifically designed to respond to the technological issues surrounding on-line databases. On the other hand, the proposed legislation is designed to deal with one specific aspect or type of misappropriation. It deals with that one issue and its various complexities.

---

[194] Statement of Charles Phelps, at 8.

The later drafts acknowledged the complexity of this issue and responded to individual issues in far more detail than the 1996 Bill. This was exemplified by the specific provisions proposed concerning a raft of individual issues, including access to government information, use of information by educational and research institutions, use of share market information, use of genealogical information and use of information for intelligence activities. In addition, a number of more general exceptions and defences were proposed that mirrored provisions concerning exceptions and defences to copyright infringement.

The end result is an approach to *sui generis* protection for databases that is a hybrid of the tort of misappropriation, copyright law, protection for sweat of the brow and protection for the interests of specific groups with sufficient lobbying power to have those interests considered by Congress. It is, in short, a far more complex piece of proposed law than the Directive.

There are some obvious reasons for this complexity. The adoption of a misappropriation approach in itself immediately introduces some complexity. It requires a consideration of economic issues, such as the market of the owner of the collection of information and harm to that market. It acknowledges the need for a balance between protection for investors and access to information, and for that balance to be determined by a judge. In contrast, the Directive's approach is more simplistic, with its exclusive property-based approach to protection coupled with a relatively small number of exceptions.

There are also some practical reasons for these differences that should be acknowledged. The nature of a Directive, as opposed to American federal legislation, is that it deals with general principles and issues that must be implemented and addressed by Member States. The details of the legislation in each Member State must be determined by that Member State in the context of its own legal system. In contrast, the American legislation is obviously more specific and detailed as it is the sole and final legislative statement on the issue of *sui generis* protection. Partly for this reason, it deals more specifically with a greater number of particular types of information. For example, the issue of access to databases containing government information is dealt with quite specifically in the American legislation. In the Directive, it receives general recognition, but the details of access to government information are left to the legislation of Member States.

Even with an acknowledgment of these differences between the nature of a Directive and specific legislation, there are some respects in which the later American proposals are clearly superior to the Directive. That superiority flows from the manner in which some drafting issues are addressed, such as the definition of a collection of information. It

also flows from the willingness to accept and address the conceptual issues associated with different types of information and different uses of
that information. For example, the equivalent of the fair use defence acknowledges the difficulty in sharply distinguishing between commercial
and non-profit activity, particularly in the education and research sectors.
These and similar points are discussed in more detail in Chapter 6.

6 International aspects of protection of databases

This chapter has two main parts. The first part examines the application of existing international copyright agreements to the protection of databases. In the course of that examination, the argument is made that the Member States of the EU may be in breach of their international copyright obligations to accord national treatment and most favoured nation status to other members of relevant international agreements, by not providing the same *sui generis* protection for foreign databases as that provided to EU databases. This argument is based on the points made in Chapter 3 concerning the overlap between the *sui generis* right and copyright. The Directive's *sui generis* protection may be categorised as copyright and, consequently, national treatment must be accorded to all databases, regardless of their geographical origin. In turn, this has implications for the argument that other countries, such as the United States, should provide similar protection in order to obtain reciprocal protection from the EU.[1] If the EU is already obliged to accord national treatment, that argument loses all merit.[2]

The second part of the chapter examines the steps taken to date towards a multilateral treaty that would deal specifically with database protection. It also discusses the myriad of bilateral agreements entered into by the EU with other countries that effectively 'export' the *sui generis* right of the Directive to those countries as part of the *acquis communitaire* of the EU. The very nature of the discussion concerning databases requires some consideration of these international legal dimensions. Geography is largely irrelevant to the computer networks that permit the almost instantaneous transmission of large amounts of information to any point

---

[1] See for example the testimony of Henry Horbaczewski on behalf of Reed Elsevier in respect of the Alternative Bill on 15 June 1999 before the Subcommittee on Telecommunications, Trade and Consumer Protection at http://thomas.loc.gov.

[2] In any event, the Clinton Administration indicated its preparedness to take action against countries that failed to protect its databases. See the Statement of Andrew Pincus, General Counsel United States Department of Commerce before the Subcommittee on Courts and Intellectual Property Concerning the 1999 Bill on 18 March 1999, at 20–1.

on the globe from anywhere else. In contrast, the actual legal protection and regulation of databases is primarily done on a territorial basis. Public international law determines the extent to which individual territorial laws may be harmonised, reducing the impact of the territoriality of legislative rights. For example, the creation of minimum standards of protection for copyright ensures that similar standards of protection are provided to databases throughout much of the world. In the absence of some international uniformity of protection, the global digital environment will work against the effectiveness of *sui generis* legislation if it is only provided in a small number of countries. This will certainly be the case for databases that have a global market. The legislation of the Member States of the EU will have its greatest effect on databases that cater primarily for national markets. An international regime of protection is therefore necessary if databases with international markets are to be adequately protected.

The initial proposal for a multilateral treaty under the auspices of WIPO was based on the Directive and the EU has continued to argue in WIPO that the Directive is a sound model for protection. The EU's promotion of the Directive as a template for international protection has encountered stern opposition from a coalition of scientific and library organisations and the majority of developing countries. While those debates in WIPO have not significantly advanced the conceptual debate for and against *sui generis* protection, they have served to identify very clearly the different stakeholders and their interests in the debate.

In response to the lack of progress in WIPO, the EU has shifted its efforts to its bilateral arrangements with other countries, especially other European countries. Within the framework of existing general bilateral arrangements, it has ensured that almost every European country and a number of other countries will have the *sui generis* right within the forseeable future.

International agreements concerning copyright protection of databases

There are three main international agreements specifically dealing with collections or compilations which consequently impact on databases. All of them relate to the copyright protection of databases. They are the Berne Convention, TRIPS and the Copyright Treaty. The Berne Convention guarantees quite minimal protection for compilations of literary and artistic works. Article 2(5) provides that:

Collections of literary and artistic works such as encyclopedias and anthologies which, by reason of the selection and arrangement of their contents, constitute intellectual creations shall be protected as such, without prejudice to the copyright in each of the works forming part of such collections.

This provision was restricted to collections of literary and artistic works rather than collections of information where the individual pieces of information were not in a form entitling them to copyright protection.

This minimal protection was expanded under TRIPS and the Copyright Treaty. Both included provisions that expanded this protection to collections of data generally. However, this protection is conditional upon the collection being selected or arranged in such a way as to constitute an intellectual creation. For example, Article 4 of the Copyright Treaty reads:

Compilations of data or other material, in any form, which by reason of the selection or arrangement of their contents constitute intellectual creations, are protected as such. This protection does not extend to the data or the material itself and is without prejudice to any copyright subsisting in the data or material contained in the compilation.

Hence, there is no requirement to provide protection for sweat of the brow under any of these international agreements, although it should be remembered that these agreements provide minimum standards of protection. Individual nations or groups of nations such as the EU are at liberty to provide higher levels of protection. However, the effect of the Directive and the decision in *Feist*, at least in theory, has been to standardise copyright protection for databases to the level described in TRIPS and the Copyright Treaty. Of course, it should be noted that the provisions in those agreements concerning collections of information are more likely to be a reflection of decisions in the EU and the United States to adopt that standard rather than the cause of those decisions.

There are also more general provisions concerning copyright protection that have an impact on the legal protection of databases, particularly electronic databases, in an indirect way. These provisions are the provisions in the Copyright Treaty concerning electronic dissemination of copyright material. In particular, there is the new right of communication to the public and the obligations concerning technological measures and rights management information. Article 8 of the Copyright Treaty provides that:

[A]uthors of literary and artistic works shall enjoy the exclusive right of authorizing any communication to the public of their works, by wire or wireless means, including the making available to the public of their works in such a way that members of the public may access these works from a place and at a time individually chosen by them.

Given the massive use of on-line databases, any *sui generis* protection must also provide either the same or a similar right to databases that are not protected by copyright. As pointed out in Chapter 3, the right of re-utilisation in the Directive incorporates this right of communication to the public. The prohibition in the 1999 Bill on making available to others and extraction for the purpose of making available to others also covers the concept encapsulated in Article 8 of the Copyright Treaty.

Article 11 of the Copyright Treaty also provides that:

Contracting Parties shall provide adequate legal protection and effective legal remedies against the circumvention of effective technological measures that are used by authors in connection with the exercise of their rights under this Treaty or the Berne Convention and that restrict acts, in respect of their works, which are not authorized by the authors concerned or permitted by law.

The subsequent laws of contracting parties that have implemented this provision have placed restrictions on the manufacture, importation, distribution and use of devices that may be used to circumvent technological measures of protection.[3] Restrictions have also been placed on the offering of services to circumvent technological protection.[4] This in turn has restricted, or will restrict, the availability of such devices for other purposes such as the circumvention of technological protection for lawful purposes such as gaining access to copyright material that has entered the public domain and to databases that do not have copyright protection. In addition, the necessary difficulties associated with applying any standard of originality other than sweat of the brow also mean that it is often difficult to determine whether a database is subject to copyright and, therefore, whether it is permissible to circumvent technological protection of it.

Article 12 of the Copyright Treaty also provides that:

Contracting Parties shall provide adequate and effective legal remedies against any person knowingly performing any of the following acts knowing, or with respect to civil remedies having reasonable grounds to know, that it will induce, enable, facilitate or conceal an infringement of any right covered by this Treaty or the Berne Convention:

---

[3] E.g. s. 116A of the Copyright Act 1968 (Australia). See also Article 6(2) of the Common Position No. 48/2000 adopted by the Council on 28 September 2000 with a view to adopting Directive 2000/EC of the European Parliament and of the Council on the harmonisation of certain aspects of copyright and related rights in the information society, OJ No. C344 1 December 2000.
[4] Ibid.

i. to remove or alter any electronic rights management information without authority;
ii. to distribute, import for distribution, broadcast or communicate to the public, without authority, works or copies of works knowing that electronic rights management information has been removed or altered without authority.

'Rights management information' is defined in Article 12(2) as:

[I]nformation which identifies the work, the author of the work, the owner of any right in the work or information about the terms and conditions of use of the work...when any of these items of information is attached to a copy of a work or appears in connection with the communication of a work to the public.

Again, owners of databases subject to copyright protection will be given protection for rights management information. One of the key purposes of this protection will be to preserve information concerning the contractual terms upon which the owner is prepared to provide access to its database. The protection therefore facilitates the contractual process for gaining access to, and use of, the databases. The information would also be relevant to issues relating to the period of protection of the database. For example, the 1999 Bill effectively required the owner of a collection of information to provide a notice stating the date at which particular information was first made commercially available. The protection of such notices would be provided by Article 12 if the collection of information in question were subject to copyright.

National treatment, most favoured nation status and the Directive

The final relevant obligation under international copyright agreements is the obligation of national treatment. The Berne Convention, the Copyright Treaty and TRIPS all ensconce the concept of national treatment and, in the case of the latter, the similar concept of most favoured nation status. National treatment requires a nation to extend the same copyright protection that it provides to its own nationals to the nationals of all other nations that are a party to the relevant international agreement. It was a fundamental part of early bilateral copyright conventions and has been part of the Berne Convention since its inception.[5] It has remained a fundamental feature of subsequent international agreements concerning copyright. For example, Article 3(1) of TRIPS provides that:

[5] S. Ricketson, *The Berne Convention for the Protection of Literary and Artistic Works: 1886–1986* (Centre for Commercial Law Studies, Queen Mary College, University of London, 1987), at p. 5.54.

Each Member shall accord to the nationals of other Members treatment no less favourable than that it accords to its own nationals with regards to the protection of intellectual property.

Article 4 of TRIPS encapsulates the concept of most favoured nation status:

With regard to intellectual property, any advantage, favour, privilege or immunity granted by a Member to the nationals of any other country shall be accorded immediately and unconditionally to the nationals of all other Members.

Article 4 then goes on to list a number of exceptions to this requirement that are not relevant to the present discussion.

An explanatory note to TRIPS states that:

For the purposes of Articles 3 and 4 of this Agreement, protection shall include matters affecting the availability, acquisition, scope, maintenance and enforcement of intellectual property rights as well as those matters affecting the use of intellectual property rights specifically addressed in this Agreement.[6]

An important point to note is that while TRIPS specifies certain minimum requirements of protection for intellectual property, the Agreement specifically provides that members may provide more extensive protection than is required by the Agreement.[7] This, coupled with the requirement to implement national treatment and to confer most favoured nation status on other members of TRIPS, seems to lead to the conclusion that if a nation chooses to provide more extensive protection to intellectual property than is required by TRIPS, then it must provide that additional protection to nationals of other nations. It cannot provide that additional protection to other nationals on a reciprocal basis, that is on the condition that the domestic legislation of those nationals also provides that additional protection to its nationals. Some argument to the contrary may flow from Article 1(3) which states: 'Members shall accord the treatment provided for in *this Agreement* to the nationals of other Members' (emphasis added). This may suggest that the obligation of national treatment only extends to the protection required by TRIPS, but Articles 3 and 4 seem to be quite clear that the requirements of national treatment and most favoured nation treatment extend to all intellectual property protection, whether advantages, favours, privileges or immunities.

A critical issue then becomes what constitutes 'intellectual property' within the meaning of TRIPS. This is addressed in part by the agreement

---

[6] See the text of TRIPS and accompanying notes at the WTO website, http://www.wto.org/english/docs_e/legal_e/27-trips.pdf, at note 3.

[7] Article 1(1) of TRIPS.

itself, which provides in Article 1 (2) that: 'For the purposes of this Agreement, the term 'intellectual property' refers to all categories of intellectual property that are the subject of Sections 1 to 7 of Part II.' Those sections refer in particular to 'Copyright and Related Rights' in s. 1, while the other sections refer to 'Trademarks', 'Geographical Indications', 'Industrial Designs', 'Patents', 'Integrated Circuits' and 'Undisclosed Information'. In addition, the categorisation of any intellectual property regime would also be influenced by international conventions such as the Berne Convention. This is because TRIPS itself requires its members to comply with many provisions of these pre-existing conventions and clearly borrows from the concepts within those conventions.[8] The definitions of intellectual property and, in particular, copyright and neighbouring rights then flow from a consideration of those conventions and the additional provisions in TRIPS. For example, the Berne Convention requires protection for compilations of artistic or literary works where their selection or arrangement involves intellectual creativity, but TRIPS has added to that requirement by requiring protection for compilations of data or other material as well as compilations of literary and artistic works.

On its face, the *sui generis* right of extraction and re-utilisation created by the Directive does not appear to fall within the category of copyright or neighbouring rights. Hence, the Directive can stipulate that *sui generis* protection to nationals of other countries is only provided on a reciprocal basis. However, a closer inspection of the Directive's provisions leads to a different conclusion. As discussed in Chapter 3, the *sui generis* protection provided for databases is arguably copyright protection under another name. That discussion will not be repeated here except to note the following aspects of the Directive's *sui generis* right.

1. The same acts by the same person would, in many instances, constitute both authorship of a database for copyright purposes and making a database for the purposes of the *sui generis* right.
2. The test for the subject matter of protection for the *sui generis* right is effectively the same as for a sweat of the brow copyright regime. More importantly in the present context, it goes further by also providing that the *sui generis* right is conferred upon the intellectual creativity associated with the selection and arrangement of a database, or a combination of sweat of the brow and intellectual creativity.
3. The rights conferred on a database maker are the same as those conferred on a copyright owner.

---

[8] For example, Article 9 of TRIPS requires members to comply with Articles 1–21 of the Berne Convention.

4. The exceptions provided are very similar and, in a number of cases, identical to those provided for copyright. In addition, these exceptions are themselves limited by the general principle adopted in the Berne Convention that any exceptions must not conflict with a normal exploitation of the work or unreasonably prejudice the legitimate interests of the author.[9]

Not only was the effect of Chapter III of the Directive to provide copyright protection, but there is considerable evidence that this was the intention. Some of the discussion within the Commission and the Council leading up to the adoption of the Directive makes this conclusion almost inescapable. The argument that *sui generis* protection was intended to be a form of copyright protection is reinforced by the views expressed by the Committee's Opinion on the First Draft, which was prepared by the Commission. The Committee actually urged that the Directive simply confer copyright protection for sweat of the brow and suggested that a *sui generis* approach was not the most appropriate approach to providing protection.[10] It also expressed the view that if a *sui generis* right was to be created it should be 'as effective a right as it would be if it were a restricted act under the copyright in the database'.[11] While the preferred approach of not creating a *sui generis* right was not adopted, the second approach was. It differed only in form rather than substance from the copyright-based approach that the Committee recommended. A copyright-based approach to *sui generis* protection was also favoured by the database industry, particularly those producers in the UK, during the process leading up to the adoption of the Directive. After the release of the First Draft, a number of organisations of database producers objected to it and lobbied for a 'British-style protection' to be extended to the rest of the EU.[12] The dramatic shift in emphasis of the Directive from one based on unfair competition principles to one based on copyright principles suggests that those lobbying activities were successful.

In short, the only difference between copyright and the *sui generis* right under the Directive is that one is called 'copyright' and the other is called '*sui generis*'. Such a difference in form cannot mask the substantive reality that it is copyright for databases. As such, the EU Member States have an obligation to accord national treatment to the databases of all the nationals of those nations that are signatories to international agreements such as TRIPS and the Copyright Treaty.[13]

---

[9] Article 9(2) of the Berne Convention. This wording is also adopted in Article 13 of TRIPS in respect of copyright and related rights.

[10] Para. 2.6.1 of the Committee's Opinion.   [11] Para. 2.7 of the Committee's Opinion.

[12] R. Cobb, 'The Database Fightback', *Marketing*, 18 February 1993, p. 3.

[13] For a contrary view, see P. Goldstein, *International Copyright: Principles, Law and Practice* (Oxford University Press, Oxford, 2001), pp. 79–80.

The actual manner of implementation of the Directive by Member States of the EU also suggests that the individual pieces of legislation that implement the Directive come within the TRIPS definition of intellectual property, and hence national treatment must be accorded to all nationals of members of the World Trade Organization. The implementing legislation of the UK is the most obvious example of that. The UK implementation of the Directive is contained within regulations to the UK Copyright, Designs and Patents Act 1988[14] (the UK Database Regulations), reinforcing the perception that the *sui generis* protection for databases is part of copyright.[15] This is further reinforced by official UK documentation which shows that the UK government's intention was to disturb the existing UK sweat of the brow copyright regime as little as possible.[16]

There are also other consequences of categorising the *sui generis* provisions of the Directive and the legislation implementing it as copyright legislation. Once that conclusion is reached, all of the international obligations imposed by agreements such as TRIPS and the Berne Convention apply to the so-called *sui generis* rights. In particular, the minimum period of protection for most copyright material is fifty years after the death of the author.[17] Under EU law, the period is seventy years after death of the author.[18] The EU would be entitled to vary the period for its own internal purposes but it would be bound by the fifty-year minimum prescribed by the Berne Convention and TRIPS which is enforceable through the World Trade Organisation. The fifteen-year period of protection provided for in the Directive obviously falls short of that period of protection.

The major implication of such an analysis is that the attempt to pressure countries outside the EU into providing reciprocal protection will lack any

---

[14] Copyright and Rights in Databases Regulations 1997, SI 1997 No. 3032.

[15] Other Member States have placed the new provisions regarding databases in their legislation concerning copyright and neighbouring rights and identified them as a new form of neighbouring right. See, e.g. France, Law No. 98–536 of 1 July 1998 transposing the directive into the code of intellectual property; the Netherlands, Act of 8 July 1999 implementing Directive 96/9/EC 11 March 1996 concerning the legal protection of databases (Staatsblad 1999–303); Italy, Legislative Decree No. 169, of 6 May 1999, *Official Gazette* No. 138, 15 June 1999 at 5.

[16] Copyright Directorate, The Patent Office DTI, 'Directive 96/9/EC of the European Parliament and the Council of 11 March, 1996 on the Legal Protection of Databases: A Consultative Paper on United Kingdom Implementation' (London, 1997), at 10; and Copyright Directorate, The Patent Office, 'The Government's Proposals to Implement the Directive of the European Parliament and the Council on the Legal Protection of Databases (96/9/EC): Outcome of Consultations' (Patent Office, London, 1997), at 1–2.

[17] Article 7 of the Berne Convention.

[18] Council Directive of 29 October 1993 harmonizing the term of protection of Copyright and certain related rights, OJ No. C290, 24 November 1993, pp. 9–13.

clout if the EU is required to accord national treatment to the databases from those countries.

Public international obligations and the American legislation

In contrast with the Directive, the substance of the American Bills which have been presented to, but not passed by Congress, cannot be so readily categorised as being of copyright in nature. Indeed, there is very little argument that they can be. The nature of the rights conferred on an owner of a collection of information in the 1999 Bill is fundamentally different from those conferred by copyright. The reliance on misappropriation principles to define the nature of the prohibitions on extraction, and the making available of the collection of information takes the legislation outside the copyright paradigm and into the realms of misappropriation. The Alternative Bill goes even further in this regard.

Steps towards a WIPO Treaty on the Protection of Databases

There is, as yet, no multilateral agreement to provide *sui generis* protection for databases. There has been discussion of the topic under the auspices of WIPO. In particular, a proposal for a treaty on the protection of databases (the Draft Treaty)[19] was put to the same diplomatic conference convened by WIPO that led to the adoption of the Copyright Treaty.[20] This proposal was the product of preliminary drafts prepared by the EU and submitted at the February 1996 sessions of the Committees of Experts[21] and the United States in May 1996 to the same committee.[22] These drafts were then considered by the Committee of Experts in February and May of 1996[23] and a basic proposal put to the Diplomatic Conference in that same year.

The Draft Treaty did not receive any detailed consideration at the Diplomatic Conference owing to substantial opposition, particularly from developing countries. Instead, a decision was made to continue further consideration of the issue of protection of databases.[24] Partly for that reason, a detailed analysis of the provisions of the Draft Treaty is not really necessary. However, some pertinent comments on the Draft Treaty

---

[19] Basic Proposal for the Substantive Provisions of the Treaty on Intellectual Property in respect of Databases Considered by the Diplomatic Conference on Copyright and Neighbouring Rights Questions, Geneva, December 1996, CRNR/DC/6.
[20] CRNR/DC/6.   [21] BCP/CE/VI/13.   [22] BCP/CE/VII/2-INR/CE/VI/2.
[23] CRN/DC/6, at 2.   [24] WIPO Press Release, Geneva, 20 December 1996.

are provided below, followed by a discussion of the current position in WIPO concerning a treaty.

The Draft Treaty

The Draft Treaty was put forward in November 1996, soon after the adoption of the Directive. It was prepared by the Chairman of the Committees of Experts on a Possible Protocol to the Berne Convention and on a Possible Instrument for the Protection of the Rights of Performers and Producers of Phonograms together with some explanatory notes concerning the Draft Treaty.[25] This was also soon after the 1996 Bill was put before the American Congress. It is therefore not surprising that it was very similar to those two documents. It basically mirrored the Directive and the 1996 Bill which, in its turn, also mirrored the Directive.

Hence, it had the very broad definition of a database included in the Directive.[26] The basis upon which a database acquired protection was that a substantial investment had been made in the collection, assembly, verification, organisation or presentation of the contents of the database. The investment could have been either quantitative or qualitative. Explanatory notes to the Draft Treaty confirmed that the investment could 'consist of the contribution of ideas, innovation and efforts that add to the quality of the product' in addition to sweat of the brow.[27] Given that the Draft Treaty was based on the Directive, this adds weight to the suggestion (made in Chapter 3 and in the previous section of this chapter) that the Directive's *sui generis* right actually protects those aspects of the creation of the database that confer copyright on the database. In addition, the notes also stated that verification included 'subsequent verification or re-verification' (an issue that was discussed in Chapter 3 concerning the meaning of 'verifying' for the purposes of the Directive).[28]

The owner of a database was then granted the rights of extraction and utilisation that were identical to the rights of extraction and re-utilisation under the Directive.[29] Exceptions to the rights were themselves expressed to be subject to the requirement that they not conflict with the normal exploitation of the database and not unreasonably prejudice the legitimate interest of the rightsholder.[30]

As with other WIPO treaties and TRIPS, Article 6 of the Draft Treaty ensconced the concept of national treatment. This was perhaps the only significant deviation from the Directive which gave protection to

---

[25] CRNR/DC/6.   [26] Article 2 of the Draft Treaty.
[27] Explanatory Memorandum to the Draft Treaty, at 16.   [28] Ibid.
[29] Article 3 of the Draft Treaty.   [30] Article 5 of the Draft Treaty.

databases from non-EU countries, only on the basis that those countries also provided similar protection to EU databases.

The Draft Treaty provided two alternative provisions concerning the duration of protection. One proposal was to provide protection for a period of fifteen years, whereas the alternative proposal was for a period of twenty-five years. Again, this was a reflection of differing EU and American approaches on the topic at the time.

Further moves towards a database treaty by WIPO

Since the Diplomatic Conference in 1996, the issue of a database treaty has been discussed in various WIPO Committees, pursuant to a recommendation adopted at the Diplomatic Conference that the competent WIPO governing bodies decide on further preparatory work for such a treaty.[31] The issue was discussed at a meeting of the governing bodies of WIPO and the unions administered by WIPO in March 1997 in Geneva.[32] Prior to that meeting, the director-general of WIPO issued a memorandum in January 1997[33] proposing a tentative schedule for preparatory work towards adopting a database treaty. The proposed schedule involved the convening of a committee of experts to consider a draft of the proposed treaty that 'would be prepared by the International Bureau taking into account any written proposals of governments or the European Community' that were received by the end of May that year.[34] Thereafter, a further meeting of the governing bodies would consider the results of the proposed meeting of the Committee of Experts with a view to organising further preparatory meetings concerning a database treaty.[35] The clear intention behind the memorandum was to push forward with moves for a treaty on databases as quickly as possible.

At the meeting of the governing bodies, there was considerable opposition to this potential fast-tracking of a database treaty from a number of African, Asian and South American countries. For example, the Republic of Korea's delegation submitted that preparatory work on this matter should be deferred until after 1998.[36] Other delegations, from the Cote d'Ivoire and Pakistan, suggested that the contributions should be sought from 'relevant organisations, such as UNESCO, WMO and UNCTAD, in particular on the impact of a *sui generis* protection of databases on

---

[31] WIPO Press Release No. 106.
[32] See General Report adopted by the Governing Bodies (AB/XXX/4), available at http://www.wipo.org/eng/document/gov.body/wo_gb_as/30_4.htm.
[33] AB/XXX/3.   [34] Ibid., at 2.   [35] Ibid., at 3.
[36] General Report adopted by the Governing Bodies (AB/XXX/4).

development'.[37] A number of delegations supported the preparation of a technical study on existing laws and practices concerning databases.[38] In short, the overwhelming majority of represented countries favoured slowing down the process of adoption of a treaty on databases. The final decision of the meeting was to have an information meeting concerning intellectual property in databases.[39]

WIPO information meeting on intellectual property in databases, Geneva, 17–19 September 1997

The information meeting took place in September 1997. Rather than being a meeting intended to prepare a draft treaty, it was an opportunity for an exchange of information concerning existing national and regional legislation concerning databases and observations by various interested organisations such as the World Meteorological Organization (WMO)[40] and UNESCO (United Nations Educational Scientific and Cultural Organization).[41]

Observations by WMO and UNESCO

Both WMO and UNESCO submitted written observations to the meeting that expressed concerns about the potential impact of any database treaty on the free flow of scientific information.[42] Both sets of observations questioned the application of a free enterprise, competitive model to the issue of access to, and distribution of, data for scientific purposes. After describing the framework for the international exchange of meteorological data, WMO observed that: 'The activities espoused by WMO for the overall benefit of countries and peoples have required and thrived on co-operation primarily, not on competition.'[43] Similarly, UNESCO observed that there are a number of databases incorporating information relating to the earth sciences, the environment, oceanography or space[44] and that 'their success lies in the wide coverage that they can be given, together with the best conditions of access and effective use, without regard to commercial considerations'.[45] It went on to state that:

The rules that will govern exchanges involving this type of database . . . should not, therefore, be derived from the logic of competitive exploitation which is a feature of commerce . . . Data exchanges for the purposes of scientists should consequently conform to a specific model based on rules of cooperation separate from

[37] Ibid., at 3.   [38] Ibid.   [39] Ibid.
[40] DB/IN/4, available at: http://www.wipo.org/eng/meetings/infdat97/.   [41] DB/IM/5.
[42] DB/IM/4 and 5.   [43] DB/IM/4 5.   [44] DB/IM/5 at 2.   [45] Ibid.

those applicable to the commercial exploitation of databases. Scientists should be able to have free access to databases from all sources in exchange for mere participation in the cost of producing and communicating the data.[46]

Outcome of the information meeting

The report of the meeting revealed considerable opposition to any swift conclusion of a treaty on databases with a number of delegations requesting further time for study and analysis of the issue.[47] Ultimately, the information meeting adopted a number of recommendations concerning the distribution of information arising out of the meeting and the written submissions made to it. Decisions about the convocation of any further WIPO meetings on the issue were left to the competent governing bodies of WIPO.[48] Since the Information Meeting, the issue has been considered at five of the six meetings of the Standing Committee on Copyright and Related Rights (SCCR).[49]

None of these meetings has significantly advanced the cause of a treaty or the theoretical debate concerning the legal protection of databases. The first session of the SCCR was held in Geneva in November 1998. On the whole, scientific organisations opposed *sui generis* protection for databases, and developing countries expressed their concerns about the potential impact of such legislation, often repeating the points made by scientific organisations.[50]

One possibility that was raised by the Australian, Russian and Swiss delegations, apparently for the first time, was an international instrument with 'a certain degree of flexibility for Member States that allowed them to

---

[46] Ibid.   [47] DB/IM/6, 19 September 1997, at 2.   [48] Ibid., at 3.

[49] In March 1998, the Assemblies of the Member States of WIPO made some significant changes to its governance structure. Prior to these changes, WIPO had established ad hoc committees of experts on various topics, such as the committee of experts on a protocol to the Berne Convention. The role of these committees was to undertake preliminary work towards a treaty and when that work had reached an advanced stage, a diplomatic conference was convened to consider and, if possible, conclude the treaty. This was the process by which the Copyright Treaty was concluded. This system of committees of experts was replaced by a number of standing committees, including the SCCR which was given responsibility in respect of databases. See A/32/INF/2 for a discussion of these reforms; Assemblies of the Member States of WIPO, 32nd Series of Meetings. Geneva, 25–27 March 1998, 'The Governance Structure of WIPO'.

[50] See for example Report of the Permanent Committee of Author Right and Connected Right, 2–10 November 1998. Adopted by the Standing Committee, SCCR/1/9 and the views of the Indian delegation, para. 139, Egypt, para. 140, Indonesia, para. 154, Kenya, para. 146, People's Republic of China, para. 150, WMO, para. 159, UNESCO, para. 160.

choose the way they wished to implement [it]'.[51] A similar approach has been taken in the Convention for the Protection of Producers of Phonograms Against Unauthorized Duplication of their Phonograms 1971 and the proposed Treaty on Intellectual Property in Respect of Integrated Circuits 1989.

The meeting made two major recommendations in respect of future work concerning the protection of databases. First, that 'the International Bureau should organize regional consultations, whether in the form of regional meetings, seminars or round tables, during the second quarter of 1999', and second, that 'the International Bureau should commission a study on the economic impact of the protection of databases on developing countries, with a special emphasis on the impact on least developed countries'.[52]

Neither these regional consultations nor further meetings of the SCCR revealed any real changes in the attitudes or arguments of either governments or non-governmental bodies.[53] The study on the impact on developing countries is still under preparation. No date for its submission has been given and it is unlikely that further substantial discussion will be resumed until the study is completed.[54]

Summary of moves to adopt a database treaty

The initial moves to fast-track the adoption of a database treaty at the Diplomatic Conference in 1996 have been replaced by delay and continued requests for more information about the issue of databases. One of the difficulties with advancing the process is that there is no organised bloc of nations behind a treaty, or at least, a particular form of treaty. There are a number of nations and organisations that support some form of *sui generis* protection, but they have a diverse range of views on the form. The EU and its Member States have continued to support *sui generis* protection in the form that it exists in the Directive. Support for this approach from other nations has been limited to that from the Central European and Baltic states, which presumably have a political agenda of support-

---

[51] Ibid., at paras. 134, 137 and 145.   [52] Ibid., at para. 204(b).
[53] See the reports on the second and third meetings of the Standing Committee on Copyright and Related Rights, 4–11 May 1999, at SCCR/2/11, SCCR 2/10 Rev, a report on the regional round table for Central European and Baltic States on the protection of the rights of broadcasting organisations not on the protection of databases, and the Standing Committee on Royalty and Related Rights SCCR3/11 for reports on four of the six round table meetings. The Arab Group of countries and the Caribbean and Latin American countries did not provide a report of their regional meetings.
[54] E-mail to the writer from Carlos Claa, WIPO, 5 September 2000.

ing the EU as they may wish to become part of it.[55] There has also been some conditional support from a small number of African nations.[56] The Directive's approach has been supported by a number of non-government organisations such as the International Publishers Association (IPA).[57]

The United States has also indicated its ongoing support for some form of *sui generis* protection. However, in the absence of any domestic American legislation, the form of that support cannot be specified with precision. The position of the American administration certainly shifted dramatically from its original support for a treaty based on the Directive and the 1996 Bill.[58] By the time of the second session of the SCCR in May 1999, the position of the US delegation had moved to one of clear support for a misappropriation based national law concerning databases.[59] In addition, it appears inevitable that the form of any final American legislation on the topic enacted by Congress will reflect that view, and it will be very different from the Directive's exclusive property-based approach. Hence, even if consensus could be achieved on the desirability of additional protection for databases, the form of that protection is a matter of some debate.

This leaves open the possibility raised by Switzerland, the Russian Federation and Australia of a treaty that adopts a flexible approach to protection of databases. This may involve imposing a general requirement to protect the investment in the obtaining, verifying and presenting of the contents of a database, without prescribing the exact nature of the protection or unduly restricting the exceptions to any rights provided to database owners. This would allow individual nations to adopt either an exclusive rights regime or a misappropriation-based approach to protection. However, achieving a consensus on a flexible approach that actually provides any significant protection for non-original databases would not be easy.

The lack of a cohesive approach within the ranks of those supporting some form of *sui generis* protection is in sharp contrast to what appears to be a solid bloc of opposition to the approach taken in the Directive. This opposition has come from the Asian and Pacific nations, a majority of the African nations and a number of international scientific and educational organisations.[60] There is an almost uniform concern about the effects of

---

[55] SCCR/2/10 Rev, at 2.
[56] E.g. SCCR/2/11, submission from Ghana.
[57] SCCR/3/11 paras. 112, 114, 115, 116 and 117.
[58] E.g. Statement of Andrew Pincus ibid.   [59] SCCR/2/11, para. 96.
[60] In addition to the views expressed by WMO and UNESCO, the International Council of Scientific Unions (ICSU) indicated its concerns with *sui generis* protection, see SCR/2/11, para. 113; as did the International Federation of Library Associations and Institutions (IFLA), see SCCR/1/9 at para. 165.

any *sui generis* protection on developing nations and access to information for educational, scientific and research purposes, as well as access to information produced with public funds. This concern has been expressed in a number of different ways that ultimately resulted in considerable delays in progress towards a treaty. For example, there have been repeated calls for more information and justification for any *sui generis* protection at all. The most populous countries have all recorded their concerns with proposals for more protection. These include India, Russia, People's Republic of China and Indonesia[61] which, between them, account for well over half of the world's population. In particular, the International Bureau has been charged with commissioning a study into the impact of greater protection on developing and transition economies and that process has itself been a slow one.

The African nations have also attempted to use the issue of databases to gain leverage on a quite separate topic of protection of expressions of folklore and traditional knowledge. The original linkage of the two issues may have occurred due to the almost casual reference to it in the Memorandum of the Director General concerning the original draft of a proposed treaty in 1996.[62] However, the African nations have raised a connection between the two issues on more than one occasion, indicating their desire to ensure that issues of more relevance to developing countries are addressed before greater intellectual property protection is provided to developed countries.[63]

What cannot be ignored is that the proposal for the creation of a new regime of intellectual property in respect of databases is only the second major proposal for a new intellectual property regime that will have significant input from developing countries.[64] The other traditional forms of intellectual property, patents, designs, copyright and trademarks were well established before any of the major developing countries of today were engaged in any significant manner in the international processes for establishing international norms of protection. The interests and concerns of developing countries regarding existing intellectual property regimes have been dealt with as an afterthought, supplement or exception to established regimes. Naturally, the consequence of this has been considerable

[61] See, for example, Report adopted by the Standing Committee, SCCR/1/9 and the views of the Indian delegation, para. 139, Indonesia, para. 154, People's Republic of China, para. 150 and the views of the Russian delegation at SCCR/3/11, para. 74.
[62] CRNR/DC/6, notes on Article 2 of the Draft Treaty, at 8.
[63] General Report adopted by the Governing Bodies (AB/XXX/4) at 4, and SCCR/3/2 at para. 76.
[64] The first was *sui generis* protection for circuit layouts although it is arguable that this was merely a variation on copyright protection.

opposition to changes to existing regimes and rights to meet the concerns of developing countries, as nothing is more difficult than change to an existing scheme of rights and entitlements. An obvious example of this is the difficulty that was experienced in achieving a consensus on the adoption of the Stockholm Protocol to the Berne Convention concerning copyright in developing countries.[65]

Therefore, it is critical, from the perspective of developing countries and those organisations with concerns about the issue of *sui generis* protection of databases, that the initial establishment of any new intellectual property regime takes proper account of the concerns of those countries and organisations, as any subsequent changes will be extremely difficult to achieve. One particular aspect of this debate that may affect developing countries more than developed countries is the control of information created with government funds. In developed countries, the government and non-profit sector contributes about one-third of the funds used in research and development. In developing countries that percentage seems to be significantly higher.[66] In the next chapter, there is some discussion of the relationship between information generated by government funds and *sui generis* protection.

Given the concerns and particular interests of developing countries, the process of establishing a multilateral database treaty is likely to be a long and complex one, and it is extremely unlikely that the highly protectionist model adopted by the EU will be accepted internationally, at least in the forseeable future.

EU and bilateral arrangements

The EU's response to a lack of progress at a multilateral level has been to pursue database protection as part of the bilateral arrangements with particular countries with which it has existing special relationships. For example, the EU has a myriad of association agreements with various countries, including a number seeking membership of the EU. A condition of these agreements and membership itself is that laws of those countries comply with the *acquis communitaire*, the entire body of EU law. Examples of such agreements are the European agreements formed

---

[65] See Chapter 11 in S. Ricketson, *The Berne Convention 1886–1986*.
[66] E.g. in India in 1995/6, 83.6 per cent of funds for research and development came from the non-profit sector. UNESCO, *World Science Report* (UNESCO, Paris, 1998) at pp. 197–8.

between the EU and ten Central and East European countries.[67] Other
agreements are in place that commit nations such as Cyprus, Malta,
Turkey, Israel and South Africa to adoption of EU laws, including the
laws protecting databases. Other countries are also likely voluntarily to
adopt laws similar to the Directive because of their close relations to the
EU or members of the EU. Mexico and some Latin American countries
are examples of these countries.

In total, more than fifty nations have or will have in the forseeable
future, the *sui generis* right created by the Directive. In most cases, this
will occur as part of the process of adopting all EU laws rather than
specific consideration of database protection.

Conclusion

The end result is that while a multilateral treaty seems to be a long way
off, the EU's model has spread to almost all of Europe, South Africa,
parts of South America and other countries such as Israel and Turkey.
On the other hand, very considerable resistance to the model exists in
North America, Asia and Africa.

As indicated at the beginning of this chapter, the debate concerning
international protection of databases has identified the key stakeholders in the debate. In WIPO discussions, the concerns of key scientific
and library organisations and many developing countries about the EU
model of protection have emerged. The concerns expressed by global
organisations such as the WMO and International Council for Science
(ICSU) reflect similar concerns expressed at a national level in the United
States. The main opposition to *sui generis* legislation in the United States
has come from scientific organisations such as the American National
Research Council, an umbrella organisation for various scientific organisations such as the National Academy of Sciences, National Academy
of Engineering and the Institute of Medicine. The consequence of this
opposition has been to delay the introduction of *sui generis* legislation
at a national level in the United States, and at a multilateral level via a
WIPO Treaty. In contrast, the Directive's model has penetrated the legal systems of more than fifty countries with what appears to have been
minimal opposition.

There appear to be three explanations for this stark contrast in attitudes to the EU's model. The first is that in the years leading up

---

[67] Poland, Hungary, the Czech Republic, Slovakia, Romania, Bulgaria, Latvia, Lithuania,
Estonia, Slovenia.

to the adoption of the Directive, there were no pan-European or pan-EU scientific organisations in existence, let alone one sufficiently organised to lobby in opposition to the publishing interests that pressed for strong database protection. In contrast, there were pan-European organisations such as the Federation of European Publishers that were well organised and able to have significant input into the final form of the Directive.

The second reason for the differences is that the publishing industry in the EU was firmly behind the Directive, whereas American publishing organisations are split on their views about *sui generis* protection, with some publishers such as Dun and Bradstreet siding with the science lobby. This split has also been evident in the various WIPO discussions.

The third reason for the spread of the Directive's model to some countries is their unquestioning acceptance in bilateral agreements of all EU laws as part of the price of closer relations with the EU. There has been virtually no debate in those countries of the appropriateness of *sui generis* protection of databases for them.

These differences in attitudes, and the manner in which the EU's model has spread without any further debate to many other countries, demonstrates the desirability of caution in establishing any new intellectual property regime such as this. In the next chapter, the discussion on the justification for *sui generis* protection for databases concludes with a list of fundamental issues that should be addressed when conferring any new protection on databases.

7   The appropriate model for the legal protection of databases

The preceding chapters have involved a detailed analysis of the legal position concerning the Directive and American proposals for *sui generis* protection of databases. Chapter 6 examined the moves by the EU to spread the Directive's model for database protection throughout Europe and to other regions via multilateral and bilateral agreements. This chapter examines some of the justifications for *sui generis* protection of databases and recommends some key aspects of any future legislation or international agreement that provide *sui generis* protection of databases.

It does so by firstly looking at the arguments for *sui generis* protection. Part of this section draws upon the economic justifications for intellectual property regimes as discussed by Posner and Landes. At the same time, the costs of creating intellectual property regimes as identified by Posner and Landes are discussed in the context of databases. In the course of this discussion, this section of the chapter deals with some of the particular problems associated with the economics of information, particularly those associated with treating information as a commodity. It is possible to treat information as a commodity and, in many cases, desirable to do so. The critical issue is determining the nature of that commodity and the nature of the rights that should be given in relation to it. One of the particular difficulties in this area is that information tends to be treated as homogenous when, in fact, it is not. Consequently, different types of databases and different uses of databases need to be treated differently.[1] For example, there are difficulties in ensuring that the chain of information production, or what may be more accurately described as the spiral of information production, is properly maintained. These concepts of chains or spirals refer to the interrelationship between database owners, database users and those who contribute information to the databases.

---

[1] '[A] policymaker who mistakenly assumes that there is only one kind of information and that there is, therefore, only one rule of property law for all markets in information will create inefficiencies, leading to the wrong amount and kinds of information being generated.' R. Cooter and T. Ulen, *Law and Economics* (Scott, Foresman and Co., Glenview, 1988), p. 115.

In some contexts, such as scientific research, users and contributors are one and the same. Consequently, excessive restrictions on database users may impact on their ability to contribute to the databases, thereby having a negative impact on the amount and quality of information available. Therefore, legal rights in databases need to be carefully defined so as to ensure the information contained within them is used to its full potential.

After examining the application of economic theories to the argument for *sui generis* protection, this chapter examines some of the anecdotal and empirical evidence that supports those arguments, and some of the evidence that suggests that *sui generis* protection may not be necessary. The primary difficulty with this evidence is that there is no conclusive empirical evidence that *sui generis* protection is required. Nevertheless, changes to the law often occur without conclusive empirical evidence.[2]

There are also non-economic considerations relating to access to information that need to be addressed. They relate primarily to the role of information in a democratic society, and the need to advance science and the arts via the maintenance of norms concerning the use of information that do not treat information as a commodity. This leads to a conclusion that some exceptions are required in relation to government information and for news reporting. In addition, some arenas of scientific endeavour and exchange of information, such as those referred to by WMO and UNESCO, should be exempted altogether from *sui generis* legislation that defines information as a commodity.

This chapter concludes that while some additional rights should be conferred via *sui generis* protection, reform in this area needs to assiduously avoid the view that some *sui generis* protection is good and therefore more *sui generis* protection is necessarily better. There are good reasons for adopting a conservative and cautious approach to conferring any *sui generis* protection. They include the following:

1. The lack of convincing empirical evidence that strong *sui generis* protection via exclusive property rights is required.
2. Once created, it is extremely unlikely that an intellectual property regime can be dismantled. On the other hand, expansion of intellectual property regimes is common and undertaken relatively easily. Any new intellectual property regime can be expanded if convincing evidence for so doing is subsequently forthcoming.
3. Some conventional economic analysis itself suggests that any *sui generis* protection should be limited in a number of respects.

---

[2] US Copyright Office Report on Legal Protection for Databases, August 1997 at 76–7, available at http:www.copyright.gov/reports/.

4. The moves for *sui generis* protection almost inevitably involve some form of rent seeking, in which those with most to gain from such protection seek greater protection than that which is necessary to obtain a return on their investment in databases. For that reason alone, claims by database owners for protection should be treated with caution.

The suggestions at the end of the chapter concerning any *sui generis* protection reflect the points made above. They also draw upon the discussion in the preceding chapters (especially Chapters 3, 4 and 5), concerning some of the drawbacks of the Directive and the various American proposals.

The argument in favour of *sui generis* protection

The argument of database owners in favour of strong *sui generis* protection of databases has been consistent and simple. They invest money in databases. If their databases can be appropriated without payment, the incentive to continue to invest will be lost or significantly diminished. The resulting lack of databases or diminished quality of existing databases needs to be avoided. This economic argument is essentially the same argument that is made for copyright protection. In the absence of some legislative rights to prevent or restrict copying, there is market failure[3] as free-riders will not pay for the product at the market price which would prevail if improper appropriation did not occur. Consequently, legislative intervention is required to facilitate a market in which buyers and sellers of information are brought together, and forces of demand and supply determine the price of the information. This market facilitation is done via the creation of property rights that prevent others from simply taking what has been created.

In the context of databases, the particular difficulty with this approach is that the precise nature and extent of the property rights to be conferred are not obvious. With physical commodities, the use of the commodities by one person precludes that same use by others. Some form of property rights is required to determine which person may use the commodities in a particular way and which people should be excluded from so doing.[4] With databases, the consumption of the commodities by one does not interfere with the consumption of them by another. Hence, it is less obvious

---

[3] 'The failure of markets to achieve an optimum resource allocation.' C. Pass and B. Lowes, *Collins Dictionary of Economics* (2nd edn, Harper Collins, Glasgow, 1998).

[4] J. Gans, P. Williams and D. Briggs, 'Clarifying the Relationship Between Intellectual Property Rights and Competition', report prepared on behalf of the National Copyright Industry Alliance for submission to the Review of Intellectual Property and Competition, February 2001, available at: http://www.ipcr.gov.an/SUBMIS/docs/78.pdf.

what property rights should be conferred on the owner of the database. The status of databases as commodities is defined by the law that protects them.[5] Similarly, their economic value as commodities is largely dependent upon the character of that law. The stronger the rights provided by the law, the more economically valuable the commodity. The weaker the rights, the less valuable the commodity.

While there is a market for databases in the sense that there is both supply of, and demand for, databases, there is no such thing as 'the' market for any particular database. There are a number of possible markets that can be artificially facilitated by legislation conferring commodity status on databases. A very simple example of the range of possibilities is that created by differing periods of protection for a database. The First Draft suggested a protection period of ten years,[6] the Directive actually conferred a protection period of fifteen years,[7] the first proposed American legislation proposed a period of twenty-five years[8] and Mexican legislation[9] presently provides protection for five years. The value of the database would vary according to the period of protection conferred on the database owner, yet that period of protection is basically an arbitrary figure.

As can be seen from the analysis in previous chapters of the Directive, its preliminary drafts and the various pieces of proposed legislation in the United States, *sui generis* protection can take a myriad of forms. At one end of the spectrum is the approach in which a database owner is given exclusive property rights in relation to their database.[10] They then have almost total control over the use of that database by any person for any reason for the duration of the period of protection. As a result, they capture almost all the commercial benefits of the use of that data. The Directive's approach to *sui generis* rights most closely approximates this approach. The approach of the 1999 Bill to *sui generis* protection would have provided more limited protection. In particular, it would not have provided protection against every person using the database, as the plaintiff would have had to demonstrate that the use caused material harm to its primary or related market. The Alternative Bill would have provided even more restricted protection. These approaches were aimed at providing a return to the database owner for its investment but not

---

[5] In addition to any *sui generis* protection that may be conferred, protection already exists via other means such as contract, copyright and the law of trade secrets.

[6] Article 9(3) of the First Draft.   [7] Article 14 of the Directive.

[8] Section 6 of the 1996 Bill.

[9] Article 108 of the Federal Mexican Copyright Law 1996.

[10] W. Landes and R. Posner, 'The Economics of Trademark Law' (1988) 78 *Trade Mark Reporter* 267 at 267: 'A property right is a legally enforceable power to exclude others from using a resource, without need to contract with them.'

to permit it capturing the entire benefit flowing from the creation of the database.

A database protected by the proposed American legislation would therefore be a less valuable commodity to its owner than the same database protected by the Directive. Whether the protection provided by the proposed American legislation is insufficient or the protection provided by the Directive is excessive, in the sense that they will provide a sub-optimal investment in databases or a sub-optimal restriction on access to them, is the vital question. The difficulty is that there is no compelling empirical evidence providing the answer.[11]

The artificial definition of a database or a collection of information as a commodity means that there is no magical process that will lead to the most optimal utilisation of information. At the moment, government intervention is sought on defining the commodity that is to be protected; an obligation then falls upon government to consider the ramifications of the definition that it has created. It cannot define the commodity to be bought and sold and then depart the scene, claiming that the market mechanism will now resolve issues of optimal allocation of resources. There is no natural market equilibrium that will be achieved or, at least, not one that is satisfactory to database owners or, indeed, most stakeholders in the debate as the natural market price is zero. Government therefore has an obligation to become involved at a detailed level in defining and regulating the commodity that its legislation is creating. The proposition put in the Committee's Opinion that:

> It would be wrong to compromise on the question of whether or not something should be protected by allowing a measure of short-term intellectual property protection with a compulsory licence. *It is preferable to take a decision on whether something qualifies for protection and, if so, then to grant intellectual property protection of a high standard.*[12] [emphasis added]

is not self-evident. It is an assertion that needs to be tested.

Economic theory

We can utilise economic theories to analyse the economic arguments for *sui generis* protection. Many of them are similar to the economic arguments for protection of copyright and so literature on economic protection of copyright is worthy of examination.

In particular, the writing of Posner has often been cited in this regard and there is no doubt that his writing and the literature of other

---

[11] US Copyright Office Report on Legal Protection for Databases, August 1997 at 76–7.
[12] Para. 2.6.2 of the Committee's Opinion.

members of the Chicago School have been influential.[13] He and Landes have identified the market failure that occurs if rights against copying of copyright material are not granted, and the arguments for providing a property-based solution to that problem.[14]

Their analysis begins by examining the benefits of property rights. They note that property rights have both static and dynamic benefits.[15] The static benefits are that the property will be maintained by the person with property rights and those rights therefore prevent degradation of the resource in question.[16] With the use of real estate for farming, for example, a lack of property rights would lead to many using and exploiting the real estate for farming purposes, but nobody would invest in the maintenance of the farm as others would profit from that investment without contributing to it. This situation is often referred to as 'the tragedy of the commons', in which users will exhaust a resource that is available to all without making any or any sufficient contribution to its maintenance or improvement. Providing property rights in the real estate that forms the farm resolves this by creating an incentive for the property right owner to maintain the real estate.

These static benefits of preventing the degradation of a resource are irrelevant to intellectual property or, in this particular case, databases. The continued or repeated use of the database does not degrade it. The lack of static benefits leaves only the dynamic benefit of a property right, that it constitutes an incentive to invest in the creation or further development of the resource in question.[17] This is the argument for *sui generis* protection put forward by database owners. However, in addition to the issue of creation of databases, there is the issue of access to the information in the databases once they are created.

Price discrimination   Some economic theory suggests that very strong property rights in databases will lead to both the production of databases and access to them. This economic theory is based on two propositions. The first proposition is that the existence of strong property rights preventing reproduction and redistribution of databases will constitute a strong incentive to create databases. The second proposition

---

[13] See W. Landes and R. Posner, 'Citations, Age, Fame and the Web' (2000) 29 *Journal of Legal Studies* 319, for a discussion of a study of citations of legal scholars that lists Posner, Landes, Bork and Easterbrook (who are all associated with the Chicago School of Economics in the top fifty of cited legal scholars).

[14] W. Landes and R. Posner, 'An Economic Analysis of Copyright Law' (1989) 18 *Journal of Legal Studies* 325.

[15] Landes and Posner, 'The Economics of Trademark Law', at 267–8.

[16] Ibid., at 268.   [17] Ibid.

is that the owner of the database will have a considerable incentive to provide access to its database if it has strong property rights that permit it to engage in price discrimination. This second proposition is based on the view that once the database is created, the marginal cost of access provision to any particular user is relatively small. Provided that the database owner can engage in price discrimination by charging according to the user's willingness to pay for use of the database, the database owner will do so in order to maximise return from its investments. Price discrimination involves practices such as pricing according to the time taken to search, limiting access to a particular part of the database and charging different prices for off-peak access to on-line databases. Different users have different requirements that affect their willingness to pay. If the database owner can tailor access to the database to meet the different users' willingness to pay, they can maximise their return from the database while at the same time meeting the demands of all potential users for access.

Some form of legal protection is necessary to facilitate this price discrimination. If the database user does not have legal rights over the database, one user who acquires access to the database cheaply could resupply or resell the information to a user who would otherwise pay a higher price to the owner. This would discourage the database owner from attempting to engage in price discrimination and providing access to as many potential users as possible. Instead, it would need to charge high prices to all its actual users on the assumption that some of them will redistribute or resell the information. Hence strong property rights are consistent with both the production of databases and access to databases.[18]

The theory is dependent on the ability of the database owner to engage in price discrimination without incurring large transaction costs in so doing. If the cost of determining users' willingness to pay is too great or the cost of the contractual process is too high, it ceases to be worthwhile for the database owner to engage in price discrimination. In the absence of the database owner's willingness and ability to engage in detailed price discrimination, those whose willingness or ability to pay is low will not obtain any access to the database. In the case of those who are reliant on public funds to obtain access, this could be a serious problem. The issue of transaction costs is discussed in more detail in the next section dealing with the costs of property rights.

---

[18] L. Tyson and E. Sherry, 'Statutory Protection for Databases: Economic and Public Policy Issues', a paper prepared on behalf of the Information Industry Association and presented to the Committee on the Judiciary on 23 October 1997, at 3–4. This argument is made in relation to copyright generally in J. Gans, P. Williams and D. Briggs, 'Clarifying the relationship'.

In addition, the theory provides no extra incentive for a database owner to make data available for productive purposes, such as a new value-added database that may compete with the original database or database owner. For example, many of the decided cases concerning the Directive relate to telephone directories. In a number of instances, telephone directories have not only been reproduced but also improved by the party reproducing the original directory.[19]

A further assumption is that there would be pressure on any database owner to keep its pricing low, so to avoid competition from new entrants to the market. This in turn assumes that there are no barriers to market entry for that particular database.[20] For various reasons discussed below in the context of rent seeking, this may not be the position with many databases.

Given these possibilities, there is some justification for fail-safe provisions permitting use of insubstantial parts of databases and fair use, particularly for research and scientific purposes. In addition, there may be some justification for mandating the licensing of data to enable productive uses of it. These suggestions are discussed in the last section of this chapter. Nevertheless, this theory certainly does support, at the very least, a prohibition on the redistribution[21] of databases for commercial purposes. Whether stronger rights over use by individuals for purposes such as research or education are necessary is questionable in circumstances where copyright and contract may already provide sufficiently strong rights.

The costs of intellectual property rights

In addition to noting the dynamic benefits of intellectual property rights, Landes and Posner also note that intellectual property rights potentially impose four types of costs as well as conferring benefits, which are:[22]

1. rent seeking. Economic rent is the surplus above the minimum necessary to create an incentive to provide the goods or service in question. If the property rights provided in respect of a product are more than necessary to provide the incentive to create it, the users of the product will have to pay the makers more than the minimum necessary to provide an incentive for investment that would lead to the creation of that product. If the rights exceed what is necessary to provide the incentive

---

[19] The decision in *Feist* that has been referred to throughout this book is an example.
[20] Tyson and Sherry, 'Statutory Protection for Databases', p. 18, although they claim that there is little evidence of the exercise of market power in database markets.
[21] 'Redistribution' in this context also includes 'making available'.
[22] Landes and Posner, 'The Economics of Trademark Law', at 268.

to create the product, potential owners will expend considerable resources in competing to secure those rights;

2. the restriction of use of property that has a public good character. As
   information is not degraded by its use and distribution, placing legal
   limits on that distribution incurs a cost associated with denying the
   public access to that information. The benefits of the rights conferred
   need to outweigh those costs;

3. transaction costs associated with the exercise and transfer of property
   rights. Time and other resources are necessarily expended in negotiating the transfer of rights or acquiring a licence to exercise rights;
   and

4. the costs of enforcing the rights.

The application of these four potential costs of property rights and *sui
generis* rights in particular in databases is considered below.

Rent seeking   The resources invested in the race to obtain property rights over the subject matter of intellectual property may consume
many of the benefits of granting the rights in the first place. This race is
very likely to occur where there is 'a large potential gap between value
and cost'.[23] Rent seeking may be a particular problem with databases
for a number of reasons. In particular, while in theory the creation of a
database containing specified information does not prevent the creation
of an identical or similar one being independently created, there are a
number of reasons why that may not be feasible. If that is the case, the
race to be first to create the database will be a fierce one and considerable
resources will be consumed in winning the race.

Examples of this may be situations in which the database is the first
one in the area in question. Economies of scale may be such that it would
be inefficient for any competitor to produce a similar database and hence
the first database owner in the area would secure a natural monopoly. The
need for comprehensiveness of information in a database suggests that
the first to create such a database will also, in many cases, acquire such a
natural monopoly. In addition, the database owner may well have secured
exclusive contractual rights from various suppliers of the information in
the database. In that case, it is impossible for a later competitor to acquire that information directly from those suppliers without the suppliers
incurring liability for breach of contract, or the competitor incurring liability for inducing that breach. This could include, for example, databases
of medical and legal journals, as the database owner usually acquires an
assignment of copyright in each individual article before publishing and

---

[23] Ibid., at 270.

placing it on its database. Alternatively, the database owner may be the person with sole access to the information in the database, as is the case with telephone and television directories.

Competition law may be able to deal with the worst of these difficulties but for reasons already explained in Chapter 2, it is a blunt instrument that cannot deal with the majority of problems associated with the market power of database owners.[24] This problem can only be addressed by a careful crafting and limitation of the rights provided to them in the first place, not by an attempt to put the genie back in the bottle after it has been released. Under a copyright regime that only provides protection for the selection and arrangement of information and permits reuse of the underlying information, the possibility of competition based on the way in which competitors select and arrange their information is obviously far greater.

Under a *sui generis* scheme, there is a further danger that database owners will invest more resources in obtaining rights in relation to the information in their databases, and less resources in selecting and arranging those contents creatively in a manner that suits the database users' needs. Hence, the provision of *sui generis* protection could result in a decreased incentive to create copyright works. This could lead to the worst of all possible worlds. The benefits of *sui generis* protection may be eroded by rent seeking while the incentive to create copyright works may be reduced by the incentive to obtain a more easily procured form of intellectual property that delivers fewer social benefits. For example, the protection of qualitative investments in the contents of a database, as provided for in the Directive, may create such a problem, depending on how a qualitative investment and a qualitatively substantial part are defined.[25] The acquisition of important, individual items and their incorporation into a database may constitute such an investment, although the cost of physically incorporating them into the database may be minimal. If a small number of pieces of such information constitute a qualitatively substantial part of the database and extraction of that small number of pieces constitutes an infringement of the *sui generis* right, one could expect the expenditure of considerable resources to obtain exclusive rights in respect of such information. This is due to the large differential between its high value, as created by *sui generis* protection, and the low cost of incorporating it into the database.

Rent seeking also takes the form of resources being expended upon not only seeking to acquire rights pursuant to existing intellectual

---

[24] Some suggestions are made at the end of this chapter about how competition law could be modified to improve this situation.
[25] See the discussion of this issue in Chapter 3.

property regimes but also expending resources on altering and expanding the scope of intellectual property rights by litigation or lobbying for new legislation.[26] The manner in which the first versions of the Directive were transformed from a limited property right over electronic databases, to one granting a very strong property right in respect of all databases, may be an example.

Loss of public good benefits   The second relevant cost of property rights is 'restricting the use of property when it has a public good character'.[27] This is related to the fact that there are no static benefits from intellectual property rights. The marginal cost of using the information in a database is zero, as there is no direct extra cost associated with permitting another person to have access to, and use, the information in question. Excluding such uses creates a loss or social cost that must be balanced against the incentive benefits of any new form of *sui generis* protection.

In addition, there is a significant issue as to whether some databases would be created in any event, even if there were no legal protection for them. This point is part of the 'spin-off' argument that has already been addressed in a number of European decisions with conflicting results.[28] Telephone directories and football fixtures are obvious examples of databases that would almost certainly be created even in the absence of protection for them.

This point is but part of the general issue of identifying the particular value that database owners add to the information in the database, and the impact that additional legal protection would have on their incentive to provide that added value. Related to this is the need to consider the entire process of database creation. As Braman states: the notion of information as a commodity requires as a complement a concept of an information production chain. The steps of such a chain, adapted from models suggested by Machlup and Boulding, include information creation (creation, generation and collection), processing (cognitive and algorithmic), storage, transportation, distribution, destruction and seeking.[29]

Proposals for *sui generis* protection focus exclusively on protection for the collection, presentation and distribution stages of that process. The process is far more complex than this. In addition to those stages, there

---

[26] P. Drahos, *A Philosophy of Intellectual Property* (Dartmouth, Aldershot, 1996), p. 133.

[27] Landes and Posner, 'The Economics of Trademark Law', at 269.

[28] See Chapter 4.

[29] S. Braman, 'Defining Information: An Approach for Policy Makers' (1989) 13 *Telecommunications Policy* 233–42.

are stages before and after which are critical to the creation of many databases, and the relationship between all of these requires attention. The first of these stages is the creation of the information that is subsequently collected, presented and distributed. Much of this may not be subject to copyright, or if it is, for various reasons the copyright owner may be prepared to sell rights in relation to it relatively cheaply. This is particularly the case where the information being created is being created for a public purpose or with the public purse. Examples of this in the legal sphere are legislation, judgments and secondary materials such as academic articles. In the scientific sphere, much information is generated by employees of public institutions or institutions that have public funding.[30] In the case of scientific publications, some scientific researchers actually pay for the privilege of having their articles and scientific data published.[31] In other areas, such as meteorological information, it is provided for free as part of the public role of the provider. Similar considerations apply to legal material such as court judgments. The motivation of those who create this information may not be a financial one or, even if it is, it is not a financial motive to derive any significant, direct reward from the inclusion of the information in a database. Hence, to the extent that scientific researchers are seeking an economic reward, they derive that reward from having their writing distributed and their reputations enhanced rather than any payment for publication. Judges, who are also driven by motives other than purely financial ones, derive their economic rewards from their employment as judges. They do not write their judgments because of any financial return flowing from having them published in Lexis or any other legal database. Database owners obtain the advantage of these different motivations for the creation of information. They have the opportunity to capture some of the positive external effects of the behaviour of members of such groups. In effect, they reap the benefits of a mismatch of economic paradigms in which they focus exclusively on the financial returns from their databases, while those creating the information do so for reasons largely unrelated to any possible financial returns from inclusion of that information in databases. Greater protection for

---

[30] E.g. between 1992 and 1997 more than 33 per cent of all research and development in the United States was funded by government, universities or other non-profit organisations. Bureau of Statistics, Statistical Abstract of the United States (Bureau of Statistics, Washington DC, 1998). The same was also true for the UK between 1992 and 1996: UK Office for National Statistics, Annual Abstract of Statistics No. 135, 1999, Table 19.1 (Office for National Statistics, London, 1999).

[31] Survey of Australian Medical Researchers' Usage of and Contributions to Databases undertaken by Keith Akers and the author, June 2000, on file with the author. Thirty-nine per cent of researchers paid to have their material published and, of those, more than half paid in excess of $500. None were paid for their publications.

owners of databases will privilege that part of the process of creation of a database that involves collection, selection and presentation of information but it does not address issues relating to creation of information. It may permit even greater capture of the benefits of information creation by its collectors at the expense of the public good in having access to that information.

A conventional economic perspective may not suggest any difficulties with this approach as the database owners are helping the information creators to maximise their reputations; that desire of the creators is an example of their choice as to how they maximise their economic welfare. There are a number of difficulties with the assumption that the market mechanism will always resolve issues concerning the relationship between information producers and database owners. One of these difficulties relates to the exploitation of the public subsidy of the creation of this information and the relationship between that subsidy and the public subsidy conferred by the provision of legislative protection of databases.[32] In particular, there are problems with any assumption that those who provide information in return for little or no financial reward, particularly information produced with public funds, are maximising their individual welfare and, consequently, the apparently low price provided for their information is not a problem that needs to be addressed.

One difficulty is that the individuals in question received a public subsidy to create the information. In pursuing their own individual objectives, such as enhancing their reputations, they do not seek a return of that public subsidy. The database owner receives the benefit of the subsidy of the creation of the information.[33] Alternatively, the information is being sold cheaply because the database owner has some market power that places pressure on the creators to deal with those database owners.

A more fundamental objection is that this approach assumes that every action of every person is based on self-interest and that they obtain utility from their actions.[34] This assumption then leads to the conclusion that the information providers have extracted the correct price for their information. This conclusion significantly downplays the possibility

---

[32] 'Examples of the governmental subsidisation of the private provision of information are the governmental funding of basic research in the sciences, humanities, and the arts and the awarding of monopoly rights to the creators of information through the patent, copyright and trademark systems', Cooter and Ulen, *Law and Economics*, at p. 113. See also J. Boyle, 'A Politics of Intellectual Property: Environmentalism For the Net' (1997) 47 *Duke Law Journal* 87 where he argues that the provision of intellectual property rights can be regarded as a tax on the community.

[33] This benefit is not passed on to the user of the database if the database owner is not subject to significant competition.

[34] R. Posner, *Economic Analysis of Law* (4th edn, Little Brown, Boston, MA, 1992), pp. 3–4.

that the actions of information providers are due to the impact of factors such as socialisation and the pursuit of social status by personal conduct such as contributing to the common good.[35] A full explanation of that proposition is beyond the scope of this book. However, the fundamental point here is that while economic theory provides some insight into the motivations of individuals, there are risks associated with the assumption that it can explain every action of every individual. This point is discussed further below in the section entitled 'The Limits of the Tragedy of the Commons'.

The end result is that while the database owners play a valuable role in distribution, there is a case for limiting their legislative property rights. Those limits would permit some return of information to the public sector via exceptions or defences such as that of fair use and provisions that ensure access to information created with public funds. This could, in theory, be achieved via greater government input into the contractual relationships between publicly subsidised producers of information and database owners. However, there are good reasons for governments to retain some public rights to information produced with government funds via legislation that ensures public access to some information, particularly given the significant government and non-profit investment in the creation of information.[36]

At the other end of the process of creation, the role of the users of databases also needs to be considered. There is a danger with an assumption that the owner of a database is the producer of the database and the user is the consumer of the database. The nature of information confounds such assumptions. The use of it does not lead to the consumption of it in the ordinary sense that it is used up in the process of consumption. Not only does it still exist after it is used, it is also transformed by its use

---

[35] 'Because they also assume self-interested behavior, economists traditionally have had difficulty explaining why individuals give to public radio, control their littering, leave tips at roadside restaurants, return items to a lost-and-found, and otherwise cooperate when a rational, unsocialized person would not.' R. Ellickson, 'Social Norms, Social Meaning, and the Economic Analysis of Law' (1998) 27 *Journal of Legal Studies* 537 at 540. See generally volume 27 of the *Journal of Legal Studies* for a series of articles on this topic and its relationship to economics and the law. See also National Research Council, *Bits of Power: Issues in Global Access to Scientific Data* (National Research Council, Washington DC, 1997), p. 22 which states 'the most valued goal of scientists is that other scientists should learn of their work and use it'.

[36] E.g. between 1992 and 1997 more than 33 per cent of all research and development in the United States was funded by government, universities or other non-profit organisations. 'Statistical Abstract of the United States'. The same was also true for the UK between 1992 and 1996, Annual Abstract of Statistics No. 135, 1999, Table 19.1. Considerable amounts of other information come from non-research-oriented activities of government such as case law, legislation, statistics on births, deaths and marriages and various other sorts of information.

while still maintaining its original form. At this point, it is worthwhile to make some distinction between data and information. A detailed discussion of those metaphysical distinctions is beyond the scope of this book, and so the following comments are offered from an heuristic perspective of considering the relevance of those distinctions to the relationship between owners and users of databases.[37]

Data is the first stage in the evolving information–knowledge chain, usually represented by shapes in the form of letters, words, numbers or symbols that require cognitive skill to decipher, and the recall of previously assimilated information to help give them meaning.[38]
[...]
The transformation of data into information is thus a process of reception, recognition and conversion, made possible by our cognitive history and our ability to decipher symbols within a particular culture. Interestingly accurate conversion of data to information can only take place when we are able to add value to it from stores of information that we have access to.[39]

Data, by itself, is information in an unprocessed state. It is little more than a group of symbols that have no meaning in the absence of a person who has the capacity to decipher it, usually as a consequence of them having some other information. It is the act of interpreting the data that transforms it into information.[40]

Until the data becomes information, it is of little or no use. It can only become information as a consequence of the process of value adding undertaken by the user. To the extent that each user provides a different value adding, the data is transformed to that same extent into different types of information. This new knowledge, the new state of being informed, that is, the consequence of the user adding value to the data that they have perceived, then has the potential to be represented as new data that can be added to existing data. This data, in its turn, can be transformed into new information. In other words, the users of databases are also often the creators of data and critical players in the process of developing new information. There is no more obvious example of this

---

[37] See, for example, the writings of Kenneth Boulding in K. Boulding, *Notes on the Information Concept* (Exploration Press, Toronto, 1955), pp. 103–12.

[38] T. Haywood, *Info-Rich – Info-Poor: Access and Exchange in the Global Information Society* (Bowker Saur, West Sussex, 1995), p. 1.

[39] Ibid., p. 3.

[40] Some writers refer to this view of data as information and to knowledge as the act of interpretation and incorporating information into an information structure. See, e.g. K. Boulding, *Notes on the Information Concept*, pp. 103–12, as summarised in R. Babe, *Communication and the Transformation of Economics: Essays in Information, Public Policy, and Political Economy* (Westview Press, Boulder, CO, 1995), p. 166. The details of the distinction are not important here. What is important is the understanding that data, information and knowledge are part of an ongoing process, not just commodities.

than the science disciplines. Those who use databases are also those who contribute to them.[41]

This has significant implications for the regulation of what is often referred to as the chain of information[42] or a stream of information.[43] While these metaphors are very useful, they have the potential to mislead in one critical respect. They suggest that there is a beginning and an end to the process of producing, collecting and disseminating information. They do not indicate the impact that the user of data may have on the creation of more data that is returned to, and contributes to, the process. The circular aspect of the process has an impact on the nature of the legal protection that should be provided at any particular point of the process. Perhaps a more useful metaphor to overcome that difficulty would be that of an expanding spiral of data and information. This exemplifies the difficulty in identifying any start or endpoint in the creation of information. Those who create information from existing data supplied by owners of databases contribute more data that is then collected, selected and presented by database owners. This, in turn, is used by the users of the databases to create more information, generating more data that, in its turn, finds its way into databases. In this way, there is a perpetual expansion of data and consequent information and knowledge. However, no group contributing to this process operates independently of the others. Creating legal incentives for one group may have a negative impact on others and their contribution to the process. For example, excessive protection for database owners may reduce access to data, and therefore have a negative impact on the incentive or capacity of those users who are also creators and therefore crucial players in the creation process. Any *sui generis* form of protection must recognise this fact.

A further complication associated with treating information as a commodity is that this hides the relevance and importance of the vast diversity of the different types of information that may be contained within a database. This is because information is not homogenous:

Evidently, there should be *something* that all the things called information have in common [but] it surely is not easy to find out whether it is much more than the name.[44]

---

[41] Survey of Australian Medical Researchers' Usage of and Contributions to Databases undertaken by Keith Akers and the author, June 2000, on file with the author. All of the researchers surveyed had contributed material that was available in databases, all used databases regularly and considered them an essential part of their research activity.

[42] S. Braman, 'Defining Information', 12.

[43] J. Reichman and P. Samuelson, 'Intellectual Property Rights in Data' (1997) 50 *Vanderbilt Law Review* 51.

[44] Braman, 'Defining Information', at 12, quoting from F. Machlup and U. Mansfield (eds.), *The Study of Information: Interdisciplinary Messages* (Wiley, New York, 1983).

Information is one universal concept, binding together many diverse phenomena.[45]

Any consideration of the differing nature of information reveals the errors in the assumption that all types of information have anything of significance in common. The information contained in a telephone directory is a very different thing from information contained in a database of the human genome. Laws that create a commodity out of information need to acknowledge and respond to the diversity of commodities thus created. This relates to the point made above concerning the relationship between the creators of information, the owners of databases and the users of the databases. In some situations, such as in the case of the telephone directory, we may be able to see the relationship as being more akin to a supplier/consumer relationship. The consumer uses the information to telephone the person they are wishing to contact. The information is utilised but not significantly transformed or improved by the consumer.[46] In other situations, such as databases of scientific data, the relationship between creators, owners and users is far more interdependent and needs to be given more attention. This is because the information may be used to increase the amount of information to be contributed to that or a similar database.

The situation may arise in which the creation of information, for example by scientific researchers, is subsidised by the public purse. The publication of this information is then subsidised by the provision of the funds paid by the researchers to publishers to publish the material. Further subsidisation is then given to the database owners via *sui generis* legislative protection. Finally, public funds are used by those researchers to obtain access to the databases containing the very information that they have collectively provided and which is necessary to ensure the creation of further information. Excessive subsidisation of the collection and presentation of material via strong *sui generis* protection can reduce the effect of the subsidies on the creation of, and access to, that information. The subsidy of creation and use may be used up in paying to access the information because of an excessive subsidy in the form of legislative protection that unduly limits access.

An example of part of this problem is the failed privatisation of Landsat, as described in *Bits of Power*.[47] Landsat is a series of remote sensing

---

[45] Babe, *Transformation of Economics*, p. 10.
[46] See Cooter and Ulen, *Law and Economics*, p. 259 where they distinguish between productive facts and redistributive facts. Redistributive facts can be used to redistribute wealth in favour of the party who obtains the information but does not lead to the creation of new wealth, whereas productive facts, such as the formula for a vaccine against polio, increase wealth. Transformative or productive uses of information receive favourable treatment under the defence of fair use.
[47] National Research Council, *Bits of Power*, at Chapter 4.

satellites. Privatisation of these satellites occurred during the Reagan administration, resulting in the price of images from the satellites increasing from $400 per image to $4,400 per image.[48] The effects of this on research were devastating;[49] one example was described as follows:

> The poor availability of Landsat Thematic Mapper imagery is not only due to cost, but also the practice of operating the satellite selectively for certain land-surface areas. The cost of imagery reduced the user base, and EOSAT had to determine which images would be most marketable prior to acquiring them. That left many scientists with a very limited, high-cost archive of TM data. Thus, for certain areas of the globe there is extensive coverage, but for others it is very poor.[50]

Scarce public funds provided for obtaining access to the information in question were used up to such an extent that Landsat itself was under-utilised and new information based on Landsat data simply dried up. *Sui generis* protection may exacerbate such a problem.

This point about the relationship between the creators of information, database owners and users again leads back to the need for the retention of some government control over information created using public funds. Again, while this can be done via contract, the use of legislation by ensuring some access via exceptions to rights over information for public good purposes may well be an appropriate and more certain means of so doing.

Transaction costs   In one sense, at least in the case of on-line databases, transaction costs may not be huge because contractual arrangements can be made to exercise property rights via electronic commerce and 'click-on contracts'.[51] Database owners can, with reasonable ease, make arrangements for potential users to contract on-line to access their databases. The introduction of digital technology has therefore decreased the transaction costs associated with acquiring licences to access databases. The opportunity to reduce transaction costs via 'click-on' contracts has led to calls for the elimination of exceptions to both copyright and *sui generis* rights, on the grounds that those exceptions are no longer justified by the need to minimise transactions costs.[52]

---

[48] Ibid., at 121.   [49] Ibid., at 122–3.   [50] Ibid.

[51] 'Standard form contracts reduce transaction costs and increase efficiency.' J. Reichman and J. Franklin, 'Privately Legislated Intellectual Property Rights: Reconciling Freedom of Contract with Public Good Uses of Information' (1999) 147 *University of Pennsylvania Law Review* 875 at 906.

[52] A submission to that effect was made by the cross-industry working party established by database producers to the UK government in 1997. See Copyright Directorate, Patent Office, 'The Government's Proposals to implement the Directive of the European

Despite these claims that transaction costs have been dramatically reduced in a digital environment, the actual process of negotiating database licences can still be protracted. For example, many database licences are negotiated between publishers and library consortia. While this process is adopted by library consortia partly in order to restore some balance in bargaining power between major publishers and libraries, publishers and libraries have also adopted this approach in order to minimise the difficulties associated with negotiating individual contracts.

A further transaction cost that may present difficulties is one that results from the approach taken in the Directive that creates an overlap between copyright and *sui generis* protection. The creation of legally distinct but, in practice, extremely similar rights in the same subject-matter generates potential problems. One party may own the copyright and another may own the *sui generis* rights. At that point, a database user would need the permission of two different legal entities in order to perform basically the same actions in respect of the same database or part of it. This problem would be exacerbated if copyright subsisted in the individual items within the database and the user had to negotiate with the owner of the copyright in the database, the owner of the *sui generis* right and the owner of the copyright in the individual items. Even if there were no dichotomy in ownership, licence agreements would have to deal with all the relevant sets of rights, adding to the transaction costs.

This difficulty is but part of a potentially greater problem that has been described by Heller as 'the tragedy of the anticommons'.[53] The tragedy of the commons as already explained is a shorthand expression for the market failure that flows from permitting free-riding, namely, in this context, that the incentive to create databases is diminished by the possibility that all may use the database without paying for it. The basic problem with a commons is that 'multiple owners are each endowed with the privilege to use a given resource, and no one has the right to exclude another'.[54] The problem with an anticommons is the reverse of this phenomenon.

In an anticommons ... multiple owners are each endowed with the right to exclude others from a scarce resource, and no one has an effective privilege of use. When too many owners hold such rights of exclusion, the resource is prone to underuse – a tragedy of the anticommons.[55]

Parliament and the Council on the Legal Protection of Databases (96/9/EC): Outcome of Consultations', (London, 1997), at 3. See also the discussion in Chapter 2 of the justification for exceptions to copyright.

[53] M. Heller, 'The Tragedy of the Anticommons: Property in the Transition from Marx to Markets' (1998) 111 *Harvard Law Review* 621.

[54] Ibid., at 622.   [55] Ibid.

In Heller's article on the anti-commons, he refers to the problems generated by an excess of rights and rights holders in respect of real estate in Moscow.[56] The effect of this is that many storefronts in Moscow are empty 'while street kiosks in front are full of goods',[57] because the transaction costs associated with obtaining exclusive rights to the storefronts are too high. In the context of databases, the potential difficulty with *sui generis* rights is that they may lead to what Reichman describes as the Balkanisation of information, and Heller refers to as the fractionation of property. The result is an anti-commons. If rights are, in effect, granted in respect of data and an incentive is thereby given to obtain those rights, there is a real risk that different database owners will acquire rights in respect of individual 'subdivisions' of blocks of data that are of some, but nevertheless limited, usefulness by themselves. The existence of a number of different owners with their own rights in respect of individual subdivisions of the whole block will lead to an underuse of the whole block. We have already examined some examples of this problem. The *Feist* case itself was a situation in which the defendant wanted to provide a more comprehensive telephone directory incorporating directories from different telephone companies and their respective geographical areas. The individual directories had their use but the larger, more comprehensive directory would have been even more useful. If the plaintiff's refusal to licence its directory had been effective, the result would have been an anti-commons in which the rights granted to individual telephone companies would lead to an underuse of the entire block of information contained in all the relevant directories. The transaction costs confronted by the defendant were, in that case, insurmountable because of the plaintiff's refusal to licence the use of its directory. Another example would be the exchange of meteorological data; discrete pieces of data relating to a limited geographical area are of limited use in comparison with the whole of the data for larger areas.

Some economic and legal theorists suggest that these difficulties with transaction costs would be overcome by the voluntary development of market processes to minimise transaction costs and bring interested parties together via contract.[58] Examples of this are the voluntary development of collecting societies for copyright material that reduce transaction

---

[56] 'In a typical Moscow storefront, one owner may be endowed initially with the right to sell, another to receive sale revenue, and still others to lease, receive lease revenue, occupy and determine use.' Ibid., at 623.

[57] Ibid.

[58] See, for example, R. Coase, 'The Problem of Social Cost' (1960) 3 *Journal of Law and Economics* 1, and R. Merges, 'Of Property Rules, Coase, and Intellectual Property' (1996) 94 *Columbia Law Review* 2655.

costs by pooling different copyrights and providing 'one stop shopping' for 'consumers'. However, Heller contends that: 'Once an anticommons emerges, collecting rights into usable private property bundles can be brutal and slow. The difficulties of overcoming a tragedy of the anticommons suggest that policy makers should pay more attention to the content of property bundles.'[59] He identifies a number of reasons why markets may not be able to convert an anticommons into useful private property.[60] Apart from the not inconsiderable problem of transaction costs, Heller identifies deviant behaviour, rent seeking and uncertainty as problems that the market will not be able to overcome easily by itself.[61]

Enforcement costs   The final difficulty of the costs of enforcing the property rights that are granted will depend, again, on the nature of how, and clarity with which, the rights are expressed. This potential cost is also associated with rent seeking and social costs, as database owners may expend resources in attempting to convince courts to place broad definitions on *sui generis* legislation and to use any ensuing decisions to restrict use of their databases. Cases such as *Mars* v. *Teknowledge* demonstrate a broad use of the *sui generis* legislation to protect computer software in a way that may not have been intended even by the EU.

On the other hand, one possible advantage of providing property rights is that it may reduce the need for reliance and expenditure on technological protection devices. With *sui generis* protection in place, the database owner may only need to monitor wholesale copying of contents of the database and take appropriate legal action. Unlike smaller works such as sound recordings of popular songs, it is unlikely that wholesale copying would be done by other than a commercial user of the database whose use could be detected and stopped by litigation.

Limiting the costs of property rights

Landes and Posner identify a number of ways in which property rights in intellectual property can be moulded so that the costs of the property can be reduced. They all relate to limiting the scope of legal protection so as to achieve a balance between the dynamic benefit of providing an

---

[59] Heller, 'The Tragedy of the Anticommons', 621 at fn. 28.
[60] Ibid., at 688.
[61] Ibid., at 656–8. See also fn. 237 in which Heller states: 'Even in a world free of transaction costs, people would not necessarily bargain to put the anticommons resource to a unique use. Because of the presence of wealth or framing effects, there may be multiple efficient uses for an anticommons resource, depending on who initially holds the rights of exclusion.'

incentive for creation, and the social costs associated with providing the property rights that generate that incentive. These views on limiting the scope of legal protection can be applied to the debate concerning *sui generis* protection.

One way is by limiting the period of protection.[62] This places a ceiling on the value of the intellectual property right and thus reduces both rent seeking and the social costs of restricting use of property that has a public good character. The EU and most American proposals have suggested a period of fifteen years but no empirical evidence has been provided to justify that period of protection. The EU period was arbitrarily selected and replaced the original proposed period of ten years which is the same as that provided in the Nordic catalogue laws.[63]

The Report of the Committee for a Study on Promoting Access to Scientific and Technical Data for the Public Interest has noted that '[t]he average high-activity life span of original data in an online commercial database is approximately 3 years'.[64] Other suggestions by Landes and Posner on how to limit the costs of providing property rights actually counteract the argument for *sui generis* protection of databases. For example, they emphasise the protection of expression rather than ideas.[65] However, their writing on this topic preceded the full effects of the digital revolution (as described in Chapter 1), and the argument for some protection for the investment in the collection of information has been strengthened by those effects. Nevertheless, Landes and Posner also emphasise the importance of permitting fair use of copyright works, especially for productive purposes.[66] Similar considerations operate in relation to any *sui generis* protection of databases.

Summary of economic theory

The net effect of the above discussion is that there is some merit in the claims of database owners based solely on economic grounds that

---

[62] Landes and Posner, 'An Economic Analysis of Copyright Law', at 362: 'There is no congestion externality in the case of information, including the text of a book, and hence no benefit (yet potentially substantial costs) in perpetuating ownership beyond the period necessary to enable the author or publisher to recoup the fixed costs of creating the work.'

[63] For example, s. 49 of the Copyright Act 1960 (Sweden). See also s. 71 of the Copyright Act 1995 (Denmark) and Article 49 of the Copyright Act 1961 (Finland).

[64] National Academy of Sciences, *A Question of Balance: Private Rights and the Public Interest in Scientific and Technical Databases* (National Academy of Sciences, Washington DC, 1999) at 85, quoting from Martha E. Williams (1984–1999), Information Market Indicators: Information Center/Library Market – Reports 1–60 (Information Market Indicators, Inc., Monticello, IL).

[65] Landes and Posner, 'An Economic Analysis of Copyright Law', at 347–9.

[66] Ibid., at 360–1.

they need some form of *sui generis* protection. It is possible to adopt a commodity-based approach to databases by the introduction of *sui generis* legislation but the implications of doing so are somewhat more complex than those suggested by some of the proponents of increased rights for database owners. In particular, the expanding spiral of production of data, information and knowledge needs to be considered when determining the nature of the protection to be conferred. So does the public subsidy provided to the creation of information. Simply providing increased protection at one point in that spiral runs the risk of causing an information implosion. For example, users who rely on public revenues to pay for access to data legitimately predict 'that any increase in the price of access to data will not be compensated by increased public subsidies'.[67] This in turn will have an impact on their capacity to act as contributors to databases.

Consequently, the concession that some form of *sui generis* protection is warranted is only a starting point in the discussion about *sui generis* protection. The devil is in the detail concerning the nature of that protection; in particular, how much protection is needed to provide an optimal mix of incentive to produce and improve databases, while at the same time avoiding undue impact on those who create the very information that is contained within them. In determining that, consideration needs to be given to the fact that protection is conferred by copyright on many, if not most databases, and further protection can be obtained from a combination of trade secret law, contract and technological restraints on access to databases.

Anecdotal and empirical evidence

Ultimately, economic theories for the provision of legal protection must be vindicated by some hard evidence. There is a considerable body of anecdotal evidence that there is a need for some form of protection over and above that presently provided by copyright, trade secret law and a combination of contract and technological protection devices. This has also been conceded by a number of independent organisations[68] and even those who have expressed concerns about *sui generis* protection.[69]

---

[67] National Academy of Sciences, *A Question of Balance*, p. 88.

[68] Ibid., and Statement of Andrew J. Pincus, General Counsel, US Department of Commerce to the Subcommittee on Courts and Intellectual Property of the Judiciary Committee on the 1999 Bill, 18 March 1999.

[69] Statements of Joshua Lederberg (on behalf of the National Academy of Science and Ors.), and Charles Phelps (on behalf of the Association of American Universities and Ors.) to the Subcommittee on Courts and Intellectual Property of the Judiciary Committee on the 1999 Bill, 18 March 1999.

A number of cases that were analysed in the previous chapters provide examples of how database users have taken a free ride on the efforts of database owners. Other examples have been given to American Congress committee hearings of businesses that invest considerable resources in databases that may not have copyright protection. A number of these examples are given in the Appendix to the Submission of the Coalition Against Database Piracy[70] (CADP) to the House Judiciary Subcommittee on Courts and Intellectual Property on 18 March 1999.[71] They include the Thomson Corporation's POISINDEX which lists about a million substances, their clinical effects, treatment measures and other relevant information for medical practitioners and poison control specialists. Reed Elsevier's MDL Information Systems 'produces a range of databases that, taken together, offer chemists an electronic library that covers chemical suppliers and pricing, handling and safety information for 100,000 chemical products'.[72] The Appendix also refers to legal and medical directories produced by Skinder-Strauss and the American Medical Association. The president of Doane Agricultural Services Company submitted that the company, which produced directories of agricultural information such as acreage and production prices, crops and supply and livestock, was heavily affected by the lack of *sui generis* protection. The company had not provided its services via the Internet for fear of appropriation by competitors. Similarly, the National Association of Realtors expressed its concerns at the uncertain extent of copyright protection for its Multiple Listing System which had already been the subject of litigation.[73] Some database owners expressed similar concerns in their discussions with the American Copyright Office in 1997.[74]

On the other hand, there is also some anecdotal evidence that investment in databases and information products generally was unaffected by the supposed lack of protection for databases. Between 1991 and 1997,

---

[70] Written Statement of Marilyn Winokur, Executive Vice-President of Micromedex on Behalf of the Coalition Against Database Piracy (CADP) on the 1999 Bill to the Subcommittee on Courts and Intellectual Property of the Judiciary Committee on 18 March 1999. CADP consists of a group of small and large US database providers, including the McGraw-Hill Companies, National Association of Securities dealers, Newsletter Publishers Association, New York Stock Exchange, Reed Elsevier Inc. and Thomson Corporation. See the description of CADP in the Written Statement of the CADP Sub-Committee on Courts and Intellectual Property of the Judiciary Committee concerning the 1997 Bill, 23 October 1997.

[71] Written Statement of Marilyn Winokur.   [72] Ibid.

[73] *Montgomery Country Association of Realtors* v. *Realty Photo Master*, 878 f. Supp. 804 (1995), *San Fernando Valley Board of Realtors Inc.* v. *Mayflower Transit Inc.*, unreported, No. CV 91-5872-WJR- (Kx) (CD Cal 1993).

[74] US Copyright Office Report on Legal Protection for Databases, August 1997 at 78.

the number of databases increased from 7,637 to 10,338 and the private sector share rose from 22 per cent in 1977 to 78 per cent in 1997.[75] An examination of the annual reports of the largest information companies[76] also reveals a strategy of ongoing and increasing investment in the supply of information. For example, the 1998 Annual Report of the Thomson Corporation states that the company has strategically transformed itself into an information company and divested itself of other interests unrelated to information.[77] Between 1993 and 1998, it invested $6.1 billion in acquisitions to supplement its core information businesses, and in 1998 alone it spent $830 million on acquiring seventy new information businesses.[78] Its 1998 Annual Report proudly states:

Over the past five years, our information revenues have grown by $2.4 billion – an achievement almost equivalent to creating a Fortune 500 company.[79]

At the time of these investments and the growth in revenue, there was no *sui generis* protection for its information businesses, in either Europe or the United States. Thomson's Annual Report for 1999 also suggests that the existence of *sui generis* protection in the EU, and the absence of it in the United States, do not pose a problem. Its report for 1999 states that its Internet-based revenues doubled to $390 million, its adjusted earnings were up by 14 per cent and it invested $470 million in capital expenditures.[80] This was despite the fact that 86 per cent of its income was derived inside the United States where there was no *sui generis* protection.[81]

A similar picture emerges in relation to other major information companies. In 1998, the Executive Board of Wolters Kluwer reported that the company had made a record number of acquisitions, and organic growth had risen from 4 per cent in 1996 and 1997 to 5 per cent in 1998.[82] Between 1994 and 1996, Reed Elsevier invested over $3 billion in the acquisition of Lexis and Shepard's citation service alone.[83]

---

[75] M. Williams, 'The State of Databases Today: 1998', *Gale Directory of Databases*. See also the testimony of Jonathan Band on behalf of the Online Banking Association before the Subcommittee on Courts and Intellectual Property of the United States House of Representatives Committee on the Judiciary on the 1999 Bill, at http://www.hyperlaw.com/band.htm.

[76] The Thomson Corporation identifies itself, Reed Elsevier and Wolters Kluwer as the major global information businesses. See the Thomson Corporation Annual Report of 1998, at 26.

[77] Ibid., at 4.   [78] Ibid., at 6.   [79] Ibid.

[80] Ibid., at 3.   [81] Ibid., at 7.

[82] Wolters Kluwer Annual Report of 1998, at 1, available at http://www.wolters-kluwer. annual report98_11.html.

[83] Reed Elsevier press release, 27 April 1998, available at http://www.reed-elsevier. com/newsreleases/nr39.htm.

It should be pointed out that these figures refer to the overall investments of these companies in information businesses, and they do not
discriminate between investment in information that is already protected
via copyright and information that would derive protection from some
form of *sui generis* protection. Nevertheless, some of the acquisitions relate to information in a form that does not have copyright protection and
their present protection flows from a combination of contract and technological protection. Lexis, or certainly parts of Lexis, is an example of
this.

It could be argued that the investment in information and databases
would have been even greater if *sui generis* protection had been conferred
in both the EU and the United States. However, the statistics do suggest
that the absence of such protection until 1998 in the EU and in the United
States altogether has not had a serious chilling effect on investment. In
addition, that argument can always be made to suggest that existing protection is insufficient and it should be expanded. In any event, the above
statistics indicate that the magnitude of any problem generated by the
gap caused by a lack of protection for sweat of the brow is a relatively
small one. Action to fill the gap needs to be correspondingly small.

A further interesting aspect of the reports by these companies is the
emphasis that they place on the form in which information is presented
to their clients. All of them see themselves operating in a global on-line
environment and providing not only information, but information in a
user-friendly manner. For example, Thomson Corporation states in its
1998 Annual Report that:

The declining cost and easy adoption of proven technology is lowering barriers
to entry as well as inviting greater competition from nimble technology 'start-
ups'. This trend heightens the need to increase product differentiation providing
unique added-value features and capabilities.[84]

Wolters Kluwer's report for 1998 notes that:

In the coming year, faster development of on-line products is expected to help
strengthen organic growth still further. Group companies have developed many
Internet services, and are continuing to do so . . .
Professional users of information services have a growing need for selection,
structuring and interpretation within the continually growing flow of information.

In its 1999 Report, Reed Elsevier stated that:

At the core of our strategy is a clear focus on Internet delivery, additional high
value added content and services, and greater ease of use and functionality.

---

[84] Thomson Corporation Annual Report of 1998, at 24.

Two points can be made from this evidence. The first is that these major information businesses perceive that their competitive advantage is derived, at least to a substantial extent, from the way in which they present information to their clients rather than just the content. Copyright already provides significant protection for that source of their competitive advantage. The second point is that the emphasis on electronic delivery via on-line services does not seem to have been diminished by the lack of international *sui generis* protection for the contents of databases. There is no detectable fear in the official documentation of these companies of mass free-riding on their efforts.

Evidence of the Directive's impact   The most comprehensive empirical survey to date of the impact of the Directive on investment in databases is a report by Stephen Maurer to Industry Canada.[85] Part of the report describes a study of the database industries in the US, UK, France and Germany between 1993 and 2001. The data for the study were taken from various editions of the *Gale Directory of Databases*.

Maurer concluded that the number of new providers entering the French, UK and German database industries rose sharply in statistics for 1998 and that the total number of databases increased significantly in statistics for 1999.[86] Yet this increase in the number of new entrants and new databases was soon followed by a return to pre-1998 levels, and he concluded that the Directive had a once-only impact on the investment in databases.[87] Even that once-only boost may have been in part a reflection of new entrants delaying their entrance until implementing legislation was in place and the legal position was more certain.[88]

On the other hand, there is some anecdotal evidence that the Directive's existence has influenced the decision about where to undertake some database projects. In addition, there is some anecdotal evidence that the availability of databases on CD-ROM increased significantly at about the time of the implementation.

All of the above discussion concerning the evidence for greater protection suggests that the existing protection, via trade secret law, copyright, contract and technological restraints on access to databases, already provides a significant incentive to invest in information products. If there is a problem with a lack of incentive for investment in databases, there is good reason to believe that the problem is smaller rather than larger.

---

[85] S. Maurer, 'Across Two Worlds: Database Protection in the US and Europe', paper prepared for Industry Canada's Conference on Intellectual Property and Innovation in the Knowledge-Based Economy, 23–24 May 2001, available at: http://www.strategis.ic.gc.ca/SSI/ipf/maurer.pdf.
[86] Ibid., at 40.   [87] Ibid., at 2.   [88] Ibid., at 37.

The response to the problem should therefore be more minimalist than maximalist.

Non-economic roles of information

So, an analysis of the neoclassical economic arguments for *sui generis* protection and the anecdotal and empirical evidence available to date reveals the weakness in the economic arguments for *sui generis* protection. Perhaps, more accurately, that analysis reveals that the economic arguments for *sui generis* protection only justify a weak form of protection. A further issue also needs to be addressed. The neoclassical economic arguments do not take account of non-economic arguments for and against *sui generis* protection. While information can be defined and treated as a commodity:

Definitions of information that treat it as a commodity work to the advantage of those who win when the game is played on economic grounds, or for whom economic values are the only values.[89]

Information also has other definitions and roles to play than as a commodity. As Braman suggests, information is not just a commodity but also a constitutive force in society.

With definitions of information that treat it as a constitutive force in society, information is not just affected by its environment, but is itself an actor affecting other elements in the environment. Information is that which is not just embedded within a social structure, but creates that structure itself.[90]

A very obvious example of this constitutive aspect of information is information that comes from services traditionally supplied by government to the population at large, free of charge or at the cost of supply of that information.

The overwhelming mass of what we know about ourselves as a society comes from the government information services. Most of this reaches us through secondary sources like the press and television, but this in no way negates the point that such information originates from government agencies . . .

[G]overnment is the only institution capable of systematically and routinely gathering and processing information on everything from patterns of divorce to infant morbidity, from occupational shifts to criminological trends, because this daunting task requires huge sums of money and, as important, the legitimacy of constitutional government. Consider, for example, the detailed and intimate information which becomes available from the census every ten years and one appreciates the point.[91]

---

[89] S. Braman, 'Defining Information', pp. 233–42.   [90] Ibid., at p. 239.
[91] F. Webster, *Theories of the Information Society* (Routledge, London, 1995), p. 120.

The points that Webster makes above concerning information are particularly pertinent to the database debate and the need to perceive information as being, in many contexts, far more than just a commodity. In many ways, it is what underpins the public sphere described by Jurgen Habermas[92] and Webster has pointed out the relevance of information to the public sphere.[93]

If we value an informed citizenry and the benefits that this brings to the way in which we are governed or are able to govern ourselves, then information is a powerful constitutive force that must be protected and channelled with goals such as the democratic process in mind. Take, for example, a recent political debate in Australia concerning the 'stolen generation', a reference to the fact that for several decades some Aboriginal children were forcibly taken pursuant to government policy from their natural parents and placed in institutions or adopted out to white Australians. Not surprisingly, there were huge sociological implications of the implementation of the policy and, in recent times, a very large political debate concerning the appropriate government response to the 'stolen generation'. That debate simply could not have taken place without government information concerning the extent and nature of the problem. Information about issues such as how many children were taken, where they were taken to and why, was available only from public sources. Its commercial value is minimal. However, its impact on a nation and its attempts to come to grips with its historical and present-day treatment of its indigenous minority is profound.

This example is but one of a plethora of political issues that simply cannot be publicly debated without access to government information. Information therefore has a huge role to play in the democratic process and forming political opinion.

A popular Government, without popular information, or the means of acquiring it, is but a prologue to a farce or a tragedy, or perhaps both. Knowledge will forever govern ignorance and a people who mean to be their own governors must arm themselves with the power knowledge gives.[94]

---

[92] J. Habermas, *The Structural Transformation of the Public Sphere: An Inquiry into a Category of Bourgeois Society*, trans. T. Berger (MIT Press, Cambridge, MA, 1989).

[93] '[A]n arena, independent of government (even if in receipt of state funds) and also enjoying autonomy from partisan economic forces, which is dedicated to rational debate (ie to debate and discussion which is not "interested", "disguised" or "manipulated") and which is both accessible to entry and open to inspection by the citizenry. It is here, in this public sphere, that public opinion is formed.' F. Webster, *Theories*, pp. 101-2.

[94] B. Jones, *SLEEPERS, WAKE: Technology and the Future of Work* (Oxford University Press, Sydney, 1982), p. 173 quoting James Madison.

Webster has noted the shift in government attitudes towards the role of information.[95] Writing with particular reference to the position in England in the 1980s, he noted the shift in government policy towards obtaining a return from the distribution of government information and away from perceiving the provision of information as a public service. He also noted similar concerns in the United States.[96]

These trends towards the commodification of information have been exacerbated by recent trends in privatisation of government services and scientific information formerly generated with public funds. Obviously these moves towards commodification of information that previously played an alternative or additional role in the public sphere existed prior to any suggestion of *sui generis* protection for databases. The proposals for *sui generis* protection may be in part a response to, or effect of, those trends rather than a cause of them. Nevertheless, *sui generis* protection that focused exclusively on the commodity nature of information would confirm and strengthen those trends. It would be part of the process of creating a culture of commodification and a culture that would be blind to the other roles of information. Alternatively, *sui generis* protection that forthrightly and positively acknowledged the differing roles of information could play a part in arresting, and possibly reversing, some of the undesirable aspects of this trend.

Limits of the tragedy of the commons

Related to this proposition is the theoretical and empirical work that suggests that the intellectual commons is not necessarily a tragedy. This in turn leads to the conclusion that the lack of a tragedy leads to the lack of a need for government intervention via the development of private property rights.[97] Ellickson studied the effects in Shasta County, CA of changes in the legal liability of cattle ranchers for accidental trespass by their cattle. Most of Shasta County was open range, effectively unfenced land and a commons in which cattle could graze and trespass without any liability being imposed on the cattle owner. However, special California legislation effectively closed parts of the range and imposed liability on the ranchers for their trespassing cattle in the closed parts. Despite the all-or-nothing liability of a rancher for trespassing cattle, depending on the open or closed status of the land in question, Ellickson discovered that this reversal in legal liability had no impact on the way in which

[95] F. Webster, *Theories*, Chapter 6.   [96] Ibid., p.123.
[97] R. Ellickson, *Order Without Law: How Neighbors Settle Disputes* (Harvard University Press, Cambridge, MA, 1991); E. Ostrom, *Governing the Commons: The Evolution of Institutions for Collective Action* (Cambridge University Press, New York, 1990).

neighbouring farmers acted or their decisions as to who should incur the costs of fencing.[98]

Neighbours developed a series of norms concerning the costs of fencing land and thus limiting trespass by cattle. These norms were developed and followed regardless of the legal position. For example, they developed a norm of proportionality in which neighbours made decisions about the allocation of fencing costs according to rough critieria such as who had the most cattle and their respective capacity to contribute to the work. Neighbouring ranchers with similar numbers of cattle split the fencing costs equally, whereas ranchers bordering 'ranchettes' with few or no cattle usually bore the entire costs of fencing. Others came to arrangements whereby one bore more than 50 per cent of the costs if they perceived that they would gain more than 50 per cent of the benefits, even though they could legally gain those benefits without incurring any cost.[99]

> Neighbors in fact are strongly inclined to cooperate, but they achieve cooperative outcomes not by bargaining from legally established entitlements... but rather by developing and enforcing adaptive norms of neighborliness that trump formal legal entitlements.[100]

This study suggests that people with access to a commons do not necessarily act as free-riders, thus generating the tragedy of the commons. Ellickson and others have identified some of the necessary conditions for effective norms to develop and operate. In particular, 'disputants are increasingly likely to turn to legal rules when the social distance between them increases, when the magnitude of what is at stake rises, and when the legal system provides an opportunity for the disputants to externalize costs to third parties'.[101] For example, Ellickson noted that the norms developed by ranchers were less likely to apply when the damage caused by trespassing cattle was to motor vehicles driven by strangers to the area.[102] Ostrom has been involved in other empirical, psychological testing that also suggests that free-riding on what she describes as common pool resources is less likely to happen when there is a social relationship between those with access to the pool of resources.[103]

Another way of putting this is that when the commons is closed to a particular group, they can and will develop their own norms that lead to

---

[98] This contrasts with the views expressed in Coase, 'The Problem of Social Cost', where he argued from a purely theoretical basis that the end result of whether land was fenced would be the same, subject to the transactions costs in achieving that result, but the legal rules of liability would dictate who would pay for the fencing.

[99] Ellickson, *Order Without Law*, pp. 71–9.

[100] Ibid., p. 4.   [101] Ibid., p. 283.   [102] Ibid.

[103] P. Keohane and E. Ostrom (eds.), *Local Commons and Global Interdependence: Heterogeneity and Cooperation in Two Domains* (Sage Publications, London, 1995), pp. 119–20.

effective utilisation of the resources in the commons. The concept of a closed commons is one that was identified by John Locke. Drahos, in his analysis of the application of Locke's theories of property to intellectual property, writes of different types of commons, including an exclusive or closed, positive commons.[104] This is a commons available to a particular group, rather than all individuals, in which no member of the group is entitled to take anything from the commons without the consent of the group. This is contrasted with an inclusive, negative commons. An inclusive or open commons includes every individual as no one is excluded from it, and a negative commons is one in which individuals may take from the commons without the permission of those with access to the commons. It is in the inclusive or open commons that the tragedy of the commons is most likely to arise. In those circumstances, the law needs to intervene in order to avoid or solve the tragedy. In the exclusive or closed, positive commons the norms spoken about by Ellickson and Ostrom can arise.

What has this to do with databases? It has particular significance in relation to the exchange of scientific information. There is a considerable body of evidence that scientific communities have developed what could be described as exclusive, positive commons in relation to the exchange of scientific information. Coupled with this are norms concerning the generation and exchange of that information.[105] As noted in Chapter 5, the emphasis of scientists and scientific organisations on the culture of exchange of scientific information has been an important aspect of the opposition to some proposals for *sui generis* protection.[106] There is a theoretical debate in academic writing on whether norms concerning collective goods enhance welfare, or whether a more efficient approach is to adopt a market-based approach to property.[107] However, the anecdotal evidence provided by scientific organisations that these norms concerning the use and exchange of scientific data should be preserved as far as possible is at least as convincing as the evidence in favour of *sui generis* protection for databases.

---

[104] Drahos, *Philosophy of Intellectual Property*, pp. 57–60.

[105] See A. Rai, 'Regulating Scientific Research: Intellectual Property Rights and the Norms of Science' (1999) 94 *Northwestern Law Review* 77.

[106] See, for example, the statements of various scientific organisations referred to in Chapter 5. See also National Research Council, *Bits of Power*.

[107] E.g. Ellickson, 'Social Norms', at 550, and E. Posner, 'Law, Economics and Inefficient Norms' (1996) 144 *University of Pennsylvania Law Review* 1697. Ellickson argues that as a general rule, norms enhance the wealth of the group following that norm. This enhancement of the group's wealth can have positive or negative externalities or effects on those outside the group. For example, the Ku Klux Klan's racist norms have negative effects on those outside the group. In contrast, it is a reasonable assumption that norms concerning exchange of scientific information have positive external effects.

Most, if not all, of the writers about the relationship between law and norms take the view that legal policies can enforce or disrupt the development and maintenance of self-regulating norm systems:[108]

[A] large literature demonstrates that behavior is governed not simply by positive law or social norms but by a complex and intimate interaction between the two systems. Lawmakers who wish to encourage particular behavior can therefore achieve their goal by using law to shape norms.[109]

Rai has identified the manner in which norms concerning the exchange of information about scientific inventions were broken down by changes to patent laws in the United States during the 1980s.[110] Those laws increased the property rights of patentees and there was a resulting breakdown in the norms of exchange of information.

The same risk exists in relation to *sui generis* protection of databases. Norms concerning the communalism of scientific information may be further eroded by laws that commodify basic scientific information. While there may also already be other pressures on these norms, inappropriately formulated *sui generis* legislation could hasten that process. While the tragedy of the commons is a real issue that needs to be considered and addressed, there is also a romance of the commons that needs to be considered. Failure to do so could lead to a farce instead of a tragedy.

Examples of scientific cooperation

Numerous examples can be given of the benefits of cooperation in the exchange of information and the costs of impeding that exchange.[111] In particular, the exchange of information not only leads to those who acquire it being better informed, but they move beyond being users of information to being contributors to the spiral of knowledge. This transformative use of information is a key issue in the area of scientific research. Two examples are discussed below.

The Health WIZ project   The Health WIZ project is undertaken by a private company on behalf of the Australian government's Department of Health and Aged Care.[112] It is a database of databases relating to healthcare in Australia. It draws upon the information contained in a number of disparate health databases such as the following:

---

[108] Rai, 'Regulating Scientific Research', at 84; Ellickson, *Order Without Law*, pp. 284–5.
[109] Rai, *Regulating Scientific Research*, p. 88.   [110] Ibid.
[111] See *Bits of Power*, pp. 205–19.
[112] See information concerning this database at http://www.prometheus.com.au/healthwiz/hwizf.htm

- population census statistics;
- hospital use statistics;
- hospital capacity;
- mortality data;
- immunisation data;
- national and state cancer data;
- social security and department of Veterans' Affairs recipients;
- childcare data
- medicare (Australia's national health scheme) data;
- aged care data; and
- map data.

By combining all these different databases, it has created a new and powerful database that can be used to consider an almost infinite number of health issues. It can produce a geographical map of health in different areas and compare that with a map of health facilities in those areas. For example, it could produce information concerning where there are large pockets of elderly people requiring geriatric care and compare that with the actual geographic location of geriatric care units or expenditure on medical assistance for the aged. Similar tracking of children and paediatric care units could be undertaken. Alternatively, the data could be used to develop a picture of the most common causes of death in different areas and to target health resources to address those different causes in different areas. The possibility exists for other databases to be integrated into the Health WIZ or some other transformative health database, such as databases of coroner's records, or even information such as the location of allegedly health threatening factors such as high-intensity power lines or coal-based electricity generators.

The databases within this larger database are public health databases maintained by either the Australian government or state governments. However, there is no reason why private databases may not also be incorporated into this or a similar database. For example, information from private health funds may also be able to make a valuable contribution. Alternatively, information that is not inherently or primarily related to health issues, such as the location of various industries that may threaten the health of nearby residents, could also be utilised. The creation of such a transformative, improved database requires the cooperation of different organisations with their own objectives and reasons for initially collecting their information. Those organisations may not have any commitment to the objectives of a larger, better database. Indeed they may be diametrically opposed to those objectives. The interpolation of a new exclusive property right may unnecessarily complicate the process by which these different organisations are brought together to cooperate. The new rights might unnecessarily frustrate new and useful ways of manipulating data that were created for entirely different purposes. In short, the creation of new rights might lead to a tragedy of the anti-commons unless they are crafted so as to prevent such frustration of productive uses of information.[113]

World Meteorological Organization (WMO)   The work of the World Meteorological Organization further exemplifies the need for caution in establishing any *sui generis* regime. WMO was established in 1947 and is a specialised agency of the United Nations.[114] Its purposes include the facilitation 'of international cooperation in the establishment of networks of stations for making meteorological, hydrological and other observations; and to promote the rapid exchange of meteorological information'.[115] Cooperation in the exchange of meteorological information exists between the 185 Member States and territories of the WMO.[116] Its major programmes include World Weather Watch, which transmits over 15 million data characters and 2,000 weather charts each day throughout WMO's distribution network. It has also played an influential role in environmental matters by providing key data concerning global warning and other environmental changes attributable to climatic changes. For example, it was 'instrumental in the negotiations for a UN Convention on Climate Change which was signed during the Rio Earth Summit in 1992'.[117] It is very possible that WMO's work on environmental matters may have a significant impact on whether humanity survives.

The cooperative nature of WMO's activities was placed under threat in the mid-1990s. Up until that time, Member States had contributed their respective data freely. However, in the mid-1990s, European meteorological organisations indicated that they may have to withdraw from that cooperative arrangement and that they wished to receive payment for the provision of meteorological information. Lengthy negotiations were held by WMO which averted that from happening.[118] However, the European attitude at the time was an example of the increasing pressure placed on governmental organisations to recoup their operating costs by commodifying their data at the expense of the other roles of those data.[119]

---

[113] The problems of an anti-commons are also discussed in Maurer, 'Across Two Worlds', at 2, 46 and fns. 204–206.
[114] http://www.wmo.ch.
[115] http://www.wmo.ch/web-en/wmofact.html.
[116] World Meteorological Organization, *Exchanging Meteorological Data: Guidelines on Relationships in Commercial Meteorological Activities: WMO Policy and Practice*, publication No. 837 (WMO, Geneva, 1996).
[117] http:///www.wmo.ch/web-en/achiev.html.
[118] J. Zillman, 'Atmospheric Science and Public Policy' (1997) 276 *Science* 1084.
[119] Ibid.

While that process of commodification is already facilitated by the use of contract and simply denying access to the data in question, the creation of specific new rights over data can exacerbate the position. The risk is that such legislation legitimates and drives a cultural and institutional change in attitude towards the role of information. The commodity role of information is perceived as being paramount at the expense of any other. This perception may arise without any proper analysis of the differences between types of information and the roles that they may play.

The example of meteorological data also demonstrates a potential difficulty with the argument of database producers that the same information can be obtained elsewhere and placed in another competing database. This is simply not the case with the observation of natural phenomena at a particular point in time. For example, there was only one opportunity to measure the maximum and minimum temperature in New York City yesterday or any other day in the past. The results cannot be replicated.

As the discussion above has explained, the commodification of information via *sui generis* legislation can lead to a situation in which information's commodity role is privileged in a manner out of proportion to its actual benefits. While commodification may have some benefits, the tendency is to assume that some commodification is good and more is better. Instead of analysing individual circumstances and attempting to understand when a commodification approach is appropriate, an assumption is made that property rights should and must be strong. All relevant information is then filtered through that assumption, which infects analysis of any particular situation. It can be regarded as a more insidious manifestation of the type of rent seeking in which claims are made for broad property rights in order to increase the value of any investment. Its insidiousness flows from its attempt to make a virtue out of a vice.

Some suggestions for protection of databases

The upshot of the preceding discussion is that there is a case for some further protection for databases over and above that provided by most existing copyright regimes. However, given the existing division between the EU and the United States on the approach to database protection and the very considerable resistance to any further protection from many members of WIPO, it is unlikely that any consensus will be reached on a specific model law such as the Directive or something similar to it. Instead, the most that is practically achievable is an agreement on some fundamental issues that each country should address via its own legislation to provide some minimal degree of protection for databases in addition to that provided by copyright.[120] Those fundamental issues are discussed below.

Defining the subject matter of protection narrowly so as to avoid unnecessary and unintended consequences

In Chapters 3 and 4, the definitions of a database under the Directive and a collection of information under the various American proposals respectively were considered. One of the difficulties with the Directive's definition, unlike the various American definitions, is that it does not include an aspect emphasising that the purpose of the database is to provide information. Hence, there is uncertainty about protection for data within computer programs, a point that should never have been raised by *sui generis* protection for databases. Any international agreement for *sui generis* protection should address this issue. It should also go further. It should specifically provide that the purpose of the database is to permit retrieval and direct perception of the contents of the database by human beings, in order to facilitate their attempts to become informed. Prior to the copyright protection of object code in computer programs this was regarded by some courts as a key element of the definition of a literary work.[121] Inserting such a requirement in the definition of a database would reinforce the point that data within computer programs that is primarily there to allow the programs to perform their functions is not within the scope of *sui generis* protection.

It would also be a manifestation of the understanding of the relationship between the owner and a user of a database. Without the user's knowledge and skills, the contents of the database are useless; the user transforms and enhances the value of the contents by their use. Including this within the definition of a database or a collection of information would be part of the process of incorporating that understanding into any *sui generis* protection, and ensuring that such protection reflects the importance of the relationship between database owner and user. For that same reason, it may be desirable to use the European term 'database' rather than the American term 'collection of information'. This would reinforce the point that the contents of the database are, by themselves, simply data and are of minimal use in the absence of a knowledgeable user who can transform the data into information and knowledge.

---

[120] Statement of Andrew J. Pincus, General Counsel, United States Department of Commerce before the Subcommittee on Courts and Intellectual Property Committee on the Judiciary, 18 March 1999 at fn. 4. See also the suggestions for such an approach made by the Australian delegation to WIPO discussed in Chapter 5.

[121] E.g. *Apple Computer Inc.* v. *Computer Edge Pty Ltd* (1984) 53 ALR 225.

Separation of the subject matter of sui generis *protection for sweat of the brow from copyright protection*

If *sui generis* protection of databases is to be conferred, there are good reasons for insisting upon a very clear separation of the protection conferred on what is essentially the sweat of the brow involved in the creation of the database from copyright protection. This involves clearly delineating between, and separating the subject matter of, copyright and the subject matter of *sui generis* protection. The former should be restricted to the structure and arrangement of databases involving a degree of originality, and the latter to the quantity of labour and resources invested in creating the database. This fits neatly with existing international copyright obligations concerning compilations that only require protection for compilations constituting an intellectual creation by virtue of their selection and arrangement, and that protection only extends to the creativity of the database.

The most obvious reason for doing this is the practical one of ensuring there is no duplication of regimes applying to the same subject matter. Copyright would be restricted to the creative aspects of a database and *sui generis* rights to the sweat of the brow involved in the database construction. This would necessarily entail eschewing any and all references to the quality of investment in the creation of a database. The difficulties of introducing qualitative issues into this area were examined in detail in Chapter 3.

In addition to those difficulties, the introduction of qualitative measures distorts the desirable symmetry between the investment in obtaining, verifying and presenting of the database and the protection provided for it. In particular, it introduces the possibility that the unauthorised use of a very small number of items will constitute an infringement of the *sui generis* right. This, in turn, creates a significant gap between the cost of incorporating these items into the database and the value of those items to a database owner. The larger the gap between cost and value, the larger the possibility of the detrimental effects of rent seeking.

Clearly separating copyright from *sui generis* protection would also leave open the possibility of privileging creativity by providing greater protection via copyright for creativity than *sui generis* protection for sweat of the brow. The reasons for so doing have been expounded in countless judicial opinions in a wide range of jurisdictions and in academic writing on the point.[122] The push for *sui generis* protection has in no way diminished the

---

[122] Landes and Posner, 'An Economic Analysis of Copyright Law', and the *Feist* decision itself which has been discussed in Chapters 2 and 4. The copyright laws of continental

argument that creativity should receive greater protection than sweat of the brow. As argued above, the case for *sui generis* protection suggests that there should be some protection via intellectual property legislation for sweat of the brow as opposed to none, but that protection should still be more limited than the copyright protection conferred on creativity. For these reasons, those jurisdictions that have provided copyright protection for sweat of the brow should seriously consider altering their copyright regimes, so as to introduce a dichotomy between the subject matter of copyright protection and the subject matter of *sui generis* protection.

Differentiation of sui generis *rights from copyright*

A corollary of the separation of the subject matter of copyright from the subject matter of *sui generis* protection is a differentiation of the nature of the rights conferred by copyright and *sui generis* legislation. The rights conferred by copyright and the minimum duration of protection are, to a large extent, defined by international agreements such as the Berne Convention, TRIPS and the Copyright Treaty. Obviously, this is not yet the case with *sui generis* protection.

The acts to be restricted will almost certainly be similar to those restricted by copyright. This is because the commercial exploitation of copyright material and database material necessarily involves similar acts. In defined circumstances, reproduction has to be prevented, as does communication to the public via transmission or making available, and rental and distribution, subject to a first sale doctrine. What then can and should differentiate copyright rights from *sui generis* rights? The first point to make here is that the rights provided for *sui generis* protection should be narrower than the rights provided by copyright. An example is the temporary reproduction of database material. There has already been considerable debate on the issue of whether temporary computer copies of copyright material made without the consent of the copyright owner are illegal reproductions.[123] Regardless of the outcome of that debate, the justification for prohibiting temporary reproductions of database material is considerably weaker than it is in relation to copyright. The circumstances in which temporary copies can be commercially exploited by the makers of such copies are limited, if not non-existent.[124] A prohibition on

---

countries also reflect this approach. See the discussion of originality in Chapter 2 and of copyright generally in Chapter 3.

[123] See the discussion of this issue in Chapter 2.

[124] There are issues of defining a temporary copy. For these purposes, reference is being made to the temporary copy in the RAM of a computer that disappears upon turning off the computer.

temporary copies of databases would be primarily a prohibition on personal users of the information contained within them. Excluding temporary copies from the right of reproduction in a scheme of *sui generis* legislation would, in itself, go a very long way to ensuring that such protection was aimed squarely at commercial redistribution of databases or substantial parts of them.[125]

In addition, while the nature of the acts to be restricted will necessarily have a close relationship to copyright, it is possible to move away from the exclusive rights model of copyright that effectively prevents everyone from performing those acts without the consent of the copyright owner. In particular, the purpose and effect of the particular actions being constrained can be key criteria in limiting and differentiating *sui generis* rights from copyright. The emphasis should be on unauthorised commercial uses of the database, in keeping with unfair competition principles that have been applied in both Europe and the United States. Almost all the anecdotal evidence to date suggests that unauthorised commercial use is the primary, if not the exclusive, problem that database owners face. A reshaping and harmonisation of European laws concerning unfair competition would have been sufficient to meet the legitimate needs of publishers.

Exceptions to copyright to permit use of underlying information

As discussed below, the period of protection under a *sui generis* right should be far shorter than it is for copyright. However, upon the expiry of that right, copyright may still operate to prevent the use of that information. If the data is in digital form, the most obvious and convenient means of extracting that information, once the *sui generis* right has expired, is by digital reproduction. The difficulty with this is that in order to reproduce the information, its structure and arrangement must be temporarily reproduced. While the structure and arrangement can then be stripped out from the underlying information, without the structure and arrangement being re-used in any significant manner, the temporary reproduction of the structure and arrangement would infringe copyright. This technical infringement would prevent the most efficient re-use of the data that had entered the public domain upon expiry of the *sui generis* right. What is needed is an exception to copyright that permits temporary reproduction of the structure, and arrangement for the purpose of obtaining and reproducing the underlying data in circumstances where the reproduction of that data is lawful.

---

[125] This possibility is acknowledged in Tyson and Sherry, 'Statutory Protection for Databases', at 9.

Exceptions to prohibitions on circumvention protection devices

Coupled with the need for an exception to copyright for the purposes described above, would be the need for an exception to the prohibition on circumvention of protection devices. The exception would apply to circumventing copyright protection devices in order to gain access to the underlying information that has fallen into the public domain. Such an exception would prevent the possibility of de facto perpetual protection for data. The general issue of circumvention of protection devices has been addressed in Chapters 3 and 5.

An equivalent to the fair use defence

A fair use defence was adapted into the 1999 Bill to apply to the *sui generis* rights conferred by that bill. As discussed in Chapter 5, a crucial aspect of that defence is its discretionary nature. The defence defines the relevant criteria that are to be considered but the weighting and application of those criteria are to be done by judges on a case-by-case basis.[126] However, the most important of these criteria relates to the purpose of the alleged fair use. In particular, it provides scope for educational and research activities that may have some commercial aspect to them. In contrast, the very limited defence in the Directive is restricted to illustration for teaching and research purposes that are purely non-profit activities. As pointed out in Chapter 4, it is extremely difficult completely to divorce commercial purposes from all educational and research activities.[127] The fair use defence acknowledges that educational and research activity may take place anywhere in the spectrum between purely non-profit and purely commercial activity. The degree to which the activity is non-profit or commercial is then weighed with other factors, particularly the extent to which the use is transformative and constitutes a new and better use of the information.

Partly for this reason, the more flexible defence of fair use is superior to the defences in the Directive. The major difficulty with the Directive's approach is that it provides a very general form of protection for investment in databases and then carves out narrowly defined exceptions. For example, while it permits exceptions to the *sui generis* right for public

---

[126] See the discussion of the defence of fair use in Chapter 5.

[127] See Library Association Copyright Alliance, 'Interpretation of terms in the Database Regulations: Supplement to a position paper submitted to the Database Market Strategy Group in 1999' (2000), on file with the author, which indicates that UK libraries are experiencing difficulties in interpreting that provision and difficulties associated with having different exceptions for the *sui generis* right and copyright.

security or administrative or judicial procedures, it provides no exception for news reporting. This is an extraordinary omission in a society based on democratic principles.

There are other good reasons for applying the general standard of fair use rather than specific rules.[128] In particular, the heterogeneity of information in databases suggests that a standard-based approach is most desirable because of the myriad of different types of information and its uses. More precise rules do not have sufficient flexibility to deal with the varying of circumstances in which the use of databases may occur.[129]

Relationship with contract law and compulsory licences

Ultimately, any provisions concerning the protection of databases are of little moment if the relationship between those provisions and contract law is not addressed. The point has already been made earlier in this book and by many academic writers, that contract law has effectively created new intellectual property rights as between the parties to contracts for the use of material that would otherwise be governed by intellectual property regimes. Unless the intellectual property regime pre-empts contract law or, more accurately, prevents contract law pre-empting it, the debate surrounding *sui generis* protection is potentially irrelevant.

This is another reason why 'exceptions' to *sui generis* rights need to be cast in terms of the positive rights of database users. This is one of the weaknesses of the proposed American legislation. It does not interfere with contractual relationships concerning access to, and use of, information unlike the Directive, which provides a positive right to use insubstantial parts of the database. However, this right is probably limited to those who have some contractual right to use the database. Any *sui generis* legislation needs to go further. It needs to require the imposition of a contractual relationship between owners and users in certain circumstances,[130] including those where:

---

[128] 'A standard indicates the kinds of circumstances that are relevant to a decision on legality and is thus open-ended.' I. Ehrlich and R. Posner, 'An Economic Analysis of Legal Rulemaking' (1974) 3 *Journal of Legal Studies* 257 at 258.

[129] See, e.g. ibid., and L. Kaplow, 'Rules versus Standards: An Economic Analysis' (1992) 42 *Duke Law Journal* 557.

[130] These compulsory licences could be crafted such that the licensee is only permitted to utilise the information in a database, not its selection or arrangement. This would avoid any difficulties with the relationship between copyright and compulsory licensing.

- the database owner has sole access to the contents of the database, or the database owner has a natural monopoly in the database;
- the information was originally created via the use of public funds and is not readily available from other sources; and
- the user intends to use the contents in a transformative wealth-creating manner by, for example, creating another database that adds value to the original database.

The introduction of compulsory licences introduces a liability-based rule rather than an exclusive property approach to database protection.[131] As many academic writers have pointed out, a liability-based approach has significant transaction costs as the decision as to what payment will be made depends upon third parties such as tribunals or courts.[132] In contrast, in a property-based situation, the parties reach their own agreement based upon their respective valuations of the property being bought or sold and there are economic efficiencies associated with such an approach. However, there are also costs associated with property rights and the mere possibility of compulsory licensing would be likely to lead to a negotiated settlement between the parties.

In some respects, the imposition of compulsory licensing would impose an obligation on the database owner to subsidise the use of its material and it would constitute a tax on the owner. However, the circumstances described above in which compulsory licences would be applicable also indicate that the database owner is itself receiving some form of subsidy, or wealth-creating uses of information are being blocked via *sui generis* protection.[133] In any event, the opportunity to obtain such a licence would be rarely invoked. For example, exclusive rights would still be in place to control the vast majority of circumstances in which someone wishes

---

[131] A liability-based rule imposes an obligation to pay for the use of the material but cannot prevent the use of the material, whereas an exclusive property approach permits the property owner to exclude others completely from using its property.

[132] R. Merges, 'Contracting into Liability Rules: Intellectual Property Rights and Collective Rights Organizations' (1996) 84 *California Law Review* 1293.

[133] See, e.g. J. Boyle, 'A Politics of Intellectual Property: Environmentalism for the Net' (1997) 47 *Duke Law Journal* 87, where he makes the argument that intellectual property rights are a tax on the general community and that provisions permitting use of information reduce the extent of that tax. The same point is made in I. Ayres and P. Klemperer, 'Limiting Patentee's Market Power without Reducing Innovation Incentives' (1999) 97 *Michigan Law Review* 985 at 991. 'In seeking an unprecedented level of state intervention, it seems only logical that publishers exchange a measure of support for the public-good uses of scientific data for lessened risk aversion and for a measure of artificial lead time in which to recoup their investments', J. Reichman and P. Samuelson, 'Intellectual Property Rights in Data' (1997) 50 *Vanderbilt Law Journal* 51 at 156 where they advocate a short period of protection followed by compulsory licensing provisions.

to reproduce the database in order to compete directly with the database owner.

Modification of competition law principles

For the reasons explained in Chapter 2, competition law or anti-trust law will not perform the task of imposing compulsory licences except in limited circumstances. Even in its restricted sphere of economics, it is a blunt instrument that only targets the most obvious and grossest abuses of economic power. There are a couple of possible responses to this inadequacy. One is to reverse the onus of proof such that a database owner would have to prove that it is not the only source of the information. It would also have to demonstrate that it did not possess substantial economic power and that its refusal to licence was not an abuse of that power. This would include requiring the database owner to demonstrate that its refusal to licence information did not have an impact on other markets for which the information may be required.[134]

A second possible response would be to modify competition law rules to restore the balance in power between database owners and users. For example, the various consortia of database users that have been formed, particularly by library groups, could be afforded some immunity from provisions concerning collective bargaining with individual database owners. The structure of most competition laws is such that joint action by buyers who together wield some market power is more likely to fall foul of competition law principles than the conduct of an individual seller with market power. Most competition laws also provide for some form of exemption from liability in limited circumstances and such exemptions could be utilised in this context.

Duration of the period of protection

The duration of protection is an obvious aspect of protection that should be narrower than that for copyright. Various timeframes have been suggested, ranging from just a few years to twenty-five years or, in the case of the Directive, effectively perpetual protection. There is no significant empirical evidence that justifies any of these terms. Perhaps the only point to

---

[134] This point was specifically raised in the submission of the Australian Consumer and Competition Commission to the Australian attorney-general's department. Undated submission from the Australian Competition and Consumer Commission to the Attorney-General's Department re: the legal protection of databases. Unpublished, a copy held on file by author.

make is that the Nordic catalogue laws provided protection for ten years and there has been no suggestion from within the EU that this period of time was insufficient. In the light of that, the argument for a term of protection beyond ten years has not been established. Given the analysis above concerning the role of information and access to it in society, a shorter period of time should be favoured.

The onus should also be on the database owner to prove that the information appropriated has been commercially available for less than the relevant period. This should include an obligation to state clearly and openly the extent of its claim and penalties for asserting protection when it is not available, such as electronically tagging information with an incorrect release date. The position under the Directive, whereby all the data in a database can effectively acquire perpetual protection if part of the database is periodically updated, is indefensible on any analysis.

Remedies

Obviously, remedies are a critical part of any regime of protection. The remedies for copyright infringement are reasonably well defined by TRIPS.[135] It would be a mistake to copy all those provisions and incorporate them into *sui generis* provisions. The layering of remedies can be used to recognise the heterogeneity of information and the different relationships between database owners and users. Various sanctions can be applied to groups of infringing users, as suggested in the 1999 Bill. For example, employees of scientific research institutions would not have been liable for punitive damages, injunctive relief and the relinquishment of infringing material.

There should also be an onus on the owner of the database to demonstrate its loss. That loss needs to be defined by reference to a loss of opportunity to recover a reasonable return on its investment in the database. It should not defined by reference to the loss of any potential profit that may have been derived from that investment if the database were treated as the exclusive property of the owner. To permit the database owner to capture all the benefits associated with its provision of the contents of the database would create a very significant gap between the cost of creating the database and its value. At that point, the potential for economic rent seeking escalates dramatically.

[135] Part III of TRIPS.

Excise some areas of scientific cooperation from any treaty or legislation

The discussion concerning the role of information in society above suggests that database protection law needs to take account of the different roles of types of information and users of information. The scientific and educational sectors are clear examples of these different types of users that need to be supported by legislation.

For this reason, any international agreement or domestic legislation on *sui generis* protection of databases needs to emphasise the purpose of such an agreement. It needs to acknowledge and celebrate various important uses of information and databases that are not driven primarily by standard economic incentives, for example, the sharing of scientific information within organisations such as the WMO and between different scientific organisations. The importance of such uses of information needs to be promoted to the forefront of any agreement rather than relegated to an exemption or exception that will be subjected to the demand for constant justification.

This should be done in two ways. First, any recitals or explanatory memoranda should acknowledge the varying roles of different types of information and the need to avoid treating some information as a commodity. They should specifically refer to arrangements for the sharing of scientific information, such as international agreements concerning the exchange of meteorological information. They should make it clear that nations are not only permitted but also expected to exempt those types of arrangements from any legislation on the topic. These recitals would then be the basis upon which national scientific organisations could argue for particular exemptions within their own national legislation. Second, provisions concerning use of databases for research and education should not be expressed as exceptions to rights of database owners, but in a form creating positive rights for scientific researchers that cannot be abrogated by the existence of *sui generis* protection or contract law. An obvious example would be a positive right to use insubstantial parts of a database for educational or research purposes.

Government information

There are other issues concerning information generated with government revenue that are related to the above proposition. Some care needs to be taken to ensure that such information can be obtained with reasonable ease. This involves adopting policies presenting government information in ways that are 'provider neutral'. An obvious example of this 'provider neutrality' is the policy adopted in the UK and Australia of releasing court judgments in paragraphs that are numbered by the court itself. References to the judgments utilise these paragraph numbers rather than the paragraph or page numbers of any particular reporting service. This sort of approach reduces the possibility of problems arising such as those relating to the protracted copyright dispute between Westlaw and Hyperlaw.[136] Different providers would be able to select and arrange the government information in their own way and none would have a virtual monopoly over the information in its raw form.

This issue is but part of a more general issue concerning the role of government in creating and disseminating information. While the question of the nature and extent of legal protection of databases is a crucial one, some of the concerns about access to information are ones that can only be addressed by governments and a commitment to public sector expenditure on creating and disseminating some types of information. Some of the proponents of *sui generis* protection for databases rightly point out that many of the concerns about access to information actually flow from a lack of public funding, rather than proposed legal regimes for protection of databases. No legislative regime can solve that problem by itself. Nevertheless, as indicated already, the legislative regime can have some influence on the general attitude towards information as a commodity or as something that may also perform other roles. This possible influence can and should be taken into account when shaping that legislation.

Conclusion

There is an obvious difficulty with the suggestions above. Some of them lead inevitably to uncertainty about, and potential complexity in determining, the precise nature of the *sui generis* protection that would be conferred on databases. This nebulousness is the price that must be paid for an acceptance of the complexity of the issues involved in the protection of databases. The attraction of simplicity and reductionism needs to be resisted. As has already been observed in this chapter, data or information is not homogenous. Different categories of information generate different issues and different relationships between producer, suppliers and users of information.

Despite this complexity and the need to respond to it, the above suggestions still give a very considerable measure of certainty in respect of the most obvious misappropriations of a database owner's investment. Wholesale copying for commercial purposes without adding any value

---

[136] See the discussion of this litigation in Chapter 5.

would be prohibited. However, the legislation would then take account of the various nuances of the debate for protection in its treatment of other forms of database use. Copying, in return for payment, would be permitted in some circumstances; and in cases where the database owner has an effective monopoly in respect of the information, payment would be required. Similarly, if the contents of the database were to be used for a derivative, value-adding purpose, there may be good reason for requiring the database owner to licence the contents to avoid a tragedy of the anti-commons. Those users who are also contributors to databases either indirectly or directly, such as researchers or educational institutions, would also be privileged above other users via exceptions and defences such as fair use. There would also be exemptions from the operation of the legislation in the case of particular examples of international cooperation in sharing scientific information.

The suggestions in the previous section obviously favour the general American approach to *sui generis* protection that is based on misappropriation principles and reject the Directive's more protectionist approach. However, as Chapter 4 and the various American legislative proposals have demonstrated, misappropriation is a nebulous term that can confer very broad or very narrow protection, depending upon the content that is given to that term in any particular context. While the suggestions made above are based on misappropriation principles, they are intended to give some content to the concept of misappropriation in this context. They are also intended to deal with the potentially difficult relationship between *sui generis* protection and copyright. In keeping with the analysis earlier in this chapter of the arguments for *sui generis* protection, the suggestions also provide for a minimalist approach.

There are other reasons for suggesting this minimalist approach. The empirical evidence justifying the establishment of extra protection for databases is limited.[137] The push for protection is based on economic theory and the lobbying of interested pressure groups that have a particular but limited perspective on the role of information. As discussed above, the latter is a form of rent seeking. All these factors suggest that, at the very least, any moves for an international treaty to protect databases should be slow and that any resulting agreement should be for minimal protection. Once created, a new intellectual property regime is difficult to do away with, even if the original justification for the intellectual property regime was questionable. Various economic analyses of patent protection,

---

[137] See Statement of Marybeth Peters, Register of Copyrights before the House Subcommittee on Courts and Intellectual Property of the Judiciary Committee, 23 October 1997, available at http://www.house.gov/judiciary/41112.htm, at 3.

for example, suggest that it would be inappropriate to install such a system today.

If we did not have a patent system, it would be irresponsible on the basis of our present knowledge of its economic consequences, to recommend instituting one.[138]

It would be regrettable if a similar error were made, on a worldwide basis, in respect of databases. On the other hand, the scope of intellectual property regimes can be (and has been) expanded with relative ease. Obvious examples of this are the extensions of the periods of copyright and patent protection via domestic legislation, the Berne Convention and TRIPS.

Chapter 1 of this book put the proposition that the Directive is not an appropriate template for international *sui generis* protection. The analysis of the Directive and the comparisons that have been made with the more sophisticated models in proposed American legislation have revealed its deficiencies, as has the theoretical analysis of *sui generis* protection that was undertaken earlier in this chapter. The model for protection offered by the Directive has significant flaws, in both its detail and overall design. If the issue of international *sui generis* protection is to be advanced at all, the EU needs to reconsider its own position before seeking approval for, and universal adoption of, that position.

Addendum

Canadian approach to originality

In *CCH Canadian Ltd* v *The Law Society of Upper Canada*,[139] the Canadian Federal Court of Appeal adopted a sweat of the brow standard of originality when it specifically rejected the proposition that copyright material requires any creative spark in order to be original. It specifically rejected the proposition that it earlier decision in *Tele-Direct (Publications) Inc.* v *American Business Information Inc.*[140] had changed the standard of originality, and it explained its decision in that case on the basis that the plaintiff had failed to establish that it had exercised more than a negligible amount of skill, labour and judgement in compiling the compilations for which it sought protection.

---

[138] F. Machlup, *An Economic Review of the Patent System* (Washington DC, 1958), p. 80.
[139] (2002) Fed. Ct Appeal LEXIS 104; (2002) FCA 187.   [140] [1998] 2 FC 22.

*Reports to WIPO on the impact of database protection
on developing countries*

In April 2002, five reports concerning the potential impact of database protection on developing countries were presented to the SCCR.[141] The conclusions reached in the five reports differ widely and reflect the arguments discussed in previous chapters of this book. For example, the report of Yale Braunstein from the School of Information, Management and Systems, University of California, Berkeley adopts a neoclassical economic approach that advocates strong property rights with limited exemptions for both developed and developing nations.[142] In contrast, the reports of Sherif El-Kassas from the Department of Computer Science, American University in Cairo and Thomas Riis from the Law Department at the Copenhagen Business School[143] both claim that particular problems will arise for developing countries, and that considerable protection already exists for databases via technological protection measures. These three reports lack any significant empirical data on the issue and are primarily based on theoretical considerations.

The reports with a specific focus on India and China[144] provide some empirical data pertaining to the issue. For example, the report by Zheng Shengli from the Intellectual Property School, Peking University undertakes a comparison of tertiary education costs in China and the United States of America. It concludes that, as a proportion of GDP per capita, Chinese students pay greatly higher costs for tertiary education. Consequently, increases in database licensing costs would have a disproportionately greater impact on Chinese tertiary education.[145] The report by Vandrevala Phiroz from the National Association of Software and Service Companies provides some information about the potential for commercialisation of government information and the development of a database industry in India.[146]

---

[141] Yale Braunstein, 'Economic Impact of Database Protection in Developing Countries and Countries in Transition', 4 April 2002, SCCR 7/2; Sherif El-Kassas, 'Study on the Protection of Unoriginal Databases', 4 April 2002, SCCR 7/3; Thomas Riis, 'Economic Impact of the Protection of Unoriginal Databases in Developing Countries and Countries in Transition', 4 April 2002, SCCR 7/4; Phiroz Vandrevala, 'A Study on the Impact of Protection of Unoriginal Databases on Developing Countries: Indian Experience', 4 April 2002, SCCR 7/5; Shengli Zheng, 'The Economic Impact of the Protection of Databases in China', 4 April 2002, SCCR 7/6.

[142] Yale, 'Economic Impact' at p. 27.

[143] Sherif, 'Study on the Protection of Unoriginal Databases', Thomas 'Economic Impact'.

[144] Phiroz, 'Developing Countries: Indian Experience'; Zheng, 'Economic Impact'.

[145] Zheng, 'Economic Impact', at pp. 48–9.

[146] Phiroz, 'Developing Countries: Indian Experience', at pp. 8–14.

These reports were discussed at the 7th Session of the SCCR held between 13 and 17 May 2002 but delegates agreed that more time was required to consider the reports.[147] While the presentation of the reports is a useful contribution to the debate, it is unlikely that the process for reaching agreement on an international treaty has been significantly accelerated by their release, especially in light of the different conclusions reached by them.

[147] Report of the Standing Committee on Copyright and Related Rights, Seventh Session, Geneva, 13–17 May 2002, SCCR 7/10 at p. 5.

Glossary

CADP	Coalition Against Database Piracy
Committee's Opinion	Opinion on the Proposal for a Council Directive on the Legal Protection of Databases of the Economic and Social Committee, 93/C/19/02.
Copyright Treaty	The WIPO Copyright Treaty of 1996
EEPROM	Electronically erasable programmable read-only memory
First Draft	Proposal for a Council Directive on the legal protection of databases COM(92) 24 final – SYN 393 Brussels, 13 May, 1992.
Green Paper	The EC Green Paper on Copyright and the Challenge of Technology 1998 (Doc. ref. COM(88) 172 Final)
ICSU	International Council for Science
IFLA	International Federation of Library Associations and Institutions
IPA	International Publishers Association
SCCR	Standing Committee on Copyright and Related Rights
The 1996 Bill	The Database Investment and Intellectual Property Antipiracy Bill of 1996 (HR 3531 of 1996)
The 1997 Bill	The Collections of Information Antipiracy Bill of 1997 (HR 2652)
The 1999 Bill	The Collections of Information Antipiracy Bill of 1999 (HR 354, 106th Congress)
The Alternative Bill	The Consumer and Investor Access to Information Bill of 1999 (HR 1858 of the 106th Congress)
The Berne Convention	The Berne Convention for the Protection of Literary and Artistic Works

The Copyright Directive	EU Directive 2001/29/EC of the European Parliament and of the Council of 22 May 2001 on the harmonisation of certain aspects of copyright and related rights in the information society
The Directive	Directive 96/9/EC of the European Parliament and of the Council of 11 March 1996 on the legal protection of databases.
The Draft Treaty	Basic Proposal for the Substantive Provisions of the Treaty on Intellectual Property in respect of Databases Considered by the Diplomatic Conference on Copyright and Neighbouring Rights Questions, Geneva, December, 1996.
TRIPS	Agreement on Trade Related Aspects of Intellectual Property
UNCTAD	United Nations Conference on Trade and Development
UNESCO	United Nations Educational Scientific and Cultural Organization
WIPO	World Intellectual Property Organization
WMO	World Meteorological Organization

Bibliography

American Law Institute, Restatement of the Law, Third, Unfair Competition, 1995

Auinger, C., 'Implementation of the Database Legislation in the EU and Plans for Review', paper presented at a Workshop conducted by the ICSU, Baveno, 14 October 2000

Australian Competition and Consumer Commission, undated submission from the Australian Competition and Consumer Commission to the Attorney-General's Department re: the legal protection of databases. unpublished, on file with the author

Ayres, I. and P. Klemperer, 'Limiting Patentee's Market Power without Reducing Innovation Incentives' (1999) 97 *Michigan Law Review* 985

Babe, R. (ed.), *Communication and the Transformation of Economics: Essays in Information, Public Policy, and Political Economy* (Westview Press, Boulder, CO, 1995)

Baird, D., 'Common Law Intellectual Property and the Legacy of *International News Service* v. *Associated Press*' (1983) 50 *University of Chicago Law Review* 411

Band, J., Testimony of Jonathan Band on behalf of the Online Banking Association before the Subcommittee on Courts and Intellectual Property of the United States House of Representatives Committee on the Judiciary on the 1999 Bill

Bittlingmayer, G., 'The Antitrust Vision Thing: How Did Bush Measure Up?' (2000) 45 *The Antitrust Bulletin* 291

Boulding, K., *Notes on the Information Concept* (Toronto, Exploration Press)

Boyle, J., 'A Politics of Intellectual Property: Environmentalism for the Net' (1997) 47 *Duke Law Journal* 87

Braman, S., 'Defining Information: An Approach for Policy Makers' (1989) 13 *Telecommunications Policy* 233–42

Brown, L. (ed.), *The New Shorter Oxford Dictionary* (4th edn, Clarendon Press, Oxford, 1998)

Chalton, S., 'The Copyright and Rights in Databases Regulations 1997: Some Outstanding Issues on Implementation of the Database Directive' (1998) 20 *European Intellectual Property Review* 178

Clark, C., 'Net Law: A Cyberspace Agenda for Publishers', paper prepared for the UK Publishers Association and the Federation of European Publishers, available at http://www.alpsp.org/netlaw5.pdf, 11 October 1999 (Publishers' Association, London, 1999)

Clauss, R., 'The French Law of Disloyal Competition' (1995) 11 *European Intellectual Property Review* 550

Coase, R., 'The Problem of Social Cost' (1960) 3 *Journal of Law and Economics* 1

Cobb, R., 'The Database Fightback', *Marketing*, 18 February 1993

Colston, C., 'Sui Generis Database Right: Ripe for Review?' 2001 (3) *Journal of Information, Law and Technology*

Committee of the Judiciary, US Congress, *Report of the Judiciary Committee on the Collections of Information Antipiracy Act*, 30 September 1999

Cooter, R. and T. Ulen, *Law and Economics* (Scott, Forseman and Co., Glenview, 1986)

Cornish, W., '1996 European Community Directive on Databases' (1996) 21 *Columbia-VLA Journal of Law and the Arts* 1

D'Amato, A. and D. Long (eds.), *International Intellectual Property Law* (Kluwer, Amsterdam, 1997)

Date, C., *An Introduction to Database Systems* (6th edn, Addison-Wesley, Reading, 1994)

Davison, M. and K. Akers, Survey of Australian Medical Researchers' Usage of and Contributions to Databases (2000) On file with the author

Dietz, A., *International Copyright Law and Practice* (Matthew Bender, New York, 1999)

Drahos, P., *A Philosophy of Intellectual Property* (Dartmouth, Aldershot, 1996)

Dreier, L. and G. Karnall, 'Originality of the Copyright Work: A European Perspective' (1992) 39 *Journal of the Copyright Society USA* 289

Dworkin, G., 'Originality in the Law of Copyright' (1962) 11 *ASCAP Copyright Law Symposium* 60

Ehrlich, I. and R. Posner, 'An Economic Analysis of Legal Rulemaking' (1974) 3 *Journal of Legal Studies* 257

Ellickson, R., *Order Without Law: How Neighbors Settle Disputes* (Harvard University Press, Cambridge, MA, 1991)

'Social Norms, Social Meaning, and the Economic Analysis of Law' (1998) 27 *Journal of Legal Studies* 537

European Union, 'Institutions of the European Union' at http://europa.eu.int/inst.en.htm

Fitzgerald, D., 'Magill Revisited' (1998) 20 *European Intellectual Property Review* 154

Franzosi, M., 'The Legal Protection of Industrial Design: Unfair Competition as a Basis of Protection' (1990) 5 *European Intellectual Property Review* 154

Gans, J., P. Williams and D. Briggs, 'Clarifying the Relationship Between Intellectual Property Rights and Competition', report prepared on behalf of the National Copyright Industry Alliance for submission to the *Review of Intellectual Property and Competition*, February 2001, available at http://www.ipcr.gov.au/SUBMIS/docs/78.pdf

Garner, B., *A Dictionary of Modern Legal Usage* (2nd edn, Oxford University Press, New York, 1995)

Gaster, J., 'European Sui Generis Right for Databases' (2001) 3 *Computer Und Recht International* 74

Gimeno, L., 'News Section: National Reports' (1996) 2 *European Intellectual Property Review* D-49

'Protection of Compilations in Spain and the UK' (1998) 29 *IIC* 907

Ginsburg, J., 'Copyright without Borders? Choice of Forum and Choice of Law for Copyright Infringement in Cyberspace' (1997) 15 *Cardozo Arts and Entertainment Law Journal* 153

'No "Sweat" Copyright and Other Protection of Works of Information after *Feist* v. *Rural Telephone*' [1992] *Columbia Law Review* 338

Goldstein, P., *International Copyright: Principles, Law and Practice* (Oxford University Press, Oxford, 2001)

Habermas, J., *The Structural Transformation of the Public Sphere: An Inquiry into a Category of Bourgeois Society* trans. T. Berger (MIT Press, Cambridge, MA, 1989)

Haywood, T., *Info-Rich – Info-Poor: Access and Exchange in the Global Information Society* (Bowker Saw, West Sussex, 1995)

Heller, M., 'The Tragedy of the Anticommons: Property in the Transition from Marx to Markets' (1998) 111 *Harvard Law Review* 621

Hertz-Eichenrode, C., 'Germany' in D. Campbell (ed.), *World Intellectual Property Rights and Remedies* (Oceana Publications, New York, 1999)

Hugenholtz, B., 'Copyright and Databases, Report on the Netherlands' in M. Dellebeke (ed.), *Copyright in Cyberspace, ALAI Study Days 1996* (Otto Cramwinckel, Amsterdam, 1997), p. 491

'Electronic Rights and Wrongs in Germany and the Netherlands' (1998) 22 *Columbia Journal of Law and the Arts* 151

'The New Database Right: Early Case Law from Europe', paper presented to the Ninth Annual Conference on International Intellectual Property Law and Policy, New York 19–20 April 2001

Jacobacci, G., 'Italian Trademark Law and Practice and the Protection of Product and Packaging' (1983) 74 *Trade Mark Reporter* 418

Jones, B., *SLEEPERS, WAKE: Technology and the Future of Work* (Oxford University Press, Sydney, 1982)

Jones, N., 'Euro-Defences: Magill Distinguished' (1998) 20 *European Intellectual Property Review* 352

Kamperman Sanders, A., *Unfair Competition Law: The Protection of Intellectual and Industrial Creativity* (Clarendon Press, Oxford, 1997)

Kaplow, L., 'Rules versus Standards: An Economic Analysis' (1992) 42 *Duke Law Journal* 557

Katzenberger, P., 'Copyright Law and Data Banks' (1990) 21 *IIC* 310

Keohane, P. and E. Ostrom (eds.), *Local Commons and Global Interdependence: Heterogeneity and Cooperation in Two Domains* (Sage Publications, London, 1995)

Kirk, M., Statement of Michael Kirk, Executive Director, American Intellectual Property Law Association to Subcommittee on Intellectual Property and the Courts of the Committee on the Judiciary, 18 March 1999

Lai, S., 'Database Protection in the United Kingdom: The New Deal and its Effects on Software Protection' (1998) 20 *European Intellectual Property Review* 32

Lamberton, D. (ed.), *The Economics of Communication and Information* (Edward Elgar, Cheltenham, 1996)

Landes, W. and R. Posner, 'An Economic Analysis of Copyright Law' (1989) 18 *Journal of Legal Studies* 325

'Citations, Age, Fame and the Web' (2000) 29 *Journal of Legal Studies* 319

'The Economics of Trademark Law' (1988) 78 *The Trademarks Reporter* 267

Lederberg, J., Statement of Joshua Lederberg before the Subcommittee on Courts and Intellectual Property of the Judiciary Committee concerning the 1999 Bill, 18 March 1999

Leistner, M., 'The Legal Protection of Telephone Directories Relating to the New Database Maker's Right' (2000) 31 *IIC* 950

Limpberg, K., 'Netherlands', in D. Campbell (ed.), *World Intellectual Property Rights and Remedies* (Oceana Publications, New York, 1999)

Lucas, A. and A. Plaisant, 'France' in M. B. Nimmer and P. E. Geller, *International Copyright Law and Practice* (Matthew Bender, New York, 1999)

Machlup, F., *An Economic Review of the Patent System* (United States Government Printing Office, Washington DC, 1958)

Maurer, S., 'Across Two Worlds: Database Protection in the US and Europe', paper prepared for Industry Canada's Conference on Intellectual Property and Innovation in the Knowledge-Based Economy, 23–24 May 2001

Maurer, S., B. Hugenholtz and H. Onsrud, 'Europe's Database Experiment' (2001) 294 *Science's Compass* 789–90

Mehrings, J., 'Wettbewerbsrechtlicher Schutz von Online-Dataenbanken' [1990] *Computer und Recht* 305, 307

Merges, R., 'Contracting into Liability Rules: Intellectual Property Rights and Collective Rights Organizations' (1996) 84 *California Law Review* 1293

'Of Property Rules, Coase, and Intellectual Property' (1994) 94 *Columbia Law Review* 2655

Monotti, A., 'The Extent of Copyright Protection For Compilations of Artistic Works' (1993) 15 *European Intellectual Property Review* 156

National Academy of Sciences, *A Question of Balance: Private Rights and the Public Interest in Scientific and Technical Databases* (National Academy Press, Washington DC, 1999)

National Research Council, *Bits of Power: Issues in Global Access to Scientific Data* (National Academy Press, Washington DC, 1997)

Nimmer, M. and D. Nimmer, *Nimmer on Copyright* (Lexis, New York, 1963)

Oosterbaan, O., 'Database Protection in the EU and the US Compared: A High-Tech Game of Chicken?' (2002) available at http://lex.oosterban.net/docs.html

Ostrom, E., *Governing the Commons: The Evolution of Institutions for Collective Action* (Cambridge University Press, New York, 1990)

Pass, C. and B. Lowes, *Collins Dictionary of Economics* (2nd edn, Harper Collins, Glasgow, 1988)

Peters, M., Statement of Marybeth Peters, Register of Copyrights, before the House Subcommittee on Courts and Intellectual Property on HR 354, 106th Congress, 1st Session, 18 March 1997

Phelps, C., Statement of Charles Phelps on behalf of the Association of American Universities, the American Council on Education and the National Association of State Universities and Land-Grant Colleges to the Subcommittee on Courts and Intellectual Property of the Judiciary Committee concerning HR 354, 18 March 1999

Pincus, A., Statement of Andrew Pincus, General Counsel, US Department of Commerce before the Subcommittee on Courts and Intellectual Property of the Judiciary Committee concerning the 1999 Bill, 18 March 1999

Posner, E., 'Law, Economics and Inefficient Norms' (1996) 144 *University of Pennsylvania Law Review* 1697

Posner, R., *Economic Analysis of Law* (4th edn, Little, Brown and Co., Boston, MA, 1992)

Rai, A., 'Regulating Scientific Research: Intellectual Property Rights and the Norms of Science' (1999) 94 *Northwestern Law Review* 77

Raubenheimer, A., 'Germany: Recent Decisions on Database Protection Under Copyright Law and Unfair Competition Rules' (1996) 1 *Communications Law* 123

Raue, P. and V. Bensinger, 'Implementation of the Sui Generis Right in Databases Pursuant to Section 87 et seq. of the German Copyright Act' (1998) 3 *Communications Law* 220

Rees, C. and Chalton, S., *Database Law* (Bristol, Jordans, 1998)

Reichman, J. and J. Franklin, 'Privately Legislated Intellectual Property Rights: Reconciling Freedom of Contract with Public Good Uses of Information' (1999) 147 *University of Pennsylvania Law Review* 875

Reichman, J. and P. Samuelson, 'Intellectual Property Rights in Data' (1997) 50 *Vanderbilt Law Review* 51

Ricketson, S., *The Berne Convention for the Protection of Literary and Artistic Works: 1886–1986* (Centre for Commercial Law Studies, Queen Mary College, University of London, London, 1987)

The Law of Intellectual Property: Copyright, Designs and Confidential Information (LBC Information Services, Sydney, 1999)

Robins, D., 'Will Massachusetts Adopt the Misappropriation Doctrine?' (1999) 43 *Boston Bar Association Boston Bar Journal* 4

Sease, E., 'Misappropriation is Seventy-five Years Old; Should We Bury it or Revive it' (1994) 70 *North Dakota Law Review* 781

Sherman, B., 'Digital Property and the Digital Commons' in C. Heath and A. K. Sanders (eds.), *Intellectual Property in the Digital Age: Challenges for Asia* (Kluwer, London, 2001)

Shughart II, W., 'The Fleeting Reagan Antitrust Revolution' (2000) 95 *The Antitrust Bulletin* 271

Steckler, B., 'Unfair Trade Practices under German Law: Slavish Imitation of Commercial and Industrial Activities' (1996) 7 *European Intellectual Property Review* 390

Sterling, J., *World Copyright Law* (Sweet and Maxwell, London, 1998)

Strowel, A., N. Dutihh and J. Gorbet, 'Belgium' in D. Nimmer and P. E. Geller (eds.), *International Copyright Law and Practice* (Matthew Bender, New York, 1999)

Thomson Corporation, Annual Report of 1998, Annual Report of 1999

Tyson, L. and E. Sherry, 'Statutory Protection for Databases: Economic & Public Policy Issues', paper prepared on behalf of the Information Industry Association and presented to the Committee on the Judiciary, 23 October 1997

UK Copyright Directorate, 'The Government's Proposals to Implement the Directive of the European Parliament and the Council on the legal protection of databases: Outcome of Consultations' on file with the author

UK Copyright Directorate, The Patent Office, 'A Consultative Paper on United Kingdom Implementation: Directive 96/9/EC of the European Parliament and the Council of 11 March 1996 on the Legal Protection of Databases'

UK Library Association Copyright Alliance, 'Interpretation of terms in the Database Regulations: Supplement to a Position Paper Submitted to the Database Market Strategy Group in 1999' (2000) on file with the author

UK Office for National Statistics, *Annual Abstract of Statistics No. 135, 1999* (UK Office for National Statistics, London, 1999)

UNESCO, *World Science Report 1998* (UNESCO, Paris, 1998)

US Bureau of Statistics, *Statistical Abstract of the United States* (Bureau of Statistics, Washington DC, 1998)

US Copyright Office, Report on Legal Protection for Databases, August 1997, available at http://www.copyright.gov/reports/

US Department of Energy, Human Genome Project Information at http://www.ornl.gov/hgmis/

Webster, F., *Theories of the Information Society* (Routledge, London, 1995)

Williams, M., 'The State of Databases Today: 1998', *Gale Directory of Databases*

Winokur, M., Written Statement of Marilyn Winokur, Executive Vice-President of Micromedex on behalf of the Coalition Against Database Piracy (CADP) on the 1999 Bill to the Subcommittee on Courts and Intellectual Property of the Judiciary Committee, 18 March 1999

WMO, 'Exchanging Meteorological Data: Guidelines on Relationships in Commercial Meteorological Activities: WMO Policy and Practice', publication no. 837 (WMO, Geneva)

Wolters Kluwer, Annual Report of 1998

Zillman, J., 'Atmospheric Science and Public Policy' (1997) 276 *Science* 1084

Index

abuse of dominant position
  Commission reports, 97
  licensing, 45, 46
  unlawful purpose, 44, 45
access
  charges, 35
  compulsory licensing, 34, 35–36
  contracts, 11, 35, 36, 40, 41
  extraction, 87
  fair dealing, 35
  fair use, 35, 42
  Green Paper (1988), 53
  incentives, 243
  marginal costs, 243, 247
  networks, 2
  non-contractual, 41
  prevention, 35, 41
  public subsidy, 5, 243, 250
  technological protection circumvention,
    41, 165
  willingness to pay, 243
advertisements
  France, 114, 116, 117
  Germany, 124, 125
  public procurement, 114, 116,
    117
advertising, telephone directories, 162
Agreement on Trade Related Aspects of
    Intellectual Property see TRIPS
    Agreement
anti-trust law
  see also competition law
  enforcement, 48
  licensing, 199, 280
  terminology, 43
artistic works
  Berne Convention, 218–219
  compulsory licensing, 34
  right of distribution, 31
assignment of copyright
  Belgium, 109
  contracts, 109

database owners, 245
  Germany, 118
Australia
  citizenship, 265
  compilations, 10, 12, 14, 18
  compulsory licensing, 34
  computer programs, 75
  Copyright Tribunal, 34
  government information, 283
  Health WIZ Project, 269–271
  infringement, 37
  sweat of brow, 14
  unfair competition, 37
authorship
  Belgium, 109
  Berne Convention, 224
  compilations, 17, 54
  Database Directive, 75, 76, 83,
    84
  definitions, 21, 76, 83
  Draft Directive, 64, 66
  emanation, 17–18, 21
  France, 114
  Germany, 118
  indexing decisions, 22, 23, 25
  Italy, 130, 131, 133
  originality, 17, 21, 37
  personality, 16, 17
  requirement, 21–24
  selection/arrangement, 18
  United Kingdom, 24

Belgium
  assignment of copyright, 109
  authorship, 109
  changes to database, 113
  communication to public, 110, 113
  copyright, 109–111
  database defined, 109, 112
  educational use, 110, 113
  employers, economic rights, 109
  equitable remuneration, 111

exceptions, 109, 111, 113
extraction, 112, 113
hardcopy databases, 110, 111, 113
insubstantial part, 112
lawful users, 110, 112
literary works, 109
maker of database, 111–112
neighbouring rights, 109
non-EU databases, 110, 112
originality, 109
parasitic copying, 111
private use, 110, 113
public lending, 110, 112
re-utilisation, 112
research, 110, 113
right of reproduction, 110, 113
selection/arrangement, 109
substantial investment, 112
sui generis right, 111–112
term of protection, 113
transposition of directive, 109–113
unfair competition, 111
Berne Convention 1971
artistic works, 218–219
authorship, 224
compilations, 52, 218–219, 223
compulsory licensing, 36
developing countries, 234
exceptions, 79, 92
exclusive rights, 76, 79
literary works, 218–219
national treatment, 221
right of reproduction, 29
Stockholm Protocol, 234
term of protection, 225
bilateral agreements
European Union (EU), 5, 217, 218,
    234–235
national treatment, 221
sui generis right, 5, 217, 218

catalogue laws
Sweden, 59, 103, 141, 142, 143,
    155
term of protection, 59, 258
CD-ROMs
fixed goods, 88
impact of Directive, 263
originality, 62, 63
substantial investment, 73
changes to database
Belgium, 113
qualitative change, 93
substantial changes, 92–93
term of protection, 59, 64, 67, 93, 192

United States, 192
updating, 22, 23
Chicago School, 242
Coalition Against Database Piracy
    (CADP), 260
collecting societies, 34, 35, 115,
    256
collections
see also compilations
France, 114
Germany, 120, 121
hardcopy databases, 72
Italy, 129, 130
Netherlands, 133, 134
Spain, 138
United States, 194, 199, 201, 273
commercial purposes
definition, 66
Draft Directive, 51, 57, 65, 66, 98
re-utilisation, 57, 66
redistribution prohibited, 244
unauthorised extraction, 57, 66, 98
unfair extraction, 57, 65
United States, 168, 191
commercial value
misappropriation, 184
time-sensitive data, 185, 186, 187
commodification
culture, 266
database defined, 241
definitions, 264
diversity, 252–253
economic development, 54
exceptions, 238
privatisation, 266
production chain, 247
property rights, 239–240
sui generis right, 266
common law
compilations, 10
economic incentives, 16
intellectual property, 6
misappropriation, 162, 175, 178, 190,
    214
news reporting, 173
unfair competition, 37
United States, 162, 175, 178, 214
communication to public
available on-line, 88
Belgium, 110, 113
Copyright Treaty (1996), 31, 77, 88,
    219
electronic distribution, 31
exclusive rights, 28, 31–32
Germany, 125

communication to public (*cont.*)
  making available to public, 29
  re-utilisation compared, 88
  sui generis right, 32
  transmission, 88
competition
  competitive excellence, 44
  direct competition, 132, 174, 180,
    183–185, 206
  perfect competition, 43–44
  unfair competition, 38, 146–147
competition law
  see also anti-trust law
  compulsory licensing, 43
  contracts, 43
  Database Directive, 97–98
  distributive justice, 48–49
  enforcement, 47–48, 246
  government policy, 48
  harmonisation, 60
  intellectual property, 43
  modification, 280
  paradigm does not fit, 43–46
  principles, 43–49
  purpose/theory, 43
  regulation, 47–48
  sui generis right, 11, 43
compilations
  see also collections
  Australia, 10, 12, 14, 18
  authorship, 17, 54
  Berne Convention, 52, 218–219, 223
  common law, 10
  copyright, 11, 274
  criteria, 12
  England, 18
  France, 114
  Germany, 119, 120
  government/public information,
    162–163, 208–209, 211
  Green Paper (1988), 52, 53, 54
  infringement, 19
  Ireland, 126
  literary works, 12, 218
  multimedia, 13
  musical works, 85
  Netherlands, 133
  originality, 16, 17–21, 163–164
  pre-existing works, 12, 86
  public domain material, 166–167
  sui generis right, 53
  Sweden, 141
  tables, 12, 13
  terminology, 12
  TRIPS Agreement, 13, 223

United Kingdom, 12, 143, 144, 145
United States, 162–164
comprehensiveness
  all available material, 19, 21
  single source, databases, 157–158
  telephone directories, 170, 256
  value to users, 170
compulsory licensing
  access, 34, 35–36
  artistic works, 34
  Australia, 34
  Berne Convention, 36
  collecting societies, 34, 35, 115, 256
  competition law, 43
  contracts, 36, 278–280
  Database Directive, 97–98
  Draft Directive, 51, 52, 57, 61, 65, 67
  educational use, 34, 49
  equitable remuneration, 34
  France, 115
  Ireland, 127, 128–129
  justification, 244
  literary works, 34
  news reporting, 34
  public interest, 34, 35, 36, 37
  requirements, 34–36
  substantial part, 34
  sui generis right, 36, 52, 58
  transaction costs, 34, 35, 245
computer programs
  Australia, 75
  compression tables, 75
  Computer Software Directive 1993,
    120–121
  copyright, 55, 71
  data content, 71, 74, 273
  database defined, 74
  Database Directive, 74, 75
  dongles, 166
  Draft Directive, 55, 71
  filtering applications, 166
  Germany, 119, 120–121
  infringement, 71, 75, 119
  literary works, 21, 75, 273
  look-up tables, 75
  malfunction/obsolescence, 166
  Mars decision, 71, 74, 75
  object code, 273
  organisation of data, 21, 23, 24
  originality, 55, 114, 120–121
  rental rights, 31
  reverse engineering, 165
  skill and judgement, 75
  substantial investment, 75
  sui generis right, 62, 198, 257, 273

United States, 198, 208
confidential information, 7
contents
  arrangement *see* selection/arrangement
  changes *see* changes to database
  comprehensive *see* comprehensiveness
  Database Directive, 74, 75, 76, 81, 84,
    86, 89, 93
  obtaining, 83, 86, 89
  presentation, 86, 89, 93
  primacy, 56
  qualitative investment, 84
  substantial investment, 86
  sui generis right, 51, 55, 57, 81,
    84
  verification, 86, 89, 93
contracts
  access, 11, 36, 40, 41
  advantages, 40
  assignment of copyright, 109
  bargaining strength, 42, 43
  click-on, 41, 254
  competition law, 43
  compulsory licensing, 36, 278–280
  conditions of use, 42
  contract law, 40–43
  contracts of adhesion, 101
  contractual arrangements, 56
  Database Directive, 42
  disadvantages, 40, 41
  Draft Directive, 56, 60
  electronic commerce, 254
  fair dealing, 42
  fair use, 42
  France, 115, 117, 156
  Germany, 125
  hardcopy databases, 41
  lawful users, 56, 156
  legislation overridden, 42
  non-derogation, 193, 199, 212
  non-negotiable, 41
  overridden by legislation, 42, 58, 78, 91,
    101
  price discrimination, 40
  public interest, 42
  re-utilisation, 58
  return on investment, 40
  technological protection circumvention,
    11
  third parties, 40, 78
  United Kingdom, 148
  United States *see* United States
copyright
  basic principles, 10, 11–37
  Belgium, 109–111

  compilations, 11, 274
  computer programs, 55, 71
  Database Directive, 3, 4, 75–76
  Draft Directive, 54–55
  European standards, 16–17, 51, 69,
    76
  exceptions, 32–34, 77–81, 152
  factual material, 170, 171
  France, 113–115
  Germany, 118–122
  Green Paper (1988), 54
  harmonisation, 3, 50, 76, 94,
    152–153
  indexing, 91
  infringed *see* infringement
  international treaties, 218–226
  Ireland, 126–127
  Italy, 129–131
  justification, 241
  licensing *see* compulsory licensing
  literary *see* literary works
  market failure, 242
  minimal protection, 218
  Netherlands, 133–134
  originality *see* originality
  protection lacking, 3, 4, 7
  rights *see* exclusive rights
  Spain, 138–139
  sui generis right: differentiation, 11;
    overlap, 6, 81–82, 84, 90, 92, 217,
    223–224, 255, 274–275
  summary conclusions, 36–37
  UK *see* United Kingdom copyright
  United States, 4, 10, 162–171
Copyright Directive 2001
  educational use, 102
  exceptions, 101–102, 153
  harmonisation, 3, 50
  insubstantial part, 101
  research, 102
  technological protection circumvention,
    3–4, 50, 100–102, 112, 129
Copyright Treaty 1996
  adoption, 29, 88
  Agreed Statements, 29
  communication to public, 31, 77, 88,
    219
  distribution of copies, 88
  electronic dissemination, 219
  exclusive rights, 76
  minimal protection, 219
  national treatment, 221, 224
  remedies, 220–221
  rental rights, 31
  right of distribution, 31, 89

Copyright Treaty 1996 (*cont.*)
  rights management information, 219,
    221
  sweat of brow, 219
  technological protection circumvention,
    32, 101, 129, 220
  United States, 197
costs
  maintenance, 86, 93, 194–195, 210
  marginal costs, access, 243, 247
  property rights *see* property rights
  sunk costs, 44–45
  transactions *see* transaction costs
creativity
  see also originality
  importance, 274
  intellectual creation *see* intellectual
    creativity
  Italy, 130
  low standard, 15
  relevance, 19–20
  selection/arrangement, 10, 15, 19, 27,
    54, 63, 84, 171
  Spain, 138
  United Kingdom, 144

data
  computer programs: content 71, 74,
    275; organisation, 21, 23, 24
  high-activity life-span, 258
  information distinguished, 251
  time-sensitive *see* time-sensitive data
database creation
  all available material, 19, 21
  economies of scale, 245
  growth, 261, 263
  incentives *see* incentives
  indexing, 22–23, 91
  investment *see* investment
  necessary arrangements, 24
  programs *see* computer programs
  rent seeking, 245
  sunk costs, 44–45
  technical aspects, 22–24
  telephone directories, 22–23, 246
  verification, 86, 89, 93
database defined
  see also subject matter of protection
  Belgium, 109, 112
  commodification, 241
  computer programs, 74
  Database Directive, 273
  dependence, 72
  Draft Directive, 54, 57, 60, 62, 63, 66
  Draft Treaty 1996, 227

fixed form, 70
France, 114, 116
Germany, 120, 124
hardcopy databases, 72
'independent', 72, 120
Ireland, 126, 128
Italy, 130, 132
purposive aspect, 73, 273
United Kingdom, 144, 147
United States, 73, 191, 192, 194, 273
Database Directive
  ambiguities, 4
  authorship, 75, 76, 83, 84
  competition law, 97–98
  compulsory licensing, 97–98
  computer programs, 74, 75
  contents, 74, 75, 76, 81, 84, 86, 89,
    93
  contracts, 42
  copyright, 3, 4, 75–76
  Copyright Treaty 1996 compared, 88
  database defined, 273
  distribution of copies, 88
  draft *see* Draft Directive
  exceptions: copyright, 77–81;
    educational use, 78, 79–80, 98;
    European standards, 51;
    harmonisation, 10–13, 33;
    insufficient, 9; interpretation, 77;
    research, 78, 79–80, 98; *sui generis*
    right, 79, 91–92
  exclusive rights, 76–77
  final provisions, 98–99
  final version, 68–102
  hardcopy databases, 78
  history, 51–68
  impact, evidence, 263–264
  information retrieval, 70
  infringement, 91
  investment protection, 6, 69, 70, 82
  lawful users, 77–78, 91
  maker of database, 82–83, 84
  national treatment, 63, 97, 217, 221
  neighbouring rights, 97, 223
  non-EU databases, 5, 97
  originality, 15, 33, 76, 94, 95
  private use, 78
  qualitative criteria, 76, 83–87, 89, 93,
    246
  reciprocity, 5, 63, 97, 223, 225
  recitals, 69, 71, 72, 73, 76, 77, 82, 85,
    93
  rental rights, 31, 77
  restricted acts, 76–77
  retrospectivity, 93–97

right of distribution, 31
saving, existing legal regimes, 98
scope, 70, 74
selection/arrangement, 50, 74, 75, 84
substantial investment, 6, 73, 81,
    83–87
substantive provisions, 70
sui generis see sui generis right
summary, 99–100
sweat of brow, 81, 83, 92, 224
term of protection, 9, 52, 77, 92,
    156–157
territorial qualification, 97
transposition: Belgium, 109–113;
    France, 113–118; Germany, 118–126;
    Ireland, 126–129; Italy, 129–133;
    lawful users, 156; legislation,
    104–108; Netherlands, 133–137;
    retrospectivity, 95; Spain, 138–141;
    summary, 152–159; Sweden,
    141–143; United Kingdom, 143–152
uniform laws, 69
US proposals compared, 192–193,
    199–200, 211–212, 215
database industry
    acquisitions, 261
    entrants *see* new entrants
    information companies, 261–263
    retrospectivity, 94, 96
    Spain, 61
    sui generis right, 236
    United Kingdom, 61
    United States, 54, 63
database markets
    entrants *see* new entrants
    international, 48, 54, 217, 218
    natural monopoly, 44, 245
    niches, 44
    power *see* market power
    property rights, 239
    United Kingdom, 61
    United States *see* United States
database owners
    assignment of copyright, 245
    Italy, 130
    power *see* market power
    public subsidy, 249
databases
    access *see* access
    boundaries, 25–26
    changes *see* changes to database
    contracts *see* contracts
    non-electronic *see* hardcopy databases
    single source, 157–158
    structure *see* selection/arrangement

Denmark, term of protection, 59
derogations, Draft Directive, 56
developing countries
    Berne Convention 1971, 234
    intellectual property, 233–234
    rental rights, 31
    World Intellectual Property Organization
        (WIPO), 5, 218, 226, 228, 232–233
differential pricing *see* price discrimination
digital environment
    access charges, 35
    access prevented, 35
    advantages, 2
    multimedia, 13
    right of reproduction, 30
    surveillance, 35
direct competition
    misappropriation, 174, 180, 183–185,
        206
    time-sensitive data, 206
distribution, exclusive rights *see* right of
    distribution
distributive justice, competition law,
    48–49
dominant position
    see also market power
    abuse *see* abuse of dominant position
    competitive excellence, 44
    intellectual property, 46
    legitimation, 46–47
Draft Directive
    see also Database Directive
    authorship, 64, 66
    commercial purposes, 51, 57, 65, 66,
        98
    Common Position 1995, 68
    compulsory licensing, 51, 52, 57, 61,
        65, 66–67
    contracts, 56, 60
    copyright, 54–55
    Council's Reasons, 68, 81
    database defined, 54, 57, 60, 62, 63,
        66
    derogations, 56
    Economic and Social Committee, 60,
        65, 70
    educational use, 55
    European Parliament amendments
        (1993), 65–68
    exceptions, 55–56, 58–59, 67, 98
    exclusive rights, 61
    Explanatory Memorandum, 53,
        61
    fair dealing, 55–56
    first draft, 53–60

Draft Directive (*cont.*)
  Green Paper *see* Green Paper 1988
  hardcopy databases, 57, 60, 62, 98
  insubstantial part, 58
  justification, 54, 65
  lawful users, 56, 58
  legal philosophy, 61
  minimalist approach, 65
  neighbouring rights, 57, 62
  non-EU databases, 59, 63
  originality, 55
  primacy, 56
  private use, 57, 58, 67
  re-utilisation, 58
  recitals, 53, 60
  retrospectivity, 59
  saving, existing legal regimes, 59–60
  selection/arrangement, 57
  substantial investment, 66, 83–87
  sui generis right, 3, 4, 37, 57, 62, 65, 66,
    67
  summary, 60
  sweat of brow, 51, 62, 65
  technological protection circumvention,
    64
  term of protection, 52, 59, 63, 64, 65,
    68, 240
  unauthorised extraction, 66
  unfair competition, 50, 51, 57, 60
  unfair extraction *see* unfair extraction
Draft Treaty 1996
  database defined, 227
  diplomatic conference (1996), 5, 226,
    228–229, 231
  EU model, 218, 226
  national treatment, 227
  preliminary drafts, 226, 227–228
  substantial investment, 227
  sweat of brow, 227
  term of protection, 228
  verification, 227
  WIPO initiatives, 228–229
duration *see* term of protection

Economic and Social Committee, 60, 65,
  70
educational use
  Belgium, 110, 113
  compulsory licensing, 34, 49
  Copyright Directive 2001, 102
  Database Directive, 78, 79–80, 98
  Draft Directive, 55
  Germany, 121, 126
  'illustration', 79

Ireland, 127, 128
Italy, 131, 133
Netherlands, 134, 137
non-commercial purpose, 79
price discrimination, 40
Spain, 138, 140
sui generis right, 6
Sweden, 141
technological protection circumvention,
  165
United Kingdom, 146, 151
United States, 165, 168, 197–198,
  205–206
effort exerted *see* sweat of brow
employers
  Belgium, 109
  Italy, 130
enforcement
  anti-trust law, 48
  competition law, 47–48, 246
  property rights, 245, 257
England
  see also United Kingdom
  compilations, 18
  infringement, 37
  test for protection, 84
  unfair competition, 37
equitable remuneration
  Belgium, 111
  compulsory licensing, 34
  Germany, 122
  Netherlands, 134
European Parliament, 65–68
European standards
  copyright, 16–17, 51, 69, 76
  Database Directive exceptions, 51
  harmonised *see* harmonisation
  originality, 16–17, 51, 76
European Union (EU)
  acquis communautaire, 217, 234
  Association Agreements, 234
  bilateral agreements, 5, 217, 218,
    234–235
  Central and East European Countries,
    231, 235
  Computer Software Directive 1993,
    120–121
  copyright *see* Copyright Directive
    2001
  databases: Directive *see* Database
    Directive; protection, 50–102
  most favoured nation, 217
  national treatment *see* national
    treatment

excellence
  competitive excellence, 44
  standard of excellence, 26–27, 76
  substantial part, 26–27
exceptions
  Belgium, 109, 111, 113
  Berne Convention, 79, 92
  copyright, 32–34, 77–81, 152
  Copyright Directive (2001), 101–102,
    153
  Directive *see* Database Directive
  Draft Directive, 55–56, 58–59, 67,
    98
  fair dealing *see* fair dealing
  fair use *see* fair use
  France, 33, 80, 114, 117–118
  Germany, 80, 121–122, 126
  government information, 238
  harmonisation, 156
  inconsistencies, 152
  Ireland, 128
  Italy, 131, 133
  Netherlands, 134, 137
  news reporting, 238
  scientific research *see* research
  Spain, 138–139, 140
  sui generis right, 58–59
  Sweden, 141, 142
  teaching *see* educational use
  technological protection circumvention,
    101–102, 165–167, 277
  TRIPS Agreement, 79
  underlying information, 276
  unfair extraction, 58
  United Kingdom, 33, 92, 145, 146, 151
  United States, 33, 161, 190
exclusions, United States, 198–199
exclusive rights
  Berne Convention, 76, 79
  communication *see* communication to
    public
  Copyright Treaty 1996, 76
  Database Directive, 76–77
  distribution *see* right of distribution
  Draft Directive, 61
  infringement, 25, 28, 38
  international treaties, 28
  originality, 89
  rental *see* rental rights
  reproduction *see* right of reproduction
  sui generis right, 52, 89, 190, 192, 193,
    240
  technological protection circumvention,
    29, 32, 35

exemptions, technological protection
  circumvention, 165–167, 277
exhaustion
  Germany, 125
  right of distribution, 31
Explanatory Memorandum, Draft
    Directive, 53
expression
  discovery compared, 19
  originality, 17, 21
  protection, 258
  United States, 164, 172, 173
extraction
  access, 87
  Belgium, 112, 113
  definition, 87
  France, 117
  Germany, 125
  infringement, 87
  Ireland, 128
  Italy, 133
  Netherlands, 136–137
  repeated and systematic, 92, 150, 191,
    197
  reproduction right compared, 87
  right to prevent, 87–89
  Spain, 140
  'transfer', 87
  unauthorized *see* unauthorized
    extraction
  unfair *see* unfair extraction
  United Kingdom, 148, 150, 151
  United States, 191, 197

fair dealing
  access, 35
  contracts, 42
  Draft Directive, 55–56
  Ireland, 127, 128
  lawful users, 78
  news reporting, 152
  reliance, 38
  research, 33, 80
  United Kingdom, 33, 80, 145, 146, 151,
    153
fair use
  access, 35, 42
  contracts, 42
  fail-safe provisions, 244
  flexibility, 33
  sui generis right, 277–278
  technological protection circumvention,
    165, 167
  United States *see* United States

films, database defined, 72
Finland, term of protection, 59
France
    advertisements, 114, 116, 117
    authorship, 114
    Civil Code, 111, 115
    collections, 114
    compilations, 114
    compulsory licensing, 115
    contracts, 115, 117, 156
    copyright, 113–115
    database defined, 114, 116
    exceptions, 33, 80, 114, 117–118
    extraction, 117
    insubstantial part, 117
    Intellectual Property Code, 114, 116
    lawful users, 115, 117
    maker of database, 116
    misappropriation, 116
    neighbouring rights, 116
    news reporting, 115
    originality, 114
    parasitic copying, 116, 117
    private use, 33, 115
    public lending, 117
    re-utilisation, 117
    right of reproduction, 115
    selection/arrangement, 114
    slavish imitation, 115
    sui generis right, 116–117
    sweat of brow, 114
    term of protection, 118
    transposition of directive, 113–118
    unfair competition, 111, 115–116, 157
free-riders
    investment protection, 3, 38
    market failure, 62, 255
    misappropriation, 171, 179, 180, 187,
        189, 239
    new entrants, 94–95
    reputation, 38, 39
    tragedy of commons, 255, 267

Germany
    advertisements, 124, 125
    assignment of copyright, 118
    authorship, 118
    collections, 120, 121
    communication to public, 125
    compilations, 119, 120
    computer programs, 119, 120–121
    contracts, 125
    copyright, 118–122
    database defined, 120, 124
    economic rights, 118

    educational use, 121, 126
    equitable remuneration, 122
    exceptions, 80, 121–122, 126
    exhaustion, 125
    extraction, 125
    good morals, 123
    hardcopy databases, 126
    insubstantial part, 125
    lawful users, 122, 156
    licensing, 119
    maker of database, 124, 125
    materials, 120
    monism, 118, 119
    moral rights, 118
    news reporting, 122
    originality, 118, 119, 120
    parasitic copying, 103
    periodicals/journals, 122
    private use, 121, 126
    re-utilisation, 125
    research, 126
    right of distribution, 125
    right of reproduction, 125
    search engines, 125
    slavish imitation, 123
    substantial investment, 124–125
    sui generis right, 124–125
    telephone directories, 119–120,
        123–124, 125
    term of protection, 126
    transposition of directive, 118–126
    unfair competition, 39, 103, 123–124
government information
    Australia, 283
    exceptions, 238
    legal databases, 162–163, 248, 283
    privatisation, 253–254, 266
    provider neutrality, 282
    society, 264
    United Kingdom, 283
    United States, 162–163, 198, 208–209,
        211
Green Paper 1988
    access, 53
    compilations, 52, 53, 54
    copyright, 54
    investment protection, 53
    sui generis right, 53

hardcopy databases
    anthologies, 72
    Belgium, 110, 111, 113
    collections, 72
    contracts, 41
    Database Directive, 78

Draft Directive, 57, 60, 62, 98
Germany, 126
Ireland, 127
originality, 63
periodicals/journals, 72
telephones *see* telephone directories
trespass, 41
harmonisation
  competition law, 60
  copyright, 3, 50, 76, 94, 152–153
  Database Directive exceptions, 10–13,
    33
  exceptions, 156
  international law, 218
  originality, 65, 94
  term of protection, 77

incentives
  access, 243
  common law, 16
  misappropriation, 171, 180, 187–188
  property rights, 242, 244
  retrospectivity, 94
  sui generis right, 239, 246, 252
  telephone directories, 187, 188
  unfair competition, 39
  value added, 244, 247
indexing
  Boolean logic, 23
  copyright, 91
  database creation, 22–23, 91
  database defined, 54
  decisions, authorship, 22, 23, 25
  intellectual creativity, 91
  substantial part, 91
  sui generis right, 91, 246
  thesaurus, 23
  updating, 23
information
  Balkanisation, 256
  chain/stream, 252
  citizenship, 265
  data distinguished, 251
  democratic society, 8, 238, 265
  diversity, 1–2, 252–253
  economic commodity *see*
    commodification
  information companies, 261–263
  non-economic roles, 1, 7, 238,
    264–272
  social force, 264
  telephone directories, 253
  uses, 250
  value added, 251–252
information economies

  issues, 1, 2
  wealth creation, 1, 5
information processing
  investment, 69, 71, 82
  software *see* computer programs
information production
  contracts, 245
  financial motives, 248
  information retrieval, 2–3
  market mechanism, 249
  market power, 249
  public subsidy, 5, 6, 8, 248, 249, 250,
    253, 259
  reputation, 248, 249
  spiral, 2, 237, 252, 259, 269
  tradeable commodity *see*
    commodification
information retrieval
  capacity, 2
  Database Directive, 70
  information production, 2–3
  selection criteria, 25
  selection/arrangement, 1
  telephone directories, 23
infringement
  Australia, 37
  compilations, 19
  computer programs, 71, 75, 119
  Database Directive, 91
  directories, 28
  EEPROMs, 71
  England, 37
  exclusive rights, 25, 28, 38
  extraction, 87
  prohibited acts
  right of distribution, 31
  right of reproduction, 29
  rights conferred, 155–156
  selection/arrangement, 27, 28
  substantial part, 25–28, 37, 89, 155–156
  Sweden, 155
insubstantial part
  see also substantial part
  Belgium, 112
  Copyright Directive 2001, 101
  Database Directive, 91, 98
  definition, 67
  Draft Directive, 58
  failsafe provisions, 244
  France, 117
  Germany, 125
  Ireland, 128
  Italy, 133
  Netherlands, 136–137
  private use, 67

insubstantial part (*cont.*)
  Spain, 140
  sui generis right, 98
  United Kingdom, 150, 151
  United States, 197
intellectual creativity
  see also originality; creativity
  Germany, 119
  indexing, 91
  meaning, 13
  natural phenomena, 19
  Netherlands, 134
  requirements, 15–16, 19–21, 24,
    27
  sporting events, 20, 86
  sui generis right, 84
  United Kingdom, 145
  United States, 15–16
intellectual property
  common law, 6
  competition law, 43
  developing countries, 233–234
  dominant position, 46
  investment protection, 6
  meaning, 222–223
intellectual property regimes
  Database Directive, 98
  Draft Directive, 59–60
  expansion, 238
  United States, 161, 181, 199
International Bureau, 231, 233
international law, harmonisation, 218
International Publishers Association (IPA),
    232
international treaties
  Berne Convention 1971 *see* Berne
    Convention 1971
  copyright, 218–226
  exclusive rights, 28
  national treatment, 5, 63, 97, 217,
    221–223, 224, 226
  right of reproduction, 29
  term of protection, 225
  TRIPS *see* TRIPS Agreement
  WIPO: copyright *see* Copyright Treaty
    1996; draft *see* Draft Treaty 1996
investment
  see also database creation
  financial, 82
  impact of Directive, 263–264
  information processing, 69, 71,
    82
  maintenance costs, 86, 93, 194–195,
    210
  originality, 18

public interest, 6
rent seeking, 244, 245–247, 257
selection/arrangement, 83, 153–154
substantial *see* substantial investment
sunk costs, 44–45
sweat of brow, 18–19, 20, 83
value of rights, 90
investment protection
  Database Directive, 6, 69, 70, 82
  exclusive rights
  free-riders, 3, 38
  Green Paper (1988), 53
  intellectual property, 6
  justification, 7
  sui generis right, 6, 10, 69, 70, 82, 89,
    153–155, 262
  types of investment, 82
Ireland
  compilations, 126
  compulsory licensing, 127, 128–129
  copyright, 126–127
  database defined, 126, 128
  educational use, 127, 128
  exceptions, 128
  extraction, 128
  fair dealing, 127, 128
  hardcopy databases, 127
  insubstantial part, 128
  lawful users, 127, 128
  literary works, 126–127
  maker of database, 128
  original database, 126–127
  originality, 126
  private use, 127, 128
  re-utilisation, 128
  research, 127, 128
  rights management information, 129
  substantial investment, 128
  sui generis right, 128
  sweat of brow, 103
  technological protection circumvention,
    129
  term of protection, 128
  transposition of directive, 126–129
  unfair competition, 127
Italy
  authorship, 130, 131, 133
  Civil Code, 132
  collections, 129, 130
  copyright, 129–131
  creativity, 130
  database defined, 130, 132
  database owners, 130
  educational use, 131, 133
  employers, 130

exceptions, 131, 133
extraction, 133
insubstantial part, 133
lawful users, 131, 133
maker of database, 132, 133
news reporting, 130, 131
originality, 130
private use, 131, 133
public lending, 131, 132
re-utilisation, 133
research, 131, 133
right of reproduction, 131
slavish imitation, 132
sui generis right, 132
transposition of directive, 129–133
unfair competition, 131–132

lawful users
acknowledgments, 58
Belgium, 110, 112
contracts, 56, 156
Database Directive, 77–78, 91
Draft Directive, 56, 58
fair dealing, 78
France, 115, 117
Germany, 122, 156
Ireland, 127, 128
Italy, 131, 133
licensing, 77–78
Netherlands, 134, 136
resale, 78
Spain, 138, 140
transposition of directive, 156
United Kingdom, 151, 156
legal databases
acquisitions, 261–262
all available material, 19
boundaries, 25
public information, 162–163, 248,
    283
libraries
copying, 131, 139, 146
databases, 73
government information, 208, 209
licensing, 255
reasonable use, 206
sui generis, opposition, 79
technological protection circumvention,
    165
licensing
abuse of dominant position, 45, 46
anti-trust law, 199, 280
compulsory *see* compulsory licensing
Germany, 119
lawful users, 77–78

libraries, 255
United Kingdom, 145, 146, 152
literary works
Belgium, 109
Berne Convention, 218–219
bingo games, 20
compilations, 12, 218
compulsory licensing, 34
computer programs, 21, 75, 273
Ireland, 126–127
Netherlands, 134
originality, 126
right of distribution, 31
Sweden, 141
tables, 12, 126
term of protection, 59
United Kingdom, 144, 145
United States, 163, 166

maker of database
Belgium, 111–112
Database Directive, 82–83, 84
France, 116
Germany, 124, 125
Ireland, 128
Italy, 132, 133
United Kingdom, 147
Malaysia, 14–15
market failure, 62, 242, 255
market power
see also dominant position
information production, 249
legitimation, 46–47
limitation, 246
unlawful purpose, 45
markets, databases *see* database markets
meteorological information
public information, 248
WMO *see* World Meteorological
    Organization
misappropriation
common law, 162, 175, 178, 190, 214
France, 116
free-riders, 171, 179, 180, 187, 189, 239
Member States, 60
Spain, 139
sui generis right, 4, 8, 171, 190, 192,
    193, 200, 212–213, 284
United States *see* United States
misrepresentation, unfair competition, 38,
    173
moral rights, Germany, 118
most favoured nation
European Union (EU), 217
TRIPS Agreement, 221, 222

musical works
  compilations, 85
  database defined, 72, 73, 85–86

national treatment
  Berne Convention, 221
  bilateral agreements, 221
  Copyright Treaty (1996), 221, 224
  Database Directive, 63, 97, 217, 221
  Draft Treaty 1996, 227
  international treaties, 5, 63, 97, 217,
    221–223, 224, 226
  meaning, 221
  TRIPS Agreement, 221, 222, 224
neighbouring rights
  Belgium, 109
  Database Directive, 97, 223
  Draft Directive, 57, 62
  France, 116
  TRIPS Agreement, 223
Netherlands
  Civil Code, 134
  collections, 133, 134
  compilations, 133
  copyright, 133–134
  educational use, 134, 137
  equitable remuneration, 134
  exceptions, 134, 137
  extraction, 136–137
  insubstantial part, 136–137
  intellectual creativity, 134
  lawful users, 134, 136
  literary works, 134
  news reporting, 135–136, 137
  obligations, 134
  originality, 133, 134
  private use, 134
  public lending, 134
  re-utilisation, 136–137
  real estate listings, 136, 137
  research, 134, 137
  search engines, 136
  spin-off argument, 135, 136, 154
  substantial investment, 135–136
  sui generis right, 135–136
  telephone directories, 136
  term of protection, 137
  transposition of directive, 133–137
  unfair competition, 134–135
networks, access, 2
new entrants
  free-riders, 94–95
  growth, 263
  market barriers, 45
  opportunities, 94

news reporting
  see also time-sensitive data
  common law, 173
  compulsory licensing, 34
  exceptions, 238
  France, 115
  Germany, 122
  hot news, 132, 175, 186
  Italy, 130, 131
  misappropriation, 132, 172–173, 183,
    184, 206
  Netherlands, 135–136, 137
  property rights, 178
  Spain, 139
  substantial investment, 173–174
  United States, 132, 172–174, 183, 184,
    186–187, 189, 206
non-EU databases
  see also national treatment; reciprocity
  Belgium, 110, 112
  Database Directive, 5, 97
  Draft Directive, 59, 63
  unfair extraction, 63

obtaining, contents, 83, 86, 89
originality
  see also creativity; intellectual creativity
  authorship, 17, 21, 37
  Belgium, 109
  compilations, 16, 17–21, 163–164
  computer programs, 55, 114, 120–121
  Database Directive, 15, 33, 76, 94, 95,
    145
  Draft Directive, 55
  European standards, 16–17, 51, 76
  exclusive rights, 89
  expression, 17, 21
  France, 114
  Germany, 118, 119, 120
  hardcopy databases, 63
  harmonisation, 65, 94
  high standard, 4, 80–81, 114, 118
  investment, 18
  Ireland, 126
  Italy, 130
  literary works, 126
  low standard, 10, 14, 18, 146
  meaning, 13
  Netherlands, 133, 134
  requirement, 13–21
  selection/arrangement, 21, 36, 55,
    274
  Spain, 138
  spectrum, 17
  standard of excellence, 26–27, 76

substantial part, 27
sweat of brow, 14–15, 27–28, 65
Sweden, 141
uncertainty, 20
uniform laws, 65
United Kingdom, 126, 143–144, 145, 146
United States, 162

parasitic copying
  Belgium, 111
  France, 116, 117
  Germany, 103
  supplementary protection, 11
  Sweden, 142
patents, United States, 181, 269
period of protection see term of protection
periodicals/journals
  assignment of copyright, 245
  Germany, 122
  hardcopy databases, 72
pre-existing works
  compilations, 12, 86
  selection see selection/arrangement
presentation
  contents, 86, 89, 93
  United Kingdom, 148
price discrimination
  contracts, 40
  educational use, 40
  property rights, 242–244
  willingness to pay, 243
primacy, contents, 56
privacy, 7
private use
  acknowledgments, 58, 67
  Belgium, 110, 113
  Database Directive, 78
  Draft Directive, 57, 58, 67
  France, 33, 115
  Germany, 121, 126
  insubstantial part, 67
  Ireland, 127, 128
  Italy, 131, 133
  Netherlands, 134
  re-utilisation, 58
  Spain, 138
  sui generis right, 57, 67
  Sweden, 141
  United Kingdom copyright, 146
privatisation, 253–254, 266
property rights
  benefits, 242
  commodification, 239–240

costs: anticommons, 255–256, 257, 284; economic, 244–257; enforcement, 245, 257; limitation, 257–258; public good benefits lost, 245, 247–254; rent seeking, 244–245, 257; transaction costs, 243, 245, 254–257
  database markets, 239
  incentives, 242, 244
  limitation, 250
  news reporting, 178
  price discrimination, 242–244
  static benefits, 242, 247
  term of protection, 258
  tragedy of the commons, 242, 255
  United States, 190, 192, 193
public, communication see communication to public
public interest
  compulsory licensing, 34, 35, 36, 37
  contracts, 42
  investment, 6
  misappropriation, 176
public lending
  Belgium, 110, 112
  France, 117
  Italy, 131, 132
  Netherlands, 134
  Spain, 139
public subsidy
  access, 5, 243, 250
  information production, 5, 6, 8, 248, 249, 250, 253, 259
  research, 253, 266

radio listings, 135
re-utilisation
  Belgium, 112
  commercial purposes, 57, 66, 98
  communication to public compared, 88
  consequences, 69
  contracts, 58
  Draft Directive, 58
  France, 117
  Germany, 125
  Ireland, 128
  Italy, 133
  lawful users, 91
  Netherlands, 136–137
  private use, 58
  right defined, 87
  right to prevent, 87–89
  Spain, 140
  substantial part, 58, 89
  term of protection, 59

re-utilisation (*cont.*)
    United Kingdom, 148, 150, 151
    United States, 191
reciprocity
    Database Directive, 5, 63, 97, 223, 225
    TRIPS Agreement, 222
    United States, 5, 97, 217
recitals
    Database Directive, 69, 71, 72, 73, 76,
        77, 82, 85, 93
    Draft Directive, 53, 60
Reed Elsevier, 260, 261–262
remedies
    Copyright Treaty (1996), 220–221
    sui generis right, 281
    TRIPS Agreement, 281
    United States, 211
remuneration, equitable *see* equitable
    remuneration
rent seeking
    database creation, 245
    entry barriers, 244
    investment, 244, 245–247, 257
    meaning, 244–245
    sui generis right, 239, 274
rental rights
    Database Directive, 31, 77
    exclusive rights, 29, 31
    fixed copies, 31
    TRIPS Agreement, 31, 77, 88, 89
reproduction, exclusive rights *see* right of
    reproduction
reputation
    free-riders, 38, 39
    information production, 248, 249
research
    see also scientific information
    Belgium, 110, 113
    Copyright Directive (2001), 102
    Database Directive, 78, 79–80, 98
    fair dealing, 33, 80
    Germany, 126
    Ireland, 127, 128
    Italy, 131, 133
    Netherlands, 134, 137
    public subsidy, 253, 266
    scientific publication, 248
    Spain, 138, 140
    sui generis right, 6
    United Kingdom, 33, 80, 146, 151, 153
    United States, 197–198, 205–206
retrospectivity
    Database Directive, 93–97
    database industry, 94, 96
    Draft Directive, 59

incentives, 94
    justification, 95–97
    protectionism, 96–97
    sui generis right, 94
    transposition of directive, 95
    United States, 211
right of distribution
    artistic works, 31
    Copyright Treaty (1996), 31, 89
    Database Directive, 31
    exclusive rights, 29, 31
    exhaustion, 31
    fixed copies, 31
    Germany, 125
    infringement, 31
    literary works, 31
right of reproduction
    Belgium, 110, 113
    Berne Convention, 29
    computer displays, 29, 30
    digital environment, 30
    exclusive rights, 28
    extraction compared, 87
    France, 115
    Germany, 125
    infringement, 29
    international treaties, 29
    Italy, 131
    storage, 30
    Sweden, 141
    temporary copies, 30
rights management information
    Copyright Treaty 1996, 219, 221
    definition
    Ireland, 129
robots, downloading, 3
rule of reason, 47

satellites, privatisation, 253–254
scientific information
    cooperation, 269–272, 282
    exchange, 268, 269
    Health WIZ Project, 269–271
    natural phenomena, 19
    positive commons, 268
    research *see* research
    scientific publication, 248
    self-regulating norms, 269
    spiral of knowledge, 237, 252, 259, 269
    sui generis right, 238
    transformative use, 169, 269
securities/commodities
    futures contracts, 184, 185, 188, 196,
        207
    time-sensitive data, 90, 185, 188

selection/arrangement
  authorship, 18
  Belgium, 109
  competition, 246
  creativity, 10, 15, 19, 27, 54, 63, 84,
    171
  Database Directive, 50, 74, 75,
    84
  Draft Directive, 57
  France, 114
  information retrieval, 1
  infringement, 27, 28
  investment, 83, 153–154
  originality, 21, 36, 55, 274
  right of reproduction, 30
  technological protection circumvention,
    32
  telephone directories, 164,
    170
  United States, 164, 170, 194
skill and judgement, computer programs,
  75
slavish imitation
  France, 115
  Germany, 123
  Italy, 132
  Spain, 139
software *see* computer programs
Spain
  collections, 138
  copyright, 138–139
  creativity, 138
  database industry, 61
  educational use, 138
  exceptions, 138–139, 140
  extraction, 140
  insubstantial part, 140
  lawful users, 138, 140
  misappropriation, 139
  news reporting, 139
  originality, 138
  private use, 138
  public lending, 139
  re-utilisation, 140
  research, 138, 140
  slavish imitation, 139
  sui generis right, 140
  term of protection, 140–141
  transposition of directive, 138–141
  unfair competition, 139–140
spin-off argument
  Netherlands, 135, 136, 154
  substantial investment, 154
  Sweden, 143
  telephone directories, 247

sporting events
  British Horseracing Board decision, 137,
    147–150, 151, 153, 154, 155,
    156–157, 159
  fixture lists, 20, 142–143, 147, 148–150
  intellectual creativity, 20, 86
  misappropriation, 183–184
subject matter of protection
  see also database defined
  misappropriation, 173–174, 181, 189
  narrow definition, 273
  sui generis right, 33, 81, 89, 255,
    274–275
  United States, 173–174, 181, 189
substantial investment
  Belgium, 112
  computer programs, 75
  contents, 86
  Database Directive, 6, 73, 81, 83–87
  Draft Directive, 66
  Draft Treaty 1996, 227
  Germany, 124–125
  Ireland, 128
  Netherlands, 135–136
  news reporting, 173–174
  obtaining/verifying/presenting, 83–87,
    89, 90, 93, 116
  qualitative criteria, 84, 246
  spin off argument, 154
  sufficiently substantial, 85
  sweat of brow, 83, 84
  Sweden, 142
  telephone directories, 155
  term of protection, 87, 92
  United Kingdom, 147
  United States, 191, 194
substantial part
  see also insubstantial part
  act in respect of whole work, 26
  compulsory licensing, 34
  excellence, 26–27
  indexing, 91
  infringement, 25–28, 37, 89, 155–156
  measurement, 26
  originality, 27
  quality/quantity, 26, 27, 89–90, 91,
    149–150
  re-utilisation, 58, 89
  sweat of brow, 27, 89
  unfair extraction, 64, 89
  United Kingdom, 148
  United States, 203–204
sui generis right
  Belgium, 111–112
  bilateral agreements, 5, 217, 218

sui generis right (*cont.*)
  caution required, 238
  commodification, 266
  communication to public, 32
  comparable rights, 142
  competition law, 11, 43
  compilations, 53
  complexity, 247
  compulsory licensing, 36, 52, 58
  computer programs, 62, 198, 257, 273
  contents, 51, 55, 57, 81, 84
  copyright: differentiation, 11, 275–276;
    overlap, 6, 81–82, 84, 90–91, 92, 217,
    223–224, 255, 274–275
  Database Directive exceptions, 79,
    91–92
  database industry, 236
  Draft Directive, 4, 37, 57, 62, 65, 66, 67
  educational use, 6
  exceptions, 58–59
  exclusive rights, 52, 89, 190, 192, 193,
    240
  extraction: right *see* extraction;
    unauthorised *see* unauthorized
    extraction
  unfair *see* unfair extraction
  fair use, 277–278
  France, 116–117
  Germany, 124–125
  Green Paper (1988), 53
  hybrid form, 51
  incentives, 239, 246, 252
  indexing, 91
  insubstantial part, 98
  intellectual creativity, 84
  investment protection, 6, 10, 69, 70, 82,
    89, 153–155, 262
  Ireland, 128
  Italy, 132
  justification: anecdotal/empirical, 7, 238;
    argument in favour, 239–264;
    economic, 6–7, 237, 238, 241–244,
    258–259, 264
  limitations, 57
  makers *see* maker of database
  misappropriation, 4, 8, 171, 190, 192,
    193, 200, 212–213, 284
  Netherlands, 135–136
  obligations, 81
  private use, 57, 67
  qualitative criteria, 89, 191, 274
  re-use *see* re-utilisation
  remedies, 281
  rent seeking, 239, 274
  research, 6

  retrospectivity, 94
  right conferred, 3
  scientific information, 238
  scientific opposition, 79, 235, 268
  scope, 4, 9, 51, 81–82
  Spain, 140
  subject matter of protection, 33, 81, 89,
    255, 274–275
  substantive provisions, 70
  sweat of brow, 81, 83, 92, 274
  Sweden, 142–143
  technological protection circumvention,
    50, 100, 101
  term of protection, 92, 280–281
  uncertainty, 283
  unfair competition, 51, 52, 57, 157
  United Kingdom, 144, 147–150,
    225
  United States *see* United States
sweat of brow
  approach rejected, 19, 23
  Australia, 14
  Copyright Treaty 1996, 219
  Database Directive, 81, 83, 92, 224
  Draft Directive, 51, 62, 65
  Draft Treaty 1996, 227
  France, 114
  investment, 18–19, 20, 83
  Ireland, 103
  Malaysia, 14–15
  originality, 14–15, 27–28, 65
  substantial investment, 83, 84
  substantial part, 27, 89
  sui generis right, 81, 83, 92, 274
  Sweden, 141
  United Kingdom, 14, 51, 103, 143,
    144
  United States, 95, 162, 175, 182, 189,
    194
Sweden
  catalogue laws, 59, 103, 141, 142, 143,
    155
  compilations, 141
  educational use, 141
  exceptions, 141, 142
  infringement, 155
  literary works, 141
  originality, 141
  parasitic copying, 142
  private use, 141
  right of reproduction, 141
  spin-off argument, 143
  substantial investment, 142
  sui generis right, 142–143
  sweat of brow, 141

term of protection, 59
transposition of directive, 141–143
unfair competition, 142

tables
  compilations, 12, 13
  literary works, 12, 126
teaching *see* educational use
technological protection circumvention
  access, 41, 165
  additional prohibition, 165
  basic prohibition, 165
  contracts, 11
  Copyright Directive 2001, 3–4, 50,
    100–102, 112, 129
  Copyright Treaty 1996, 32, 101, 129,
    220
  Draft Directive, 64
  educational use, 165
  exclusive rights, 29, 32, 35
  exemptions/exceptions, 101–102,
    165–167, 277
  fair use, 165, 167
  Ireland, 129
  libraries, 165
  protection-defeating devices, 129, 165,
    220
  selection/arrangement, 32
  sui generis right, 50, 100, 101
  United States, 164–167, 192, 197
telephone directories
  advertising, 162
  comprehensiveness, 170, 256
  contents, obtaining, 83, 86, 117
  database creation, 22–23, 246
  database definition, 62, 63
  Germany, 119–120, 123–124, 125
  incentives, 187, 188
  information, 253
  information retrieval, 23
  Netherlands, 136
  selection/arrangement, 164, 170
  spin-off argument, 247
  subscription information, 18, 86
  substantial investment, 155
  synthetic information, 157
  unfair competition, 123–124
  United States, 15–16, 83, 95, 162,
    256
  value added, 244
television listings, 45–46, 86, 154
term of protection
  Belgium, 113
  Berne Convention, 225
  catalogue laws, 59, 258

changes to database, 59, 64, 67, 93,
  192
copyright, 93
Database Directive, 9, 52, 77, 92,
  156–157
date-stamping, 64
Denmark, 59
Draft Directive, 52, 59, 63, 64, 65, 68,
  240
Draft Treaty 1996, 228
Finland, 59
France, 118
Germany, 126
harmonisation, 77
international treaties, 225
Ireland, 128
literary works, 59
Netherlands, 137
perpetual, 52, 87, 93, 177, 192, 194,
  210
property rights, 258
range of possibilities, 240
re-utilisation, 59
renewal, 59, 64, 67, 93, 192
Spain, 140–141
substantial investment, 87, 92
sui generis right, 92, 280–281
Sweden, 59
TRIPS Agreement, 225
unfair extraction
  United Kingdom, 151–152, 156–157
  United States, 64, 177, 192, 194,
    209–210, 221, 240
thesaurus
  indexing, 23
third parties, contracts, 40, 78
Thompson Corporation, 260, 261,
  262
time-sensitive data
  see also news reporting
  commercial value, 185, 186, 187
  direct competition, 206
  hot news, 132, 175, 186
  misappropriation, 132, 175, 180, 182,
    185–187, 198, 207
  qualitatively substantial, 90
  securities/commodities, 90, 185, 188
tort *see* misappropriation
trade secrets, 7, 60
tragedy of the commons
  anticommons, 255–256, 257, 284
  closed commons, 268
  limits, 266–269
  meaning, 242, 255
  negative commons, 268

tragedy of the commons (*cont.*)
  open commons, 268
  positive, 268
transaction costs
  compulsory licensing, 34, 35, 245
  property rights, 243, 245, 254–257
  reduction, 254
transposition of Database Directive *see*
    Database Directive
TRIPS Agreement
  compilations, 13, 223
  exceptions, 79
  minimal protection, 219, 222
  most favoured nation, 221, 222
  national treatment, 221, 222, 224
  neighbouring rights, 223
  reciprocity, 222
  remedies, 281
  rental rights, 31, 77, 88, 89
  term of protection, 225

unauthorized extraction
  see also extraction; unfair extraction
  commercial purposes, 57, 66, 98
  consequences, 69
  Draft Directive, 66
UNCTAD, 228
underlying information
  exceptions, 276
  unfair extraction, 63
UNESCO, 228, 229–230, 238
unfair competition
  see also competition law
  Australia, 37
  basic principles, 11, 37–40
  Belgium, 111
  common law, 37
  confusion, 38, 39, 60, 116, 127, 135,
    139, 142
  deception, 38, 39, 60, 127
  disloyal competition, 116
  Draft Directive, 50, 51, 57, 60
  England, 37
  France, 111, 115–116, 157
  Germany, 39, 103, 123–124
  incentives, 39
  Ireland, 127
  Italy, 131–132
  misappropriation *see* misappropriation
  misrepresentation, 38, 173
  Netherlands, 134–135
  parasitic *see* parasitic copying
  reaping without sowing, 39
  relationship between parties, 39
  slavish imitation, 115, 116, 132

Spain, 139–140
sui generis right, 51, 52, 57, 157
Sweden, 142
telephone directories, 123–124
United Kingdom, 38, 146–147
United States, 37, 38, 39, 173, 181–182,
    189–190
unfair extraction
  see also extraction; unauthorized
    extraction
  commercial purposes, 57, 65
  exceptions, 58
  harmonisation, 60
  insufficient protection, 61
  limitation, 57
  meaning, 57
  non-EU databases, 63
  substantial part, 64, 89
  underlying information, 63
uniform laws
  Database Directive, 69
  originality, 65
United Kingdom
  British Horseracing Board decision, 137,
    147–150, 151, 153, 154, 155,
    156–157, 159
  contracts, 148
  database defined, 144, 147
  database markets, 61
  database right, 147
  educational use, 151
  England *see* England
  exceptions, 151
  extraction, 148, 150, 151
  fair dealing, 33, 80, 145, 146, 151,
    153
  government information, 283
  insubstantial part, 150, 151
  intellectual creativity, 145
  lawful users, 151, 156
  licensing, 152
  maker of database, 147
  presentation, 148
  re-utilisation, 148, 150, 151
  research, 33, 80, 146, 151, 153
  substantial investment, 147
  substantial part, 148
  sui generis right, 144, 147–150, 225
  term of protection, 151–152, 156–157
  transposition of directive, 143–152
  unfair competition, 38, 146–147
United Kingdom copyright
  authorship, 24
  compilations, 12, 143, 144, 145
  creativity, 144

database industry, 61
educational use, 146
exceptions, 33, 92, 145, 146
fair dealing, 33, 80, 145, 146, 153
licensing, 145, 146
literary works, 144
originality, 126, 143–144, 145, 146
private use, 146
scope, 4
sweat of brow, 14, 51, 103, 143, 144
United States
  bootstrapping, 166
  collections, 194, 199, 201, 273
  commercial purposes, 168, 191
  common law, 162, 175, 178, 214
  competition *see* anti-trust law
  compilations, 162–164
  comprehensiveness, 170
  computer programs, 198, 208
  contracts
    futures contracts, 184, 185–186, 188,
      196, 207
    non-derogation, 193, 199, 212
    sui generis right, 42, 193
  copyright, 4, 10, 162–171
  Copyright Treaty (1996), 197
  database defined, 73, 191, 192, 194, 273
  database industry, 54, 63
  database management information, 192,
    197
  database markets: actual/potential
    markets, 169, 171, 191, 193,
    195–197, 199, 205; material harm,
    201–202, 212, 214, 240; primary
    markets, 202, 206; protected markets,
    202–203; related markets, 202;
    substantial harm, 162, 180, 201, 212
  digital on-line communications, 208
  direct competition, 174, 180, 183–185,
    206
  educational use, 165, 168, 197–198,
    205–206
  exceptions, 33, 161, 190
  exclusions, 198–199
  existing legal regimes, 199
  expression, 164, 172, 173
  fair use: criteria, 168–170, 205, 211;
    defence, 167–170; entire work
    reproduced, 169; equivalent defence,
    168; flexibility, 33; informational
    works, 169; justification, 167;
    non-profit, 168; potential markets,
    169, 171; productive/redistributive
    facts, 169; reasonable uses, 205–207;
    reasonableness, 204–205; standard,

  170; *sui generis* right, 160, 168, 170,
    204–205; technological protection
    circumvention, 165, 167;
    transformative use, 169; value added,
    169
Feist decision, 15–16, 28, 83, 95, 162,
    169, 171, 175, 182, 219, 256
genealogical information, 207, 211, 215
government/intelligence investigations,
    207, 211, 215
government/public information,
    162–163, 198, 208–209, 211
hot news, 132, 175, 186
insubstantial part, 197
intellectual creativity, 15–16
Librarian of Congress, 165–167
literary works, 163, 166
misappropriation: cause of action, 180;
    commercial value, 184; common law,
    162, 175, 178, 190, 214; direct
    competition, 174, 180, 183–185, 206;
    free-riders, 171, 179, 180, 187; good
    conscience, 160, 173, 178; history of
    tort, 4, 160–161, 171–190; incentives,
    171, 180, 187–188; injunctions, 175;
    intangibles, 173; intellectual property
    regimes, 161, 181; *International News
    Service* decision, 184, 198, 206;
    justification, 160, 178; natural rights,
    39, 160; nature of protection,
    174–175; news reporting, 132,
    172–174, 183, 184, 186–187, 189,
    206; perpetual protection, 177;
    pre-emption, 180–183, 189, 199;
    protection against whom, 174; public
    interest, 176; quasi-property, 174,
    176; scope limited, 179–188; sporting
    fixtures, 183–184; state laws,
    178–179, 180–183, 189, 199; subject
    matter of protection, 173–174, 181,
    189; substantial harm, 162, 212; *sui
    generis* right, 4, 8, 11, 171, 190, 192,
    193, 200, 212–213, 284;
    time-sensitive data, 132, 175, 180,
    182, 185–187, 198, 207; unfairness,
    39
monetary relief, 206, 209
originality, 162
patents, 181, 269
perpetual protection, 177, 192, 194
real estate directories, 164
reciprocity, 5, 97
remedies, 211
research, 197–198, 205–206
restraint of trade, 176

United States (*cont.*)
    retrospectivity, 211, 217
    securities/commodities, 184, 207
    selection/arrangement, 164, 170, 194
    substantial part, 203–204
    sui generis right: 1996 Bill, 191–193;
        1997 Bill, 194–195; 1999 Alternative
        Bill, 213; 1999 bills, 200–213;
        contracts, 42, 193; EU Directive
        compared, 192–193, 199–200,
        211–212, 215; exclusive rights, 190,
        192, 193; extraction, 191, 197; fair
        use, 160, 168, 170, 204–205;
        legislative proposals, 161–162,
        190–213, 226, 232, 240–241;
        misappropriation, 4, 8, 11, 190, 192,
        193, 200, 212–213, 284; nature, 195;
        permitted acts, 197–198; prerequisite,
        194–195; re-utilisation, 191;
        reciprocity, 97; substantial investment,
        191, 194; summary of position,
        213–216; unfair competition, 37
    sweat of brow, 95, 162, 175, 182, 189,
        194
    technological protection circumvention,
        164–167, 192, 197
    telephone directories, 15–16, 83, 95,
        162, 256
    temporary copies, 30
    term of protection, 64, 177, 192, 194,
        209–210, 221, 240
    unfair competition, 37, 38, 39, 173,
        181–182, 189–190
uses
    commercial *see* commercial purposes
    conditions, 42

educational *see* educational use
fair *see* fair use
information, 250
lawful *see* lawful users
private *see* private use
re-use *see* re-utilisation
research *see* research

value added
    fair use, 169
    incentives, 244, 247
    information, 251–252
    telephone directories, 244
    users, 169, 273
verification
    database creation, 86, 89, 93
    Draft Treaty 1996, 227
websites, filtering applications, 166
Wolters Kluwer, 261, 262
World Intellectual Property Organization
    (WIPO)
    1996 draft *see* Draft Treaty 1996
    1996 Treaty *see* Copyright Treaty 1996
    database protection, 226–234, 272
    developing countries, 5, 218, 226, 228,
        232–233
    Information Meeting 1997, 229
    Standing Committee on Copyright and
        Related Rights (SCCR), 230, 232
World Meteorological Organization
    (WMO)
    Draft Treaty 1996, 228, 229–230
    scientific cooperation, 271–272,
        282
    scientific information, 238
World Trade Organization, 225

Cambridge Studies in Intellectual Property
Titles in the Series

Brad Sherman and Lionel Bently
The Making of Modern Intellectual Property Law
0 521 56363 1

Irini A. Stamatoudi
Copyright and Multimedia Works
0 521 80819 7

Pascal Kamina
Film Copyright and the European Union
0 521 77053 X

Huw Beverley-Smith
The Commercial Appropriation of Personality
0 521 80014 5